D0166987

Croatia

THE BRADT TRAVEL GUIDE

Second Edition

Piers Letcher

Bradt Travel Guides Ltd, UK
The Globe Pequot Press Inc, USA

Second edition 2005
Reprinted March 2006

First published 2003

Bradt Travel Guides Ltd
19 High Street, Chalfont St Peter, Bucks SL9 9QE, England
Published in the USA by The Globe Pequot Press Inc, 246 Goose Lane,
PO Box 480, Guilford, Connecticut 06437-0480

ISBN-10: 1 84162 113 7
ISBN-13: 978184162 113 5

British Library Cataloguing in Publication Data
A catalogue record for this book is available from the British Library

Photographs
Cover Lubenice Bay, Cres Island (Johanna Huber/Fototeca 9x12)
Text Tricia Hayne (TH), Piers Letcher (PL),

Illustrations Carole Vincer
Maps Steve Munns, Matt Honour

Typeset from the author's disc by Wakewing
Printed and bound in Italy by Legoprint SpA, Trento

Author

Born and educated in the UK, Piers Letcher has lived in France for the past 20 years. As an independent writer and photographer he has published 15 books, more than a thousand newspaper and magazine articles and hundreds of photographs. From the mid-90s he spent several years as a speechwriter at the United Nations in Geneva, before returning to his freelance career in 2002. He is the author of *Eccentric France* and *Dubrovnik: The Bradt City Guide* and contributes irregularly to *The Guardian Unlimited*.

DEDICATION

To Sarah Parkes – and to the people of Croatia.

Contents

LIST OF MAPS

Acknowledgements

For this second edition, special thanks must go to Dražen Hochecker, Nevenka Fuchs and Danijela Miletić in Zagreb as well as Lidija Mišćin in Zagreb County; Suzana Ivanković in Požega; Biljana Lončarić in Slavonski Brod; Rujana Busić, Jesna Babuć and Velimir Radović in Vukovar; and Bosanka Savić Mitrović at the Vukovar Town Museum. Along the coast and on the islands I'd like to thank Dino Matešić and Nataša Matošević in Rijeka; Kristina Maškarin on Rab; Karmen Poljak on Hvar; Marc and Silva van Bloemen, Iris and Dan Bear, Igor Bulum, Sanja Čimić, Niko Čučković, Helena Deranja, Wade Goddard, Zrinka Jelavić, Niko Kobila, Kathy Ljubojević, Antun Maračić, Bridget and Dominic Medley, Niko Radić, Slobodan Varezić, and - Deni Vokojević in Dubrovnik; Marje Musladin on Koločep; Vicko Radić and Don Ivan Vlašić on Lopud; Stanley Stjepović and Brian and Jane Foster on Šipan; Zeljko Resetar on Mljet; and Stanka Berković, Dino Četinic, Mihaljo Grgić, Stanka Kraljević and Vladimir de Polo on Korčula. A heartfelt thank you, too, to all the people whose names I never caught, who offered help, hospitality and kindness along the way.

For keeping body and soul together on a breathtaking research trip to the islands of the Kvarner Bay, and then deep into inland Croatia and back via Zagreb, and for providing a million laughs, my very special thanks to Stuart Panes. Back in France I'd like to express my gratitude to Shirley Parkes for all her help while updating this guide; Dale Madsen for being as charming as they come; Phillip Mannion for his email barrages; Geoff Hill for his insight; and Steve McClelland for simply being a great person to work with. For all sorts of reasons I'd also like to thank Alex Rossi, Matt Finn, Amélie Passot, Mathilde Chevee, Charlotte Doyle and Dawn Elmore at SITA.

For helping out with the new edition but also for being a great friend I'd like once again to thank Rajko Zorić (and his wife Ksenija and daughter Ema). For their feedback and input I'm grateful to Kris Dehamers, Lisa Fuller, Arlene and Lee Goldsmith, A Hensley, Gary Jarvis, Rosemary Mullan, Andries and Benita Nieuwoudt, Michael Shaw, Peter van Steenkiste and Sally Ann Whetherly, and as always I'd like to thank all the people at Bradt Travel Guides whose hard work makes these books the best in their field.

Finally, as always, I am indebted to Sarah Parkes (my sun and moon) for her kindness and thoughtfulness, her company and help in researching this new edition, and her generous spirit. Thanks too must go to Brice and Alec, who do a great deal, in the best possible sense, to distract me, and to my parents, who are more supportive than they probably realise.

Thanks again also to all those who made the first edition possible. In particular I'd like again to thank Slavica Alajbeg, Zdravko Banović, Vinko Bartolac, Marija Čavlek, Dragica Jović, Vesna Jovičić, Darko Kovačić, Lana Lončarević-Jadrešić, Dubravka Kovačević, Svjetlena Lupret-Obradović, Damir Macanić, Drago Marguš, Stjepan Matoš, Milan Medak, Tibor Mikuška, Morena Milevoj, Tatjana Petranović, Goran Radonić, Sara Salamunić, Roberta Surać, Keith Stimpson, Branka Tropp and Lisa Winters.

Introduction

I've had a love affair with Croatia for over 20 years, ever since I first inter-railed round Europe in 1982 and got stranded in Split for four days, waiting for someone to show up who never showed. It wasn't difficult to find my way out to the islands of Brač and Hvar, and from there to Korčula and on to Dubrovnik, by which time I was off the inter-rail map, and into a different place altogether.

Three years later I got diverted in Trieste and ended up in Pula instead of Athens, and worked my way down the coast as far as Split again, stopping in at Rab, and then for a week at the lovely Paklenica National Park (still a Croatian favourite). To get back to where I was going I went up through the country to Zagreb, and saw the Plitvice Lakes for the first time. I travelled inland, and visited the pretty baroque town of Vukovar, then wandered up through Osijek into Hungary.

It wasn't long before I was hammering at Bradt's door and clamouring to write about (what was then) Yugoslavia. The book came out in 1989, just in time to be washed away by the war – I spent 1991 glued to the television set, watching in horror as Vukovar fell and Dubrovnik was shelled, and had to wait a decade for my second chance.

My guide to Croatia was published in 2003 and now, two years later, here's the second edition – the most comprehensive and (I hope) useful guide to the country, and the only one which covers all the national parks and nature reserves.

FEEDBACK REQUEST

At Bradt Travel Guides we're well aware that guidebooks start to go out of date on the day they're published – and that you, our readers, are out there in the field, doing research of your own. You'll find out before us when a fine new family-run hotel opens or a favourite restaurant changes hands and goes downhill. So why not write to us and tell us about your experiences, for the next edition? We'll personally reply to your emails so send them to info@bradtguides.com – we'll look forward to hearing from you!

For personal correspondence and feedback, please feel free to email Piers Letcher at bradtcroatia@yahoo.co.uk.

KEY TO STANDARD SYMBOLS

—·—·—	International boundary	🏛	Historic building
------	District boundary	✝	Church or cathedral
- - - -	National park boundary	♨	Buddhist temple
✈	Airport (international)	🏠	Buddhist monastery
✦	Airport (other)	⚕	Hindu temple
✛	Airstrip	⸦	Mosque
🚁	Helicopter service	▶	Golf course
▭▭▭	Railway	🏃	Stadium
----------	Footpath	▲	Summit
--🚗--	Car ferry	△	Boundary beacon
--🚢--	Passenger ferry	◉	Outpost
⛽	Petrol station or garage	⤬⤬	Border post
🅿	Car park	⌂	Rock shelter
🚌	Bus station etc	⊏⊶	Cable car, funicular
🚲	Cycle hire	⩵	Mountain pass
M	Underground station	○	Waterhole
⌂	Hotel, inn etc	✷	Scenic viewpoint
⛺	Campsite	✤	Botanical site
♦	Hut	♧	Specific woodland feature
⚲	Wine bar	🏛	Lighthouse
✕	Restaurant, café etc	⚘	Marsh
✉	Post office	🌴	Mangrove
✆	Telephone	🦅	Bird nesting site
⒠	Internet café	🐢	Turtle nesting site
⊞	Hospital, clinic etc	〰〰	Coral reef
⚱	Museum	➤	Beach
🐂	Zoo	⤳	Scuba diving
𝒾	Tourist information	🐟	Fishing sites
$	Bank		
⚐	Statue or monument		
⁙	Archaeological or historic site		

Other map symbols are sometimes shown in separate key boxes with individual explanations for their meanings.

Part One

General Information

CROATIA AT A GLANCE

Country name Republic of Croatia
Croatian name Republika Hrvatska.
Language Croatian
Population 4.44 million (2001)
Religion Roman Catholic (87.8%), Orthodox Christian (4.4%), Muslim
(1.3%)
President Stjepan (Stipe) Mesić
Capital Zagreb (population 780,000)
Other major cities and towns Split, Rijeka, Osijek, Zadar, Slavonski
Brod, Karlovac, Pula, Sisak, Varaždin, Dubrovnik
Border countries Slovenia, Hungary, Serbia, Bosnia & Herzegovina,
Montenegro
Land area 56,542km^2
Islands, reefs and islets 1,185
Inhabited islands 67
Coastline 5,835km (1,777km mainland and 4,058km islands)
High point Mount Dinara, 1,831m
National parks Eight
Nature parks Ten
Protected species 380 (fauna), 44 (flora)
Time CET (GMT + 1 hour)
Currency Kuna (£1 = 10.7 kuna; €1 = 7.3 kuna; US$1 = 6.1 kuna:
February 2006)
International telephone code +385
Tourist board website www.croatia.hr

Background Information

FACTS AND FIGURES

Croatia's curious shape – wishbone, boomerang, croissant, or what you will – tells you immediately about its historical past. Between the Austro-Hungarian Empire to the north and the Ottoman Empire to the southeast, Byzantium to the east and Rome and Venice to the west, Croatia sits at the crossroads of Europe.

Name

It's one of those countries like Finland or Albania whose name appears quite differently to foreigners from the way it appears to locals. For us it's the Republic of Croatia – for them, it's *Republika Hrvatska*. Which is why the top-level domain name (TLD) for Croatia on the Internet is .hr.

Area

The country covers 56,542km^2 of southeastern Europe. It also claims 31,067km^2 of territorial waters in the Adriatic Sea.

Location

Southeastern Europe bordered by the Adriatic Sea and Italy to the west and southwest, Slovenia and Hungary to the north, Serbia to the east, Bosnia & Herzegovina along Croatia's inside arc, and Montenegro for all of 25km in the far south.

A Bosnian corridor to the sea cuts Dubrovnik and the south coast off from the rest of the country – though now Bosnia has harmonised its visa requirements with Croatia, this shouldn't cause you any problems (see page 29 for further details).

The westernmost point of Croatia is the settlement of Bašanija near Umag, at 13°30'E; the easternmost point is Ilok, in Slavonia, at 19°27'E. Croatia also stretches from Žabnik in the Međimurje in the north (46°33'N) to Lastovo in the south (42°23'N).

Population

The 2001 census measured a population of 4.44 million people, down from the Croatian Central Bureau of Statistics' mid year estimate for 1999 of 4.55 million – partly due to the displacements of people during the turbulent 1990s, but partly due to changes in the census methodology.

Cities

Croatia's administrative, cultural, academic and communications centre is the city of Zagreb, with 780,000 inhabitants in town – though over a million people live in and around the capital.

The next largest city, Split, is only a quarter of the size of Zagreb, with 189,000 inhabitants. This is followed (2001 census) by Rijeka (144,000), Osijek (115,000), Zadar (75,000), Slavonski Brod (65,000), Karlovac (60,000), Pula (59,000), Sisak (52,000), Varaždin (49,000) and Dubrovnik (44,000).

Coast and islands

Croatia has 5,835km of coastline, including 4,058km on the 1,185 islands, islets and reefs. There are 67 inhabited islands, the largest of which are Krk (the largest island in the Adriatic, at 409km^2, pop 16,400) and Cres (404km^2, pop 3,200).

Mountain highs

Croatia starts at sea level and peaks at Dinara (1,831m, near the Bosnian border, inland from Šibenik), the highest point on the eponymous Dinara range, which runs down almost the whole length of the coast.

The other eight peaks over 1,500m are: Kamešnica (1,809m), Sv Jure (Biokovo, 1,762m), Vaganski Vrh (Paklenica, Velebit, 1,758m), Lička Plješevica (Ozeblin, 1,657m), Bjelolasica (Velika Kapela, 1,534m), Risnjak (Gorski Kotar, 1,528m), Svilaja (Dalmatia, 1,508m) and Snježnik (Gorski Kotar, 1,505m).

GEOGRAPHY AND CLIMATE
Geography

The country is perhaps most famous for its enormous – relative to the country's size – coastline and wealth of islands, but it's also geographically diverse away from the beaches. A long ridge of mountains – peaking at Dinara – stretches from the northwest to the southeast of the country, while the plains of Pannonia dominate the Hungarian border to the north. Rolling hills dominate much of the rest of the country from behind the Dinara mountains to the Pannonian plain, while the Adriatic islands can be surprisingly mountainous, with peaks up to 778m (Brač), and Cres, Hvar, Lošinj, Vis, Krk, Korčula and Mljet all rising to over 500m.

The coast and islands are Croatia's natural selling point (especially when it comes to tourism), and they provide the country with an astonishing 5,835km coastline. Although it's only about 500km in a straight line from Trieste, the last town in Italy, to Herceg Novi, the first town in Montenegro, the Croatian coast itself is 1,777km long, with the remaining 4,058km accounted for by 1,185 islands, islets and reefs. See *Coast and islands* above.

Climate

If you're seeking an escape from a wet winter, then Croatia's probably not for you – most of the rain here falls in the cooler months, making it chilly and damp in the interior and mild but drippy along the coast. Outside the long, dry summers, Croatia is wetter than you might think, with an average annual countrywide precipitation of close to 1,100mm (compared to about 600mm on average for London and 1,400mm for Scotland as a whole), but the humid winters are more than compensated for by warm, early springs, hot dry summers and prolonged autumns.

Croatia's climate falls into three distinct patterns, varying from northern to central Croatia, and different again for the coast and islands.

The north has a moderate continental climate, equating to hot, dry summers and cold, damp winters. Average daily winter temperatures vary from around −1 to +3°C, while in summer they range from 22 to 26°C. The capital, Zagreb, is coldest in January, when the daily average barely creeps above freezing, and warmest in August, when it's 21°C. You can expect about 24mm of rainfall in the capital in August, but closer to 100mm a month from September through to November.

Central Croatia has a semi-highland and highland climate, making for cool summers and hard winters, with plenty of snow. Average daily winter temperatures run from −5 to 0°C, while in summer they bounce up to 15–20°C.

KARST

The geological term *Velebit Karst* came from the rock formations of the Velebit mountain range in Dalmatia, and the term karst is now used to describe any similar terrain – very useful as that includes most of the limestone mountains along Croatia's coast and on its islands.

Karst is grey, wild and very dry. It is formed by the absorption of water into porous limestone, which then corrodes and finally erodes the harder limestone underneath – this, combined with a history of earthquakes, is the geological reason for the shape of the Adriatic and its islands.

Young karst is typically characterised by small fissures in the rock, while more developed areas contain long underground caves, rivers that appear from the rock and then disappear again almost immediately, and highly porous limestone which is completely dry only a few minutes after rain has fallen. Karst is irregularly sculptured into sharp and wild shapes, and is extremely abrasive.

Croatia's karst was once almost entirely covered in vegetation, but large parts, particularly along the coast and on the islands, were deforested (the Venetians, in particular, needed a lot of wood) and then lost their soil from wind, erosion and over-grazing. This is known as naked karst, and can be seen at its most spectacular and barren on the island of Pag and on some of the islands of the Kornati archipelago. It's incredibly poor land, on which it seems unlikely that anything could survive – but people do live here, and somehow eke out a living from the wilderness.

When an underground cave collapses the surface is flattened, and soil gradually accumulates. Usually this is then cleared of rocks, walled in, and cultivated. One of the hazards of this type of field (known as *polje*) is that they don't always drain as quickly as they fill up, creating lakes of a few days' or weeks' duration. Every so often you'll be surprised by a boat at the edge of a field or pasture, even in the mountains. It's also the reason why you'll never see houses built on the *polje* itself, but always to one side.

Up in the mountains you need to be well equipped for the weather. In Risnjak National Park, at around 1,500m, you can expect precipitation in the sort of quantities you'd be unlucky to find even in the wettest parts of England's Lake District – though here much of the annual 3,579mm falls as snow. At the mountain lodge in the park, at 1,418m, snow stays on the ground for an average of 157 days a year, and can be up to 4m deep.

Weather in the mountains is unpredictable all year round, so plan accordingly. Snow can fall in every month of the year at 1,700m, and I've been caught in terrible hail in June on the Velebit massif at 1,200m, just a few kilometres inland from the coast.

Down at sea-level, of course, the coast and islands have a Mediterranean climate, with wet, mild winters, and long, hot and very dry summers. Daily averages range from 5 to 10°C in winter and from 25 to 30°C in summer, though almost never exceed 35°C – and daily maximums in Dubrovnik never fall below 12°C. The coast gets most of its precipitation in the autumn months, with 508mm falling in Rijeka and 377mm falling in Dubrovnik from October to December, but only 10mm of rainfall expected in Split in July.

The sea is for many the main attraction, so you should remember that it cools down to a chilly 8°C at Pula in winter, although from mid June to early September it stays above 20°C, making for pleasant swimming (especially in August, when the water reaches its maximum temperature of 26°C).

There's also no shortage of sunshine on the Adriatic – Pula's pleased with its 2,480 hours annually, while Brač brags about its 2,700 sunny hours per year. Bring plenty of suncream.

NATURAL HISTORY AND CONSERVATION

Croatia is blessed with unpolluted lakes, spectacular limestone scenery, and the cleanest coastline on the Mediterranean. During Tito's days, Yugoslavia embarked on a progressive programme of tourist development, and although some of the resorts along the coast might be considered over-developed there's also a wealth of national parks and other protected areas.

Natural history

In the remoter forests of the interior and in the inland national parks there are still bears and wolves at large, though you're unlikely to see them – bears are notoriously cautious, while wolves only come down from the mountains to raid villages for scraps during the depths of winter. Wild boar, however, are still common in the northern and eastern forests, along with red, fallow and roe deer. You might also be lucky enough to see chamois and mouflon in the mountains along the Slovenian border and through Dalmatia. But you're more likely to see eagles and griffon vultures than lynxes – lynx being almost shyer than bears.

Snakes are reasonably common, but there are very few which are poisonous, and the old saying is worth repeating: they're much more frightened of you than you are of them. Snakes will mostly avoid regularly walked paths or roads, but if you're heading across country it's as well to wear sensible shoes or boots. In accumulated months of walking in Croatia I've seen several dozen snakes of four or five species, but never anything dangerous, so please don't kill them out of ignorance or fear.

You'll see a number of charming species of lizard if you're out walking, or even sightseeing – they love to bask on warm stone the moment the sun's shining. Look out, too, for frogs if you're near water, and several varieties of toad which are peculiar to the woods which grow on limestone mountains. Martens, wild cats and squirrels also live in these forests, but they're pretty shy.

From early summer onwards Croatia features several species of butterfly you won't see often in the UK – look out for swallowtails in the mountains, white admirals on the islands, and hosts of butterflies of all species if you're here in late spring or early summer.

A total of 44 species of vegetation and 380 species of animal are protected in Croatia. Most endangered of all is the fast-disappearing Mediterranean monk seal, with a Croatian population of 25 or less according to the IUCN (International Union for the Conservation of Nature). The seals can only be found on the small island of Šćedro, off the south coast of Hvar, and on the uninhabited islands of Brusnik and Svetac in the Vis archipelago. These elegant dark brown seals grow to around 2.4m in length and weigh up to 300kg or more.

Croatia's flora is also delightful. Along the coast and on the islands you'll find aromatic herbs and abundant Bougainvillea. In the woods and forests there's a wide variety of plants and trees ranging from orchids to holm oak to pine and beech woods, while higher up in the mountains you'll find beautiful summer pastures, home to tiny flowers and fragrant herbs.

As the summer wears on, the colours fade and everything dries out, leaving an arid impression across much of the country, which doesn't really wear off until the leaves change to their superb autumnal colours.

Environmental issues

In spite of the long-standing promotion of eco-tourism, the creation and maintenance of a whole crop of national parks and protected areas (see below), and its pride in having the cleanest waters of the Mediterranean, Croatia hasn't entirely escaped the blights of the modern world. Metal works, refineries and other factories have damaged some forests with acid rain, while coastal pollution from industrial and domestic waste has been experienced in some areas.

Much more significant, in environmental terms, however, has been the destruction of both infrastructure and natural resources by the civil strife of the early 1990s. In spite of the quick repairs in tourist centres like Dubrovnik, it will take some time before the damage is entirely fixed country-wide, and longer still before the countryside returns to its natural state – there are still a handful of minefields which haven't yet been fully cleared along the front lines of the war zone.

Fire is another environmental hazard – a landscape which quickly absorbs what little water there is and a hot dry summer is a recipe for accidental combustion. The starting of any kind of fire in Croatia in summer is strongly discouraged in most areas, and is usually forbidden in the national parks. If you're going to be barbecuing, do so carefully, and be sure you have what it takes to put the flames out if things get out of control.

Croatia is also strongly exposed to one other environmental risk: earthquakes. A major and active earthquake fault network runs through Italy and the Balkans, and it was an earthquake in 1667 that killed more than 5,000 people in Dubrovnik and levelled most of the public buildings. In 1880 another major earthquake destroyed much of Zagreb, and most of what you see in the capital today dates from the post-1880 reconstruction of the city.

The most recent serious earthquake in Croatia occurred in 1996, with its epicentre in the area of Slano and Ston, 50km up the coast from Dubrovnik. The historical town of Ston – now famous for its excellent oysters – was almost completely destroyed. Although there were no fatalities, around 2,000 people in the area lost their homes to the earthquake damage.

National parks, nature parks and other protected areas

Croatia has an impressive range of national parks, nature parks and other protected areas. Below you'll find a summary of what's on offer – more detail can be found in the relevant chapters.

National parks

Croatia has eight national parks covering a total of 98,697 hectares (987km^2).

The **Brijuni Islands** (often written Brioni in English, see page 146) were the government's (ie: Tito's) private retreat for decades, off limits to the general public and used for entertaining heads of state and the like. The group of two larger and 12 smaller islands lies off the west coast of Istria, and was once a fashionable holiday destination for the upper classes. Now it's a pretty national park featuring ruins from antiquity and a large open-air zoo – many of the animals are the descendants of gifts to the former Yugoslavia. Be warned however that it's on the package-tour circuit – it's the closest and most accessible park to Croatia's busiest stretch of coast.

The **Kornati** archipelago (see page 222) is a scattered group of 147 uninhabited islands, islets and reefs south of Zadar, and 89 of the islands were declared a national park in 1980. Popular with the yachting community, it's relatively difficult to access for other visitors to Croatia, but is nonetheless one of the most striking national parks I've ever seen, with sheer cliffs, unusually indented coastlines, clear seas and no water sources at all.

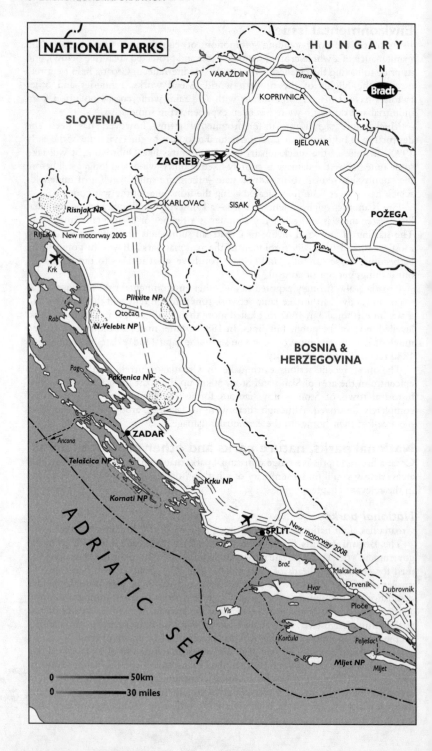

The **Krka** River and waterfalls (see page 214) run from Knin to Skradin, just inland from Šibenik. The park – which is mainly visited by boat – features stunning karst scenery of lakes, waterfalls, canyons and deep forests. At the river's widest point you'll find a lovely Franciscan monastery on an island.

The western part of the island of **Mljet** (see page 298), between Korčula and Dubrovnik, has been designated a national park with good reason. Featuring Europe's only wild mongooses, lush vegetation, and a former monastery on an island on one of two saltwater lakes, Mljet is a delight.

Paklenica National Park (see page 203) is a pair of fabulous limestone gorges running up from the sea into the Velebit massif not far from Zadar. Popular with Croatian climbers and walkers, it's one of my personal favourites and offers hiking from the merely gentle to the seriously strenuous.

The **Plitvice Lakes** (see page 114) are one of Croatia's best known and biggest draws. Situated inland, half way between Zagreb and Zadar, the national park features 16 lakes at different levels, inter-connected by waterfalls. Excellent walking trails keep you away from the crowds, but fun can be had too on the mini-train and organised boat rides.

Risnjak (see page 173), situated north of Rijeka, where the Alps and the Dinara meet, is the perfect national park for mountaineers and naturalists alike, featuring as it does Croatia's biggest diversity of flora and fauna. The beautiful forests and magnificent views here are understandably popular with locals, but you're surprisingly unlikely to bump into foreign visitors.

Between Senj and Karlobag, where the Kvarner Bay turns into northern Dalmatia, lies the forbidding ridge of **North Velebit** National Park (see page 176). Here you'll find some of the remotest hiking in Croatia just inland from one of the most deserted parts of the coast. There's a good reason for that, of course – there's little room along the narrow coast for development, while the massif behind it can be a wild, unwelcoming place, cold in spring and autumn and baking hot in summer. It's not for the faint-hearted, but it is your best chance of seeing a bear in the wild – around 500 live up here.

Nature parks

Croatia also boasts ten designated nature parks covering a further 404,702 hectares (4,047km^2) of the country.

Biokovo (see page 239) is the name of the massif overhanging the Makarska Riviera, between Split and Dubrovnik, and although it's a hard walk to the summit it offers the most breathtaking views out over the islands of Brač and Hvar.

Kopački Rit (see page 129), on Croatia's eastern border, where the river Drava flows into the Danube, is an area of swampland featuring superb bird and plant life, along with plenty of deer and wild boar. It's a birdwatchers' paradise, but take serious mosquito-repellent.

Lonjsko Polje (see page 119), running along the river Sava in Slavonia, is one of the biggest swamps in Europe, and features huge oak forests and excellent birdlife (some 240 species) – and in particular, storks. It's still well off the tourist trail.

Medvednica (see page 89), just north of Zagreb, is a low-key mountainous area which provides the capital's nearest refuge from city life for the locals. Pleasant beech and fir forests, steep-sided valleys, and well-maintained walking paths make this a lovely and quiet alternative to some of the more strenuous parks, and it's very easy to get to.

Papuk (see page 123) is eastern Slavonia's biggest mountain. At under 1,000m high, its forested slopes make for some lovely summer walking, with well-marked and well-maintained trails, burbling brooks, and even thermal baths to swim in.

Bordering on the northern end of the Kornati archipelago, and hogging the cleft-stick inlet at the southern end of Dugi Otok (Long Island), **Telaščica** Park (see page 223) features Croatia's biggest cliffs, rising a dramatic 180m out of the sea. It's naturally popular with anyone lucky enough to be on a sailing holiday.

Učka Park (see page 160) is the name given to the massif above Opatija, in Istria. Rising to 1,400m, the park provides excellent views out over Rijeka and the islands of the Kvarner Bay, and a welcome relief from the crowds along the shore. Well-marked trails and pleasant oak and beech forests make this an excellent day trip from the coast.

Stretching for more than 100km, from Senj to Zadar, the 2,000km² **Velebit** Park (see page 176) includes both the Paklenica and North Velebit National Parks, the latter being home to the **Velebitski Botanički Vrt** botanical gardens and the strictly protected **Hajdučki Kukovi** nature reserve. The gardens, established in 1967, are some of the remotest in Croatia, being situated at around 1,500m in the most inaccessible part of the Velebit, and featuring flora unique to the region. The Hajdučki Kukovi nature reserve shelters one of the dozen deepest caves in the world, **Lukina Jama**, which was only discovered in 1993, and has now been explored to a depth of nearly 1,400m. In the same cave complex you'll find **Atkov Gust**, the second deepest vertical shaft in the world, dropping a dizzying 553m. Take a torch – and a rope.

Between Zadar and Šibenik, in northern Dalmatia, lies Croatia's largest natural lake, **Vransko Jezero** (see page 203), famous for its mix of sea and freshwater fish, and an ornithological reserve, which is home to a wide variety of wading birds and a colony of rare purple herons.

West of Zagreb, across the Sava River and nestled up against the Slovenian border, lies the **Žumberak-Samoborsko Gorje** (see page 106), a protected area of pretty villages connected by well-marked trails, and popular with weekend hikers from the capital.

Other protected areas

This section wouldn't be complete without a brief mention of some of Croatia's other protected areas.

Probably the most famous – and the one you may have seen photographed from the air – is **Zlatni Rat** (Golden Cape), at Bol, on the island of Brač, one of the prettiest beaches on the Adriatic. The 600m spit of fine gravel, backed by pine forests, changes shape according to the sea currents and seasonal winds.

Apart from the famous Krka (see above), four other rivers in Croatia deserve a mention here. The **Drava**, starting in Slovenia and running along the border between Croatia and Hungary, is one of Europe's best-protected large rivers, and a candidate for being nominated as a world biosphere. The fast-flowing **Dobra**, near Karlovac (50km west of Zagreb), is popular for rafting, kayaking and canoeing, while the **Mrežnica**, nearby – a tributary of the Kupa River – is all the rage with bathers. Finally, the 30km-long **Gacka**, near Otočac, inland from Senj, is a trout-fisher's paradise, with clear waters flowing past picturesque old water mills.

On the west coast of Istria is the fjord-like 10km inlet of **Limski Zaljev**. A nature reserve since 1979, it's an important haven for fish over-wintering or spawning. The low salinity and high plankton count make it popular too with mussel and oyster farmers – and eaters.

Down at the other end of the coast, between Makarska and Dubrovnik, is the **Neretva Delta**, one of the Adriatic's most important waterfowl reserves, featuring swampy salt marshes, lagoons, reeds and meadows. Inland from Makarska, near Imotski, are the Red and Blue Lakes (**Crveno Jezero** and **Modro Jezero**), a pair of unusually deep water-filled holes in the karst. The bottom of Red Lake is only

19m above sea-level, with a depth varying from 280 to 320m, and Blue Lake really is blue. As indeed is the Blue Cave (**Modra Špilja**), of course, on the island of Biševo, off the western end of Vis. The cave – like the Blue Grotto on Capri – is visitable only by boat, and many rate it as highly as its Capri counterpart.

Finally, a mention should be given to **Gorski Kotar**, the strictly protected nature reserve east of Rijeka, which contains Risnjak National Park (see above). In the forests here, which are among Europe's most unspoiled, wolves, brown bear, lynx and wild boar can still be found in the wild, along with a wide variety of bird species and plantlife. Gorski Kotar also features such striking natural phenomena as the extraordinary karst rock formations at Bijele and Samarske Stijene, or Vražji Prolaz (the Devil's Pass) near Skrad, a narrow canyon with a perilous footpath running through it.

HISTORY

Croatia is at once a very old country and a very young one. Inhabited since the early Stone Age, and a lynchpin of the Roman Empire, it only became a modern nation in 1991, and parts of the country were still under UN control – following the war – until 1998. And whilst it was a respectable kingdom of its own in medieval times, Croatia has spent most of the past millennium attached to (or subjugated by) its near neighbours. As a result the country's history is unbelievably turbulent; fraught with foreign intervention, plagued by constant strife from pre-Roman times on, and richly textured with assassinations, intrigues, piracy and treachery.

Over the past 2,500 years a succession of empires invaded, annexed or occupied Croatia, and each left its mark. For example islands along the Adriatic coast which were deforested by the Venetians in the 18th century are still barren, yet the coastal towns and cities wouldn't be half as lovely if it weren't for the Venetian Gothic architecture.

Croatian independence today is remarkable given the sheer numbers of land grabs it's been subjected to, with Greeks, Romans, Ostrogoths, Avars, Slavs, Franks, Byzantines, Venetians, Hungarians, Tartars, Austrians, French, Italians, Turks, Germans and Serbs all having had their eye on a piece of the Croatian action.

Which is hardly surprising: the Adriatic has been the most practical trade route between Europe and the East since trade began there, around 3,000 years ago. Croatia has also been a buffer zone between east and west and between north and south for centuries.

Illyrians, Greeks and Romans

In spite of lots of early Stone Age finds, recorded history in Croatia starts with the Illyrians, a group of tribes that shared techniques for building and burying their dead but not much else, it seems. By the 7th century BC they were trading with the ancient Greeks, and within two centuries the Greeks had established colonies in the area, notably at Pharos (now Stari Grad, on the island of Hvar) and Salona, and on the island of Vis.

By 229BC the Greeks were calling on Rome to help them in their quest to dominate the Illyrians, and the Romans pitched in with enthusiasm – though it took them more than two centuries to complete the job. In AD9, five years before becoming emperor, Tiberius finally annexed the area for Rome, thereby becoming the first (and last, until 1918) person to unify this bit of the Balkans.

Under Roman rule the Balkans – and Dalmatia in particular – prospered, providing the empire with troops and provisions and receiving the protection of a major world power in return, setting something of a pattern for the region. The Romans built (or reinforced) many of the existing settlements, with their principal cities being Pola (Pula), Jadera (Zadar) and Salona (Solin). As was their wont, they also constructed summer palaces along the coast and on the islands, and reinforced trade links all the way from Pula to Cavtat.

The most famous Dalmatians to make it big at this time were the three who went on to become Roman emperors, most notably Diocletian, who ruled from AD284–305 – an astonishingly long period given that more than a dozen emperors had come and gone in the generation before he came to power. Diocletian ruled from Nicomedia (now Izmít, in Turkey), but started building himself a fabulously swanky retirement home just along the coast from his native Salona within months of taking the purple. Diocletian's palace in Split remains one of Croatia's most impressive monuments, with its corridors today being streets and its rooms entire houses.

In AD293, Diocletian partitioned the empire into the western and eastern parts, with the river Drina being the boundary, thus sealing Croatia's fate forever as a province on the frontline. Diocletian's frontier ran through the cities of Budva and Belgrade, and a rough approximation of this can still be seen on maps today, marking the eastern border of Slavonia in Croatia, and running down the eastern side of Bosnia & Herzegovina and Albania. Everything east of this line ultimately became Byzantium, and Orthodox, while everything west became part of Rome (and the eventual Holy Roman Empire), and Catholic. The division is also clearly visible today in the use of the Latin alphabet to the west and Cyrillic to the east.

Diocletian abdicated in AD305 and retired to Split, spending the last 11 years of his life in palatial splendour, rousing himself only to throw Christians to the lions; having tolerated the religion for most of his reign he spent the rest of his life in relentless persecution of it.

Arrival of the Slavs

The Roman Empire imploded in the 5th century, leaving the way clear for invasions by Huns, Goths, Vlachs, Avars, Bulgars and – most importantly for this guide – Slavs.

One group of Slavs, coming from what is now Poland, was the Croats. They conquered Roman Pannonia (now roughly the area known as Slavonia) and much of Dalmatia, and drove the inhabitants from the Dalmatian capital Salona to the nearby islands of Šolta, Brač, Hvar, Vis and Korčula.

During the same period, other Slavic ethnic groups, the Slovenes and the Serbs, settled the areas roughly corresponding to Slovenia and Serbia.

After a series of tussles with the Franks, Avars and Byzantines, the Croats finally managed to unite Dalmatian and Pannonian Croatia in AD925, under the crown of King Tomislav. For more than a century the kingdom prospered, with the greatest Croatian king being Petar Krešimir IV, who ruled over Bosnia, Slavonia and the Dalmatian towns and islands from 1058 to 1074.

Byzantium and Venice were already encroaching on the southern and northern coastlands, however, and Hungary soon captured most of the interior, driving a corridor through to the sea by 1089. After the death of King Stjepan II in 1091, it all fell apart. A decade later, in 1102, the Hungarian King Kalman knocked together the heads of the 12 most powerful Croatian clans, persuading them to sign up to the *Pacta Conventa*, under which they would accept the Hungarian monarch's rule but were able to maintain Croatia's traditions and customs. Amazingly the treaty held until 1918.

Venetians, Austro-Hungarians, and the Illyrian Provinces

Over the next 700 years Croatian history largely depended on which of its neighbours was the most powerful *du jour*, with Hungary/Austria driving down from the north, the Ottoman Empire steaming in from the southeast, and Venice ever expansive from its corner of the Adriatic. Much of the architectural heritage of the country dates from this period, with the coast and islands still looking remarkably Venetian, and the interior retaining a monumental Habsburg feel.

During the 16th century, Austria created the Krajina (literally 'zone'), as a buffer against the advance of the Ottoman Turks, and Serbs who had escaped Ottoman rule were given land in the Krajina in exchange for military service.

In 1558 the Croatian and Slavonian diets were united, and Zagreb became Croatia's capital. Just 15 years later the peasants revolted and – as you'd expect – were ruthlessly suppressed. Their leader, Matija Gubec, was executed in Zagreb (see page 84).

A century later, in 1671, another rebellion was set in motion against the Habsburgs, this time led by the aristocratic Petar Zrinski and Fran Krsto Frankopan. Expecting help from abroad which never materialised, they were swiftly brought to task and they too were executed.

Uskoks

For much of the 16th century, the regional balance of power along the coast had been in the hands of a small third party, the Uskoks, who were pirates, based in the port of Senj from the 1530s until the Uskok war of 1615–17.

The Uskoks (from the Croatian word *uskočiti*, to 'jump in' or 'to board') were refugees who had been driven north by the advancing Ottoman Turks, but as their swashbuckling exploits grew they attracted rebels from all quarters. When a party of Uskoks was hanged in Venice in 1618, nine of them turned out to be English – of whom six were apparently of noble birth.

At first, until the mid 1560s, the Uskoks attacked the Ottoman Turks on land and sea, but after this anyone appears to have been fair game, especially the Venetians, who were accused by the Uskoks of being un-Christian. This suited the Habsburgs just fine. Even though they paid lip service to condemning piratical exploits (they were after all the nominal rulers of Senj at the time) anyone that was harassing their enemies was a friend rather than a foe.

The Uskoks however, appear to have been reluctant pirates, and pleas for tillable land in the interior fell on deaf ears for more than 50 years. They also had an honourable reputation amongst their immediate neighbours, the Kvarner Bay islanders of Krk, Cres, Rab and Pag, redistributing their booty whenever possible and paying for provisions when they had the money to do so.

The unwilling pirates were finally crushed during the eponymously named Uskok War from 1615-17, after which the Habsburgs agreed to a military occupation of Senj. The surviving Uskoks were impelled 30km inland to Otočac, which they had wanted all along. They disappeared without trace.

Ragusa

At the same time, another city, Ragusa, was at the height of its fame and powers. Ragusa was one of the most important – and independent – of the Dalmatian cities, fending off unwanted interference by successfully paying off the Ottoman Turks and the Hungarians. Ragusa, in fact, remains one of Croatia's most fashionable tourist attractions…under its Croatian name, Dubrovnik.

The Illyrian Provinces

Venice and Ragusa alike were swept aside by Napoleon, who created the Illyrian Provinces, a region running all the way from Trieste and Slovenia in the north to Dubrovnik in the south. The region was administered by Marshal Marmont, and for a few brief years benefited from the French passion for building roads, fortifying towns and encouraging the local south Slav culture – in a bid to create a buffer against undue Russian and Austro-Hungarian ambitions. 'Though Marmont was a self-satisfied prig, he was an extremely competent and honourable man, and he loved Dalmatia,' as Rebecca West so succinctly put it when she came through in 1937.

Austro-Hungarians

But it was for nought; Napoleon fell, and Habsburg rule was restored in 1815, albeit within a separate Kingdom of Croatia and Slavonia. By the middle of the 19th century an educated elite, led by Ljudevit Gaj started defending Croatian nationality and sovereignty and worked towards a national revival, under the moniker of the Illyrian Movement. Count Janko Drašković helped the movement along in 1832 by publishing the first political pamphlet in Croatian.

In 1848 the viceroy of Croatia, Ban Josip Jelačić, led an army of 50,000 soldiers towards Hungary, but instead of winning independence for his country he unfortunately allowed Austria to take over both countries instead. Nonetheless he was a great hero, having abolished feudalism and brought in reforms allowing elected officials to join the nobility in parliament (the Sabor). After his death in 1859 a great statue of him on horseback was raised in Zagreb's central square. A year later a new constitution allowed Croatian to become the national language.

The Kingdom of Croatia and Slavonia continued under Austro-Hungarian rule until the 525th anniversary of the Ottoman defeat of Lazar at the battle of Kosovo Polje, last of the independent Serbian rulers, in 1389.

On that day (June 28 1914) Archduke Franz Ferdinand, heir to the Austro-Hungarian Empire – in a remarkable display of hubris, given that it was a day of national mourning – ignored all warnings and paid an official visit to Sarajevo. And with his wife, Sophie Chotek, was shot dead by a 19-year-old student called Gavrilo Princip, thus kicking off World War I. Austria had long been looking to declare war on Serbia, and this provided the perfect excuse. Russia took offence; Germany supported Austria; Britain and France piled in with Russia; and the world's bloodiest war to date was underway.

The Kingdom of the Serbs, Croats and Slovenes

Aware that the Austro-Hungarian Empire was going to come out of the war at best badly diminished, Slovenia and Croatia threw in their lot with Serbia in 1918, resulting in the creation of the Kingdom of Serbs, Croats and Slovenes, under the Crown of King Petar I from the dynastic Karađorđević family.

Petar was succeeded on his death, three years later, by his son King Aleksandar I, in the face of increasing irritation on the part of the Croats that they had so little power in Belgrade. The Croatian Republican Peasant Party, led by firebrand Stjepan Radić, had won local elections in 1920, but this wasn't of any use to the party in the capital.

Tension remained high through the 1920s, until, on June 20 1928, Radić was shot in Belgrade's parliamentary chamber by a Montenegrin deputy. Six weeks later Radić died and more than 100,000 turned up to his funeral in Zagreb. The king suspended parliament 'reluctantly' at the beginning of 1929 and established a dictatorship in its place, promising to restore democracy once unity had been achieved. In October that year he also finally put diplomats and letter-writers across the continent out of their misery by changing the country's name to the more manageable Yugoslavia.

So much for the good news – 1929 also saw the founding of the Ustaše by Ante Pavelić, a party dedicated to the violent overthrow of the Yugoslav state, and one which would later have a dramatic effect on Croatia's future.

Croatian national sentiment continued to run high, and in 1934, King Aleksandar, aged 46, was assassinated in Marseille, in a plot sponsored by the Ustaše but executed by a Macedonian with Italian support. Aleksandar's death left the ill-equipped Prince Petar to run the country – aged only 11. His uncle, Prince Pavle, was drafted in to help, but Yugoslavia was in no state to prosper. And war was once again on the horizon.

World War II

By the time World War II broke out – not the Balkans' fault this time round – the country was in a mess. The Ustaše fascists wanted complete independence for Croatia, Macedonia was trying to secede, and only the Yugoslav Communist Party, founded in 1919 and outlawed nine years later, had any kind of countrywide support.

Yugoslavia managed to remain neutral for the first year and a half of the war, but increasing axis pressure resulted in Prince Pavle signing a pact on March 25 1941,

KARAÐORÐEVIĆ ROYALTY

Having been born in the Royal Palace in Belgrade in September 1923 and been pronounced king at the age of 11 after his father's assassination, it must have been a shock for the 17-year-old monarch, King Petar II, to find himself sitting out the war in London.

Fortunately for the Karaðorðević dynasty, Petar married Princess Aleksandra of Greece (the daughter of King Alexander) at the Yugoslav Embassy in London in 1944, and on July 17 the following year she bore him a son, Crown Prince Aleksandar II of Yugoslavia.

Parliament, under the orders of Winston Churchill, stepped in quickly and proclaimed Suite 212 of Claridges as Yugoslav territory, so that the putative heir would have the right to be king some day, and the child was baptised in Westminster Abbey by the Patriarch of Serbia. No prizes for guessing the godparents: King George VI and his daughter Princess Elizabeth (QE II, to you).

An auspicious start to Aleksandar's life, perhaps, but in November 1945 the Yugoslav monarchy was abolished by the communists, under the leadership of Tito, and although King Petar II never abdicated, he never saw Yugoslavia again, either. He died after a long illness at the Colorado General Hospital, in Denver, in 1970, only a year older than his father had been when he was assassinated in Marseille in 1934.

Since the summer of 2001, post-Milošević, Crown Prince Aleksandar, for his part, has been living in the Royal Palace in Belgrade, with his family, returned from lifelong exile. As the great-great-grandson of Queen Victoria and the cousin of King Juan Carlos of Spain, he half expects to see the monarchy restored – on constitutional lines, of course – but he has one major disadvantage: he apparently speaks Serbian very poorly.

aligning Yugoslavia with fascist Germany and Italy, in spite of his personal pro-British sentiments. Two days later a group of air force officers, backed by both the communists and the Orthodox Church, staged a coup d'état, deposed Prince Pavle and installed King Petar II, now aged $17^1/_2$, in his place.

The pact was annulled and Yugoslavia reaffirmed its neutrality; Hitler responded by bombing Belgrade on April 6. On the same day massive German and Italian armies entered the country, and Yugoslavia capitulated ten days later. King Petar II escaped to London with the Yugoslav government and set up house in Claridges, never to return to his former kingdom.

The Ustaše

Once Yugoslavia had thrown in the towel in 1941, the Ustaše declared the Independent State of Croatia (*Nezavisna Država Hrvatska*, NDH), leaving the rest of Yugoslavia to be carved up between Germany, Hungary, Bulgaria and Italy – something for which the Ustaše has never really been forgiven by many. Contrary to what has been claimed by some, resistance to the Ustaše was strong across Croatia throughout the war, but it was often the subject of ruthless suppression.

From the start, the Ustaše tried to clear the Serbs out of Croatia. When this proved impossible, they set up a number of concentration camps, the most notorious being the Jasenovac complex, a string of five camps on the bank of the Sava River, about 100km south of Zagreb. The camps were used from 1942 to 1945 to eliminate not just Serbs but also religious minorities and political opponents of the Ustaše, and reports are that they were just as bad as the more notorious German camps at Auschwitz, Belsen or Treblinka. Scenes of unbelievable barbarism were reported at the Jasenovac 'death factory', including contests to see who could kill the most people in a single night.

Nobody will ever know for sure how many people were killed by the Ustaše, but it's now thought that between 300,000 and 400,000 Serbs were killed in total, with 40,000–50,000 being murdered at Jasenovac alone. One of the unfortunate reasons for the confusion over the numbers is that Jasenovac has long been used by both sides in a propaganda war between Serbia and Croatia, with some Croatians calling the Serbian numbers (up to a million) inflated, while many Serbs feel that Croats have tried to whitewash the past.

The Resistance

After the fall of Yugoslavia, in April 1941, resistance was immediately organised, but divided into two fiercely opposed groups, the Četniks and the partisans. The royalist, pro-Serbian, Četniks supported the government in exile in London, and hated just about everybody else – Croats (both Ustaše and resistance), Germans, Italians, communists, and a host of non-Serb minorities.

As anti-Germans, the Četniks were aided at first by the allies, but they were regarded with distrust by many Yugoslavs. The partisans, on the other hand, led by Josip Broz 'Tito', were the army of the communist party, and although only 42,000 strong at the outset, their effective resistance and daring attacks earned them wide support from communists and non-communists alike.

Unfortunately, however, the desire of the two resistance groups to rid Yugoslavia of invaders – and indeed the Ustaše – was at times exceeded by their determination to kill each other, resulting in a long and bloody civil war being run in parallel with the greater conflict. The partisans themselves are thought to have murdered up to 100,000 of their opponents at the end of the war, interring them in caves, never to be mentioned again.

When the end of the war was close, Ustaše-founder Ante Pavelić mobilised large numbers of Croat reservists and civilians and persuaded them to go to Bleiburg, in Austria (the British HQ), to surrender to the allies. The British, to whom they surrendered, immediately handed them back (against American orders) to Tito's troops, who had some shot and buried in mass graves on the spot and marched the rest to the other end of Yugoslavia along what Croats now call the *Križni Put* (Way of the Cross). Contemporary Croat history tells us that at least 50,000 died along the way. Ante Pavelić wasn't one of them: he escaped to South America and then on to Franco's Spain, where he died in 1959.

Yugoslavia paid a terrible price during World War II, with more than a tenth of its citizens being killed. Among them were at least 300,000 Croats, 300,000 partisans and nearly 400,000 Bosnians. But the resistance had successfully tied up enormous numbers of axis soldiers, and it's quite possible that the allies couldn't have won the war without Yugoslavia.

With the help of the British (aid was transferred from the Četniks to the partisans in 1943), and the Red Army, Belgrade was finally liberated in 1944, and by 1945 a provisional government, in temporary accord with the government in exile, was in force.

Tito and a non-aligned Yugoslavia
Post-war elections not surprisingly gave the communists 90% of the vote – with separate ballot boxes provided for those who cared to vote against them. That gave the government the freedom to set up on the lines adopted by Stalinist Russia, and to embark on a disastrous experiment with collectivisation.

Stalin, however, was wary of Yugoslavia, as it was the only country in the Eastern Bloc to have made its way entirely independently. And indeed, in 1948, Tito broke with the Cominform, the economic ground base for the countries allied to the Soviet Union. This declaration of non-alignment was arguably the greatest political act of Tito's career, allowing Yugoslavia to develop its own brand of communism. And it's the main reason why Serbs, Croats, Slovenes, Montenegrins and Macedonians get huffy even today if you lump them in with the Eastern Bloc.

Tito's was a brave political move, for sure, but it brought hard times for Yugoslavia in the 1950s, starting with an economic blockade by the Soviet Union. Credits from the west and the launch of mass tourism in the 1960s saved the country, however. Tito introduced the idea of workers' self-management, putting the country's hospitals, schools and factories in the hands of those who staffed them, and despite leading to sometimes excessive decentralisation, it allowed competition within the framework of communism, proving reasonably effective during the 1960s and 1970s.

In an attempt to solve Yugoslavia's nationalist problems Tito had also decentralised the state itself, giving each of the six republics complete control over its internal affairs. While Tito lived this was a remarkably effective strategy, mainly because he was ruthless in suppressing opposition. Croatian writers and intellectuals had issued a declaration in 1967 stating that Croatian was a different language from Serbian, and Croatian Serbs had quickly counter-declared their right to be taught in Serbian, but Tito would have none of it, and was quick to quash the so-called 'Croatian Spring' in 1971.

After being declared President for Life in 1974, Tito died in 1980, three days before his 88th birthday. He made one more trip around the country in funeral state, in the Blue Train made famous during the early post-war days when he toured the country tirelessly promoting his programme of Brotherhood and

Unity. This time it was mourners who lined the tracks in their thousands, and it's difficult now to conjure up just how important Tito's funeral was. It still stands as one of the best attended ever, from an international perspective, with official mourners coming from more than 120 countries, including four kings, 32 presidents and other heads of state, 22 prime ministers, and more than 100 representatives or secretaries of communist and workers' parties.

Post-Tito

Like so many singularly powerful men, Tito left his country with a weak succession. Each of the republics would, in theory, get a year as head man, but without Tito's personal charisma and unifying strength it was never going to work well. It wasn't long before the old problems of nationalism, unfair distribution of wealth between the republics, and corruption in government resurfaced.

Onto this scene arrived Slobodan Milošević, who rapidly gained popularity in Serbia after defending Serb protestors against mostly ethnic Albanian police in Kosovo in 1987. Two years later, on June 28 1989 – that date, again (see page 14) – Milošević addressed a million Serbs at Kosovo Polje and was elected president of Serbia in the autumn.

This was the beginning of the end for a united Yugoslavia. Milošević's talk of an ethnically pure Greater Serbia was never going to sit well with Slovenes, Croats, Bosnians, Macedonians – or indeed most Kosovars.

War – and Croatian Independence

The fall of the Berlin Wall in 1989 and the collapse of communist governments across Europe encouraged several republics, led by Slovenia and Croatia, to try and change the political structure of Yugoslavia.

In 1990, led by former army general and dissident (some would prefer revisionist) historian Franjo Tuđman, the Croatian Democratic Union (HDZ), won elections. Once in power, the HDZ pushed parliament to drop the word 'Socialist' from the Croatian republic's name, and the red star was quietly removed from public symbols. The HDZ also put Croatia's 600,000 Serbs on the defensive by changing their status from 'constituent nation' in Croatia to 'national minority', and many Serbs in government lost their jobs. The HDZ didn't improve matters by making itself an easy target for Serb propaganda, party members playing straight into Serb hands by attempting to rehabilitate the Ustaše or by saying that the numbers of people killed at Jasenovac were inflated (whether or not that was true).

At the same time, most of the republics tried to negotiate a transition to a confederation, on the Swiss model, but this went completely against the Milošević view of a Greater Serbia, with money and power concentrated in Belgrade. As a result, the rebellious republics raised their sights, aiming for independent statehood instead. Trouble was inevitable.

During the summer of 1990, encouraged by Belgrade into fearing real danger, Croatia's Serbs (armed by the Yugoslav People's Army, the JNA) declared an autonomous region around Knin, 50km inland from Šibenik. Croatian police helicopters, sent in to sort out the trouble, were soon scuttled by Yugoslav air force MIGs. Tension continued to mount until March 1991, when Knin paramilitaries took control of the Plitvice Lakes, resulting in the first casualties of the conflict.

Slovenia, meanwhile, had unilaterally decided to declare independence on June 25 1991, so Croatia declared independence on the same day – after a referendum held in May had delivered a 94% verdict in favour of a sovereign and independent Croatian state. Milošević immediately sent tanks into

FRANJO TUĐMAN – CROATIA'S FIRST PRESIDENT

Franjo Tuđman was born in 1922 and at the age of 19 joined Tito's partisans, becoming a decorated hero by the end of World War II. His youngest brother was killed as a partisan in 1943, and his depressed father is said to have shot himself and his second wife in 1946 – though Tuđman himself claimed first that they were victims of the Ustaše and later that they had been killed by the communists. (As a curious parallel, both of Milošević's parents committed suicide; his mother when Milošević was a child; his father when he was 18.)

After the war, Tuđman was sent to the advanced military academy in Belgrade, and he stayed in the army until 1961, when he retired at the age of 38, with the rank of Major-General. During the 1960s, as a historian, Tuđman gradually began to fall out of favour with the communists, and in 1971, following the suppression of the 'Croatian Spring' he was jailed for a short time, escaping a longer sentence only through the intervention with Tito of the respected Croatian writer Miroslav Krleža. He served nine months in prison in 1972.

A decade later and more strongly nationalist than ever, Tuđman was sentenced in 1981 to a three-year sentence and banned from all public activity for his dissident/revisionist views on history and for advocating a pluralist democracy. He served about half of this before being released because of failing health.

In 1987, having finally got his passport back after 17 years, he travelled in the west, widely promoting the cause of Croatian independence, and in 1989 he founded the Croatian Democratic Union (HDZ), which became the dominant political force in the first multi-party parliamentary election in the spring of 1990. The tenor of the campaign can be measured by Tuđman's reportedly having said 'Thank God my wife is neither a Serb nor a Jew'.

In spite of the strong words, Tuđman nonetheless found time for a secret meeting with Milošević in March 1991, to discuss how Croatia and Serbia might carve up Bosnia & Herzegovina for themselves. Nonetheless, Tuđman was hugely popular, as the first person since the Middle Ages to gain international recognition for Croatia as an independent state. At his funeral, in December 1999, thousands filed past his coffin – but only his death may have saved him from being indicted, like Milošević, by the Tribunal in The Hague.

Ljubljana, in Slovenia (and I'll never forget the phone call I had from a friend in the Slovene Mountain Association, who had a tank outside his office), and to the Italian and Austrian borders. The world sat up and took notice, and the EU introduced sanctions; within a week Serbia realised it didn't stand a chance (with Italy and Austria so close) and the war in Slovenia was over. Within a month the army had left the country – though it only retreated as far as Croatia, and later distributed many weapons to the local Serb population.

Croatia, with a significant Serb minority, wasn't as fortunate as Slovenia. As soon as it proclaimed independence, the Serbs countered by proclaiming the independent state of Republika Srpska Krajina (RSK) within Croatia, declaring loyalty to Belgrade and Milošević (the commander of the army), and choosing Knin as its capital.

In six months at the end of 1991 – with the help of the JNA, and heavy fighting, bombardments and air-strikes – the Serbs ethnically 'cleansed' nearly a third of Croatia, re-awakening memories of the brutality of the 1940s. Thousands of Croats were forced to leave their homes and many were killed by the JNA or loosely associated paramilitary forces.

Many towns were besieged and bombarded for months, with wholesale destruction and local suffering involved. Worst of all was the siege of Vukovar, which ended with appalling atrocities being carried out on the local Croatian population. Dubrovnik was also besieged, suffering huge damage and considerable loss of life.

Local industry across the country was effectively destroyed, and Croatia was paralysed by the RSK, which controlled most of the country's oil resources, the land routes to the Dalmatian coastal cities, and the main access road from Zagreb into Slavonia. The tourist trade – one of Croatia's main sources of foreign earnings – came to a complete halt.

By the time the UN was able to broker a cease-fire in January 1992, thousands of people had died, tens of thousands of homes had been destroyed, and Croatia had hundreds of thousands of local refugees, placing a huge burden on the main cities. Only then did the European Union (in spite of French and British reluctance) recognise Slovenian and Croatian independence. In May, after amending its constitution to protect minority groups and human rights, Croatia joined the United Nations.

It was not a happy country, however. Croatia was all but impossible to administrate with its newly fragmented borders, and from 1994 it lobbied hard, against intense European opposition, to end the UN policing of the cease-fire line. Failing on that front, it took matters into its own hands. From June 1995, Croatia 'liberated' the Krajina in a series of lightning assaults, first reclaiming the main road into Slavonia, and then focusing on the main part of the RSK in August.

WESTERN TIES

Most men dressing for work in the morning don't spare a thought for Croatia – which is a pity, as the ubiquitous neck-tie they put on not just originated there but is named after the country.

The origins of one of fashion's most durable accessories date back to the Thirty Years War in Europe, which ran from 1618 to 1648. The story goes that Croatian mercenaries of the period wore a colourful silk scarf tied around the neck. Some of their number were stationed in Paris, and were presented to the court (whether that of Louis XIII, who died in 1643, or Louis XIV, who succeeded him, is debatable), triggering off a copycat craze for cravates – the word coming from dressing à la Croat (or Hrvat, in Croatian).

During the dandyish reign of Louis XIV the wearing of cravates by French men became widespread, and the new fashion soon spread right across Europe – indeed the French word 'cravate' exists in one form or another in almost every European language, from 'gravata' in Greek to 'krawatte' in German.

Today, businessmen across the whole world consider the tie as a basic part of their wardrobe, though for the most part they probably aren't wearing the enormously expensive long and floppy silk scarves favoured by Croatian soldiers, but the rather more sober ties launched in England at the end of the 19th century.

In just three days, fuelled by both fear and propaganda from Belgrade, most of the civilian Serb population fled the land they had lived on for centuries, in perhaps the biggest example of ethnic cleansing in the war so far. The leaders of the RSK launched rocket attacks on Zagreb and Sisak as a parting shot, before retreating to Serbia. In the vacuum left in the Krajina, however, Serb houses across the RSK were looted and destroyed, while the authorities turned a blind eye.

The December 1995 Dayton Peace Agreement finally helped to restore stability to the region, reinforced at the end of 1996 by the signing of a peace treaty between Croatia and Yugoslavia, although the last bit of eastern Slavonia which was still in Serb hands was only returned to Croatia, under UN supervision, in January 1998.

A vast reconstruction programme has meant that most houses have now been rebuilt, and Serbs have been encouraged to return – though nobody's sure quite how many have actually done so. What is clear is that with so much bloodshed, anguish and suffering across the region, reconciliation is a painful process, and it's not surprising that some people are still bitter about the failure of Britain in particular to support Croatia early on during the conflict.

POLITICS

Independence brought Croatia a new constitution (online in English at www.vlada.hr/english/docs-constitution.html if you're interested) and a new political system which – as the Ministry of Foreign Affairs says on its website (www.mvp.hr) – is now 'democratic and based on a respect for human rights, law, national equality, social justice and multiple political parties'. The last part is certainly true enough, with a bewildering array of three- and four-letter acronyms to deal with. At the elections in the year 2000, following the death of Franjo Tuđman (see box on page 19), more than 4,000 candidates from 55 political parties stood for office. As Rebecca West said witheringly, when she was here in 1937, 'There is no end to political disputation in Croatia. None.'

Croatia's independence also brought it a new flag, known locally, irreverently, as the 'zoo' – above the chequerboard of the main flag are the old coats of arms from the regions, featuring Dalmatia's three crowned-leopards, Istria's goat, and Slavonia's marten.

Croatia's legislature consists of a parliament, the Sabor, with 151 MPs elected for a four-year period. The president (re-elected in 2005), is the colourful Stjepan (Stipe) Mesić – a former Secretary of the HDZ, and Croatia's first prime minister. If you can read Croatian, it's worth visiting his chatty website at www.stipemesic.com; English readers will find www.president.hr more rewarding.

Like Tuđman, Mesić had also been condemned in the repression of the 'Croatian Spring' in 1971, and he served a one-year jail sentence at the notorious Stara Gradiska prison. Later, however, he later went on to be elected to the Sabor, the body from which Yugoslav presidents were appointed in rotation, following Tito's death in 1980. As a result, Mesić also became the last president of a united Yugoslavia, until his resignation in December 1991.

In 1994, disagreeing with the HDZ policy on Bosnia & Herzegovina – Tuđman still appearing to be keen to carve it up between Serbia and Croatia – Mesić left the party and set up the rival Croatian Independent Democrats (HND). Three years later he joined the Croatian People's Party (HNS) and became the HNS executive vice president.

In the most recent parliamentary elections, held at the end of 2003, the HDZ saw a return to form, winning 66 of the 151 seats available in the Sabor (parliament), and able to form a government via an informal coalition with other smaller parties. Both the president and the prime minister, Ivo Sanader, are keen to join NATO and the EU – although hopes that this might happen in 2006 for NATO and 2007 for the EU may nonetheless be overly optimistic.

ECONOMY

Croatia is still paying the price of a legacy of communist mismanagement of the economy, as well as its more recent war, which left infrastructure damaged and large numbers of people displaced. Progress towards economic reform has been hampered by coalition politics and resistance on the street, mainly from trade unions, but the government is now keen to achieve EU membership, and the economy is looking in better shape than it has for years.

Inflation dropped to just 2.1% in 2003, and GDP, at close to US$40 billion (at purchasing power parity, PPP) grew by 4.3% from 2002 to 2003. Nonetheless, Croatian GDP per capita, at around US$8,800, is still under half that in Spain and around a third of that in the UK. Average gross salary in April 2004 had risen to 5,962 kuna per month (around €800), but unemployment, at 18.6%, was still stubbornly high.

Vital to the economy – especially along the coast – is tourism. In the year 2000 revenue from tourism finally exceeded the 1990 figures for the first time, and in 2003 was worth something like US$8 billion annually to Croatia's economy. The government expects this figure to reach US$20 billion within ten years.

TOURISM

In 1990 more than 16 million tourist nights were spent in Istria alone, and 3.5 million nights were spent in Dubrovnik – more than 814,000 of them by the British. The following year people stayed away in droves. In Istria – the part of the country least affected by the war – tourist nights plummeted by more than three-quarters, to below 4 million.

Since 1998, however, the recovery has been rapid and continuous, and the number of tourist nights in Croatia as a whole grew from 31.9 million in 1998 to 46.6 million in 2003. The number of foreign visitors to the country over the same period grew from under 4.5 million to over 8.9 million, staying in around 800,000 beds in some 300,000 rooms. Visitor figures have now overtaken their 1990 peak, when 8.5 million tourists came to Croatia.

Istria is Croatia's undisputed tourist capital, registering a staggering 16.2 million tourist nights from 2.4 million visitors in 2003. In the same year Dubrovnik county, one of the next busiest places on the tourist map, registered 697,000 visitors, staying for an average of five nights each.

The vast majority (over 85%) of Croatia's tourists are foreigners from the north in search of sea and sunshine, leaving most of the wonderful national parks and nature reserves remarkably empty, even at the height of the season. The most numerous visitors in 2003 were Germans (1.5 million), Italians (1.2 million), Austrians (710,000), and Czechs (700,000); the UK, for its part, was a long way down the list, with 153,000 visitors to Croatia in 2003, although the figure was up by nearly half on the year 2001.

PEOPLE

In spite of the large displacement of people – both Serbs and Croats – during the war of the 1990s, Croatia's total population has remained fairly stable (at around 4.4 million) over the past 20 years. Ethnic demographics have changed however.

In the 1991 census, around three-quarters of people considered themselves Croats, while 12.2% said they were Serbs. A decade later, the 2001 census showed that almost 90% of people thought of themselves as Croats, while Serbs only accounted for 4.5% of the population. There are a number of reasons for the decline in Serb numbers, including the introduction of a new category, 'ethnically uncommitted' (which attracted 2% of the population in 2001), changes in the census methodology, especially relating to Croatians living abroad (ethnic Croats were counted; ethnic Serbs weren't), and the exodus of Serbs from Croatia during 1995. It will be interesting indeed to see the results in 2011.

Croatia also has a whole host of other national minority populations, as follows (2001 census): Bosnians 0.5%, Hungarians 0.4%, Italians 0.4%, Slovenians 0.3%, Albanians 0.3%, Czechs 0.2%, Montenegrins 0.1%, Macedonians 0.1% and Slovaks 0.1%.

However they describe themselves, I've always found the people of Croatia to be warm, hospitable and generous, though inevitably this varies from place to place and person to person. In the interior, and especially in the national parks and nature reserves, people tend to have more time for you, whereas along the coast you might sometimes mistake a certain efficiency for brusqueness, especially at the height of the season. But in Croatia, as everywhere, you'll find that people on the whole will treat you right, if you treat them right.

LANGUAGE

The official language is Croatian, written using a Latin alphabet. For 96% of the population this is their first language, with the remaining 4% mostly speaking Italian, Hungarian, Czech, Slovak or German.

Croatian is a tough language to learn, but words are nothing like as difficult to pronounce as you'd think, since every letter always has a unique pronunciation – albeit not always the same as in English. Although you're unlikely to have time to learn much Croatian, grab at least a handful of words and phrases to take with you – the effort will be richly rewarded (see *Appendix 1* for some essentials).

The language comes from the group described by linguists as Serbo-Croat, meaning that Serbs, Croats and Bosnians can readily understand each other – not that you'd necessarily know this, judging by the strife of the past 20 (or even 2,000) years. Within Croatia itself there are also regional variations and dialects, with the one you'll most likely notice being the three different ways Croats have of saying 'what?'. The official version – used in the media – is the Slavonian '*što?*', but in Zagreb you'll hear '*kaj?*' and along the coast it's invariably '*ča?*'.

The use of the Latin alphabet is largely to do with religion, and the east–west division of the Roman Empire – it was in Croatia in the 9th century that Sts Cyril and Methodius invented the Glagolitic alphabet (see *Glagolitic Alley*, in Istria), which was converted by St Clement, in Ohrid (now in the Former Yugoslav Republic of Macedonia), into the Cyrillic alphabet, variants of which are now used throughout the Orthodox world. You won't see Cyrillic unless you venture into neighbouring Serbia, Bosnia or Montenegro.

Most people – especially in the capital and along the coast – speak at least one foreign language, with German very widely spoken, and English being increasingly taught and popular among the young. Italian is understood by many on the coast and islands.

RELIGION

In the 2001 census, some 87.8% of the population labelled themselves as Roman Catholics (up from three-quarters in 1991), and Catholicism has long been tied to national identity here – it's as much a statement against Tito's brand of socialism or Serbia's Orthodox Church as it's a credo in itself. As a result, church attendance was hugely popular in the first years of Croatian independence, though has tailed off somewhat in recent years.

Outside of church service times there are often people worshipping privately at the bigger churches and cathedrals, and their quiet and privacy should of course be respected. Smaller churches – and even some of the bigger ones – may well be closed outside of the periods immediately before and after mass.

Beyond Catholicism, 4.4% of the population say they're Orthodox Christians, while Muslims account for 1.3% of the population.

CULTURE

Millennia of foreign occupation have left Croatia with an impressive architectural heritage, ranging from Greek and Roman ruins to a wealth of Venetian Gothic to the Habsburg splendour of the cities in the north. See the individual chapters for specific sights (and sites).

By contrast, there are very few Croatian artists, writers or composers who are well known outside the country, the most famous probably being the sculptor Ivan Meštrović. Which is not to say the Croats are an uncultured lot, simply that most of the country's culture hasn't been exported.

What you will see – and hear – plenty of is Croatia's abundant folk music. Across the country the rich heritage has been preserved, and Tito's communist government was unusual in encouraging people to retain their folk tradition. Most of the popular tourist destinations – notably Dubrovnik and Split, and many of the islands – have summer music festivals which highlight the very best in folk songs and dancing, along with jazz and classical music too.

You should also focus on what's happening at the local level. Some of the very best traditional music I've heard has been at Croatian weddings, so keep your ears pinned back on Saturdays.

Practical Information

2

WHEN TO VISIT

High summer is a great time to be in the higher parks, such as Risnjak, in the north, or to visit the capital and other towns away from the coast, as lots of locals are themselves on holiday then. But bear in mind that inland Croatia can get pretty hot and sweaty in the absence of sea-breezes – and you'll need to book tickets on public transport in advance.

If you have a choice, September is the best month to be on the coast or visit the islands. The weather is fine, the school holidays are over and the sea is still easily warm enough for swimming. October is also fine, but by November the sunshine hours are down and the rainfall hours up. May and early June, too, are absolutely gorgeous along the coast, though there's an increasing tendency for accommodation and ferries to fill up as June progresses.

September and June are the best months for walkers and hikers, closely followed by October and May, and autumn in the inland parks provides stunning visuals as the leaves change colour. Earlier than May and you may find it damp in the lowlands and freezing higher up; later than October and you run the risk of being caught by the first snows.

Yachting, sailing and motor-cruising have a season running from the beginning of May to the first week of October. Outside this period charters won't be possible and you'll find the weather in any case less pleasant, with a more frequent gale-force *bora* blowing between September and May.

July and August are easily the most popular months with all types of visitor, so you may want to leave well alone, unless you're absolutely set on clubbing, or that deep sun tan. These are the months when you'll be competing for rooms with up to six million others, and if you're travelling by car you'll find parking a hassle, and queues for the car ferries measured in hours – on weekends you can even find yourself waiting a whole day or night. That said, July and August are *easily* the best months for being on the beach, and Croatia's coastal nightlife only really comes alive in summer.

If you're not bothered by the damp and cold, winter is a great time for cultural exploration – the coast and islands are deserted and you'll have museums and churches to yourself. Waiters and hoteliers will be delighted you're there rather than hassled by the next customer, and you may have to wait a day for the next ferry, but you won't have to queue to get on it. If you're in inland Croatia in winter, however, do wrap up warm. Finally, if you're planning winter trips to any of the islands, especially the smaller and remoter ones, bear in mind that from November until Easter (and sometimes right through to the beginning of May) they're simply not expecting you. That means accommodation can be hard or impossible to find and restaurants may be closed for the duration – book ahead before you catch the ferry.

HIGHLIGHTS
Scenic interest
For wild karst scenery right on the seashore you can't beat the Velebit massif, at its most accessible in Paklenica National Park, which has well-marked trails for all grades of walking. Less rugged scenery, punctuated by falling water, is provided by the rightly famous Plitvice Lakes National Park and the Krka River and falls, both of which easily outshine the crowds.

Offshore, the island of Mljet is a personal favourite, with its saltwater lake and roaming mongooses, while if you have no time to do anything at all you'll still have time to take the ten-minute ride from Dubrovnik to the island of Lokrum. The country's most famous beach is Zlatni Rat, near Bol, on the island of Brač, while anyone with their own boat will find the beauty of the Kornati archipelago irresistible.

Inland, there's little to match the rugged beauty of the Istrian interior, with its hilltop villages, or the Zagorje and Žumberak regions to the north and southwest of Zagreb, where rolling hills are home to dozens of castles from the late Middle Ages onwards.

Wildlife and botany
Gorski Kotar, the strictly protected nature reserve to the east of Rijeka, has the country's rarest fauna, with bear, lynx, wild boar and wolves on the hoof, and various species of eagle and vulture in the air. In the Velebit you'll also find chamois and mouflon, along with red, fallow and roe deer.

Ornithologists really are spoiled for choice, from the waterfowl and wading birds on the Neretva Delta, south of Makarska, and Vransko Jezero, near Zadar, to the storks at Lonjsko Polje and the abundant birdlife at Kopački Rit, in Slavonia. Botanists, for their part, can head up to the remote Velebitski Botanički Vrt gardens and their unique mountain flora.

By boat
Croatia's section of the Adriatic is a sailor's paradise, with more than a thousand islands to choose from, and spectacular scenery all along the way. Remote, uninhabited islands compete with the charm of old towns like Hvar, Korčula and Rab on the islands and Rovinj and Zadar along the coast. With a boat you can sail alongside Croatia's most spectacular cliffs at Telašćica (on the island of Dugi Otok), or lose yourself amongst the thousands of inlets and harbours of the islands of the Kvarner Bay. And there are few greater pleasures than being thrown a mooring line from a private jetty belonging to a tiny restaurant, with an evening of eating, drinking and music ahead of you.

Art and architecture
From the Austro-Hungarian magnificence of the northern cities like Zagreb and Osijek, to the Venetian Gothic of towns along the coast and islands, visitors to Croatia are spoiled for choice. Add one-offs like Roman Pula, medieval Dubrovnik, palatial Split and Renaissance Šibenik, and you'll find yourself having to pick and choose – or come back again next year. Croatia's place at the crossroads of Europe means you can find anything here, from Habsburg palaces to Greek and Roman ruins, from fortified churches to Venetian loggias and from Byzantine mosaics to medieval frescos.

Transport dependent
Almost everything in this guide can be reached on public transport, which in Croatia mostly means by the regular and inexpensive buses. A good train network

also connects the main cities together, but doesn't go as far as Dubrovnik. Some parts of the mountains, obviously, are a whole lot easier to reach by car than by bus, but having a car won't solve all your problems, as driving in Croatia can be pretty hard going – ask anyone who's been stuck on the endless coast road in August.

A personal (baker's) dozen

This list isn't in any particular order but represents the 13 places I've been most taken with in Croatia.

Plitvice Lakes Much-hyped, these 16 lakes interconnected by waterfalls never fail to impress, and deserve their UNESCO classification as a World Heritage Site.

Diocletian's Palace, Split Spreading out from the *peristyle*, the streets of the old town of Split were once palatial corridors and the houses huge reception rooms for the former Roman emperor in retirement. It's difficult not to be captivated.

Risnjak National Park Situated within the confines of Gorski Kotar, and featuring Croatia's biggest diversity of flora and fauna, this is the perfect park for mountaineers and naturalists alike.

Šibenik Cathedral Šibenik itself is lovely, but the 15th/16th-century cathedral here – Croatia's most important Renaissance monument – is terrific.

Biokovo Overhanging the Makarska Riviera, Biokovo is Croatia's answer to Cape Town's Table Mountain, offering fabulous views out over Brač and Hvar.

Lokrum This is a haven, just a short boat-ride away from the bustle of Dubrovnik, offering rocks to swim from, woods to picnic in, and a small café set in a ruined Benedictine monastery.

Roman Amphitheatre, Pula It may look like a cliché on a postcard, but the world's sixth biggest extant Roman amphitheatre is a wonderful monument all the same.

Lonjsko Polje One of Europe's largest concentrations of storks – more than 500 pairs – make this wetland park a stunning place to visit. Go by boat, when it floods in spring.

Krka River and Falls Several sets of travertine waterfalls you can walk over, across and around, a monastery on an island in the river, and boat trips up and down, along with the chance to swim at the base of the falls, make Krka a delight.

Trogir The traffic-free old town of Trogir is one of the most charming on the whole Adriatic coast. A medieval island settlement, it's astonishingly well preserved and well deserving of its classification as a UNESCO World Heritage Site.

Paklenica National Park Twin karst canyons running up from the sea into the Velebit massif, offering some of the best and most accessible walking and hiking in Croatia.

Rovinj The site that has graced a million postcards is Istria's jewel. The organically medieval historic centre of Croatia's most Italian town stands on a former island, with red-tiled roofs crowned by a Venetian campanile.

Mljet Lush vegetation, an abandoned monastery on an island on a lake on an island, Europe's only wild mongooses and relatively few visitors make Mljet a treasure not to be missed.

TOUR OPERATORS
In the UK

There's a long history of package tourism as well as independent travel from the UK to Croatia, and there are plenty of operators to choose from – beyond those listed below it's worth seeing what your local travel agent has to offer, as well as visiting www.visit-croatia.co.uk/touroperators and www.tourist-offices.org.uk/croatia/uktourops.html.

Activity Holidays Tel: 01932 867418; fax: 01932 865179; www.activity-holidays.co.uk. Small company offering a variety of sailing holidays in Croatia, mainly based on the flotilla concept. PDF brochures are available at the website.

Adriatic Holidays Tel: 01865 516577; www.adriaticholidaysonline.com. Adriatic Holidays specialises in sailing in the Croatian Adriatic with boats out of every major port in the country – sailing boats or motor boats. Based in Britain, the company is staffed primarily by Croatians and prides itself on its unrivalled local knowledge.

Balkan Holidays Tel: 020 7543 5555; fax: 020 7543 5577; www.balkanholidays.co.uk. Has a wide variety of package destinations on offer along the coast and on the islands. You can order brochures and book online, or through your local travel agent.

Bond Tours Tel: 01372 745300; fax: 01372 749111; www.bondtours.com. An excellent variety of packages as well as city breaks. Highly recommended.

Bosmere Travel Tel: 01473 831518; fax: 01473 831574; www.bosmeretravel.co.uk. Specialist operator with a whole variety of themed holidays from old-timer sailing to naturist, with accommodation usually in small hotels.

Cosmos Holidays Tel: 0800 093 3134; www.cosmos-holidays.co.uk. Claims to be the UK's largest independent tour operator; flights from London, Manchester, Birmingham and Glasgow.

Croatia For Travellers Tel: 020 7226 4460; fax: 020 7226 7906; www.croatiafortravellers.co.uk. Aimed squarely at independent travellers, they can tailor a holiday to your precise requirements, or just book you the flights and hotels you want.

First Choice Tel: 0870 576 8373; www.firstchoice.co.uk. Specialises in southern Dalmatia, with packages to Koločep and Cavtat as well as Dubrovnik. Also offers 'Exclusive top Dubrovnik Hotels' under its Sovereign Holidays brand. Flights from London and Manchester.

Headwater Holidays Tel: 01606 720099; fax: 01606 720034; www.headwater.com. Specialises in walking and sightseeing tours in Dalmatia.

Hidden Croatia Tel: 020 7736 6066; fax: 020 7384 9347; www.hiddencroatia.com. Offers flights-only as well as tailor-made trips. Flights from London and Manchester.

Holiday Options Tel: 0870 013 0450; fax: 01444 242454; www.holidayoptions.co.uk. One of the biggest and best-known operators, with flights from London, Manchester, Birmingham, Norwich and Glasgow.

Nautilus Yachting Tel: 01732 867445; fax: 01732 867446; www.nautilus-yachting.com. Well-established company offering good learning-to-sail and flotilla holidays.

Saga Holidays Tel: 0800 300 500; www.saga.co.uk. Aimed at the over-50s, Saga has a fair range of Croatian destinations on offer along the coast and a loyal following, though their website's a navigational nightmare.

Sailing Holidays Tel: 020 8459 8787; fax: 020 8459 8798; www.sailingholidays.co.uk. Specialists in flotilla sailing in central and southern Dalmatia.

Simply Croatia Tel: 020 8541 2214; fax: 020 8541 2280; www.simplytravel.co.uk. Offers individual packages to villas, small hotels etc. Flights from London and Manchester.

Sunway Holidays UK – Tel: 01628 660001; fax: 01628 602859; www.sunwayholidays.co.uk. Ireland – Tel: +353 (0)1 288 6828; fax: +353 (9)1 288 5187; www.sunway.ie. Regular flights from Dublin and Cork and UK airports to Dubrovnik plus accommodation and complete packages.

Thomson Lakes and Mountains Tel: 0870 606 1470; www.thomsonlakesandmountains.co.uk. A subsidiary of the UK's biggest tour operator, with flights from London and Manchester.

In North America

There are very few North American operators specialising in Croatia, though some of the bigger companies sometimes offer one or more tours, usually combined with neighbouring countries – an example is Adventures Abroad (tel: 1 800 665 3998 in the USA and Canada, 1 800 147 827 in Australia; www.adventures-abroad.com), which offers a handful of interesting itineraries featuring Croatia.

Otherwise you can contact the New York office of the Croatia National Tourist Board (tel: +1 212 279 8672; fax: +1 212 279 8683), though a quicker route to a Croatian holiday may be via one of the UK operators (see above), or directly through the big Croatian companies (see below). You should also check what's available with your local travel agent.

In Croatia

There are a number of well-established tour operators and travel agents within Croatia who can organise holidays from abroad, including the travel to and from your home country. Unless you're coming from the particularly well-served UK, you may want to try one of the following.

Atlas Tel: 442 222; fax: 411 100; www.atlas-croatia.com. The Dubrovnik-based company has been around since 1923, and offers everything from tailor-made holidays to coach tours around various parts of the country. Atlas is behind the huge Plava Laguna resort company at Poreč, and owns the only hotel on Mljet, the Odisej.

Generalturist Tel: 480 5555; fax: 492 0206; www.generalturist.com. Also founded in 1923, Generalturist has been owned by Diners Club since 1999, and offers a full range of holiday, though these are usually booked through travel agents rather than direct with the company.

Marcopolo Tel/fax: 816 616; www.marcopolo.hr. Rovinj-based operator, specialising in individual and activity-based holidays in the northern Adriatic.

RED TAPE
Passports/visas

Nationals of most English-speaking (UK, Ireland, USA, Canada, Australia and New Zealand) or west European countries only need a valid passport to visit Croatia for up to three months – and it's far easier to leave the country and come back in again than it is to get an extension, if you want to stay for longer.

If you don't need a visa for Croatia you shouldn't need one for hops across the border to neighbouring Slovenia, Bosnia & Herzegovina and Montenegro, which apply the same three-month visa exemption for tourists as Croatia. For getting across Bosnia & Herzegovina towards Dubrovnik (which is technically cut off from the rest of Croatia by Bosnia's sea corridor, see page 260) – you may still not need a visa if all you're doing is transiting.

A complete list of who does and doesn't need a visa for Croatia, as well as up-to-date addresses and phone numbers of all the Croatian diplomatic missions worldwide – and foreign diplomatic missions in Croatia – can be found on the Ministry of Foreign Affairs' website at www.mvp.hr. The addresses for the main English-speaking countries are listed below.

Croatian diplomatic missions abroad

Australia Embassy of the Republic of Croatia (also covers New Zealand), 14 Jindalee Crescent, O'Malley Act, 2606, Canberra; tel: +61 2 6286 6988; fax: +61 2 6286 3544; email:

croemb@bigpond.com. Consulate General of the Republic of Croatia, 9/24 Albert Rd, South Melbourne, 3205, Victoria; tel: +61 3 9699 2633; fax: +61 3 9696 8271; email: concro@labyrinth.com.au. Consulate General of the Republic of Croatia in Australia, St George's Terrace, Perth, 6831, Western Australia; PO Box Z5366; tel: +61 8 9321 6044; fax: +61 8 9321 6240; email: crocons.perth@mvp.hr. Consulate General of the Republic of Croatia, 4/379 Kent St, Sydney, 2001, New South Wales; tel: +61 2 9299 8899; fax: +61 2 9299 8855; email: cro_con_Sydney@speednet.com.au

Canada Embassy of the Republic of Croatia, 229 Chapel St, Ottawa, Ontario, K1N 7Y6; tel: +1 613 562 7820; fax: +1 613 562 7821; email: croatia.emb@bellnet.ca; www.croatiaemb.net

Ireland Embassy of the Republic of Croatia, Adelaide Chambers, Peter Street, Dublin 8; tel: +353 1 476 7181; fax: +353 1 476 7183; email: croatianembassy@eircom.net

New Zealand Consulate General of the Republic of Croatia, 131 Lincoln Rd, Henderson/PO Box 83200, Edmonton, Auckland; tel: +64 9 836 5581; fax: +64 9 836 5481; email: cro-consulate@xtra.co.nz

UK Embassy of the Republic of Croatia (also covers Ireland), 21 Conway St, London W1T 6BN; tel: +44 20 7387 1144; fax: +44 20 7387 0936; email: consular.dept.London@mvp.hr

USA Embassy of the Republic of Croatia, 2343 Massachusetts Av, NW, Washington DC, 20008; tel: +1 202 588 5899; fax: +1 202 588 8937; email: public@croatiaemb.org. Consulate General of the Republic of Croatia, 737 North Michigan Av, Suite 1030, Chicago, IL 60611; tel: +1 312 482 9902; fax: +1 312 482 9987; email: crochicago@sbcglobal.net. Consulate General of the Republic of Croatia, 11766 Wilshire Bd, Suite 1250, Los Angeles, CA 90025; tel: +1 310 477 1009; fax: +1 310 477 1866; email: croconla@aol.com. Consulate General of the Republic of Croatia, 369 Lexington Av, New York, NY 10017; tel: +1 212 599 3066; fax: +1 212 599 3106; email: Croatian.consulate@gte.net. Consulate General of the Republic of Croatia, 4119 White Bear Parkway, Suite 210, St Paul, Minnesota, MN 55110; tel: +1 612 429 4183; fax: +1 612 429 6079; email: info@cortecvpci.com. Consulate of the Republic of Croatia, 321 St Charles Av, 10th Floor, New Orleans, LA 70130; tel: +1 504 586 8300, ext 316; fax: +1 504 586 9911; email: joc@imtt.com. Consulate of the Republic of Croatia, 100 Delaney Drive, Pittsburgh, PA 15235; tel: +1 412 843 0380; fax: +1 412 823 1594; email: cfuofa@usaor.net

Foreign diplomatic missions in Croatia

Australia Embassy of Australia, Kaptol Centar, 3 kat, Nova Ves 11, 10000 Zagreb; tel: 489 1200; fax: 489 1216

Bosnia & Herzegovina Embassy of Bosnia & Herzegovina, Department for Consular Affairs, Ul Pavla Hatza 3, 10000 Zagreb; tel: 481 9418; fax: 481 9420

Canada Embassy of Canada, Prilaz Gjure Deželića 4, 10000 Zagreb; tel: 488 1200; fax: 488 1230

Ireland Consulate General of Ireland, Trg NŠ Zrinskog 6, 10000 Zagreb; tel: 487 7900; fax: 487 7901

New Zealand Consulate of New Zealand, Av Dubrovnik 15, c/o WTC Zagreb, 10000 Zagreb; tel: 652 0888; fax: 652 7260

UK The British Consulate, Bunićeva poljana 3/I, 20000 Dubrovnik; tel/fax: 324 597. The British Consulate, Obala hrvatskog narodnog preporoda 10/III, 21000 Split; tel: 346 007; fax: +385 21 362 905. Embassy of the Kingdom of Great Britain and Northern Ireland, I. Lučića 4, 10000 Zagreb; tel: 600 9100; fax: 600 9111. British Council for Cultural Relations, Humbaldtova 4, 10000 Zagreb; tel: 600 9122; fax: 600 9298

USA Embassy of the United States of America, Ulica Thomasa Jeffersona 2, 10010 Zagreb; tel: 661 2200; fax: 661 2373

Police registration

The law in Croatia is that all visitors must register with the police within 24 hours of arrival. If you're staying in a hotel, hostel or campsite, or in a private room arranged through an agency, then this will be done for you automatically.

If you're in a private room you've found for yourself, or you're staying with friends, then they're supposed to register you. This doesn't always happen and unless you're picked up by the police, that shouldn't be a problem. Even if you are questioned, if it's clear you're just a tourist then the police will usually turn a blind eye. But if you've been unregistered for a while, particularly off the beaten track, then you could be in trouble, and even deported.

Customs

There are no restrictions on the personal belongings you can bring into Croatia, though the government recommends you declare big-ticket items (boats, laptop computers, expensive camera or movie equipment etc) to be sure of being able to re-export them hassle-free. Crossing into or out of Croatia in your own non-Balkan- registered vehicle, it's incredibly rare to be stopped or seriously questioned for any length of time, however.

Standard customs allowances apply for duty-free tobacco and alcohol – 200 cigarettes and one litre of spirits per person – and you're restricted to half a kilo of coffee, if that's your fix. If you're taking your pets then make sure they have an international veterinary certificate showing that it's been at least two weeks but not more than six months since they've been vaccinated.

You can take as much foreign currency as you want in and out of the country, but you can't export more than 2,000 kuna. For goods costing over 500 kuna you can claim a tax refund on the way out of Croatia on presentation of the tax cheque the merchant will have given you for this purpose, but it can be a lengthy procedure. Any questions you have can be answered by the helpful people at the Customs Administration in Zagreb (tel/fax: 610 2333).

GETTING THERE AND AWAY

There are five main ways of travelling to Croatia: plane, train, bus, car or boat. You could also arrive on foot, by bicycle or by hitching a lift (but see page 46).

By air

Flying to Croatia is easily the quickest way of arriving – Zagreb is just two hours from London, and Dubrovnik is only half an hour further. Both British Airways (www.britishairways.com) and Croatia Airlines (www.croatiaairlines.hr) fly to Croatia, though not always direct or every day – though summer flights tend to be both direct and a good deal more frequent. Expect to pay anything between £200 and £500 for a scheduled return flight, including taxes.

For the time being there aren't any budget airlines serving Croatia, though it can only be a matter of time (one hopes). Several do go to Italy, however, and that can be an option – see below.

There are also charter flights available, with Airtours (www.airtours.co.uk) offering flights from London Gatwick and Manchester to Pula; First Choice (www.firstchoice.co.uk) from London Gatwick and Manchester to Dubrovnik; Hidden Croatia (Air Adriatic; www.hiddencroatia.com) from London Stansted and Manchester to Pula, Rijeka, Split or Dubrovnik; Holiday Options (www.holidayoptions.co.uk) from London Gatwick, Birmingham, Bristol, Manchester, Norwich and Glasgow to Split or Dubrovnik; Newmarket Holidays (www.newmarket-group.co.uk) from London Gatwick, Belfast, Exeter,

Newcastle, Glasgow, Cardiff, Manchester, Edinburgh and Liverpool to Dubrovnik (but not in July and August, bizarrely); Palmair (tel: 01202 200700 – no website, apparently) from Bournemouth to Split and Dubrovnik; Sunsail Holidays (www.sunsailflights.co.uk) from London Gatwick to Dubrovnik; Thomas Cook (www.thomascook.com) from London Gatwick and Manchester to Split and Dubrovnik; and Thomson Holidays (www.thomson.co.uk) from London Gatwick and Manchester to Pula.

There are no direct flights from the USA, Canada, Australia or New Zealand, but most airlines will be able to route you through a European hub, usually in conjunction with Croatia Airlines. Return tickets from New York to Croatia start at under US$1,000 out of season, though they tend to rise to over US$1,500 in summer.

If you're having trouble finding a reasonably priced flight through the usual channels (newspapers, travel agents etc) there are a number of alternatives. One is to take a package tour – see the list of travel agents on page 28. Even if you want to sort out your own accommodation, some operators will be happy to arrange a 'flights-only' package for you. Even if this isn't the case, it can sometimes still work out cheaper to book yourself on a package and then not use the entire accommodation segment – though if you do this you should check the conditions very carefully to ensure you still have a return flight home. Charter operators flying to Dubrovnik from the UK are listed above.

You should also surf the Internet, as it can be a great place to shop around for flights. UK sites such as www.cheapflights.co.uk, www.lastminute.co.uk, or www.travelocity.co.uk, or US sites like www.expedia.com or www.farebeater.com will give you a quick idea about what's really available and how much it costs. But don't imagine that just because it's on the Internet it's necessarily the cheapest – you may find the fare in your local travel agent's window is still better.

Budget flights to Italy

With budget airlines increasingly popular and Italy being far better served than Croatia – Ryanair (www.ryanair.com) and Go (www.go-fly.com) both fly to northeastern Italy – a great option is to get a cheap flight to Venice or Trieste and then jump on the even cheaper bus or train to Rijeka or Zagreb. It's only $2\frac{1}{2}$ hours by bus from Trieste to Rijeka, and the one-way fare is around €10 (£7). Zagreb is about four hours from Trieste by bus, or $5\frac{1}{2}$ hours by train – add 2 hours if you're coming from Venice. Ryanair also flies to Ancona twice a day, meaning you can then hop on the night ferry to Split or Dubrovnik, a lovely way to arrive in central or southern Dalmatia.

By rail

The train is a slow and difficult way of getting to Croatia, and not significantly cheaper than the plane. The journey from London to Zagreb or Rijeka takes over 24 hours non-stop, and involves at least three or four changes – and there's no railway to Dubrovnik. But if you're a train lover, have access to a cheap ticket or are planning on stopping off at various places on the way, it's nonetheless a great way of travelling.

If you're roving round Europe on a Eurail pass (bought outside Europe – see www.eurail.com), bear in mind it doesn't cover Croatia. This shouldn't be a show-stopper – you'll just have to pay the (inexpensive) fare from the Slovenian or Hungarian border onwards.

International connections come in to Zagreb from Ljubljana (5 daily, $2\frac{1}{2}$ hours), Belgrade (4 daily, 6–7 hours), Budapest (3 daily, 5–7 hours), Munich (2 daily, 9 hours), Trieste (4 connecting trains daily, 1 direct, $5\frac{1}{2}$ hours), Venice (2 daily, 1 direct,

7–8 hours), Innsbruck, Salzburg and Vienna (1 daily, 9, 8½ and 6½ hours), Sarajevo (1 daily, 9 hours) and Skopje (1 daily, 9 hours).

By bus
Luxury coaches cruise between most cities in Europe, but it's a long journey (London to Zagreb takes between 30 and 40 hours) and buses aren't as cheap as they used to be (sample fares, without student discount, range from £120 upwards). That said, if you can get a discount this may be the cheapest way to go. A vast range of bus-related websites are available from www.budgettravel.com/eurobus.htm.

In the old days the cheapest way of getting to Croatia was to get on one of the many Athens-bound buses and ask the driver to let you off in Zagreb. It's still an option of sorts, though a risky one. It may be cheap, but there's a very real risk of never seeing your luggage again – not to mention being dumped miles out of town in the middle of the night.

By car
In spite of the long drive (London to Zagreb is 1,640km by road; London to Dubrovnik 2,175km) and the expense (tolls and fuel in Europe are expensive), having your own car in Croatia can certainly be an advantage, especially if you're travelling as a family, or planning on moving around a great deal and wanting to visit remote places – in this case you may still find a fly/drive package more advantageous than taking your own car. But if you're only going to the main centres – especially in high season, when coastal traffic is terrible – you're far better off using public transport.

That said, with the fast road from Ljubljana to Zagreb nearly complete at the time of writing (summer 2004), and the new motorway from Zagreb to Split already open, Dalmatia is already a whole lot easier to drive to than it used to be. By 2008, the motorway should run all the way to Dubrovnik.

Another option – slower, but with its merits – is to drive down through Italy and then take the car ferry across. At around €90 (£60) for the passage (car + driver), it's more pricey than coming through Slovenia and Croatia – especially if you take a cabin – but Italian motorways (believe it or not) are easier on the driver than Croatia's coast road.

Ferries run from Rimini, Ancona and Bari, in Italy, direct to Zadar, Split and Dubrovnik, as well as to some of the larger islands. If you're doing this in summer it's essential to have a ferry booking – Italians simply love Croatia, and tend to bring their cars with them. The four main companies plying the Adriatic are Adriatica Navigazione (www.adriatica.it), Azzurra Line (www.agestea.com/azzurra-eng.htm), Jadrolinija (www.jadrolinija.hr) and SEM (www.sem-marina.hr). There's also a new fast catamaran which runs from Pescara to Split, via Hvar, in just five hours – check out www.sanmar.it.

By boat
You can travel across and up and down the Adriatic on one of the many ferries which ply the Croatian coast all the way from Pula and Rijeka in the north to Split and Dubrovnik in the south. The ferries are a slow but very attractive way of getting around, and a reminder of the only way people travelled any distance here as recently as the 1930s. Long-distance ferries aren't especially cheap, however, with a typical passenger fare across the Adriatic in summer starting at €40 (£25) – see the previous section for details of the various ferry companies operating between Italy and Croatia.

If you're travelling down through Italy by train and planning to cross the Adriatic from Ancona, make sure you get off at the Ancona Maritime stop rather than the main train station. And if you're coming through Bari by plane, then bear in mind that the port is a long way from the airport, and you'll need to factor in moderately expensive taxi rides (or inconvenient buses).

Ferry travel is the only way to get between the coast and islands, and the main centres are well-connected all year round, though ferries are generally more frequent in summer. If you're on foot there's no need to book, on the whole, and the short-hop ferries aren't expensive at all.

One of the most attractive ways of seeing the Adriatic and the Croatian coast and islands of course is from your own – or a chartered – boat. There is an extensive network of nearly 50 marinas offering around 12,500 berths, while a whole raft of companies offers charters, from skippered motor launches to self-sail yachts. Prices vary enormously depending on what you're looking for (see page 47 for more details) and you should book well ahead, as it's becoming increasingly popular.

MAPS AND TOURIST INFORMATION

Croatia has an active national tourist board and dozens of tourist organisations locally, so there's usually no shortage of information available. Maps, on the other hand, while often great at the town or regional level, are less satisfactory when it comes to providing for walkers or hikers.

Maps

The national tourist board can provide you with a useful reversible 1:1,000,000 (1cm = 10km) road map/tourist map which is good for situating yourself and planning an itinerary, and is perfectly acceptable for most users. This can be complemented with Michelin map #736 (the same scale), which covers all the countries formerly in Yugoslavia – some drivers prefer it over the tourist office's map, though there's frankly not that much to choose between them.

More detail – at a higher price – is provided by Freytag and Berndt's 1:250,000 Croatia/Slovenia road atlas, or the separate maps covering the various parts of the country, available from the Austrian publisher in 1:250,000, 1:500,000 and 1:600,000 sections. Two chunks of the Dalmatian coast are even covered at 1:100,000.

Kümmerly and Frey, the Swiss publisher, also does a reasonable 1:500,000 map covering Slovenia, Croatia and Bosnia & Herzegovina, while Belletti Editore has a similar offering, but only covering Croatia and Slovenia. You may also see the Hungarian Cartographia (1:850,000) on offer, but it's not great, to be honest.

Far and away the best map for drivers is the 1:300,000 two-sided map of 'Bosnia Erzegovina', which is published by Studio FMB Bologna – it covers all of Croatia except eastern Slavonia, and is a good deal more accurate than any of the others, though unfolding it and turning it over on the move is no joke, as it's enormous. Finally, there's a pretty good 1:100,000 scale map of Istria published by Bruno Fachin Editore in Trieste, which also includes the only accurate map of the island of Krk I've ever seen.

None of these of course is much use for walkers or hikers looking to stretch their legs in the national parks or nature reserves. Some parks are usefully mapped in 1:25,000 or 1:50,000, but others still have either no map at all or inaccurate 1:100,000 sketches. There is however an excellent series of maps published under the Trsat Polo imprint of the Geodetski zavod Slovinje (Slovenian Institute of Surveyors), which covers the whole coast at 1:100,000, with separate maps for Istria, Kvarner and Dalmatia 1-4. The series is aimed at sailors, hikers and drivers, and includes plans of the marinas as well as sea and mooring guidance, along with clearly marked footpaths and contours. They're available in most Croatian bookshops and at around 30 kuna a pop they're a bargain.

Town and city plans are generally available cheaply or for free at local tourist offices, and will get you round the main sights, though they may not be all that much help if it's a particular street address you're looking for.

Tourist information

The Croatian National Tourist Board is an excellent source of information and can provide you with maps, brochures and accommodation details. The website at www.croatia.hr is a great place to start, but if you don't have easy access to the internet you may want to contact one of the following offices for information:

Head office Croatian National Tourist Board, Iblerov trg 10/IV, Zagreb; tel: +385 1 455 6455; fax: +385 1 455 7827; email: info@htz.hr

UK office Croatian National Tourist Office, 162–164 Fulham Palace Rd, London W6 9ER; tel: +44 208 563 7979; fax: +44 208 563 2616; email: info@cnto.freeserve.co.uk

USA office Croatian National Tourist Office Inc, 350 Fifth Av, Suite 4003, New York 10118; tel: +1 212 279 8672/8674; fax: +1 212 279 8683; email: cntony@earthlink.net

(These are the only English-language offices. For other European regional offices see www.croatia.hr.)

Once in Croatia you're likely to find that most tourist or information offices – in reality and on the map – are actually closer to travel agents; they'll be keen to help you find accommodation and arrange excursions, but may not be so useful when it comes to maps or finding local information. Official tourist information offices, where they exist, are listed throughout this guide.

HEALTH, INSURANCE AND SAFETY

You can save yourself a lot of time, hassle and money by being well prepared. And don't forget these three phone numbers: 94 for an ambulance, 92 for the police and 93 for fire.

Health

A reciprocal agreement between the EU countries and Croatia means that in theory EU citizens shouldn't have to pay for public hospital care, but in practice you may well be told that the service you need isn't available, and that you can only obtain it privately. Don't expect this to be any cheaper than it would be at home – in other words, take out health insurance for major emergencies.

For minor treatment, a visit to one of the ubiquitous pharmacies (*ljekarna*) should sort you out and there's very often someone who speaks some English. For more serious problems get yourself to a clinic or hospital (*klinika* or *bolnica*).

There are no legal requirements for vaccinations for Croatia, but most doctors would advise immunisation against diphtheria (ten-yearly), tetanus (ten-yearly), hepatitis A (Havrix Monodose or Avaxim) and typhoid (with one of the newer vaccines, eg: Typhim Vi). For longer trips (six weeks or more) or for those working in the medical field or with children, vaccination against hepatitis B is advised. Ideally a course of three injections is required, the minimum time for which is over three weeks.

Similarly a course of rabies injections (three doses over a minimum of three weeks) is advisable for those working with animals, or spending a longer time in Croatia.

Travellers planning to go rambling or trekking in the countryside during the spring–autumn period are at risk of tick-borne encephalitis. The ticks that transmit this potentially fatal disease live in long grass and overhanging tree branches. Precautions include wearing long trousers tucked into boots, and a hat. Using tick repellents and checking for ticks at the end of the day can also help. Remove any ticks with tweezers taking care not to damage the mouth area. Once the tick is removed, go as soon as possible to a doctor for treatment. Pre-exposure vaccine is in short supply in the UK, but if you do manage to track some down it is worth having. Three doses can be given over two weeks. However, it is still important to seek medical help in the event of a tick bite.

If you use needles for any reason you should bring a doctor's note explaining why, and if you wear contact lenses or glasses, bring spares; repairs and replacements aren't a problem, but can take time. It also does no harm at all to have a doctor's and dentist's check-up before you go – far easier at home than abroad.

You can drink the water, if it's from a public supply.

Fitness

Many a walking, hiking or cycling holiday has been ruined by a lack of form, so if you're planning one, try and get fit before you go. The best exercises are cycling and hill-walking – far preferable to running or jogging. If you're surrounded by a dearth of hills, stairs make for easily the best substitute.

Common problems

You're less resistant to disease during your first weeks abroad, so make sure your diet contains enough vitamins – take supplements if you're not sure. Drink bottled water if the source is suspect – publicly supplied water is fine, but in the mountains, rivers and streams should be treated with caution; use iodine-based water purification tablets if you're a long way off the beaten track. You may also want to bring with you a mild laxative and something for diarrhoea, although both problems can normally be fixed with a change in diet (soft fruit for the first; dry-skinned fruits for the second). If you are afflicted with diarrhoea your biggest danger is dehydration, so make sure you drink plenty – soft drinks are good.

Even if you're not heading into the wilds, it's a good idea to bring along a small supply of sticking plasters (Band-aids), antiseptic cream and mild painkillers (aspirin or paracetamol) – you can top up your supplies of these at any pharmacy.

From May onwards you should also think about protecting yourself against mosquitoes. Along the coast and on the islands all you'll need is a gizmo which plugs into a wall socket at night (with the screw-in bottle of fluid; the ones that take tablets aren't effective) and you can buy these anywhere where mosquitoes are present. But in parts of the country – and notably in the wetlands of the Lonjsko Polje and Kopački Rit – you'll be confronted with evil, savage beasts, which will attack you day or night, and are perfectly capable of puncturing light clothing. Use the gizmo at night, but double up with an effective spray-on repellent during the day.

Finally, don't hesitate to see a pharmacist or doctor if you're even slightly unsure about a diagnosis or cure. But know your source if you need a blood transfusion – HIV/AIDS is less prevalent in Croatia than in many countries, but you can't be too careful.

Mountain health

Prevention being far better than cure, walkers and hikers should be conversant with first aid – or at the very least carry a booklet covering the basics. It's especially important to know how to deal with injuries and hypothermia. If you're in real trouble call the police or alert the mountain rescue service (see *Mountain safety*, page 46).

Hypothermia

This is responsible for the deaths of more walkers, hikers and climbers than any other cause. It occurs when the body loses heat faster than it can be generated, and the commonest cause is a combination of wet or inadequate clothing, and cold wind. It's easily avoided by making sure you always have a waterproof, a sweater or fleece, and a survival bag with you – even if you're hiking with only a daypack.

If one of your party shows signs of hypothermia – uncomfortable shivering, followed by drowsiness or confusion – it's essential that he or she is warmed up immediately. Exercise is not the way to do this. Wrap the victim in warm clothing, or even better a sleeping bag, then increase blood-sugar levels with food, and hot, sweet drinks.

Injury

Again, prevention is better than cure. Try and avoid walking or climbing beyond your limits – the majority of accidents happen when you're tired. If scrambling or bouldering, avoid using your knees or elbows, and keep at least three points of contact with the rock (two hands and a foot, or vice versa). In the event of being injured, use surgical tape for cuts that would normally be stitched, and then bind the wound laterally with zinc-oxide tape. If you're going a long way off the trail, take an inflatable splint.

Altitude sickness

Croatia's lack of very high mountains means this is one problem you're unlikely to face, but if you've trekked up from sea-level to 1,500m and feel dizzy or confused you should stop and rest. If this doesn't work, return to a lower altitude. And remember, altitude sickness doesn't discriminate – youth and fitness don't help at all.

Sunburn

Altitude and wind combined tend to make you forget you're being burned – a problem which is exacerbated by the sun being that much stronger in Croatia than in northern Europe. Take high-protection suncream, reapply regularly, and don't be afraid to use a hat and sunglasses. If you get badly burned, use an after-sun lotion and then apply a total-block cream until the skin's recovered.

Snakes

In the extremely unlikely event of being bitten by a snake, try not to panic, as a racing heart speeds up the spread of venom – much easier said than done, of course. Most first-aid techniques do more harm than good. If possible, splint the bitten limb and keep below the height of the heart, then get the victim to hospital immediately.

Insurance

A good idea – it's reassuring to know you can be flown home if necessary. Read the fine print and make sure it covers what you'll be doing (walking in the mountains, for example). A general policy, covering health, theft and third party insurance, is usually cheaper and less hassle than multiple policies, though you may find you're already covered for some or all of the risks by existing insurance, such as private healthcare (which sometimes includes foreign travel) or that provided to holders of credit cards.

If you need to claim, you'll have to provide supporting evidence in the form of medical bills, in the case of health, or a police statement, in the case of theft. Obtaining the latter can be very hard work, but essential if you're hoping for reimbursement.

Travel policies are issued by banks, travel agents and others, and it's worth shopping around amongst reputable providers, as the price varies considerably. Arrange for the insurance to cover your full journey time, and keep the policy safe with your other travel documents.

Safety

Croatia is safer and freer of crime than most EU countries, though the normal precautions you'd apply at home apply here too – don't be showy with money, jewellery or flashy possessions, and avoid the seedier or ill-lit parts of cities at night. You're more likely to be robbed by fellow travellers than by Croats, so be especially careful in hostels, campsites and overnight trains or buses, and keep your valuables close to you and separate from the rest of your luggage.

Car theft, however, is increasingly prevalent, and foreign-registered cars – and especially expensive foreign-registered cars, such as Audis, BMWs and Mercedes – are attractive to thieves. Generally speaking you wouldn't expect problems along the coast, though be careful where you leave your car in any big city, and don't leave your vehicle unattended for more than a day anywhere – it's tantamount to painting a 'Steal Me' notice on it.

You'll see lots of police around, and they have rather fearsome powers – freedom of dissension shouldn't be taken for granted. The police carry out occasional spot checks on locals and foreigners alike for identification, so make sure you have your passport or identity card with you at all times. Otherwise you'll find the police friendly and helpful, though apart from along the coast and in the capital, few speak any English.

If you're driving, keep to the speed limits. There are an astonishing number of speed traps – especially along the *Magistrala*, the coast road running all the way from Opatija to Dubrovnik – and foreigners attract police attention. If you're stopped for a traffic violation, you may find the police negotiate a lower penalty with you – the heavier fine for speeding, for example, may be traded down to the lower fine (payable in cash) for not wearing your seatbelt.

Turning into a one-way street the wrong way in Dubrovnik, I was immediately stopped by the police, and told to park the car in a spot reserved for the disabled. I was then given a choice of having my licence taken away and a 1,500 kuna fine (for driving the wrong way down a one-way street – unmarked as such, I might add), or paying the 150 kuna fine for parking in a disabled spot. I'll leave you to guess which I chose (clue: I still have my licence).

If you do get closely involved with the police, stay courteous, even (especially) when it's difficult to do so. Stand, rather than sit, if you can (it puts you on an even footing), and establish eye contact – if you can do so without being brazen or offensive about it. Some people recommend shaking hands with officialdom, but it depends very much on the circumstances. Wait until an interpreter arrives (or anyone who understands you clearly) rather than be misunderstood, though this may not happen on the same day. And remember that you can be held at a police station for up to 24 hours without being charged. Your consulate will be informed of your arrest, normally within the first day.

Minefields

Along the frontlines of the war of the early 1990s – and that means in about a third of the country – minefields were laid down and they haven't all been completely cleared yet. Most are plainly marked off with barbed wire and skull-and-crossbone signs saying 'Mine', and it would be plainly stupid to explore further.

Not every minefield is labelled, however. If you see villages which seem to have been abandoned for five years or more, or fields which haven't been cultivated, there's a real risk of uncleared mines, and it's best to leave well alone – I was going to say 'tread carefully' but that hardly seems appropriate where mines are involved.

Finally, if you're travelling in the former war zone – most of Slavonia, and pretty much anywhere inland between Karlovac and Split – it's wise to stick to roads and tracks that carry regular traffic, or to marked footpaths in the national parks and nature reserves.

Sexual harassment

Croatia is a safe country for women travellers, though like anywhere with a big influx of holidaymakers it has its fair share of local men on the make. This tends to come in the form of courteous persistence rather than aggression, and is usually easily rebuffed. Speaking firmly – in any language – should make your intentions clear.

People dress here the same way as they do anywhere in Europe, so there's nothing to worry about as far as dressing modestly is concerned – though wandering around churches in beachwear is likely to offend. If you want to get your kit off, head for the nearest naturist beach (usually marked FKK) – you won't be pestered.

WHAT TO TAKE

The best way for packing for anywhere – and Croatia's no exception – is to set out all the things you think you'll need and then take only about a third of it. How much you eventually end up taking will depend to a large extent on whether you have your own transport (everyone takes more in their own car) and whether or not you're planning on camping (camping comes with a list of irreducibles – see below, and page 54). But be realistic, especially if you're going to have to carry all your own stuff – what feels like an easy 15kg pack in your living room can be more like a sack of rocks half way up a mountainside.

If you're coming to Croatia for a beach holiday, it's worth remembering that the majority of the beaches are rocks or pebbles, so bring appropriate beach footwear – along with the usual hat, sunglasses, suncream etc. Summer evenings along the coast can be cool but are rarely cold, so a light sweater should be sufficient, but if you're coming here in winter bring warm clothes, especially if you're going inland or into the mountains.

Don't forget the usual range of documents you'll need – passport, tickets, travellers' cheques, cash, insurance papers, credit card, driving licence – and something to carry them in. A belt-bag or pouch is practical, but also draws attention to where you're keeping your valuables; I prefer a zipped pocket for the essentials, whether that's in a daypack or trousers, but it's a personal choice. And bring any books you want to read – except in the major cities and tourist centres you'll have trouble finding much more than yesterday's papers.

Also, bring spare glasses if you wear them, along with any special medicines you need. You may also find it handy to have a tube of travel detergent with you for rinsing out your smalls, and a travel alarm for those early starts. And last but not least, if you're bringing any electrical appliances – even just a hairdryer or a phone charger – remember an adaptor. Croatian sockets are the same round two-pinned variety you find all across Europe.

Walkers and hikers

Walkers and hikers need adequate clothes from the ground up, so make sure you have decent footwear – light, waterproof boots with good ankle support and a strong sole can make the difference between comfort and misery. But bring another pair of lighter, more flexible shoes, too, as you can get seriously fed up with wearing boots night and day. Proper hiking socks, whilst expensive, are worth every penny, but again make sure you have alternatives, not just for washing, but for those evenings out or for travelling to and from your hiking destination.

For hiking in the mountains you'll need hard-wearing trousers, especially if you come into contact with karst. Jeans are tough, but not ideal, as they're heavy and uncomfortable when wet and take ages to dry. Unless you're travelling in winter you'll also need shorts, as it can warm up quickly during the day.

Take a variety of tops, so you can wear more thin layers rather than fewer thicker ones, and don't forget the all-important fleece and waterproof jacket. It's definitely worth spending more on these last items – breathable, workable clothes are the difference between being warm and dry and cold and wet.

If you're using a rucksack as your main luggage you might prefer to go for tall and narrow rather than short and wide – not only is this easier for walking but it's also a whole lot more manageable for going through doorways and along narrow corridors, notably on trains.

Whatever your luggage make sure you also have a good daypack, with adequate space for everything you might need on a full day's walk – extra clothing, survival bag, water bottle(s), food, camera, maps, compass, penknife, medical kit, sunglasses, etc (see also *Mountain health*, page 36). If you're going high into the steeper national parks (notably Paklenica), you should definitely have walking poles or a stick with you, as the paths can be slippery. The best sort are retractable poles, which can fit into your bag.

Camping

It sounds obvious, but if you're camping, take a tent that's easy to pitch (and practise at home before you leave) – trying to assemble an unfamiliar model on a windy and rainy night is suffering itself. I know: I've been there. Bring tent sealant and repair material; both are hard to find outside Zagreb.

What you have in the way of a sleeping bag and sleeping mat will define the shape of your nights – and again it's worth testing these before you leave home. Buy a down-filled bag if you can afford it, as they're warmer and more comfortable in use, and more compact when rolled, although care should be taken to keep them dry, as they lose their insulating properties when wet and take a long time to dry.

It can be worth dispensing with cooking materials, eating utensils and pre-packed food altogether. Given that freelance camping is illegal, you're generally going to be close to both restaurants and supermarkets, and in summer three hot meals a day aren't essential. Again, it's a personal choice, but the business of finding fuel, the weight and bulk, and the overriding cheapness and cheerfulness of cafés and restaurants, has always put me off doing my own cooking while camping in Croatia.

MONEY

Since May 1994, Croatia's currency has been the *kuna* – literally a marten, named after the trade in marten skins in Roman times, and first struck as a Croatian coin in AD1256. It's one of the few currencies in the world still officially named after an animal (the American *buck* was never legal tender, even if the word's still in fashion an awful long time since trading in deer skins was a measure of anything in the USA).

The kuna (HRK is the international three-letter code) is divided up into 100 *lipa* (literally lime tree, or linden). There are 1, 2, 5, 10, 20 and 50 lipa coins, 1, 2 and 5 kuna coins and 5, 10, 20, 50, 100, 200, 500 and 1,000 kuna

Above The old red-roofed town of Korčula (PL)
Below Veli Lošinj's charming, diminutive port (PL)

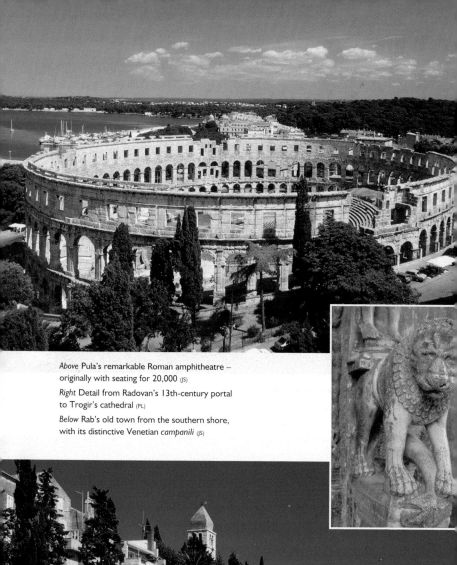

Above Pula's remarkable Roman amphitheatre –
originally with seating for 20,000 (JS)

Right Detail from Radovan's 13th-century portal
to Trogir's cathedral (PL)

Below Rab's old town from the southern shore,
with its distinctive Venetian *campanili* (JS)

banknotes. There's also a 25 kuna coin, but the chances are you'll never see one. On the whole, people aren't comfortable with the two largest notes, and you may have trouble breaking them – ask for 100s and 200s when you're changing money.

The euro has also increasingly been used as a parallel currency – the vast majority of Croatia's visitors switched to the euro at the beginning of 2002. Most people are comfortable with euro pricing, and you can pay with euros almost everywhere – but don't necessarily expect the right (or complete) change. Only accommodation is actively priced in euros, but most people are familiar with the currency and happy to let you pay with it. Nonetheless, you're much better off changing enough money for a couple of days at a time and getting used to the kuna. The kuna is pretty stable, averaging around 7.6 to the euro and 11 to the English pound.

Finding a place to buy kuna is a doddle – all banks, exchange offices and post offices, and most travel agencies and hotels will happily let you turn in your money, though you're better off with euros or sterling than US dollars, as there are so many dollar forgeries in circulation. Exchange rates are (remarkably) almost the same wherever you choose to change your money – fractionally worse at hotels, perhaps, but the difference is minimal. The black market for currency exchange – which thrived in the former Yugoslavia in spite of being one of the least efficient known to man – was mercifully put out of its misery.

Banks – unusually for Europe – are often open from seven in the morning to seven in the evening on weekdays and until one o'clock on Saturdays, though many close for lunch. At major train stations and airports, and in the bigger cities, some banks even open on Sundays.

Major credit cards (notably Visa, Eurocard/Mastercard and American Express) are accepted by most big hotels, restaurants and shops, though away from the coast their use isn't ubiquitous – and if you're staying in private rooms (see page 53) you'll find cash is king. Credit cards can also be used for raiding cash dispensers (widespread on the mainland, less so on the islands), though most take either Visa or Eurocard but not both.

Money is safest brought in the form of travellers' cheques, which are worth the small commission you pay for the peace of mind. You lose about the same percentage of your money if you use a credit card, but it's easier to keep track of cheques. American Express cheques are still the most widely used, easily recognised and most quickly refunded in case of loss or theft, and your local bank will issue them to you (though you may have to insist).

Finally, have enough money/resources with you – having money wired to you from home is an expensive hassle.

OPENING TIMES

Croats are industrious and hard-working, but like to knock off early and enjoy the evening. So you'll find people up at dawn, and many offices and shops open from 07.30 or even 07.00, but you may well find businesses shut after 16.00. Supermarkets and pharmacies have fairly long hours, and tend to be open all day, while smaller shops may take an extended lunch hour.

Generally speaking, things tend to be open when they're needed – if there's a real demand then it'll be met. So you'll find tourist agencies in the main resorts open from early in the morning until late at night, seven days a week, in summer, but probably only open in the morning and on weekdays for the rest of the year. To be sure of finding a tourist office open, the 08.00–11.00 slot is far and away the most reliable time, year-round.

If everything's closed and you're looking for accommodation, you can almost always find something by asking at the nearest bar or café – there's usually someone who knows somebody with a spare room.

Museums are also almost always open in the morning, but many close at 13.00 or 14.00 – so again, your sightseeing should be programmed around morning visits followed by a late lunch. Opening times are sometimes extended in summer, but not always.

Many churches – even some of the bigger ones – are only opened for church services, and the periods just before and after them. The tourist office can sometimes help you find the person with the key, however, if there's something you absolutely must see.

BUDGETING

How much you'll spend will depend mostly on what level of luxury you're looking for, and to some extent on the season. Camping and using public transport is going to cost a lot less than staying in swanky hotels and cabbing it around town. That said, Croatia is neither particularly cheap nor expensive – broadly speaking you should expect to pay about the same as in western Europe. Hotel accommodation and restaurants are on average slightly cheaper than in the UK, but about the same as in France – though house wine is considerably cheaper than in either. Supermarket prices on the other hand are slightly higher than they would be in the UK.

After the cost of getting to Croatia, your biggest single expense will be accommodation. Expect to pay €40–100 per night for a double room in private accommodation in summer, while doubles in hotels start at around €40 and go right up to €500 (room prices are always quoted in euros though paid in kuna). Single rooms are relatively scarce, but when available go for about 70% of the cost of a double. Off season along the coast those establishments (both hotels and private rooms) which don't close up altogether will discount by up to 20% in spring and autumn and as much as 50% in winter.

For a couple, daily food and drink costs from around 250 kuna for picnic food bought in supermarkets and maybe one meal a day in a cheap restaurant or pizzeria, to 600 kuna for breakfast in a café and lunch and dinner with wine in more upmarket restaurants. An average grill-type restaurant meal for two, with salad, skewers of meat, and wine, averages around 100 kuna a head. A nice fish dinner on the Adriatic, on the other hand, can easily set two of you back 750 kuna or more.

Public transport is fairly inexpensive by EU standards, with a single-zone Zagreb bus ticket going for 9 kuna in the summer of 2004, while the train-ride from Zagreb to Split came in at 87 kuna one-way. Typical bus fares at the time were 90–110 kuna for the 285km from Zagreb to Zadar, and 180–220 kuna for the 565km from Zagreb to Dubrovnik.

If you're really eking out the kuna (camping, picnic food) you could get away with a budget of 150 kuna per person per day. Twice that would get you into private rooms and cheap restaurants, while 500 kuna would buy you a nice holiday, but not fish every day. For that, and upper-end hotels, you'd need to count on 1,000 kuna per person per day.

Two weeks in May 2004, using public transport and staying in private rooms, cost two of us 560 kuna per day, while a 4,000km fortnight in June with our own car, staying in a mix of small hotels and private rooms, came in at a daily average of 820 kuna – in both cases not counting the cost of getting to Croatia.

Entry fees for attractions are reasonably inexpensive, but in a constant state of flux, so haven't been specifically included with each sight here – in 2004, however, you could expect to pay 5 kuna to see the treasury in Dubrovnik Cathedral, 10 kuna to climb Poreč church tower or visit the Strossmayer Gallery in Zagreb, 30 kuna to walk around the walls of Dubrovnik, and 20 kuna to visit the Meštrović atelier in Zagreb or Trakošćan Castle. Entry to the national parks ranges from 30 kuna (North Velebit) to 90 kuna (Plitvice).

GETTING AROUND

You can get around Croatia by plane, train, bus, car, bicycle and hitch-hiking – or on foot – and around the Adriatic by ferry, or on your own (or a rented) boat. The train network is good to points connected to Zagreb, but poor (non-existent) along the coast, where you'll find yourself on the ubiquitous buses or ferries. Public transport is regular, effective and good value for money, but can be slow and is sometimes overcrowded – notably in summer.

By air

Croatia Airlines' (www.croatiaairlines.hr) domestic flights are pretty good value, and a great way of getting from one end of the country to the other, especially if you've already seen it all from the bus. One way from Zagreb to Dubrovnik went for under 600 kuna in 2004, and took around 55 minutes, compared with the 12–14-hour, 200-kuna bus ride. Buy tickets from any travel agent or online at the website, but if you're planning on flying in summer make sure you book well ahead and bear in mind that if you do so from a travel agent outside Croatia, the price could be considerably higher.

By rail

Trains have greatly improved in the past decade, and cover the north and east of the country fairly comprehensively. They're about the same price as buses, for any given distance, but can be faster (inter-city, *brzi*) or slower (local trains, *putnički*). Trains can get very crowded, especially in summer, but they tend to be reasonably punctual. Local trains (the ones not marked in red on timetables) are usually much less crowded, and much less punctual. For all trains buy tickets in advance (unless there's no ticket office); you'll pay a surcharge if you wait until you're on board. *Dolazak* means arrivals, while both *odlazak* and *polazak* mean departures. *Blagajna* is where you buy your tickets.

Major railway stations all have left-luggage facilities, normally costing around 10 kuna a day per piece of luggage. Don't lose your receipts or you'll have a terrible time recovering your bags.

If you have access to the internet, you'll find all the timetables at the most excellent Croatia Railways website, at www.hznet.hr.

By bus

The bus network is wide-ranging, reliable and regular, and operated – as in Switzerland – by a well-organised federated system of inter-connected small companies. Buses offer the best way of coming into contact with local people, and are the only way of travelling on public transport along the coast and on the islands. The hourly average speed clocks in at about 45km/h, and costs around 40–50 kuna per 100km, though prices and speeds vary quite a bit depending on the route. Buses that go on ferries to the islands include the ferry fare in the cost of the ticket.

On major routes – such as Zagreb to Rijeka or Zadar, for example – buses leave every hour or even more frequently; in remoter areas they may only run once or twice a day, or even once or twice a week, to coincide with local needs.

If a bus originates in the town you're leaving from then you can buy tickets and make reservations at the bus station and you should do this a day or more ahead if you can. Otherwise wait for the bus to arrive and either pay the conductor as you get on or pay once you're underway. If you can't get a reservation, don't buy a ticket – with several companies often plying each route, it's sensible not to lock yourself in to any particular one until you're sure of being able to travel.

Luggage is stored in the holds under the bus, and you'll pay a small supplement (often around 10 kuna) for this. The price seems to be entirely arbitrary and provides you with paltry insurance, but it's an amount sufficiently large for the bus company not to want to lose, however, so your luggage should be guarded safely.

If your bus breaks down – it happens – the chances are it will be taken away and repaired enough for your journey to be completed. Your luggage won't be returned to you until repairs are complete, however, so keep out anything you might conceivably need in the next few hours, even on short journeys.

Buses stop every two hours or so for a *pausa*, and the conductor shouts out the duration of this above the din: *pet*, *deset*, *petnaest* and *dvadeset minuta* are the commonest break lengths (5, 10, 15, 20 min). These invariably occur where you can grab a quick drink/snack/meal. Watch the driver and you won't go far wrong, but be warned that the bus will go without you if you've made a mistake. Buses sometimes change drivers at these stops – this would have caught me out on a couple of occasions, were it not for the helpfulness of fellow passengers.

It's sometimes difficult – particularly inland – to obtain reliable information on bus departures. Sometimes this is out of helpful ignorance, sometimes from a willingness to please. If it's known you want a bus at 11.00 you may be told there is one, just to make you feel better. Ask open rather than closed questions (ie: 'What time is the bus to Plitvice?' as opposed to 'Is there a bus to Plitvice early tomorrow morning?') to several sources and you may find a consensus building up.

Another problem you may encounter is localised information, meaning that if you have to change buses to get to your destination, you may not be able to find out the timings for the second part of the journey before you get there. There's not much you can do about this.

By car

The most comfortable and often quickest way of travelling is by car, and sometimes it's the only way to get somewhere really remote. Road quality has improved enormously in the 20 years since I first drove in Croatia, and there are now several sections of motorway open – you'll pay tolls on these, though they're never excessive. The most expensive stretch, the 380km from Zagreb to Split, costs 115 kuna, while the 40km bit of motorway from Karlovac to Zagreb is 20 kuna. The toll bridge across to the island of Krk is charged at 20 kuna a time, while the Učka tunnel, above Opatija, costs 30 kuna. Fuel costs around 7 kuna per litre.

Inland the roads are less well maintained than you'd expect in western Europe (and often unpaved in really remote areas), while along the coast the single-lane *Magistrala*, running from Rijeka to Dubrovnik, inevitably clogs up in summer with holiday traffic – though the opening of the new motorway to Split in 2004 should do a lot to alleviate the problem. By 2008 the fast road should extend all the way to Dubrovnik. Street parking in cities is a non-starter (pay instead for public parking) and parking anywhere along the coast can be a major hassle in high season.

You may find Croatian drivers rather ambitious – to the extent that blind corners and oncoming traffic aren't seen as a natural impediment to overtaking – but don't be competitive; the omnipresent (and omnipotent) traffic police are quick to keep drivers in line with steep fines and worse. Speed limits – 50km/h in

IN THE EVENT OF AN ACCIDENT

If you have an accident – even a small one – there's a 99% chance the police will be called, and (just my opinion, this) a 95% chance that you'll be found to be in the wrong. When I had a minor crash in Đakovo, I was told by the only English speaker in town, a 14-year-old boy, that what would happen next is that I would be charged, and then taken to court the following day and punished. He was right – but he hadn't seen the accident, or assessed the damage.

If you're away from the coast (as I was) and a non-German speaker (as I am), the police process after an accident can be long, confusing and traumatic – probably for the police, as well. It can't be easy when even the simplest questions aren't eliciting responses.

From the time of the accident, until the court hearing 24 hours later, I had no idea what was going on, through hours of questioning and the confiscation of my passport. I wasn't allowed to phone anyone myself (any of my Croatian friends would have been able to help me) and the police wouldn't call anyone for me, though it's important to say that they were courteous at all times. I wasn't allowed to go to the hotel until I'd signed various incomprehensible statements – though these turned out to be anodyne, I didn't know this until the following day.

At the court, an English-speaking interpreter was provided, and she talked me through the accusation, and translated my responses to the judge. After some reflection, the judge explained that if I pleaded guilty I would probably get the minimum fine, but that if I pleaded not guilty I would have to wait for the full court to be in session. Given that it was Saturday, I pleaded guilty, was fined €100 plus (very reasonable) court costs, and was soon on my way.

built-up areas; 90km/h out of town (locally variable; keep your eyes peeled) and 130km/h on the motorway – are strictly enforced.

In the event of an accident or breakdown you can call the Croatian Automobile Club's hotline by dialling 987. If you see someone *else* in need of assistance you're legally obliged to stop and help. And remember that it's illegal for drunks or children under 12 to sit in the front of the car. The drink-driving limit, previously 50mg/100ml, was changed in 2004 to zero tolerance.

To source car parts or fix problems your first port of call should be a petrol station – these are usually open from dawn until dusk, though on some main roads there are 24-hour outlets. Try and ensure your car's roadworthy and insured against fatal breakdown, however. Although parts are in better supply and repairs more quickly effected than they used to be, it can still be an expensive and time-consuming business.

Car rental

Car rental in Croatia is fairly expensive, even if pre-booked from outside the country – you need to reckon on spending upwards of 2,500 kuna a week with full insurance and unlimited mileage. The major companies are represented in all the main population centres and the most popular tourist destinations.

By bicycle

Sadly, as a keen cyclist, I have to report that main-road mainland Croatia's really not very cycle-friendly. Courtesy is in short supply, traffic density is too high for comfort, and along the coast there isn't even the alternative of small roads or cycle-paths to choose from. You should do anything you possibly can to avoid the *Magistrala* – it's not just busy, but downright dangerous, particularly in summer.

One way of doing this is to be clever with ferries and the islands, which are absolutely superb for cyclists. Central Dalmatia, in particular, has taken an excellent initiative in publishing a great series of maps entitled *'Central Dalmatia by Bike'* which covers the islands of Šolta, Brač, Hvar and Vis, with suggested routes and route-profiles provided. Zagreb County has also just published a fine series of cycle routes/maps – see page 90 for details.

Cycle-touring can also be a great way of visiting the interior, and remains an excellent way of getting to meet local people. There are innumerable little Croatian villages connected by roads that aren't even on the map because they don't carry any traffic, but you do need to be good at navigating, and well-provisioned, as road signs are in short supply. Make sure you have decent off-road tyres, too, as the road surfaces are highly variable.

Hitch-hiking
Definitely not a recommended option. Tourists are unlikely to pick you up and locals tend to be travelling very short distances.

Walking and hiking
Walking is the slowest but most interesting way of getting around – you could follow in the footsteps of Patrick Leigh Fermor, who walked from the Hook of Holland to Constantinople in 18 months in 1933 and 1934. Plan on taking more money than he did though – he survived on a pound a week.

Croatia is a country ideally suited to the walker, with lots of national parks and nature reserves, and marked trails that range from the gentle stroll to the strenuous hike. A network of local and national walking, climbing and mountain associations keeps the paths in good repair, and staffs and maintains the mountain huts and lodges.

Hiking in the Velebit karst is a lot like walking in the Alps or the Dolomites. Even though the Velebit is considerably lower, it shares the fairly hard climate and there is generally not much surface water around, winter or summer. You need to be well equipped and have plenty of food and water with you if you're hiking here, but it is some of the most rewarding walking I've ever done.

Towards the northern end of the Velebit the mountains are lower and less harsh (in Gorski Kotar, for example), while the mountains of Slavonia, between the Drava and Sava rivers are different altogether. Here, you can find rich vegetation and plenty of water, and the softer, older mountains make for excellent hill walking.

Mountain safety
Up in the mountains, in regions where the regular emergency services don't operate, you can call on the help of Croatia's Mountain Rescue Service, the GSS (Gorska Služba Spašavanja), if you're in real trouble. Like mountain rescue people anywhere, the volunteers who staff the service won't be amused if you call them out for no good reason, but will willingly risk life and limb to bring you to safety if needed.

You can reach the GSS through the nearest information point or via a police station (call 92), or through the GSS offices in Split or Rijeka (tel: 021 569 666/051 212 302), or through the head office of the Croatian Mountaineering Association (HPS, tel: 01 482 4142). If you're well equipped with enough clothing, food, water, maps and a compass, the chances are you won't need to make that call.

Marked trails

Most of the trails in the national parks and nature reserves are well marked using a painted red circle with a white dot in the middle, or occasionally two red lines separated by a white line. The markings are maintained by local hiking and mountaineering associations, and are usually very clear, but if you're in a remote or rarely accessed part of the mountains then you may find markings worn or damaged, especially if there's no mountain lodge nearby. Occasionally you'll find trails where trees have been cut down, leaving the way ahead uncertain – try to make sure you have a local map and a compass with you in any case.

Ferries

There are few experiences more pleasant than a ferry-ride on the Adriatic, and in Croatia they're plentiful, economical, regular and reliable. Most domestic services are run by state-owned Jadrolinija (www.jadrolinija.hr). They vary from the roll-on, roll-off ferries used for very short hops between the coast and the nearest islands, to the huge ships that ply the whole length of the coast from Pula and Rijeka to Split and Dubrovnik, once a day in each direction.

Local ferries are inexpensive – typical passenger fares are rarely more than 20 or 30 kuna – while the main coastline service, which involves a night on board, can be pricey or not depending on what accommodation option you've taken. The fare for the whole length of the coast was around 200 kuna in the summer of 2004 for a place on deck or in one of the bars; a couchette went for 400 kuna; while a cabin cost 700 kuna a head.

Taking your car to the islands needn't break the bank. Short hops are charged at under 100 kuna, while medium-length journeys cost from 200 to 300 kuna. On the main coastal service, you'll pay a supplement of around 600 kuna to bring your car on the 20-hour journey.

Boat – sailing, yachting and motor-cruising

Whether you have your own boat or whether you've chartered one, and whether you're travelling by steam or by sail, there's really no better way of seeing Croatia's wealth of islands. Once you've swallowed the costs associated with the boat itself (and here the sky really is the limit), a sailing or boating holiday is (or can be) quite reasonable, with the only significant outlays being food, drink, and marina expenses.

The coast and islands between Split and Dubrovnik are on the whole less crowded than the north, and are most popular with English speakers – though English is widely spoken among the whole sailing community. The Kvarner Bay is understandably preferred by Germans and Austrians, being much closer to home, while the Italians love it all, from north to south. Friends who sailed here recently have compared it to sailing in Greece 15 years ago, with uncrowded waters, hospitable marinas and local restaurants, and wonderfully picturesque villages and fortified historical towns.

Sailing and yachting experience

The type of sailing or yachting holiday you embark on will depend at least to some extent on your level of experience. Beginners can be catered for either by a pre-arranged package (see page 28) or by having more experienced friends, but bear in mind that a week on board in a confined space can strain even close friendships, so choose carefully. Once you're on board, the Captain's word really is final – if he or she says jump, you jump.

Learning-to-sail holidays cost from around £450–650 per person for a week, or £700–900 for a fortnight, including flights from London.

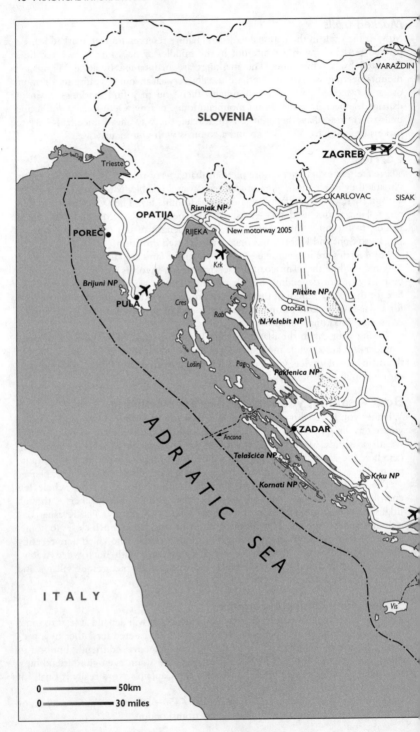

CROATIA : FERRY ROUTES

HUNGARY

N

Bradt

KOPRIVNICA

BJELOVAR

Drava

OSIJEK

POŽEGA

ĐAKOVO

VUKOVAR

SLAVONSKI BROD

Sava

BOSNIA &
HERZEGOVINA

SERBIA

SPLIT

New motorway 2008

Brač

Makarska

Hvar

Drvenik

Ploče

Korčula

Pelješac

MLJET NP

Mljet

DUBROVNIK

MONTENEGRO

Beri

If you're at an intermediate level, and at least one member of your crew is reasonably experienced, then sailing in a flotilla is an excellent way of improving your sailing skills, while not having to worry too much about navigation or the *bora* (gusty northeasterly wind) around the corner. Boats can be chartered by between two and eight people, with the cost decreasing as the numbers go up. Expect to pay close to £1,000 per person for a week at the height of the season if there are just two of you, but under £500 per person if you're a party of eight in May or September, both including flights from London.

Take the experience requirements for renting a boat seriously, even if not all the charter companies are as thorough about checking as they might be. Sailing is a tremendous activity, but it's also potentially hazardous and even life-threatening, so make sure you – or people in your party – have the necessary experience. Most charter companies won't need to see certificates (not all countries issue them anyway) but you may be asked to demonstrate your skills before heading out into open waters unaccompanied.

An alternative is to hire a local skipper with your boat – a good idea if no-one in your group has the requisite experience, and a great way of finding hidden nooks and crannies in the islands. Expect to pay £350–500 a week for the services of a skipper.

Charters

Most people will end up chartering a boat, and there's an excellent (and comprehensive) list of charter companies – over 150 at the time of writing – complete with full contact details and type and size of boats for rental on the tourist board's website. Around 14,000 vessels are available in total, with 10,000 of these being sailing boats and the rest motorboats. Go to www.croatia.hr then select *Tourism PLUS*, *Nautics*, and then *charters*. People I know have recommended Ecker Yachting for their well-maintained boats – Ecker is based in Zadar (tel/fax: 881 999), and has a range of sailing boats from 11 to 16 metres.

During the war of the early 1990s, many boats left Croatia for havens in Italy and Greece, and not all have yet returned. As a result there's a greater demand than supply for charters, so book early. Even if you do, you may find boats in less good condition than you were expecting, with the charter business still in recovery mode.

Price depends on model, size, capacity and season, starting from around £500 a week for a three- to four-berth boat in low season and escalating rapidly up to the thousands for an eight-berth yacht in August. In the summer of 2004 you could expect to pay £1,000–1,300 per week for a five-cabin, 11.4m Bavaria 36 sailing boat.

Mooring

Croatia's Association of Nautical Tourism, based in Rijeka, has a total of 48 marinas with some 12,500 sea moorings. The full list, along with all their facilities and individual websites (where available), can be found on the tourist board's website. Go to www.croatia.hr then select *Tourism PLUS*, *Nautics*, and *marinas*. The Adriatic Croatia International Club (known everywhere as ACI), based in Opatija, runs 21 of these (17 year-round) and has an excellent website listing fees, locations and facilities at www.aci-club.hr.

Marinas tend to be well equipped, with restaurants, bars and shops either on-site or nearby, and good technical services. Be aware that not all charter boats have shore power installations, even though electricity is usually available. Many marinas also have hot showers and some have laundry facilities. ACI day rates run from around €20 (£12) for small craft to €40 (£25) for boats up to 15m.

An alternative to marinas is mooring 'stern-to' in the smaller ports. You can also find mooring lines in some harbours, while remoter restaurants seeking sea-trade will put out mooring lines to encourage you in. Ports and bays are sometimes free but can charge variable fees depending on the length of the boat and how much jetty you're occupying – they are meant to provide services (such as rubbish collection, and the supply of groceries), and a receipt, in return.

Provisions/restaurants

Keeping yourself in food and drink shouldn't be a problem. You can stock up on speciality items in supermarkets in towns, but you'll also find plenty of street markets and small shops in the villages on the islands. If there's been a prolonged spell of bad weather and there isn't a ferry service you may find it hard to get bread or fresh fruit, but it's very unlikely to affect you during the summer sailing season.

Restaurants, especially on the smaller islands, tend to be good value, with wine and cheeses recommended, and you're more likely to find the homely *konoba* here than on the mainland.

Water and fuel

Watering and fuelling isn't usually a problem, with all marinas and most ports having abundant supplies of both, though you may have to scout around to find the right person responsible for supplying water to boats. Some islands, however, have no water supply of their own, so don't expect to fill up here.

Charts and guides

Croatian waters are very well charted, and Croatian, English, German and Italian charts are available. The Croatian sea charts come well recommended, and can be bought in most marinas and harbours once you're there. If you want to do some advance reconnoitring, you should be able to order charts from Kelvin Hughes Charts & Maritime Supplies, New North Road, Hainault, Essex, UK IG6 2UR; tel: +44 208 502 6887, fax: +44 208 500 0837.

If that doesn't work out (or you're not based in the UK), you can go direct to the publisher (Hrvatski Hidrografski Institut, Zrinsko-Frankopanska 161, pp291, 21000 Split; tel: 361 840; fax: 347 242; email: office@hhi.hr; www.hhi.hr), or Plovput, the government agency that looks after all the lighthouses, beacons etc (Plovput, Obala Lazareta 1, 21000 Split; tel: 355 900; fax: 585 782; email: info@plovput.hr; www.plovput.hr).

Also highly recommended comes the *Adriatic Pilot* (Imray Laurie Norie and Wilson, tel: +44 1480 462114; fax: +44 1480 496109), which is now in its third edition. This 440-page nautical guide to the Adriatic comes in at £32.50, but is well worth the expense.

Winds

If you're sailing outside the summer months, you'll need to keep a weather-eye out for the *bora* (the gutsy northeasterly which can blow at gale-force from September to May for anything from four days to a fortnight), and the *jugo-scirocco* (a warm, humid, east-southeasterly, accompanied by heavy clouds and rain).

Once winter's over you can expect lighter winds and better weather, though during July and August storms are more frequent, and during September winds strengthen again.

Summer is characterised by the prevailing *mistral* (*maestral*), which is no relation of the Provençal horror. The *mistral* here is a sailor's dream, a fair-weather wind which springs up locally mid morning, strengthens until the early afternoon and then dies down at sunset.

The summer *bora* is more localised and much less persistent than the winter version, springing up in sudden squalls and capable of gale-force strength, particularly in the Gulf of Trieste and the Velebit Channel. Fortunately it's very reliably forecast, so listen carefully to the weather bulletins on the radio and head for a well-sheltered port if a *bora*'s on the way.

The summer *jugo* is also mostly a local wind, and is more frequent in the south than the north. Be warned it can switch quickly to a *bora* – something to be borne in mind if you're in a mooring exposed to the northeast.

Weather forecasts/safety

Marinas always have the latest forecasts available, but Croatia also has three coastal radio stations which broadcast excellent weather reports – particularly for the *bora* – and warning announcements in both Croatian and English, several times a day. They receive radio-telephone messages round the clock and re-broadcast these, so stay tuned to whichever station is nearest. All three operate on VHF channel 16. They also operate on the following channels, with weather updates at the following times:

Rijeka Radio VHF channels 16, 24, 20, 21, 40, 04 – at 05.35, 14.35 and 19.35
Split Radio VHF channels 16, 21, 23, 07, 28, 70, 81 – at 05.45, 12.45 and 19.45
Dubrovnik Radio VHF channels 16, 04, 07 – at 06.25, 13.20 and 21.20

After the weather, the coastal radio stations broadcast nautical warning messages, with information on obstacles to navigation, lighthouse failures, prohibited areas, etc.

During the day you can usually contact marinas on VHF channel 17, while harbourmasters' offices are on channel 10. Harbourmasters tend to have their own patrol boats, which can be used to help boats in distress, and (as elsewhere) they can also call on the help of any suitable ship in the vicinity, including foreign boats.

If you run into trouble it's worth knowing that the radio-telephone is more likely to get you help than a CB-radio distress signal, as the authorities aren't tuned into CB-channels.

ACCOMMODATION

Thanks to its popularity with tourists in the 1970s and 1980s, Croatia has a good supply of accommodation, coming in five flavours – private rooms, hotels, campsites, hostels and mountain lodges. A total of around 800,000 beds are available in some 300,000 rooms. In 2003, nearly four million people – 45% of the total visitors – stayed in hotels or hotel villages, 1.9 million camped, 1.7 million lodged in private rooms and 700,000 slept on boats.

Private rooms offer the best value for money, but if you're in the mood to splash out there's little to beat the old-fashioned luxury of the grand hotels of the Austro-Hungarian era in the capital and in old resorts like Opatija. Most hotels on the coast and islands were built in the tourist boom of the 1970s, though the great majority have been upgraded and well restored since the war of the early 1990s.

Hotel accommodation and campsites in the main resorts fill up fast in summer, so you need to reserve well ahead of time (phone ahead – weekdays 08.00–14.00 are your best bet – and confirm by fax). Turning up on the fly in high season in Poreč can be a disappointing experience.

In a category all of its own, you could also choose to holiday in a lighthouse, of which 11 are available. Pictures and descriptions are available at www.croatia.hr –

for further information and bookings you should contact Adriatica.Net, Slavonska avenija 26/9, 10000 Zagreb; tel: 241 5600; fax: 245 2909; email: info@adriatica.net; www.adriatica.net.

Note Accommodation prices throughout the guide are given in euros, as this is the currency used in pre-negotiations, reservations and official accommodation quotations – although your final bill will be in kuna. All prices were correct as of summer 2004.

Private rooms/apartments

Anywhere that sees regular tourists has a supply of private rooms (*privatne sobe*) available, and for most independent travellers these represent the best accommodation option. They are the equivalent of B&Bs in the UK (though usually breakfastless), and are generally clean, comfortable and friendly. Their big advantage over hotels – other than reduced cost (many private rooms go for under €40 a night) – is that they offer you a chance to meet local people, though in the most popular places families are showing a tendency to insulate themselves from their lodgers.

Rooms can be sourced through local travel agencies (or through the tourist office, where there aren't agencies), but you can often save money by stopping anywhere you see signs saying *sobe/zimmer/chambre/camere/rooms/privat*.

Where buses, trains and ferries arrive in the main destinations – and notably in Split and Dubrovnik – gaggles of old women will be on hand to offer you rooms. Check both the price and location carefully, but these can be a good bargain, especially if you're staying for only a couple of nights. Through official channels a 30–50% surcharge is usually applied for stays of only one or two nights, but if you're negotiating direct with the owner a lot will depend on the time of year and how busy a place is. Singles in theory get a double room for around 70% of the full price, but in a seller's market you may end up paying the full whack.

Private rooms are classified by the local tourist office and come in three categories, I, II and III. Category I rooms will be clean and functional, but you'll almost certainly be sharing a bathroom. In Category II you'll be bathing en suite and may even have a TV, while in Category III you'll be in some luxury.

Private accommodation also includes apartments, which can be great value for families or small groups, but check how many beds have been crammed into each room before you buy. More expensive apartments tend to be better located rather than roomier.

Inland there's also a healthy move towards eco- or agro-tourism, with rooms being available in farmhouses and small villages. This is a nascent trend and not yet well established, but look out for signs if you're in the countryside.

Finally, with both private rooms and apartments don't be afraid to say no if you don't like the look of the place – staying somewhere which doesn't suit you can really spoil your holiday.

Hotels

Croatia's numerous hotels are classified by the standard international one- to five-star system, though at the lower end they don't represent very good value for money when compared with the better private rooms, which generally cost around half the price of the worst hotel in any particular town.

Most establishments are still of the large, modern and functional variety, though there is a groundswell of smaller, family-run hotels appearing. Assuming you can't afford the Habsburg opulence of one of the few pre-World War I hotels still in operation, the smaller hotels are often the nicest places to stay, though rooms need to be booked well in advance. Most of the bigger hotels – which is where you're likely to be if you're on a package – have been substantially upgraded since 1995, so you're unlikely to experience the cracked plaster, 70s light fittings and intermittent hot water which made Croatian hotels such a lucky-dip in the 1980s.

Breakfast is almost invariably included in the room price, and ranges from rolls, butter and jam to a full buffet, with a strong correlation between the quality of the food and the number of stars. You can save a fair amount of money by opting for half or full board – the supplement is usually only a small one – but bear in mind you'll also be condemning yourself to eating largely unexciting meals in the hotel, rather than getting out and about.

Camping

In a country with fine weather and beautiful countryside, camping ought to be the ideal option. It ought to be, but it's not. Campsites are not especially cheap, and sites are often huge and far removed from easy access by public transport. Some of the places you're most likely to visit – notably Split – don't have campsites at all.

The explanation is a simple one – camping is mainly aimed at northern Europeans with their own transport, who come for a week or two and set up a temporary base on the beach. And if that's what you want to do, then you'll find Croatia's campsites friendly, clean and very well-equipped. Expect to pay around €20 a night for two people, a pitch and a parking space at an *autokamp*.

Freelance camping in Croatia is illegal and if you're caught you'll be subject to an immediate and fairly hefty fine. If you're off the beaten track and camping freelance, however, then please, please don't let it be you that starts off the forest fire. Many areas of the country, especially in the mountains and on the islands, have no free water supply, and fires are a major hazard – so much so that in some areas even smoking is forbidden.

Youth hostels and student dormitories

Croatia has only a handful of officially recognised youth hostels (see www.hfhs.hr), but with summer prices averaging under €15 a head it can be easily the most economical option for single travellers (if you're in Zagreb, Pula, Zadar, Dubrovnik, Vel, Lošinj, Krk or Punat). For two or more people travelling together, private accommodation tends to be both more convenient – no daytime lockout, for example – and competitive on price.

At Zagreb University, there's some access to student accommodation in summer, but again, it's not especially good value unless you're travelling alone. Rooms go for around €20 a head, and can be booked through the tourist office.

Mountain lodges

Croatia has over 100 mountain huts and lodges, with facilities ranging from the basic (roof and walls) to the positively hotel-like. They're excellent value for money and are usually run by the local mountain associations under the auspices of the Croatian Mountaineering Association (Hrvatski Planinarski Savez, HPS, Kozarčeva 22, Zagreb; tel/fax: 01 482 4142 or tel: 01 482 3624; email: hps@zg.tel.hr; www.hps.inet.hr – where you'll find a full list of the accommodation available, along with altitudes and contact numbers). You can also ask at the various park offices around the country.

EATING AND DRINKING

What you eat and drink in Croatia will depend on where you are – in Slavonia, along the Hungarian border, you can expect to find spicy sausages and heavy, meaty soups, while along the coast you'll find an Italian flavour to the food, with plentiful pizza, pasta and fish dishes, followed by lashings of ice-cream. What you're unlikely to find these days, sadly, is *Hoppel Poppel* on the menu. According to my trusty 1966 *Gateway Guide*, 'Hoppel Poppel, which the visitor feels inclined to tackle straight away because the name sounds so amusing and exotic, turns out to be a well-known international dish – hash.' Each region has its own wines and beers to be proud of, and across the country you'll find a range of fearsome spirits, designed to warm the cockles and cement friendships.

Eating

The day starts for most of us with breakfast, though it practically doesn't exist as a meal per se in Croatia. If you're in a hotel, however, then breakfast of some sort will invariably be included in the price – usually in the form of a self-service buffet, with the quality and variety of fare on offer closely correlating to the number of stars.

If you're in a private room you can rely on cafés and *slastičarnice* (cake shops) to sell you pastries and cakes for breakfast, and if you're outside the most touristed areas you may still find *burek*, a pastry filled with cheese (*sa sirom*), meat (*sa mesom*) and just occasionally spinach (*špinat*). *Burek* is cheap, filling and usually delicious – if occasionally too greasy for comfort – but a good deal harder to find than it was a decade or so ago.

You'll also find cheap restaurants and snack bars everywhere – often billed as *bife* (bar) or *roštilj* (grill bar) – serving up lunch or dinner of *ćevapi* or *ćevapčići* (spiced meatballs or small sausages, usually accompanied by spring onions and spicy green peppers), *pljeskavica* (a wad of minced meat often served in pitta bread – the Croatian hamburger), or *ražnjiči* (kebab). Try any of these dishes with fiery *ajvar*, a sauce made from tomatoes, peppers and aubergines, with a dash of chilli.

Bakeries (*pekarnica*) sell a wide variety of breads (though occasionally only powdery white rolls and plain loaves) and sometimes offer ready-made sandwiches (*sendviči*) available with cheese (*sir*) or ham (*šunka*) fillings. Street markets (*tržnica*) will provide you with the usual fare for picnics etc, and you can ask for sandwiches to be made up to order at any deli-counter in a supermarket (*samopluga*) – just point at the type of bread you want filled, say '*sendvič*' and point at your choice of filling.

Pizzerias are the next step up the food chain, and represent great value for money. Pizza here is close to what you get in Italy, with a thin crust and a variety of toppings – including excellent chilli peppers. Pizzerias also tend to do good (and keenly priced) pasta dishes – though I've yet to eat pasta anywhere in Croatia that wasn't (by Italian standards, anyway) slightly overcooked.

Restaurants (*restoran*, *konoba* or *gostiona*) tend to focus on meat and/or fish dishes. Meat isn't especially exciting, tending towards pork and lamb chops and cutlets, pan-fried veal, or steak, but it's generally tasty enough. Fish for its part is ubiquitous and delicious – but can turn out to be surprisingly pricey. For most white fish you'll pay by the raw weight, and a decent-sized fish for two can come in at as much as 400 kuna on its own. Whitebait, blue fish (sardines, mackerel, etc) and squid are, on the other hand, great value.

Shellfish is especially popular on the coast, with steamed mussels on many menus and cockles appearing in pasta dishes and starters, and in winter (through to mid May) you can get great oysters in the south (from Ston) priced at 5 to 10 kuna apiece. You may also see crab and lobster on the menu – but mind the price tag (and watch out for mis-translations; crayfish is often billed as lobster). Finally, you'll see plenty of *crni rižot* (literally black risotto) on offer; it's a pungent dish, made with squid ink, and though it's popular it's not to everyone's taste.

You'll also see lots of *pršut*, Croatia's answer to Italy's *prosciutto*, and pronounced (and produced) in almost exactly the same way. The air-dried ham is an Istrian and Dalmatian speciality and practically melts in the mouth when sliced thinly enough – which sadly it isn't always.

Of course if you're vegetarian, *pršut*, like much else on the menu, is a non-starter – indeed it's a non-main and a non-dessert, too. Vegetarianism is no longer off the menu altogether, however, and even where restaurants don't offer specific vegetarian options, you can always get a cheese omelette (*omlet sa sirom*), a meat-free pasta dish, or a pizza, along with a range of salads. There are also a number of home-made cheeses (*sir*), often kept in oil, which vary from the tastily pungent to the surprisingly bland.

For basic restaurant vocabulary, see *Appendix 1, Language*, from page 317.

Drinking

The most important thing you need to know is that you *can* drink the water – all publicly supplied water is safe unless it explicitly says otherwise. The next piece of good news for drinkers is that alcohol is pretty inexpensive when compared to northern Europe, with a half-litre of draught beer (*pivo*) costing anything from 10–20 kuna, depending on the establishment. Premium brands go for a little more, but local beers are just great, my personal favourite being *karlovačko pivo*, from Karlovac.

Wine

Croatia makes lots of wine, and the quality – always drinkable – continues to improve. Almost the entire production is guzzled down domestically, however, so you're very unlikely to see it on your supermarket shelves at home. In shops you can pay anything from 20–100 kuna for a bottle, while in most pizzerias and restaurants a litre of the house red goes for 50–80 kuna; bottled wines start from around 80 kuna and head rapidly up from there to over 200 kuna in the swankiest establishments.

Spirits (Rakija)

Spirits are common, dangerous, and fairly cheap. In supermarkets you'll find brandies and other spirits at around 70–100 kuna a bottle, but you can also buy fiery and frequently excellent home-distilled spirits – especially *travarica*, a drink featuring a lot of alcohol and a few herbs – in the markets for anything from 50 to 100 kuna a bottle. The quality of spirits varies enormously and can't usually be determined from the label – price is a reasonable (but far from infallible) indicator. A personal favourite is *Velebitska Travarica*, which is made by monks up in the mountains and comes in an especially attractive bottle. On the other hand do anything you can to avoid a drink called *Pelinkovac*. I once had three in a row in Zagreb, convinced that at some point the apparently re-bottled wood-stain would become palatable – but it never did. It brings a bad taste to the mouth even now, just writing about it.

Friendships, business deals and meetings are all cemented with *rakija*, and it's surprising how often you'll find yourself expected to down lethal drinks. If you don't drink at all, then it's not a bad idea to come up with a plausible reason why not (health is always a reliable standby), as Croatians tend to be suspicious of anyone who won't join in.

Soft drinks

In marked contrast to the abundance of alcoholic choice, there are surprisingly few soft drinks available. Cola is of course mind-numbingly popular – but don't expect to find it that easy to source in sugar-free versions – and bottles of sweet fizzy orange are ubiquitous. If you're asked if you'd like one from the freezer on the hottest day in summer – as I was once in Cavtat, waiting for a broken-down bus to be repaired – check the freezer is actually operational before you buy.

In the most popular tourist spots along the coast there's a better range of drinks now available – largely due to the presence of Italians here – but otherwise the most exotic thing you'll find will be the delicious home-made lemonade sometimes available with your morning *burek*.

Coffee and tea
Coffee is as popular here as everywhere, and in cafés tends to be excellent – though what you'll be served with breakfast in the lower-end hotels can be frankly disgusting. Tea is most often of the fruit variety or comes in dodgy-looking bags which tend to work better with lemon than milk. Ordinary 'English' tea is known as black tea (*crni caj*), but don't expect to find anything you'll be able to stand a spoon in unless you bring your own. Tea and coffee will cost anything from 5 to 15 kuna in a café, depending on the upmarketness (or otherwise) of the establishment.

PUBLIC HOLIDAYS AND FESTIVALS
Croatia has the usual mix of religious and secular public holidays, as well as innumerable feast days, folk festivals, and annual cultural events. Specifics are covered in the relevant sections, but the national holidays and a few of the festivals are included here.

National holidays
You should expect banks and shops to be closed on Croatia's national holidays, which fall as follows:

January 1	New Year's Day
Easter Sunday and Easter Monday	Easter falls on Sunday March 27 in 2005, Sunday April 16 in 2006 and Sunday April 8 in 2007.
May 1	Labour Day
Corpus Christi	60 days after Easter Sunday, and taken seriously in Croatia, with processions and lots of first communions. Corpus Christi falls on Thursday May 26 in 2005, Thursday June 15 in 2006 and Thursday June 7 in 2007.
June 22	Day of Antifascist Struggle (celebrating the uprising of Croatian antifascist partisans on this day in 1941)
June 25	Statehood Day
August 5	Homeland Thanksgiving Day
August 15	Assumption of the Virgin Mary
October 8	Independence Day
November 1	All Saints' Day
December 25–26	Christmas holidays

Festivals
Croatia's robust Catholic heritage was built on the back of a strong pagan culture, and you'll find lots of the festivals and celebrations here owing more than a little to each. The calendar of festivities is based around both Christian (Easter, Corpus Christi, Saints' Days) and seasonal (spring, solstices, harvest) events, with Croats ready and willing to celebrate them all.

On religious holidays and feast days – not to mention the local patron saint's day – locals will hold processions, masses and major celebrations, and they're a great thing to be a part of if you're in the neighbourhood.

There are also innumerable festivals relating to the business of survival on the land or sea. Most seaside towns, villages and ports have at least one annual fisherman's festival (where the sea is treated with the usual mix of fear and due respect, and blessed by the local priest), while inland you can still find people casting away bad luck after the winter (using bells or branches as talismans against misfortune).

Pretty much every island and town along the coast now has a 'cultural summer' and 'musical nights' which keep things lively once the sun's gone down, with Dubrovnik's summer festival being the largest and most famous. Concerts and theatre productions are held most evenings in the old town, through six weeks of July and August, and the festival culminates in spectacular fireworks.

You'll also find two main types of folk music on show. First off are the big festivals which bring together hundreds – or even thousands – of performers. The most celebrated of these is the Zagreb Folk Festival in July, a five-day extravaganza drawing huge crowds and mirrored on a smaller scale across much of Slavonia. The second is the lower-key folk entertainments put on wherever tourists are to be found. Whilst these certainly aren't to be scorned, neither do they have the originality or the authenticity of the big festivals inland. You may be better off keeping your ears pricked for a wedding party, almost invariably featuring vibrant local costumes and music.

The festival year kicks off (or closes, depending on your viewpoint) with the New Year's Regatta on the island of Hvar, held annually and running from December 28 to 31 , and featuring seriously competitive dinghy racing.

Things are reasonably quiet from then until the wildly popular carnival season gets underway in February, culminating on Shrove Tuesday – or sometimes on the weekend before. Masked parades and gaudy floats can be found in many Croatian towns, but Rijeka takes the biscuit for the biggest and most showy event. Rijeka's carnival is now second only in Europe to the one in Venice, attracting more than 10,000 active participants and 100,000 spectators. At the same time men wearing sheepskins drive evil spirits away from Rijeka's hinterland villages, using bells.

In April, in odd-numbered years, Zagreb holds its *biennale*, the International Festival of Contemporary Music. This draws the biggest names in contemporary classical music (past stars have included Stravinsky, Stockhausen, Cage and Shostakovich) and is an absolute must for those trailing music's leading edge. Check out www.biennale-zagreb.hr for more information.

By the end of July, bikers across the continent will be revving up and heading towards Pula for the annual Istria Bikers' Rally, which draws not just rock musicians and heavy-metal bands but also more than 10,000 leathered motorcyclists. Barely a week later, on the first Sunday in August, 18th-century-uniformed cavalrymen charge around the town of Sinj, inland from Split, on horseback with lances, in the colourful *Sinjska Alka* festival which celebrates the town's 1715 victory over an army of Turks.

August sees snow as well – or at least the celebration of it – in the village of Kukljica, on the island of Ugljan, where the Feast of Our Lady of the Snows features both a parade and a flotilla of fishing boats setting off in honour of the snow said to have fallen there one August centuries ago. Throughout July and August on the islands you'll also have the chance to see one of the festivals of sword dances. The most famous of these is the *moreška* on the island of Korčula, which continues a tradition dating back at least 1,000 years.

In the autumn, once the harvest is in, the biggest festival is All Saints' Day, when every graveyard and cemetery in the country becomes a mass of flowers. The year then closes with Christmas, which is much as you'd expect, though a big fish rather than a turkey is the thing to have during the main celebration on Christmas Eve.

SHOPPING

Croatia's not a great place for bargain hunters, with prices for most goods pretty much in line with those across the EU, though you'll find an unbelievable number of shoe shops and people selling beachwear, both at prices about 20% less than in London or Milan. If you've forgotten to bring something with you, it'll be fairly easy to replace, but you're probably not going to need to buy extra suitcases for all the things you bought here on the cheap.

Opening hours and PDV (VAT)

Opening hours vary but you can expect most shops to be open from eight or nine in the morning until eight in the evening in the summer. In winter, opening hours tend to be shorter and shops may well close for lunch.

Purchase tax (PDV, or VAT) is set at a flat rate of 22% on all goods except essentials and books. In theory foreigners can get this reimbursed on single-ticket items costing over 500 kuna, but you have to really want the money. Fill in the PDV-P form at the point of sale and get it stamped, so that when you leave Croatia, you can have the goods, receipts and forms certified by the Croatian Customs Service – not a process for the impatient.

And that's the easy part. You then post back the certified receipts etc to the shop, along with your bank account details. Within a year or so, bingo: the money reappears. It's worth the hassle, of course, on really big-ticket items, but bear in mind when you're bringing goods back into your home country you may be subject to import duties or asked to prove you've actually paid the VAT…

Books

If you run out of holiday reading along the coast or in the capital, you shouldn't have too much trouble finding something to read, though expect to pay about 20% over the cover price. Inland, and especially in eastern Slavonia, it's a different matter, with school textbooks often being the only English-language reading material available.

Music

If you get hooked on the local music – and it happens – make sure you buy this before you leave the country. Even in an online world, Croatian folk music is pretty hard to come by. If you don't know exactly what you're looking for, most shops will be helpful in playing you a selection of CDs or cassettes, if you get talking with the staff (though don't try this half an hour before closing on a Saturday afternoon in a shop full of students in Zagreb). As a matter of principle, if you can't decide, the tackier the cover, the better the music inside. CDs are about the same price as in the rest of the EU – perhaps 10% cheaper than in the UK.

Handicrafts

When Rebecca West travelled round Croatia in 1937, she spent a good part of her trip buying up antique peasant costumes, while noting that fewer and fewer people were wearing them. This trend has continued unabated to the present day, meaning you're unlikely to see traditional dress at anything other than folk festivals or weddings. The beautifully embroidered waistcoats and skirts are still being made, but only really to fill a tourist need. Genuinely old costumes are now sufficiently hard to find – and precious – that you'd have to treat anything for sale with a dash of scepticism.

ARTS AND ENTERTAINMENT

With more than a nod to Austria in the north and Italy to the west, Croats love going to the theatre, and there are excellent productions to be seen at the professional theatres in Zagreb, Osijek, Rijeka, Split and Dubrovnik.

The Croatian National Theatre in Zagreb isn't just a theatre, it's an entire experience. The fabulous building (inside and out) sees more than 200 performances annually, in a season that runs all year except August, and includes excellent ballet, opera and theatre productions in a mix of premières and revivals. Theatre productions tend to be in Croatian, but all opera is put on in the original language.

Tickets can be hard to get (though some tickets are kept aside for sale on the day), partly because – by the standards of most countries, and especially for opera – they're inexpensive, costing from 30 to 200 kuna apiece. The current programme can be found in English at the theatre's website at www.hnk.hr.

Croats are also great cinema-goers. Fortunately for English-speakers, most of the films are subtitled rather than dubbed, straight from Hollywood. This makes going to the cinema easy enough, and tickets are cheap, but you'll be lucky to find films made outside the USA which you'll be able to understand without good language skills. I once sat through the full six hours of Bertolucci's *Novocento* in Italian, with Croatian subtitles, but it's not something I'd necessarily recommend.

Croatia has more than its fair share of concerts and festivals, too. See *Festivals*, page 57, as well as individual entries throughout the guide for more information.

Most towns of any size have at least one museum or gallery, though the quality of these varies greatly – there are very few modern art galleries, for example. Mostly, too, galleries and museums reflect Croatia's long history of attachment to one empire or another, so you'll see a lot of Austro-Hungarian and Venetian influences in the art and architecture. The most notable exception is the sculptor Ivan Meštrović, whose work you'll see everywhere, and in particular at the eponymous collections in both Zagreb and Split.

PHOTOGRAPHY

Croatia has some of the best photo opportunities you'll find anywhere, with great weather, good light, and a wide variety of photogenic subjects. While there are lots of opportunities to shoot wild flowers and the like, wildlife photography itself can be difficult, since the most interesting animals (bear, wolves, lynx, eagles etc) tend to shy well clear of people. Even the longest-focus lens isn't going to be much help here.

With a long history of tourism, you're unlikely to run into people-problems with photography in Croatia – they're used to it – but that doesn't mean you shouldn't apply the usual ethical standards. Respect people's privacy, don't take pictures you know will offend, and especially don't take pictures when you're asked not to. The one thing you should be aware of, however, is that with war memories still fresh, don't even think of photographing places that might have military significance. Spending the rest of your holiday being questioned by the authorities is no fun at all.

Digital photography is increasingly popular – but bear in mind the usual limitations of memory size, battery life etc, and know your camera well. In spite of their point-and-shoot reputation, it's still quite hard to get really first-class pictures with digital cameras unless you've gone the professional route and bought a top-range digital SLR.

If you're using standard equipment it's worth noting that while print film is easily available (if a bit more expensive than at home), slide film is relatively hard to find – especially if you have a particular brand preference. If you're buying film check the use-by date; some of the rolls you see for sale expired years ago. Finally, take films home for processing.

MEDIA AND COMMUNICATIONS

For a country of under 4.5 million people, Croatia has a surprisingly vigorous and wide-ranging press, though it's only very recently that the main newspapers, TV and radio stations have been anything other than a mouthpiece for the state.

Communications also suffered from the heritage of state communism, but the rapid uptake of mobile telephony and the internet in the first two years of the new millennium, and the increased integration of Croatia with the rest of Europe, means Croatia now has services worthy of its status as an EU supplicant. Electricity comes in the European standard size and shape, at 220V and 50Hz, and twin round-pinned plugs are used.

Media

Croatian independence in 1991 did little to bring freedom to the media, and it's only since the election of Stipe Mesić (in February 2000) that any real efforts have been made to liberate editors and journalists from half a century of government puppet-hood. Since then the president himself has spoken out in favour of keeping the media free from politics, and has encouraged journalists to practice their profession independently, as public servants rather than government acolytes. It won't happen overnight, but the signs are already encouraging.

The dominant media provider is Croatian Radio and Television, HRT, which attracts an audience in excess of two million a day to its three TV channels and its national and local radio stations. HRT 1 & 2 produce the usual mix of news, documentaries, entertainment and game shows, while HRT 3 is dedicated almost exclusively to sport. The website, at www.hrt.hr, has an English-language site-map which will help you find the various web-streamed audio services on offer – useful for helping learn Croatian.

The most important daily newspaper is *Vjesnik* (online at www.vjesnik.com), which until recently was about as dry and unbiased as TASS in pre-Gorbachev days. With a change of management after the 2000 elections, the paper seems to be finding its independence – though it can still be a heavy read.

Right at the other end of the publishing spectrum is the weekly *Feral Tribune*, which even uses a cod *Herald Tribune* masthead (see www.feral.hr). Originally a satirical supplement to Dalmatia's largest daily, *Slobodna Dalmacija*, before the mother paper was closed down by the government in 1992, *Feral Tribune* gradually became more serious, and was a regular thorn in the side of the Tuđman government.

For news in English your options are fairly limited. You can tune in to the BBC World Service on a short-wave radio, or – if you're lucky – catch one of the intermittent English-language news bulletins on HRT radio. In the bigger centres you can pick up the main English papers a day or two (or more) out of date. Otherwise the internet's your best bet, either by going through one of the two biggest Croatian news portals at www.htnet.hr or www.hic.hr, or by tuning in directly to the BBC or another English-language news provider (www.news.bbc.co.uk, www.cnn.com, www.abcnews.go.com, etc.).

Post

Mail out of the former Yugoslavia used to take anything from two weeks to three months, and post out of 21st-century Croatia isn't all that much better – postcards within Europe tend to drift home in around two to three weeks, while airmail letters are quicker, but not enormously so. Just occasionally, something slips through a hole in the space-time continuum – a letter from Brač once arrived home in three days, and a card I sent to Australia from Zadar got there in eight – but you should reckon on post being fairly slow unless you pay for a premium, guaranteed-delivery service.

Post offices (*pošta*, or HPT) are open from 07.00 to 19.00 (or 08.00 to 20.00) in most areas, and until 13.00 on Saturdays. Parcels are reasonably cheap to send, but don't seal them until you've given the cashier time to check you're not posting bombs or contraband. If you send anything valuable you may have to pay duty on it when you get home.

If you want mail sent to you, have it addressed to *Poste Restante, Pošta, Town Name*. It will be delivered to the town's main post office if there's more than one. If your family name is underlined and/or in capitals your mail is more likely to be filed correctly, but if there's nothing for you it's always worth asking them to look under your first name as well. Incoming post takes around ten days from most European destinations, and about two weeks from North America, but can be quicker, or indeed slower.

Stamps (*marke*) are also sold at news stands, tobacconists and anywhere you can buy postcards, which can save you quite a queue at the post office. In 2004 it cost 3.50 kuna to send a card to Europe, and 7 kuna to send one to Australia or America.

Phone

The Croatian telephone network has vastly improved in the last 15 years, and you'll no longer be faced with multiple attempts to get access to the outside world. The international access code of 00 has finally been adopted here, too, meaning that for any international call you simply dial 00 followed by your country code (+44 for the UK, +1 for the USA and Canada, +61 for Australia and +64 for New Zealand) followed by the local phone number (without the leading zero in most cases, but not in Italy or Russia, for example).

The international code for calls into Croatia is +385. Area codes within Croatia are for the most part refreshingly simple, covering large geographical areas (the whole of central Dalmatia is within the 021 area code, for example), though there are one or two anomalies, with the island of Pag being cut in two (served by 023 in the south and 053 in the north), and a whole clutch of codes used in the north. The map here shows the regional codes across the country; they're also included at the beginning of each chapter.

Phone boxes are plentiful, and operated by 25- to 500-unit phonecards, with the 50-unit card costing 24 kuna and the 100-unit card costing 38 kuna in the summer of 2004. Local calls normally cost one unit, with long-distance calls being quite a bit more expensive, especially at peak time (Monday to Saturday, 07.00–22.00). You can buy phonecards at post offices, news stands and the bigger hotels. For international calls of any duration you may prefer to phone from a post office, where you'll be allocated a metered phone and charged after the call. International calls mostly aren't exorbitant, but it does depend on the destination.

Croats, like most other Europeans, have gone mobile-mad, and more than half the population has a mobile phone. The network is comprehensive and the local operators have roaming agreements with their foreign counterparts, so unless you're in the wilderness or up in the mountains you should find your

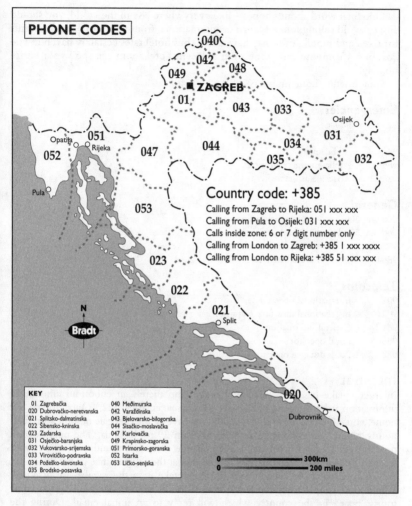

PHONE CODES

040
042
049 048
■ ZAGREB
01
043 033
Osijek
051 031
Opatija Rijeka
052 047 044 034 032
035

Country code: +385

Calling from Zagreb to Rijeka: 051 xxx xxx
Calling from Pula to Osijek: 031 xxx xxx
Calls inside zone: 6 or 7 digit number only
Calling from London to Zagreb: +385 1 xxx xxxx
Calling from London to Rijeka: +385 51 xxx xxx

Pula

053

023

022

021
N Split

KEY

01	Zagrebačka	040	Međimurska
020	Dubrovačko-neretvanska	042	Varaždinska
021	Splitsko-dalmatinska	043	Bjelovarsko-bilogorska
022	Šibensko-kninska	044	Sisačko-moslavačka
023	Zadarska	047	Karlovačka
031	Osječko-baranjska	049	Krapinsko-zagorska
032	Vukovarsko-srijemska	051	Primorsko-goranska
033	Virovitičko-podravska	052	Istarka
034	Požeško-slavonska	053	Ličko-senjska
035	Brodsko-posavska		

020
Dubrovnik

0 ━━━━ 300km
0 ━━━━ 200 miles

own mobile works, as long as you're on GSM (the principal standard across Europe and most of the rest of the world, except the Americas and Japan). If you're using your own mobile, however, remember that international calls will be expensive and local ones more so – you'll be calling from Croatia to home and back again, and paying for the whole lot.

If you're going to be glued to the phone, one option is to buy a local pre-paid subscription and top up your SIM card as needed – if you do this, keep the SIM card for your home subscription in a safe place. Not only is a local pre-paid number convenient for your outgoing calls, but it also means you can easily be called by family etc if necessary.

A local pre-paid subscription can be bought at any phone shop – the *Simpa* SIM card from Cronet costs just 300 kuna, which includes your first 100 kuna-worth of calls, after which top-up cards cost 50, 100 and 200 kuna. There are three local GSM operators, Cronet (prefix 098), Mobitel (099) and Vipnet (091), and they're all reasonable value and offer full coverage.

One final word about phones – like everywhere else in the world, you should aim to avoid calling long distance or international from your hotel room. Tariffs for fixed and mobile calls may have fallen, but hotel rates certainly haven't. The cost of a 15-minute call home from a decent hotel room can spoil your entire holiday.

Some useful phone numbers:

Emergencies
92	Police
93	Fire
94	Ambulance
985	Public emergency centre
987	Roadside assistance

General
060 300 300	Croatian Airlines
060 520 520	Weather forecast
95	Speaking clock
9864	Exchange rates

Telecoms
901	International operator
902	International directory enquiries
981	General information
988	Local operator
989	Long-distance operator

Internet

Internet uptake has been rapid in Croatia, and there's an enormous amount of information now available online (see *Web resources*, page 322). Once you've left home, you'll find that most towns and resorts have an internet café of some sort, with hourly online fees coming in at anything from 20 to 40 kuna. The public access points haven't been listed here, as they change every few months, but the nearest internet café *du jour* should be easy to find (ask at the tourist office or hotels).

Where Croatia has been slower on the uptake is in the regular use of email. While some people are instantly responsive, there's unfortunately barely a hotel or tourist board in the country which will reply to an initial email. During the

WRONG NUMBER?

There's nothing worse than buying a guidebook and then finding out some of the phone numbers are wrong, but the sad truth is that (even though every single number is checked before going to print) numbers change. And it seems they change more frequently in Croatia than other countries – numbers throughout this book migrated during the research and writing of it.

So what to do? Your best option when we fail you (my apologies) is to log on to **http://imenik.t-com.hr**, Croatia's outstanding online phone directory. There's an English-language option, and it's fast and accurate. Another option is to call the local tourist office in the town – assuming their number hasn't changed.

research for this book, many hundreds of emails were sent, the vast majority into the void. The frustrating thing is that when you do follow up with a phone call, the first response is all too often: 'Ah, yes, we saw your email!'.

So – with certain exceptions – I haven't listed email addresses in the guide, but I've included comprehensive phone and fax details, which at least have a proven reliability, along with web addresses.

BUSINESS/TIME

Most Croatian businesses operate from 08.30 to 16.30, Monday to Friday. If you're calling ahead of your journey – or having people call you in Croatia – it's useful to know that Croatia's on Central European Time (CET). That's an hour ahead of GMT, six hours ahead of New York and Washington, nine hours ahead of California, and eight hours behind Sydney and Melbourne (ten in the European winter). Summertime dates in Croatia are the same as in most other European countries, with the clocks going forward an hour in spring and back an hour in autumn.

The working environment – dress, culture etc – is similar to that in most European countries, but if you're doing business don't be surprised if you're expected to cement deals or friendships with a shot (or several) of *rakija*. If you don't drink out of choice, you need to invent a good reason why – the culture isn't particularly tolerant of non-drinkers.

CULTURAL DOS AND DON'TS

All visitors have an effect not just on a country but on its people too. There are numerous arguments for and against this which don't need to be enumerated here – suffice to say that it's worth considering both the environmental and sociological effects of your visit.

Environment

Croatia's environment is in good shape (see *Environmental issues*, page 7), so don't spoil it – preserving it is in everyone's interests.

The biggest impact you personally can have on the environment is to start a fire. There's almost nothing that can be done once a fire's out of control in Croatia's drier areas, so be especially careful here. Unless there's a plentiful supply of water nearby, in fact, it's advisable to avoid fires, or even naked flames, altogether.

Litter, by comparison, is a simple question of ugliness. Paper tissues take months to deteriorate, orange peel positively glows, and tin cans always look horrible. Take your litter with you – and if you collect any you find along the way you can feel suitably saintly about yourself. If you're in the wilds, and you can't find a toilet, do at least bury your doings – there are few sights (or sensations) more unpleasant than coming across someone else's.

Dress/naturism

In summer you won't look out of place in shorts and a T-shirt, but you won't be able to visit churches if you're too skimpily dressed – there are signs outside churches along the coast and islands giving you a pretty good idea of the dress code. Seaside topless sunbathing won't offend, but you shouldn't really be anywhere off the beach in your swimsuit (or indeed out of it).

Inland, you'll find local people more modestly dressed, though things have changed a lot in the last 15 years – you'll no longer look or feel out of place dressing the way you do back home (well, it depends on how outrageous you are back home, of course), or attract unwanted attention if you don't make an effort to conform. Quite the opposite is true these days – as a visitor you'll probably get strange looks if you're a woman in your fifties dressed all in black, or decked out entirely in retro denim if you're a man.

Back on the coast, Croatia is the main homing ground for the great European naturist – hundreds of thousands come here every year just to get their kit off. There are entire naturist resorts (the most popular are in Istria), campsites and apartment complexes, and most towns have a dedicated beach. Just look out for the FKK signs if you're interested. Croatia's also the only place I've been where you can go on a naturist sailing holiday. Mind your tackle.

Gay/lesbian

Homosexuality may have been legalised a generation ago in Croatia, but you won't find people particularly tolerant or open about it. Zagreb's first-ever gay parade wasn't held until June 2002, and only a few hundred people took part – heavily protected from hecklers by a slew of riot police.

Most activity is still very much underground, and there isn't any kind of gay/lesbian scene even in Dubrovnik, one of Croatia's most tolerant and liberal cities. Same-sex couples (men in particular) can still raise eyebrows (or even hackles) when checking into hotels. How you handle this will of course be up to you – some may be happy with a plausible cover story; others might find this stance too hypocritical.

As everywhere, younger people tend to be more tolerant than older, and urban people more tolerant than rural, but that doesn't mean you should stay away from the countryside.

Drugs

Illegal drugs are best avoided in Croatia. They're available, but the penalties are stiff, and harsher still for smuggling – don't be tempted or tricked into carrying anything across borders. Slavonia in particular has something of a reputation with the authorities for being part of a drugs corridor from Asia to the West, so be especially vigilant, and – without excessive paranoia – make sure you know exactly what's in your bags.

Tipping

A service charge isn't included in your restaurant bill, so – assuming the service has been good – it's appropriate to round up the bill to the nearest 10 kuna or so. Don't be afraid not to tip if you think the service has been terrible, but equally don't be stingy – waiting staff in Croatia aren't as well off as you are. Taxi drivers the world over expect fares to be rounded up, and Croatia's no exception.

INTERACTING WITH LOCAL PEOPLE

Croatia has been affected hugely by tourism, which has brought an improved standard of living to the country as a whole and to hundreds of thousands of individuals along the coast and on the islands. Tourism has also destroyed a way of life which was poorer and harsher, and yet, paradoxically, is often fondly remembered. Your surly, inattentive waiter at the dog-end of the summer season is probably dreaming of being the fisherman his father was – even though he knows how hard a fisherman's life really is. Don't expect to be able to unravel this contradiction.

Away from the tourist spots – and especially in the mountains, and in smaller communities inland – there are opportunities aplenty to build bridges between foreigners and local people. Take the time to talk to chance acquaintances, show people what life's like back home (photographs and postcards say more than words ever can, even if you do speak the language) and share in a cup of coffee, or a drink and a cigarette, if invited.

Off the beaten track in Croatia I've been asked into the homes of people who have virtually nothing, only to be offered the little they do. Bring pictures to show, perhaps a frisbee or sketchbook to share with the children, and Western cigarettes for the adults – most Croatians smoke and, whatever your personal feelings, cigarettes are appreciated everywhere. There are good arguments against giving gifts to kids on the street, or handing out largesse to beggars – both encourage dependence – but in people's homes, there's very little else you can do to return an extraordinary level of hospitality.

In Croatia as a whole – and especially in the parts of the country directly affected – it's a good idea not to discuss the recent war. It's a conversational minefield, and the last thing you want is to step on a conversational landmine. Even with a population that's now 90% Croat, as a foreigner you won't always know immediately whether you're talking to a Croat or a Serb, and even if you are sure, opinions are sufficiently divergent to be dangerous. The only really safe thing you can say, if you're asked directly, is that you're pleased it's all over, and that peace should bring prosperity.

GIVING SOMETHING BACK

After travelling in Croatia (and possibly even before you go) you may want to do something for the country – the two obvious ways you can help are through voluntary work or through supporting a Croatian charity.

Voluntary work

There are a number of well-established voluntary programmes operating in Croatia, though happily they're all popular and you need to book well ahead if you want to participate. Below are a few, but you can find many more if you do your own research.

One of the best-known organisations is **Suncokret** (literally, sunflower), which was founded in 1992 in response to Croatia's refugee crisis. Suncokret works in a number of refugee centres around the country and also organises working camps for volunteers. More information is available from Šeferova 10, 10000 Zagreb; tel: 211 104 or 219 460; email: suncokret@public.srce.hr. Further information can also be found at an independent website at www.ljudmila.org/~damjan/suncokret.html.

Another well-established organisation is **Volunteers Centre Zagreb** (Volonterski Centar Zagreb, VCZ), which was started in 1996, and has been working to promote peace and human rights since the war ended. VCZ organises working camps in Croatia and can be contacted at Republike Austrije 19, 10000 Zagreb; tel: 3705 641; email: vc@zamir.net. More information is available on its website at www.vcz.hr.

It's also worth getting in touch with the **Croatian Red Cross**, which is not just active in its own right but also works with many other partners. Contact Hrvatski crveni kriz, Ulica Crvenog kriza 14, 10000 Zagreb; tel: 465 5814; fax: 455 0072; email: redcross@hck.hr; www.hck.hr.

The **Croatian Heritage Foundation** (Hrvatska Matica Iseljenika), for its part, caters mainly for the Croatian diaspora of 3.5 million people around the world. The foundation organises a summer 'Task Force' which focuses on a different project each year, such as restoring medieval town walls, replanting damaged botanical gardens, or rebuilding paths in the national parks. Contact Trg Stjepana

Radića 3, 10000 Zagreb; tel: 6115 116; email: hmi-info@matis.hr or visit the (English) website at www.matis.hr/english/index.php.

Charities

The single most important thing you can do to improve life in Croatia is to support any of the many organisations involved in mine clearance. In the UK, Heather Mills has done a lot in getting prosthetic limbs and financial aid to mine victims in Croatia, and has also been instrumental in setting up the **Adopt-A-Minefield** programme. Visit the website at www.landmines.org.uk, which co-ordinates anti-landmine activity and fundraising, and is directly involved in Croatia, raising money for mine clearance and for the survivors of landmine accidents.

The **Croatian Mine Action Centre** (Hrvatski Centar za Razminiranje, HCR) does a huge amount of work on the ground and keeps up-to-date statistics and maps on mine clearance at its website www.hcr.hr.

Another active organisation is the **American Chamber of Commerce in Croatia** (AmCham Croatia; www.amcham.hr). Founded in 1998, and based in Zagreb, AmCham Croatia stresses its independence from the US Government, and has various fundraising programmes for Croatian charities, in addition to its main mandate of promoting mutual co-operation and friendship between Croatia and the USA.

Part Two

The Guide

Chamois

Zagreb

Rebecca West sized up Croatia's capital nicely when she was here in 1937: 'Zagreb makes from its featureless handsomeness something that pleases like a Schubert song, a delight that begins quietly and never definitely ends. It has the endearing characteristic noticeable in many French towns of remaining a small town when it is in fact quite large.' Indeed, with a population fast approaching a million, today, Zagreb is easily Croatia's largest and most cosmopolitan city, though the centre is agreeably manageable on foot.

Its heart is a fine, clean example of solid Habsburg architecture, tending towards palatial elegance and large squares from which to view it – though if you move away from the city centre you'll find sprawling suburbs and high rises, thrown up to accommodate waves of incoming workers over the past 50 years, and a good number of economic migrants and refugees following the 1991–92 war.

For more than six months of the year Zagreb is a lively outdoor city, with café tables spilling out across the pavements and flowers everywhere, but in winter it can be cold and oppressive, the streets of the lower town seeming too large for their occupants, and the city's emotions reined in.

Until the early 19th century, Zagreb was two small hill towns – the religious community of Kaptol, dominated by the cathedral, and the secular one of Gradec, above and beside it. The two are still separated clearly by Radićeva and Tkalčićeva, a pair of parallel streets running north out of Trg Bana Josipa Jelačića, the huge central square.

The cathedral is off to the northeast of Trg Jelačića, the old town is to the northwest, and most of the museums and other sights are to the south and southwest, within walking distance. The regular blocks and streets of Donji Grad, the lower town, were made possible by the construction of the railway embankment in 1860, and indeed lead to the train station today. On the other side of the tracks – literally – are the suburbs built between the two World Wars, while across the river Sava is Novi Zagreb, the residential area which sprang up in the 1950s and 1960s, and Pleso Airport.

Zagreb is particularly strong on classical culture, with regular opera, ballet, theatre and musical performances of international standard.

The telephone code is 01 (+385 1 from abroad).

HISTORY

Zagreb doesn't appear on the map until it was established as a diocese in AD1094 by the Hungarians. Even then, for the first centuries of Zagreb's history it was the rival communities of Kaptol and Gradec which made the running. After the Tartars laid waste to both settlements in 1242, Gradec (home to the Hungarian

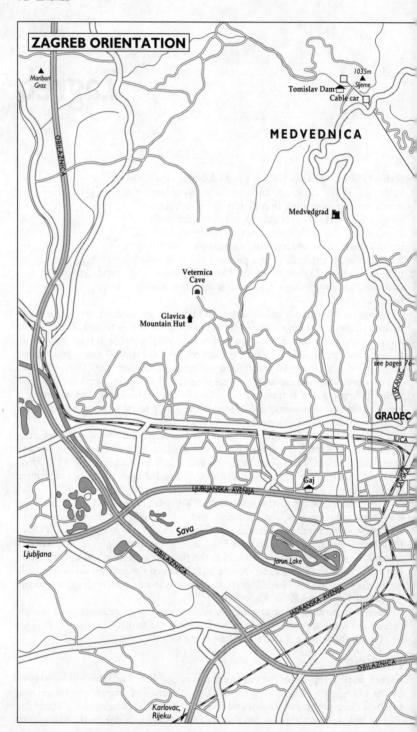

ZAGREB ORIENTATION

Maribor
Graz

1035m
Sljeme

Tomislav Dam
Cable car

MEDVEDNICA

Medvedgrad

Veternica
Cave

Glavica
Mountain Hut

OBILAZNICA

TUŠKANAC

see pages 76

GRADEC

ILICA

SAVA

Gaj

LJUBLJANSKA AVENIJA

Sava

Ljubljana

OBILAZNICA

Jarun Lake

JADRANSKA AVENIJA

OBILAZNICA

Karlovac,
Rijeku

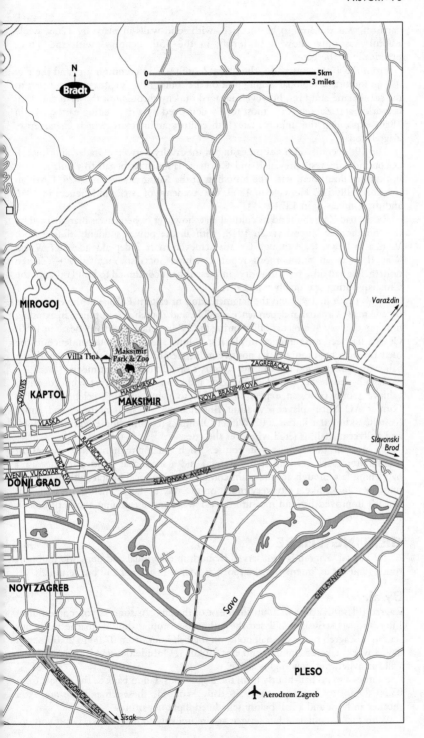

garrison) was the first to be fortified, with solid walls in place by 1266, while Kaptol was only allowed to fortify in the 15th century, with the Turks practically at the gates.

From the 16th century on, the name Zagreb was in common use, and the city was an important regional staging post on the routes from Vienna and Budapest to the sea. Plague and fires, however, ravaged the city throughout the 17th and 18th centuries, and Zagreb was almost totally destroyed by a devastating earthquake in 1880, explaining the uniform late 19th-century architecture which characterises Zagreb today.

The 19th century also saw an easing of the rivalry between Gradec and Kaptol, as common interests prevailed and Croatian nationalism began to resurge. New institutions flourished, with the founding of the Music Society in 1826, Croatian (originally Illyrian) Heritage in 1839, the Academy of Arts and Sciences in 1866 and the University in 1874.

Barely had Zagreb found its cultural feet, however, when it was marginalised by the founding of Yugoslavia in 1918, with all the power suddenly shifted from Vienna to Belgrade. Although Croatia achieved more independence after World War II – as an autonomous republic within socialist Yugoslavia – Zagreb nonetheless had little real authority, and resentment continued to build up until the Croatian Spring was quashed in 1971.

Tito's death in 1980 and the fragmentation of eastern Europe at the end of the decade made Croatian independence possible, and Zagreb was fortunate in avoiding much in the way of direct conflict during the 1990s. Since Tuđman's death in 1999, Croatia has seen a resurgence in pluralist politics and a new independence in the media, which has mostly had a positive influence on the capital, home to both the Sabor (parliament) and most of the country's broadcast and print media.

Zagreb people are proud of the city and those of its natives who go on to achieve world fame, so expect to be able to name sporting celebrities. Clue: Former AC Milan player Zvonimir Boban owns a restaurant here, and Janica Kostelić, skiing star in the 2002 Winter Olympics (coming home with three golds and a silver medal), is fêted wherever she goes.

It's not all good news, of course. High unemployment, new waves of immigration, a clogged-up traffic system, and a sense that political change isn't happening fast enough are the main complaints from local people, although to an outsider it looks like a city very much on the way up rather than the way down, and it's improved beyond measure since I was here researching another book in the late 1980s.

GETTING THERE
As the capital, Zagreb is well served by both international and domestic transport routes, and has an international airport, as well as major rail and bus terminals.

By air
Zagreb (Pleso) Airport is 10km southeast of the city. As soon as you come out of International Arrivals you'll see the airline bus stop – shuttles to the main bus station in Zagreb run every half hour, on the half hour, from 07.00 to 20.00, seven days a week, take 25 minutes and cost 30 kuna. Outside the standard times, buses will run whenever new flights arrive.

Shuttles also go half-hourly from the Zagreb bus station back to the airport from 05.30 (06.00 on Sundays) to 19.30 daily – outside these times there are extra shuttles an hour and a half before scheduled flight departures.

With such an efficient bus service you're unlikely to need a taxi, but if you do, the stand's right next to the bus stop. Make sure the meter's switched on, and expect to pay upwards of 150 kuna to the main Zagreb hotels, bearing in mind there's also a 20% surcharge at night, as well as on Sundays and public holidays.

More information on the airport, including live flight arrival and departure times (look under *Timetable* on the home page), can be found at www.zagreb-airport.hr.

By rail

The first train arrived in Zagreb in 1862 and they've been running ever since. International connections come in at least once a day from each of Slovenia, Italy, Austria, Germany, Hungary, Yugoslavia, Bosnia & Herzegovina and Macedonia – see *By rail* on page 32 in the *Practical Information* chapter, for more details about frequency and journey times.

Long-distance domestic trains run east to Osijek (five daily, 4–5 hours), southwest to Rijeka (six daily, 4–5 hours) and south to Split (once daily, 7½ hours). Local trains make up the rest of the traffic, but whilst these are picturesque, they're also slow and not especially punctual.

Make sure you get off the train at the central station, Zagreb Glavni Kolodvor – there are two other stations which trains may stop at (but which you don't want); Zagreb Klara and Zagreb Zapadni Kolodvor.

At the station there's a 24-hour left-luggage office, which charges 10 kuna per piece per 24 hours, a much better deal than the left-luggage at the bus station (see below). There's also a fairly shabby but reasonably priced station restaurant which has very long hours (from 05.00 to 23.00), and up on the west end of the main platform there are public toilets (2 kuna) and shower facilities.

To get to the centre of town from the train station, just head straight up through the big squares right in front of you – Trg Jelačića is a 10–15-minute walk away.

By bus

Zagreb's bus station is the largest and busiest in the country, as you'd expect, with around 200 arrivals a day, from destinations both home and abroad. The formerly shabby but characterful bus station was replaced some time in the 1990s with today's spanking new and usually spotless building, which also comprises a shopping mall. You should try and book your departure ticket on arrival, if you possibly can, as long-distance buses tend to be booked out ahead of time, especially in summer.

There are more than a dozen departures a day to each of Split (8 hours), Pula (6 hours), Zadar (5 hours), Rijeka (4 hours), Plitvice (2½ hours) and Varaždin (2 hours), at least six a day to Dubrovnik (11 hours), Rovinj (5 hours), Poreč (5 hours) and Osijek (4 hours), and two or more a day to practically every other destination in the country.

The bus station has a 24-hour left-luggage facility, but it's nearly three times the price of the one at the train station, which is a dull 15-minute walk away (cross the railway lines, then walk west along Branimirova) – this can easily be avoided by a quick ride on the #2 or #6 tram. Tram #6 also goes on past the station to Trg Jelačića, Zagreb's central square.

By car

Zagreb is easily reached by car, being well served by a constantly improving motorway network. Driving in town itself, however – like in most capital cities – can be a bit of a nightmare, and parking is hell. Park in the wrong place and there's a strong chance the infamous 'spider' will take your car away. Before calling the police, if your car disappears, try calling the spider, on 615 8932, to see if they have

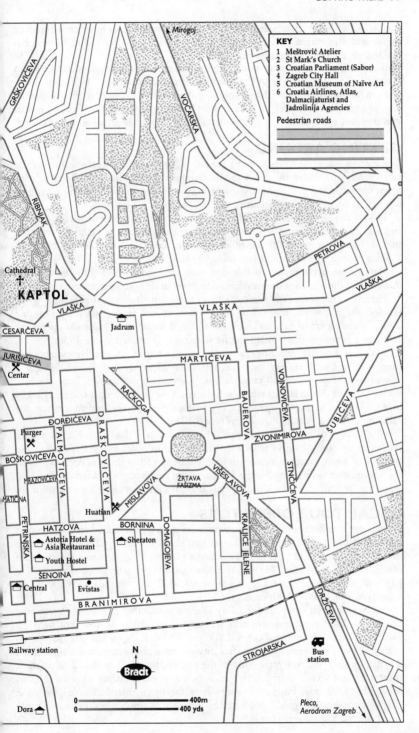

KEY
1 Meštrović Atelier
2 St Mark's Church
3 Croatian Parliament (Sabor)
4 Zagreb City Hall
5 Croatian Museum of Naïve Art
6 Croatia Airlines, Atlas,
  Dalmacijaturist and
  Jadrolinija Agencies

Pedestrian roads

Mirogoj

GRSKOVIĆEVA

VOĆARSKA

RIBNJAK

PETROVA

VLAŠKA

Cathedral
KAPTOL

VLAŠKA

VLAŠKA

CESARČEVA

Jadrum

JURIŠIĆEVA
Centar

MARTIĆEVA

RAČKOGA

VOJNOVIĆEVA

ŠUBIĆEVA

ĐORĐIĆEVA

DRAŠKOVIĆEVA

BAUEROVA

ZVONIMIROVA

Burger

PALMOTIĆEVA

STINČIĆEVA

BOŠKOVIĆEVA

MRAZOVIĆEVA

ŽRTAVA
FAŠIZMA

VIŠESLAVOVA

MATIČINA

MISLAVOVA

Huatian

PETRINJSKA

HATZOVA

BORNINA

KRALJICE JELENE

Astoria Hotel &
Asia Restaurant

Sheraton

DOMAGOJEVA

Youth Hostel

ŠENOINA

Central

Evistas

BRANIMIROVA

DRŽIĆEVA

Railway station

N

Bradt

STROJARSKA

Bus
station

0 _____ 400m
0 _____ 400 yds

Dora

Pleco,
Aerodrom Zagreb

your vehicle. Many streets are closed to traffic, and open only to pedestrians or trams, and a government credit on new cars, while good for the economy, has choked up Zagreb's thoroughfares.

If you can find a way of avoiding driving in town, then it's well worth doing so – consider leaving your car in the suburbs, where there's ample daytime parking, and catching a tram or bus. Bear in mind, however, that car theft is unfortunately a growing problem in Zagreb (as in the rest of Croatia), and if you have a classy model you may not want to leave it unattended for too long in an area you don't know.

GETTING AROUND

The electric tram was introduced to Zagreb in 1910 and it's been a feature of the city ever since. Today the city's public transport is crowded but effective, with trams covering the centre of town and buses running to the suburbs, and most homing in on either Trg Jelačića or the train station.

Tickets can be bought in advance at kiosks for 7 kuna or on board for 9 kuna, and are valid for 90 minutes in any one direction. Day tickets, valid for travel in the city centre until 04.00 the following day, are excellent value at 18 kuna. Validate tickets by punching them using the machine on board.

Maps of the network are published at most tram stops, making the system easy to navigate, though almost everything described in this guide is walkable.

There's a charming little funicular from the main shopping street, Ilica, up to Gradec, the old town. It's said to be the shortest in Europe, and it's a plausible claim, but it's a bit of fun, and well worth the 3 kuna fare. Originally opened in 1891, as a steam-powered affair, the funicular was electrified in the 1930s.

Taxis are a pretty expensive way of getting around, as you'll inevitably get caught in traffic. Fares for radio taxis start at 25 kuna, and charge 7 kuna a kilometre on top of that, 80 kuna an hour for waiting time, and 5 kuna per bag, with a 20% surcharge at night and on holidays. You can pick up a taxi fairly easily in a number of locations, including Trg Maršala Tita, by the theatre, or near the cathedral – or call 668 2505/660 0671/660 1235.

Finally, as you wander round, you'll begin to notice that Zagreb's street signs don't exactly correspond to what's on the map, as mapmakers have tended to use the spoken form, which is almost invariably different from the sign itself. So while the square is in reality Trg Svetog Marka, you'll be directed to Markov Trg, and while you're walking down Ulica Pavla Radića, it's Radićeva you'll see on the map.

LOCAL TOUR OPERATORS

Zagreb has excellent tourist information, with a number of good free guides and maps available. Coming up from the station, the first office you'll come to is on the left-hand side, just past the Strossmayer Gallery, at Zrinjevac 14. The main office (tel: 481 4051; fax: 481 4056) is less than five minutes further on, on Trg Jelačića, with longer opening hours – 08.30–20.00 weekdays, 09.00–17.00 Saturdays, and 10.00–14.00 Sundays.

Ask here for a city map, and the *City Walks* and monthly *Events and Performances* brochures. Tourist information will also give you advice on (but not help in) finding accommodation, and can sell you the 72-hour *Zagreb Card*, which for 60 kuna gives you tremendous value – free city-centre transport for the duration (itself worth 54 kuna), and half-price entry to the city's museums, as well as 20% off most theatre tickets. The tourist office also has a good walking map of Mount Medvednica for sale. Finally, if you're here for more than half a day then the '*Zagreb: in your pocket*' guide, published bi-monthly, is absolutely superb, and easily worth the 20 kuna cover charge.

The Plitvice Lakes National Park (tel/fax: 461 3586) also has an office in Zagreb, open weekdays, just up from the station at Tomislava 19, and can arrange trips to the park and accommodation there for you.

A couple of blocks further up the same street, between the two tourist offices, are several travel agencies and the main Croatia Airlines (Zrinjevac 17) and Jadrolinija (Zrinjevac 20) offices, where you can find out everything you need to know about flights and ferries respectively, as well as booking tickets.

Next door to Croatia Airlines is the Atlas travel agency (tel: 481 3933; fax: 487 3049), which is the local representative of American Express. It has offices all along the coast, owns many hotels, and can make most travel arrangements for you. Next door again is Dalmacijaturist (tel: 487 3073; fax: 487 3075), which as the name implies specialises in the Dalmatian coast, and can organise holidays in that part of Croatia. Heading back up the street towards Trg Jelačića, there's also Generalturist (tel: 481 0033; fax: 481 0428), at Praška 5. Generalturist is ubiquitous in Croatia, and can book tickets, excursions and hotels for you. Around the corner, at Teslina 4, is Croatia Express (tel/fax: 481 1842), which specialises in bus and train tickets, but also has all the other functions of a good travel agency.

All six offices above are open weekdays and for a shorter time on Saturdays.

Finally, the Croatian Youth Hostel Association (HFHS) is at Dežmanova 9 (tel: 484 7474; fax: 484 7472; www.hfhs.hr), off to the right, five minutes west along Ilica. You can make advance bookings for Croatia's (few) youth hostels here, as well as getting an ISIC student card (proof of being a student required).

WHERE TO STAY
Budget
As a bustling, business-oriented capital city, Zagreb presents a problem if you're looking for budget accommodation. Private rooms are in short supply (and twice the price of anywhere else in the country) and there's no campsite within easy reach. There are plenty of hotels, but they don't come cheap.

In summer it's possible to get a bed in the university student dorms (ask at the tourist office), but again, you'll pay more than you might expect. Finally, there's a youth hostel (tel: 484 1261; fax: 484 1269, Petrinjska 77) near the station, but it's almost invariably full, and even if it's not, it can be a bit rough, especially if you're travelling alone.

The only agency within reasonable walking distance which handles private rooms is Evistas (tel: 483 9546; fax: 483 9554), which is at Šenoina 28, a block north of Branimirova, the main road running between the train and bus stations. The agency is open from Monday to Saturday, but rooms go quickly, so try to arrive early, and expect to pay €50–80 for a double in town, or €70–100 for an apartment.

There's nowhere within easy reach of Zagreb where you'll find a hotel room for under €60 a night, either, and the top three hotels all charge a fairly breathtaking €250 plus per night for a double, year-round.

Mid-range
Hotel Ilica Tel: 377 7622; fax: 377 7722; www.hotel-ilica.hr. At Ilica 102, two tram stops west of Trg Jelačića. At the bottom end of the price-scale is this lovely little hotel. A dozen nice double rooms go for a bargain €60 a night – naturally they go very fast indeed.
Astoria Tel: 484 1222; fax: 484 1212. On Petrinjska, just up from the hostel. Barely more expensive than the Hotel Ilica, the rooms are nothing special, but the location is good and the price (€65 doubles) is right.

Dora Tel: 631 1900; fax: 631 1909; www.zug.hr. A 10-minute walk south of the station, just off Vukovarska, and 20 minutes south of Trg Jelačića. Another great-value option is the charming Dora which has 24 rooms (€86 doubles) and opened in the summer of 2001.

Gaj Tel: 381 7222; fax: 381 7225. The only other hotel at this price offering three-star quality is the Gaj. It looks like it's out of town, but it's actually only three minutes' walk from the terminus of the #118 bus, which sets off every ten minutes from Trg Mažuranić. Walk back to the first street on the right, and cross the stream over the footbridge at the end, and you'll see the hotel on your left. It's quiet, with modern air-conditioned doubles at €74. It's an excellent option if you've come in by car, as it's easy to get to and has plenty of secure parking.

Central Tel: 484 1122; fax: 484 1303; www.hotel-central.hr. The Central is one of three affordable three-star hotels in town. It is extremely well-located just across from the railway station, and has good, comfortable air-conditioned doubles €88–106, though the building itself is a bit of an eyesore.

International Tel: 610 8800; fax: 615 9459; www.hup-zagreb.hr. Ten minutes' walk south of the train station on Miramarska, you will find this reasonable three-star. The building is a bit of an eyesore again, but the €92 double rooms are fine.

Villa Tina Tel/fax: 244 5138. This hotel is a bit out of the way, on Bukovačka, up near Maksimir. It has a dozen nice quiet rooms (€85 doubles), and even features a small swimming pool.

Dubrovnik Tel: 487 3555; fax: 481 8447; www.hotel-dubrovnik.htnet.hr. Moving up the price scale is the mirrored glass building right on Trg Jelačića. It has around 250 rooms, all of which were refurbished in 2000, with smart doubles going for €140.

Palace Hotel Tel: 481 4611; fax: 481 1358; www.palace.hr. Down the road, on Strossmayerov Trg, is the Palace Hotel, which was built in 1891 and has been a hotel since 1907. While it retains much of its old-fashioned secession-era charm, the 125 rooms have all been modernised and have air conditioning. Doubles go for €135–150.

Jadran Tel: 455 3777; fax: 461 2151; www.hup-zagreb.hr. Also well located is the Jadran on Vlaška, just a few minutes east of Trg Jelačića and just round the corner from the cathedral. The hotel looks a bit run-down from the outside, but the 48 rooms have all been refurbished, and doubles go for €160 a night.

Luxury

From here it's a big leap upwards in price to Zagreb's three five-star hotels, which are almost exclusively used by business-people on expenses, few ordinary mortals having around €250 or more a night to spend on accommodation.

Regent Esplanade Tel: 456 6666; fax: 456 6050; www.regenthotels.com. Located right by the train station – as you'd expect, since it was built in 1925 as a swanky stopover for the *Orient Express*. It's still full of character, and though the public rooms can be a bit overpowering, it's a marvellous throwback to between-the-wars elegance. Check out the fabulous Emerald Ballroom, and the clocks above the main entrance, inside the door, which tell you the time in New York, Buenos Aires, London, Zagreb, Moscow, Tokyo and Sydney.

Sheraton Tel: 455 3535; fax: 455 3035; www.sheraton.com/zagreb. Two blocks up from the station and three blocks east is the Sheraton, a glass-fronted city block with 300 rooms offering as much luxury as anyone's going to need, including a gym and an indoor pool – though you have to ask yourself which humorist was responsible for putting the fitness centre on the smokers' floor.

Westin Zagreb Tel: 489 2000; fax: 489 2001; www.westin.com. Also featuring a gym and pool is this luxurious hotel which was formerly the Hotel Opera. It's a bit of a monstrosity, architecturally, but inside it's all opulence, in a tasteful way, and the rooms are lovely. Breakfast is absolutely without rival in Croatia – unlimited *Pršut*, *Paški Sir*, smoked salmon and the like, and dishes cooked to order – but this isn't included in the €250 room rate, costing an extra €20 a head.

WHERE TO EAT

Food isn't a problem in Zagreb, with restaurants for all tastes – and budgets – and a wonderful seven-day-a-week open market in Dolac, the square just down from the cathedral. Locals still come here to sell their home-grown vegetables, while underneath the market square (actually a large terrace) you can buy home-made pasta, delicious *Pršut* sliced wafer-thin, and dairy goods.

As you'd expect in a fast-moving city, there are plenty of places where you can get a bite on the hoof, fast food coming in traditional (*burek* etc) or contemporary (burgers and the like) formats. Reasonably priced pizzerias and pasta parlours are also plentiful, while more formal restaurants tend towards standard Croatian fare, with grilled meat, stews and fish being high on the menu.

Restaurants

The restaurants are listed alphabetically below and phone numbers are provided when it's wise to reserve.

Asia At the Hotel Astoria, Petrinjska 71. This is one of the very few places to serve Asian food, which has yet to catch on in Zagreb in any meaningful sense. Good Chinese food, though if you're used to take-away prices back home you'll find it expensive.

Baltazar Nova Ves 4, a couple of minutes' walk north of the cathedral. A cheerful and friendly traditional Croatian restaurant which is popular with locals and visitors alike – as you come into the courtyard, Baltazar's famous meats and grills are to the left, while fish specialities are off to the right, in the Gašpar section.

Boban At Gajeva 3. This popular place is owned by Croatian national team and AC Milan football superstar Zvonimir Boban. Underneath the café you'll find a busy Italian-themed restaurant in a brick-vaulted cellar, with truly excellent pasta dishes.

Dubravkin Put Tel: 483 4970; fax: 481 9882. Northwest of the old town, in the woods, is one of Zagreb's most fashionable restaurants, which serves up excellent fish, shellfish and meat dishes – all specialities of the Dubrovnik area. Reservations are essential, and a flexible friend comes in very handy.

Hrvatski Kulturni Klub Tel: 482 8084; fax: 482 6916. Tucked away in the basement of the Arts and Crafts Museum, with a lovely terrace at the back, is this traditional restaurant, which is popular with intellectuals and serves up solid Croatian fare. Reservations recommended.

Huatian Opposite the Sheraton. A Chinese restaurant (signed Kineski Restoran), which serves up unpretentious dishes at a reasonable price. Don't on any account be tempted by a shot of Pelinkovac as your after-dinner treat.

Kaptol Also trading on the Kaptol name is the Westin Zagreb's restaurant, which is surprisingly good value (steady on the extensive and expensive wine list, however) and mixes international dishes with good Croatian staples.

Kaptolska Klet Right opposite the cathedral is the unpretentious Kaptolska Klet. Although marked down by local journalists for resting on its laurels somewhat, it is invariably busy, and serves fine soup and excellent duck and turkey dishes.

Kapuciner Next door to Kaptolska Klet, this restaurant is worth a visit if the former is full – which can happen as it tends to attract the tour-bus market. It has a big terrace and serves up great pizza and pasta dishes with a view of the cathedral.

Kerempuh Tel: 481 9000; fax: 481 9001. Right on the corner of the Dolac market square is my favourite restaurant in all of Zagreb. Run by the ever-cheerful Nikica

Vuksan, it's only open at lunchtime and at least half the tables are permanently reserved by an eclectic bunch of retired university professors, former footballers and journalists. The food varies depending on what Nikica finds best in the market that morning, and the view out over the market square is wonderful. Booking essential.

Lopud Tel: 481 8775; fax: 481 9882. At Kaptol 10, just up from the cathedral is the Lopud. The menu's limited to whatever fish has come in that day, the wine list is positively spartan, and it's far from cheap, but it's nonetheless one of the best fish places in town – reservations are advised.

Nokturno Round the corner from Lopud, on Skalinska, you'll find the ever-popular Nokturno, which serves up good pizzas and a wide range of pasta dishes in a simple setting. There's a minuscule terrace (it's on a steep, narrow street), and their crisp Đakovo Riesling is among the most keenly priced in Zagreb, at 50 kuna a litre.

Paviljon Tel: 481 3066; fax: 484 1073. Down in the new town, opposite the station, in the former exhibition pavilion, is this upmarket restaurant, whose spacious dining room and outdoor terrace tend to attract people with a decent expense account, which you'll certainly need if you're going for the vintage champagnes. You can still get a first-rate plate of pasta here for a reasonable price, however.

Pivnica Medvedgrad On the other side of the tracks, at Savska 56, five minutes south of the Westin Zagreb, is an on-the-spot brewery which serves up its own range of beers and wholesome platefuls of local food – it's not especially cheap, but it's exceptionally good value for money. It's a half-hour walk from the centre of town, or take tram #4 or #17 towards Novi Zagreb.

Purger Petrinjska 33. A wholesome Croatian place named after the local word for 'citizen' (a variant on burgher). It's not too expensive, popular with local politicians, and has a terrace at the back in summer.

Zinfandel's Tel: 456 6666; fax: 456 6050. Finally, in the Hotel Esplanade you'll find this swish restaurant, offering a mix of Croatian and Californian cuisine. As at the Kaptol, you need to tread gingerly with the wine list – or hope you're being treated.

Cafés/ice-cream

Café society is firmly centred in the area around Trg Jelačića – the pedestrianised streets and squares to the southwest become one vast terrace in summer, and the ambiance is wonderful. There's often more or less impromptu live music in the area.

North of the main square, the long winding street called Tkalčićeva marks the path of a former river bed – the river was diverted after the smells from the tannery upstream became too noxious. The houses along here are now almost all cafés, bars and cheap restaurants, and it's great place to see and be seen.

Centar On Jurišićeva, the street running east out of Trg Jelačića. Spare a little room, after your meal, for ice-cream, which is almost as popular in Croatia as in Italy – and at its best rivals the finest *gelati*. There are plenty of ice-cream parlours (*slastičarnica*) in Zagreb, but my absolute favourite is Centar which has a good range of flavours and is always justifiably packed.

CAFÉ CULTURE

On Sunday mornings, Trg Jelačića plays host to one of the most unusual spectacles in the world, with the entire Croatian political elite – from the president down – coming out to sit at the café terraces and chew the fat. Blasé locals have been known to criticise this overt populism, but it's a refreshing change from the aloof remoteness of most of the world's politicians.

Hemingway Bar Over on Tuškanec, west of the old town. Local cocktail enthusiasts favour this ritzy bar. The drinks are fine, but heaven knows what the old man himself would have thought of it all.

Kavana Žabica At Opatička 5, in Gornji Grad. For something a good deal more traditional, try this genuinely old haunt, with lots of authentic detail and fabulous hot chocolate. It also doubles as a sometime Internet café.

WHAT TO SEE

To see all of Zagreb's sights would take several weeks – there are an astonishing 57 varieties of museum and gallery open to the public. Even to see the main attractions would take three or four days, not least because the opening hours are fairly limited, with some places only open until 14.00. The best thing about Zagreb, however, is the city itself, and there's little to beat a leisurely stroll through the old town. The route suggested below is an unhurried two- to four-hour tour, depending on how long you spend on each attraction.

Everything in Zagreb begins and ends in **Trg Jelačića**, the outsized central square. The main attraction here is the terrific equestrian statue of Ban Josip Jelačić himself. As the viceroy of Croatia in the middle of the 19th century, Jelačić was a natural reformer, and did a great deal to advance the causes of Croatian statehood. After he died, the statue (by the Austrian sculptor, Fernkorn) was erected in 1866, with Jelačić's drawn sword facing Budapest as a sign of defiance – by this time Croatia was already losing what little independence it had.

After World War II, the statue was torn down because it was considered unpatriotic within Tito's Yugoslavia, and the square was renamed Trg Republike. For more than 40 years, Ban Jelačić languished in bits, in a cellar. When the statue was restored to its former glory, on Croatian independence, in 1991, it was put up facing the other way, towards Belgrade rather than Budapest, and today the drawn sword points uncompromisingly towards Knin, short-lived capital of the erstwhile Republika Srpska Krajina (RSK). (For more history, see pages 11–21.)

Running west out of Trg Jelačića is Zagreb's main shopping street, Ilica, and not far down here is a dead-end street leading to the funicular, the easiest route up to Gornji Grad.

Gornji Grad – the old town

The funicular leads straight up to **Strossmayerovo Šetalište**, a lovely promenade giving magnificent views south out over the city, and the **Lotrščak Tower**, one of the few vestiges of the original 13th-century city fortifications. In summer the tower's tiny rooftop terrace gives even finer panoramic views.

For centuries a bell was rung from the tower every evening to announce the closing of the city's four gates (only one survives), but now it's the midday cannon which is the main attraction. If you climb the tower shortly before noon you can see it being fired by Stjepan Možar, in his distinctive Zagreb-blue uniform – he hasn't missed a day's work since he took on the job in 1975.

Heading north, the first place you come to is **St Catherine's Square** (Katerinski Trg). The northern side of the square is taken up with the Kulmer Palace, formerly the Museum of Modern Art and now a space for temporary exhibitions. In the square, check out the small but dramatic sculpture of a fisherman wrestling with a vicious-looking snake, by Simeon Roksandić. There's a much larger version of the same statue in Belgrade's main park, up above the confluence of the Sava and Danube rivers. On the southern side you'll find the Dverce Mansion and the Jesuit College, the 1607 Gymnasium, which is still a grammar school today.

The Jesuits were also responsible for the square's main attraction, **St Catherine's Church**. Zagreb's finest baroque church was built between 1620 and 1632, and features some superior 18th-century stucco work and an amazing *trompe l'oeil* altarpiece (those aren't real pillars), an extraordinary work from 1762, by the Slovene painter Kristof Andrej Jelovšek.

The street running north, Ćirilometodska, leads to St Mark's Square, the heart of Zagreb's political life. On the way up the street notice the Greek Orthodox **Church of Sts Cyril and Methodius**, the people responsible for the Glagolitic alphabet. If you have time, you should also definitely pop in and see the **Croatian Museum of Naïve Art**, (open Tue–Fri 10.00–17.00; Sat and Sun 10.00–13.00) which houses an unusual collection of naïve painting from the 1930s onwards, bracketed by the dreamy works of Generalić, father, and the more graphic art of Generalić, son.

At the corner of the street, as you come onto St Mark's Square, is the **Zagreb City Hall**, which was originally built as a theatre in 1835 by a man called Stanković who had won a huge lottery the year before. It was used for various historic parliament meetings in the 19th century, and is today a place for ceremonial gatherings – and weddings, upstairs in the registry office.

St Mark's Square (Markov Trg) itself was originally the town square of Gradec, and it was here that Matija Gubec, leader of the 16th-century peasant uprising, was supposedly put dramatically to death – the Austro-Hungarians held a mock coronation for him, with a crown of red-hot iron. The sculpted head on the corner of Ćirilometodska #8 is said to be that of the peasant leader. Today the square is dominated by swanky German cars and lots of police – hardly surprising since it's the seat of the Croatian government.

On the left-hand side of the square is the original **Ban's Palace** (Jelačić himself lived and died here), which was the target of a Serb rocket attack on Zagreb in 1991 – Tuđman, Mesić and the Croatian prime minister were all inside when it happened, so it's lucky there were no casualties. On the other side of the square is the **Croatian Parliament**, the Sabor.

Between the two is **St Mark's Church**, its distinctive roof gaudily tiled in the fashion of seaside resorts with clock flowerbeds. The left-hand coat of arms is that of the Kingdom of Croatia, Slavonia and Dalmatia, while on the right is the city of Zagreb's.

The original church here was built in the 13th century, with 14th- and 15th-century additions. Most of the church of this era has long since disappeared, though the southern portal, with 15 beautifully carved statues by the Parler family, from Prague, dates from 1420 – if they ever finish restoring it, have a look.

The rest of the church is a late 19th-century Gothic reconstruction. Like so much of the post-1880 earthquake Zagreb, it's by the Viennese architect Herman Bollé, though the belltower is an 1841 original. The interior was refurbished in the late 1930s by Meštrović, the sculptor, and Kljaković, the painter. Look out for the imposing Meštrović crucifix.

More Meštrović is on display just up the road, at Mletačka 8, where you'll find the **Meštrović Atelier** (open Tue–Fri 09.00–14.00; Sat and Sun 10.00–18.00), the sculptor's former home and studio. Inside there's an excellent collection of his work, in a more intimate setting than the vast Meštrović Gallery in Split. The house itself is excellent, with the collection spread across three floors and showing the diversity of Meštrović's sculpture.

If you're kicking your heels there are two more museums just near here, the **Natural History Museum** (open Tue-Fri 10.00–17.00; Sat and Sun 10.00–13.00), with its display of *Krapina Man*, and the **Croatia Historical**

Museum (open Tue–Fri 10.00–17.00; Sat and Sun 10.00–13.00), which has temporary exhibitions focusing on – you guessed it – Croatia's history.

At the top of the old town is the **Popov Tower** (Popov Toranj), which was originally the only defence allowed to be used by neighbouring Kaptol, which had no defences of its own. It's now part of the **Museum of the City of Zagreb** (open Tue–Fri 10.00–18.00; Sat and Sun 10.00–13.00), which was opened in 1907, and has a comprehensive collection from Neolithic times right up to the damaged furniture from the 1991 rocket attack on the Ban's Palace. It's in a wonderful building and well worth a visit. Check out the bits of sculpture from the original pre-earthquake cathedral, the reconstructions of various shops from the past, and in particular a fabulous room with a coloured map of the city inlaid into the floor, with models of the main buildings on small pedestals.

From here it's all downhill, along Radićeva (originally called Duga Ulica, meaning 'long street', and if you're coming uphill it certainly is), until you branch right onto Kamenita, where you'll see a statue of St George, on the ramp up to the 13th-century **Stone Gate**. This is the only one of the four original 13th-century city gates, although it owes its present appearance to the building of a church here in 1760, to commemorate the survival of an icon of the Virgin Mary, which miraculously escaped a fire in 1731. It's still a major place of pilgrimage – notice all the votive plaques, and the atmospheric candles constantly being lit.

Just inside the gate are two curiosities. On the right is a section of heavy black chain, which is supposed to have come from Nelson's ship, HMS *Victory*, though nobody seems to have the faintest idea how or why. On the other side of the street is a **pharmacy**, which has been in business since 1355, apparently, when it was opened by one of Dante's family, making it the second oldest in Europe, after Dubrovnik's.

Back outside the Stone Gate, Radićeva continues downhill until it meets **Krvavi Most** (Blood Bridge), named for the bloody feuds between Gradec and Kaptol long ago.

Kaptol

Krvavi Most connects the bottom of Radićeva with the bottom of Tkalčićeva, which is more or less one continuous café. Cross this and head up the steps to the market square, **Dolac**, which was built in 1926 as a market hall with a big terrace roof. The seven-day-a-week market here is not just picturesque, but a great shopping experience. Inside, downstairs, there's a fabulous selection of hams, sausages and dried meats at various stalls, while beside the fruit and vegetables you'll find the fishmongers' hall – come very early indeed to trawl for the best of the fresh fish here.

Across the square are the unmistakable twin spires of the **cathedral** (currently undergoing restoration – up close you can see just how badly worn the sculpture has become after a mere century of existence), in front of which stands another Fernkorn statue, this time a gilt Madonna, surrounded by four angels.

Around three sides of the cathedral stands the 18th-century Archbishop's Palace, and the canons' distinctive houses, all that's now left of the fortress which once dominated Kaptol.

The cathedral itself was built from the 13th to the 15th centuries on the site of an earlier Romanesque church, but what you see today is mostly the work of Bollé, following the 1880 earthquake, including the neo-Gothic façade, and the 104m and 105m spires. Inside it's in striking contrast to St Mark's – the cathedral's a light, spacious building, with an uncluttered feel to it. A touch of drama is added by the enormous 1941 Glagolitic Memorial, commemorating the 1,300th anniversary of the first contacts with the Holy See, during the reign of Pope John IV (AD640–642). It takes up most of the wall behind you as you come into the cathedral, and it really is a strange script, even to eyes used to Cyrillic.

(Just in case your Glagolitic's really rusty, the inscription reads: 'Glory to God in the highest! In memory of the 1,300th anniversary of the conversion of the Croatian people, who promised an eternal allegiance to Peter the Rock, having received from him the promised protection in every trial. Placed by The Society of the Brotherhood of the Croatian Dragon – conserving the relics of our ancestors and commending the Croatian homeland to the Mother of God – 641-1941.')

There isn't a great deal in the cathedral which pre-dates the earthquake, though the inlaid choir stalls are early 16th-century, and several of the altars and the pulpit are baroque, from the beginning of the 18th century. There are also a few faded medieval fresco fragments in the sacristy, which dates from the 13th century, along with an interesting triptych featuring the 'Crucifixion of Golgotha' by Albrecht Dürer.

The biggest draws, however, are the monument and tomb of **Alojzije Stepinac**. Nominated as archbishop of Zagreb in 1937, Stepinac courted controversy during World War II by not being quick enough to denounce the Ustaše fascists or the Independent State of Croatia (NDH) – though he subsequently not only criticised the regime but also helped Jews escape from it, and spoke out in favour of persecuted minorities, much to the ire of the NDH, and later the Germans.

He was no friend of Tito's communists, either, refusing to separate the Croatian Catholic Church from Rome, and after the war he was arrested. After a disgraceful show trial in 1948, he was condemned to 16 years' hard labour. He served five years of the sentence, in total isolation, and was then released, only to spend the rest of his life under house arrest in Krašić (see page 109).

In spite of being forbidden from pursuing his religious duties by the state, Stepinac was made a cardinal by the Pope in 1953, though he never went to Rome to receive the crimson, as he was certain he'd never be allowed home to his beloved Croatia. He died in 1960 (quite possibly of poisoning), and in 1998 was beatified by the Pope.

His monument is a great casket, with a life-size effigy of the archbishop, behind the altar, while his tomb is over on the north wall, with a touching Meštrović sculpture of Stepinac. Until 1991, and Croatia's independence, you'd have been unwise to spend much time near either; these days you'll only be one of many people paying your respects.

On your way out of the cathedral check out the enormous organ, made by Walcker of Ludwigsburg, which was first installed in 1855, and expanded and renewed in 1912, 1939 and 1987. It's reckoned to be among the ten most valuable in the world.

Donji Grad – the lower town

Once the swamp below Kaptol and Gradec was drained and the railway embankment had been built during the second half of the 19th century, lower Zagreb was ripe for development. Trg Jelačića and Ilica soon gave way to the planned urban munificence of the great squares running south to the train station. These had originally been envisaged as one side of a 'green horseshoe' – the other side should have continued up from the Botanical Gardens, but never quite came off.

Heading south down Praška brings you to the three main park-squares of Zrinjevac, Strossmayerov and Tomislava, lined with sober, imposing buildings, and closed off at the southern end with the formal elegance of the **railway station**, completed in 1891 by the Hungarian architect Ferenc Pfaff (who presumably had to endure a lifetime of wags telling him to stop faffing about).

The first attraction you come to – beyond the squares themselves, of course – is the **Archaeological Museum** (open Tue–Fri 10.00–17.00; Sat and Sun 10.00–13.00), on the west side of Zrinjevac. It's been re-vamped to deliver the best in modern multi-media displays, though it can still be a bit overwhelming. The Egyptian mummies on the third floor, however, are excellent, and the coin collection will doubtless leave numismatists agape – it's one of the world's best. It's also the repository of the *Vučedol Dove*, which you'll see everywhere, jointly acting as a symbol for peace and a memorial to Vukovar (see page 131). When you've had enough – or even if you just fancy a break during the visit – scope out the museum's café, where you can sit outside amongst ancient sculptures and enjoy a glass of wine. Outside the museum, on the north side of the square itself, there's a rather charming 19th-century meteorological station, where you can check out the weather.

At the beginning of Strossmayerov is the **Modern Art Gallery** (open Tue–Fri 10.00–18.00; Sat and Sun 10.00–13.00) which houses a big collection of Croatian paintings and sculpture from the middle of the 19th century to the middle of the 20th.

Centre stage in the square is the **Croatian Academy of Arts and Sciences** building, which houses the real *Baška Tablet*, from the island of Krk (see page 190 – the one actually at Baška is just a good copy), in the atrium downstairs, along with a good copy of *St Simeon's Sarcophagus* from Zadar (see page 202 – but here you can see what the back looks like, too, including a fine medieval scene of a woman fainting melodramatically at the sight of a dead body).

Upstairs is the excellent **Strossmayer Gallery of Old Masters** (open Tue 10.00–13.00 and 17.00–19.00; Wed–Sun 10.00–13.00). Strossmayer (1815–1905) himself was a fervently pro-Croat bishop, and was the founder of the Academy, and there's a first-class statue of Strossmayer by Meštrović on the square behind the gallery.

PENKALA THE INVENTOR

Largely forgotten now, but enormously influential at the time, was a man called Eduard Slavoljub Penkala (1871–1922). An inveterate inventor, he was forever looking for ways to improve day-to-day life. In 1906 he patented the world's first 'mechanical pencil', the pioneer in a whole range of writing devices which actually worked, and from 1914 to 1926, as a direct result, Zagreb became the European capital for the production of writing instruments.

Penkala himself never gave up his job at the Ministry of Finance (where he was Royal Technical Controller), but seems to have had plenty of time to work on his inventions, leaving him free to become Croatia's first aviator, in 1909, and the inventor of its first two-seater aircraft the following year. He also patented a hovercraft design in 1908, half a century ahead of Christopher Cockerell's antics on the Isle of Wight, and a rotating toothbrush the same year, when dental hygiene was still barely a blip on the horizon.

In a short life – he died of pneumonia, aged only 50 – Penkala came up with hundreds of inventions and registered over 70 patents.

Strossmayer was a serious art collector, and his private collection must have been one of the best anywhere. Look out for a dramatic *Resurrection* from the 16th-century Ferrara school, with Jesus positively leaping out of the grave and stepping on the sleeping soldiers on the way out, an inspiringly simple *Ecco Homo* by Filippo Mazzolo, and a wonderful *Mary Magdalene* by El Greco, centuries ahead of his time as usual. There's also a great treatment of *Salome* by Elisabetta Sirani, one of the fastest painters of all time, who managed to churn out more than 170 oils by the time of her death, aged just 27, in 1665.

The last square, leading to the station, is the perfect setting for the grand equestrian statue of **King Tomislav**, who was crowned in AD925 as medieval Croatia's first king.

Heading west from the station, it's a couple of blocks to the **Botanical Gardens**, which have been providing an oasis of calm to generations of visitors since being opened to the public in 1894. It's a low-key affair, and the glasshouses are for botany enthusiasts only, but it's a good place for a break.

Running north from here are another three big squares, Marulića, Mažuranića, and Maršala Tita. The first big building you'll see here is the **Croatian State Archives**, which seems sober and formal enough until you see the giant owls perched on the roof. In the square itself there's a statue of Marko Marulić, the father of Croatian literature, who was from Split.

In the next square north you'll find the curiously deserted **Ethnographic Museum** (open Tue–Thu 10.00–18.00; Fri–Sun 10.00–13.00), which has a comprehensive collection of Croatia's myriad national costumes. Unless you're in Zagreb at the beginning of July, when there's a big folk parade (details from the tourist office), come and see the costumes here, as they're now only rarely worn around the country, even on the remoter islands, which were Croatia's last bastions of denim-resistance.

Over to the west, unmissable on Roosevelt Square, is the palatial neo-classical building (formerly a school) housing the extraordinary **Mimara** collection (open

MIROGOJ CEMETERY

Bus #106 runs up from the cathedral to Mirogoj, which was opened in 1876 as the city's municipal cemetery. The main feature is a series of divine cupola-ed arcades running either way along the inside of the cemetery walls – they're the work of Herman Bollé, and in their own way are every bit as impressive as the cathedral. To the right of the entrance is the poignant memorial to Stjepan Radić, who was shot in Belgrade's parliament in 1928.

The cemetery is not just non-denominational but a positive Pantheon, housing Jews and Muslims, Orthodox Christians and Catholics, and communist partisans. There are literally thousands of touching memorials to individuals, families, and historical tragedies, including Bleiburg (see page 17), but the largest and most impressive of all is right at the top of the main avenue, where Croatia's first president, Franjo Tuđman, is honoured by a vast expanse of black marble.

Once you've paid your respects, you can return to the city on the bus, or simply walk down the hill – it takes around half an hour, heading down Mirogojska (head straight out of the cemetery, not down Grobna, which the bus came up) until you reach the tram stop, and then make your way across to the top end of Tkalčićeva.

Above The memorial at Jasenovac, a stark reminder of the concentration camp here in World War II (PL)

Below left The cross on the banks of the Danube, in Vukovar, commemorating the 1991 siege (PL)

Below right The classic lines of Varaždin, Croatia's former capital (PL)

Above St Mark's Church, Zagreb, with the decorative tiled crests of the Kingdom of Croatia, Slavonia and Dalmatia on the left, and the City of Zagreb on the right (PL)

Right Zagreb's colourful daily flower market (PL)

Below Jelačić square – right at the heart of Croatia's capital (PL)

Tue, Wed, Fri, Sat 10.00–17.00; Thu 10.00–19.00; Sun 10.00–14.00). Donated by Ante Topić Mimara and his wife Wiltrud, the diverse collection covers everything from Greek and Roman glassware to old masters to French impressionists. There are lots of speculative and fanciful ideas about how Mimara came by such a wealth of treasures, but little concrete evidence – though it's whispered that some of the more famous paintings here may be (shush!)…fakes.

Up from here, coming onto Maršala Tita, is the **Arts and Crafts Museum** (open Tue–Thu 10.00–18.00; Fri–Sun 10.00–13.00), in yet another huge, late 19th-century building (Bollé, again). The collection is an interesting one, ranging from classical furniture, porcelain and glassware to clothes, textiles, clocks and silverware – and all the Biedermeier you can eat. In the greenery, as you come out of the museum, look out for yet another Fernkorn sculpture, this time of St George slaying the dragon.

Across the square is the **Croatian National Theatre**, which was designed by the Viennese architects Ferdinand Fellner and Hermann Helmer, who made something of a career of theatre design, being responsible for over 40 across central Europe, from Switzerland to the Ukraine. An opportunity to see one of the frequent performances here (theatre, ballet, opera) shouldn't be missed.

In front of the theatre is Meštrović's sculpture, the *Well of Life* (Zdenac Života), dating from 1905, and one of the clearest indicators that his early work was influenced by Rodin, whom he'd met and studied with – in this case the source of inspiration is clearly *The Burghers of Calais*, though the *Well of Life* itself couldn't be mistaken for a Rodin. Across the road, in front of the university's elegant Faculty of Law, is another Meštrović masterpiece, the *History of the Croats*, a simple composition of a single, seated woman, serene but stern, holding a stone tablet.

Surrounds

If you need to get out of town and away from the hustle and bustle, there are a number of options. Close to the city is one of the best cemeteries anywhere, **Mirogoj** (see box opposite), while a little further north there's a cable car up to Sljeme, the peak of **Mount Medvednica**. To the east of town is the huge city park, **Maksimir**, while to the southwest is **Jarun Lake**, the nearest Zagreb gets to a beach. There's also a host of cycling opportunities in Zagreb County.

Mount Medvednica

If you want a real breath of country air, take tram #8 or #14 to the Mihaljevac terminus, followed by #15 to the end of the line at Dolje. From here it's a ten-minute walk to the cable-car station (Žičara), and a half-hour ride (hourly) up to the 1,035m peak of Sljeme, the highest point on Mount Medvednica.

There's some pleasant, not-too-strenuous walking to be had round here (a map is available from the tourist office), and in winter you can ski down the back. There's also a hotel, five minutes from the top of the lift, the **Tomislav Dom** (tel: 456 0400; fax: 456 0401), which has recently been refurbished and offers 45 rooms with chalet-like doubles costing €100-120 per night.

From the Tomislav Dom it's a little under an hour on foot to the 13th-century **Medvedgrad Fortress**. This was abandoned in the late 16th century and fell into ruin, but was expensively restored in the 1990s, as a patriotic gesture by Franjo Tuđman – it's become something of a nationalist symbol, and as such is mildly controversial: could the money have been better spent on something else, the locals ask. It's an atmospheric place in a great location, all the same, with lovely views out over the city, and a fine restaurant in the vaults.

If you're coming by car, Medvedgrad is ludicrously hard to find, however. If you get as far as the **Šestinski Lagvić** restaurant (another nice place to stop for a meal), then turn left here, steeply up the hill, and then turn hard left again at the only junction on this road – the fortress is a few hundred metres up this path. If you get back to the main road you've gone too far, and you'll have to repeat the circuit.

On the western corner of the Medvednica, a 20-minute hike up from the Glavica mountain hut, is the **Veternica Cave**, which is almost 7km deep. The first 400m is open to visitors on Sundays for a half-hour guided tour, and the path up from the hut and the electric lighting inside the cave were both fully refurbished during 2002. The cave was home to Neanderthals and bears, thousands of years ago, though presumably not at the same time. Contact the Medvednica Nature Park (tel: 458 0699; fax: 458 0599) for more detailed information.

Maksimir Park
A few kilometres east of Zagreb city centre is the sprawling Maksimir Park, easily reached on tram #4, #7, #11 or #12 (get off at the Bukovačka stop, heading towards Dubrava or Dubec). Landscaped in the manner of a 19th-century English park, it's a great place for a stroll, and there are follies, lakes and even a zoo to divert you.

Jarun Lake
On the other side of Zagreb, about 5km from the city centre, is Jarun Lake, an artificial playground with cycle paths, jogging tracks and even a beach (at the lake's eastern end). Tram #17 gets you most of the way there.

Cycling in Zagreb County
Cyclists should jump at the opportunity of taking advantage of an excellent new series of six maps entitled 'Biking Routes of Zagreb County' which were published for the first time in 2004 by the Zagreb County Tourist Board (tel: 487 3665; fax: 487 3670; www.tzzz.hr). These describe a series of routes to the north and west of the capital following low-traffic-density roads across beautiful rolling countryside, and range from the easy to the moderately strenuous. Altitude and distance profiles let you know exactly what you're up for and full details are provided of everything you could possibly need along the way from restaurants and accommodation options to bike repair shops. It's a wonderful initiative.

Inland Croatia

Inland Croatia is in complete contrast to the dramatic karstic landscapes of the coast and the holiday resorts on the islands. With the exception of the famous **Plitvice Lakes**, Croatia's most popular national park, the area is largely unvisited – and unjustly so.

North of Zagreb is the delightful **Zagorje** region, with hundreds of churches and dozens of castles and country houses set amongst wooded hills, while the country's northern provincial capital, **Varaždin**, is a baroque masterpiece. Southwest of the capital are the low mountains, remote villages and excellent vineyards of the **Žumberak**, bracketed by the lovely little town of **Samobor** on one side and the purpose-built Renaissance fortress town of **Karlovac** on the other.

South of Karlovac are the Plitvice Lakes, while to the southeast are the marshes and wetlands loved by birdlife – practically anywhere south and east of Zagreb you'll see nesting storks, but most notably in the **Lonjsko Polje**.

Further east of here you're into Slavonia, where hunting castles and deep forests contrast with the big Pannonian plains. The fine provincial town of **Požega** is the obvious access point to the **Papuk** Nature Park, where you'll find burbling streams and shady woods to walk in, while **Slavonski Brod** and **Đakovo** offer some of the region's most interesting folk events.

Here, you're in the heart of Slavonia, bordered by the three great rivers, the Sava, the Drava and the Danube. The region's busy capital, **Osijek**, is the gateway to the huge wetlands of **Kopački Rit**, one of Europe's most important bird sanctuaries, and the breeding ground for some of the world's most vicious mosquitoes. Make sure you wear repellent, even in the daytime, and use one of those protective wall-socket plug-ins at night – you can buy them anywhere round here, not surprisingly. Finally, at the eastern end of Slavonia is **Vukovar**, which suffered terribly during the war in 1991, but is now gradually finding its feet once again.

With few tourists, once you're inland you'll find a general lack of accommodation facilities, though in the Zagorje and Žumberak there are more and more agro-tourism offerings available. It's well worth contacting the Zagreb county tourist office (tel: 01 487 3665; fax: 01 487 3670; www.tzzz.hr) ahead of time for the latest information.

Further east, there are really only a handful of places to stay (they're listed in the text), with the whole of Slavonia boasting fewer than half the number of hotels you can find in Poreč alone.

Phone codes vary across the region – they're included within each listing.

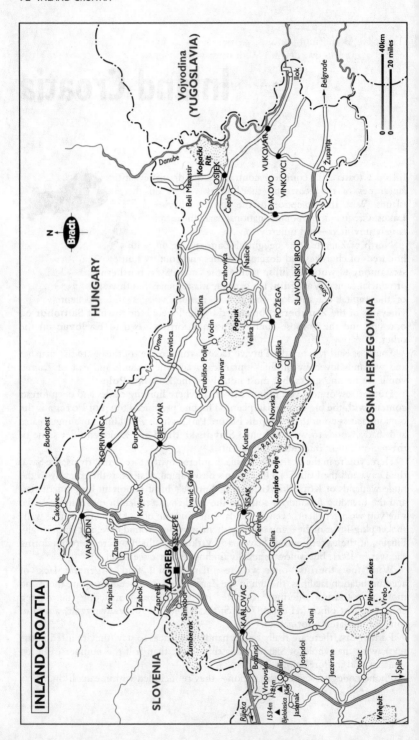

VARAŽDIN

Tucked into the northernmost corner of the country, Varaždin is a provincial capital and a baroque delight. With most people heading straight on to the coast, it sees remarkably few visitors – but deserves many more.

The telephone code is 042 (+385 42 from abroad).

History

Known as Garestin in Roman times, little of importance happened here until Varaždin was recognised by Hungary in AD1181, and then developed first as an administrative and later as a defensive centre – from the 15th century on, the city was on the frontline against the Ottoman Empire.

With the Turkish threat under control by the early 17th century, Varaždin became an affluent and influential city, and in 1756 even became the capital of Croatia. It wasn't to last – after a catastrophic fire in 1776, the Ban (the local governor) moved to Zagreb. Varaždin was still a prosperous city, however, and its wealthy merchants didn't miss the opportunity of rebuilding their houses and palaces according to the latest fashion of the day.

Today, the baroque centre of Varaždin has been beautifully restored, and it deserves to win its bid to be included on UNESCO's World Heritage list. With everything comfortably within walking distance in the centre, and plaques on many of the buildings in Croatian, English and German, it's also an easy place to visit.

Getting there and around

Situated just 80km north of Zagreb, Varaždin is simple to reach, with buses running at least once an hour from the capital, and trains making the journey a dozen times a day. Buses take around 1½ hours, while trains rarely achieve the distance in under 2½, though the notoriously slow train-ride is a much more picturesque way of making the journey. Varaždin is also a stop on the major international bus and train routes north to Austria and Hungary.

The bus station is five minutes southwest of the town centre, while the train station is ten minutes away to the east. Most of the old town is pedestrianised, with the curving shopping street Gundulića leading up to the main square Trg Kralja Tomislava. A block northwest, on Ivana Padovca, you'll find a friendly and helpful tourist information office. The newly expanded city map is well worth the 25 kuna, though if you're on a tight budget you can certainly get by with the free materials.

Where to stay and eat

Varaždin has a fairly limited supply of private rooms, though you'd be unlucky not to find one in town or the surrounding countryside. Stop in at T-Tours (tel: 042 210 989; fax: 042 210 990) on Gundulića, which is the only agency handling rooms, and expect to pay €25–30 year-round – for once there's no surcharge for short stays.

The town's three hotels are all situated within five minutes of the bus station. Best value of the three is the refurbished **Garestin** (tel/fax: 042 214 314), which has a dozen clean, comfortable double rooms with all facilities for €55. Only slightly less well appointed, and in the same price range, is the **Maltar** (tel: 042 311 100; fax: 042 211 190). Much bigger and slightly swankier than either of these two is the **Turist** (tel: 042 395 395; fax: 042 214 479), which has some doubles at €56, though most are at €80. All three hotels cater primarily to business people passing through, so you should reserve ahead if you're coming midweek, particularly at the Garestin or Maltar.

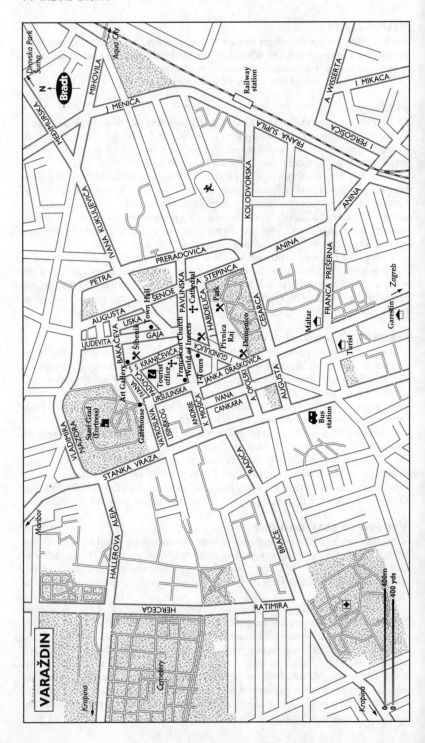

As a prosperous town, Varaždin is blessed with lots of places to eat and drink, and some of the restaurants and bars have terraces in pleasant courtyards hidden away behind the baroque façades. For good food, a fine terrace, and a view out over the park you can't beat...well, the **Park**. Nearby, on Trg Slobode, is Varaždin's most popular pizzeria, **Domenico**, while on Gundulića you'll find the cheerful **Pivnica Raj**, which as you'd expect (*pivnica* being a brewery) serves up its own beer and various grills. Further up the town and further upmarket is the **Šibenik**, which boasts excellent seafood – though predictably the white fish doesn't come cheap.

What to see

The main thing to see in Varaždin is the harmonious old town, centred on Trg Kralja Tomislava. Dominating the square you'll find the **town hall**, dating from 1523, with an unlikely spire rising from its centre.

A block south is Varaždin's 17th-century **cathedral**, with a plain baroque façade giving away few secrets about the riotous over-the-top altarpiece inside. Multi-coloured pillars frame dramatic saints in late-medieval garb, overlooked by gesticulating angels and overflown by abundant *putti*. It's absolutely marvellous – but you wouldn't want one at home.

Outside the Franciscan church, 150m west of the cathedral, anyone who's been to Split will recognise the pint-sized version of Ivan Meštrović's most distinctive statue, **Grgur Ninski** – strangely undramatic in its reduced form. As in Split, the erstwhile bishop's big toe has been worn golden by people hoping their wishes will come true.

Almost next door, and an absolute must for entomologists, is Varaždin's **World of Insects** museum, featuring a thousand species of bugs and more than 4,000 exhibits. It's one of the best collections of its kind, demonstrating not only Croatia's endemic species, but also the life-cycle and habitats of various insects.

From here it's two minutes north to the park housing Varaždin's trademark whitewashed fortress, the **Stari Grad**. Set amongst defensive earthworks which have pleasantly metamorphosed into lovely gardens, the fortress was originally built in the 14th century, before becoming a major defence against the Turks in the 15th century and evolving into its present shape during the 16th century.

The fortress now houses the **town museum**, a not especially inspiring collection of paintings, weaponry and furnishings, though the entry fee is amply repaid by the chance to wander round the rooms and the two three-tiered courtyards; the lapidarium is particularly interesting, with various Roman and religious fragments.

From the fortress it's a ten-minute stroll west to the town's **cemetery**, which has much more in common with a landscaped garden than a traditional resting place for the dead. Its avenues and promenades make for a very pleasant wander.

On the other side of the fortress you can walk out through the gatehouse and across the drawbridge on to Trg Miljenka Stančića, where you'll find the municipal **art gallery** in a gaudily fronted palace. The collection mostly consists of old masters by artists you won't have heard of, but it's none the less interesting for that.

If all the sightseeing's left you hot and bothered, and you have your own transport, head a few kilometres east out of town to **Aqua City**, where you'll find a lake to swim in, a shingle beach to sun yourself on, and a restaurant. Without wheels you can still get the shore-side experience by walking 20 minutes northeast of the old town to the **Dravska Park Šuma**, where you'll find jogging paths along the banks of the great, still river Drava.

Finally, if you're here in September or early October, it's well worth trying to get tickets (ask at the tourist office) for one of the many concerts which make up Varaždin's excellent *Festival of Baroque Music*. Most of the concerts are held in the churches around town, and they're usually first-rate.

Across the river Drava, 13km north of Varaždin, is **Čakovec**, the northernmost town in Croatia. Easily reachable several times a day on the bus from Varaždin, there's not a whole lot to do or see, though it's worth coming just for the 17th-century castle which now houses the fine **Museum of the Međimurje**, an eclectic collection ranging from Neolithic finds to period furniture to a reconstructed pharmacy. The castle was home for centuries to the influential and colourful Zrinski dynasty. Back in the centre of town check out the **Trade Union Hall**, which was built in the secessionist style in 1904 as a casino, a function which seems far more appropriate to the frivolous decorative work on the façade than the serious business of organised labour.

Southwest of Varaždin, up into the low wooded hills 15km away, and only accessible with your own transport, is the mysterious and hard-to-find **Maruševac Castle**. Originally dating from the 16th century, today's version is a 19th-century neo-Gothic pile, home to a theology school of the Adventist Church. You can allegedly visit by appointment, from 15.00–17.00 on Sundays, by calling 042 729 314 or 042 729 696 – but it didn't work for me.

THE ZAGORJE

The northwestern corner of Croatia, known as the Zagorje, is one of the most beautiful parts of the country, with scores of castles, country houses and hilltop churches looking down across rolling wooded hills and vineyards. It's largely neglected by foreigners on their way to the beach, but it's no secret to locals, who come out here at weekends to relax.

Many of the old houses – and especially the little buildings adjoining the vineyards (*klets*) – have been converted into weekenders for people escaping Zagreb, but the great majority of the castles (the French word *châteaux* is more appropriate, really) are in ill-repair, empty and abandoned, and could do with fixing up. Of the few which have been restored, most are in private hands and can't be visited. It's to be hoped, as Croatia becomes more prosperous, that more of this wonderful heritage will be restored and opened to the public, but even now there's a great deal to do and see.

It's difficult to get the most out of the Zagorje without your own wheels – even though many of the sights can be reached on public transport, it may take you all day to see a place worth only an hour of your time. Consider renting a car for a couple of days – but bear in mind that the roads can be very narrow and windy.

There aren't many places to stay, with most of the area's hotels being attached to the various spas in the region, although agro-tourism is on the rise, and there are a number of other options listed within this section. Zagorje eating is almost always a treat, on the other hand, whether you stick to the simple standards or try the local dishes, such as *štrukli*, parcels of cottage cheese wrapped in pasta, somewhere on the food chain between big ravioli and cheese dumplings. Intended for decoration rather than eating are the *licitarsko srce*, iced gingerbread hearts usually featuring the name of the town they come from. As gifts they're keenly priced; as snacks go they're pretty expensive.

The following attractions are ordered here in an itinerary heading very roughly clockwise from Zagreb towards Varaždin and back again, with those to the east of the main road to Hungary appearing at the end of the section. Covering the whole lot would make for a fairly hectic two- or more relaxed three-day tour.

Klanjec

Heading northwest out of Zagreb, it's about 40km to the small town of Klanjec, nestled right up against the Slovenian border. Buses make the journey two or three times a day and there's also a train – change at Savski Marof. The main reason to

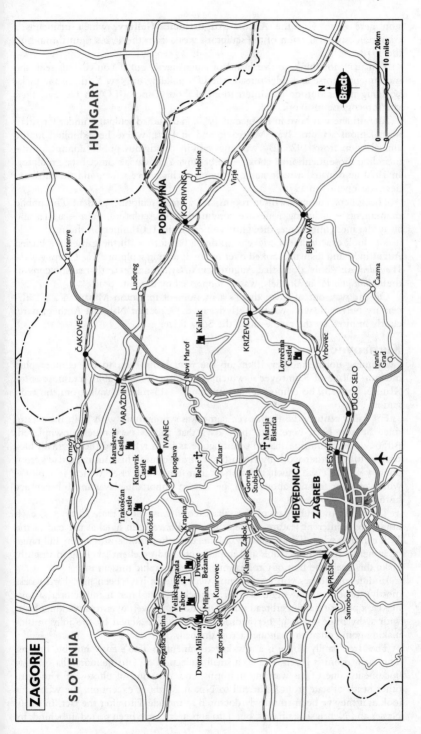

stop here is to visit the **Antun Augustinčić Gallery**, which maintains a comprehensive collection of the sculptor's work from the 1920s right through to the 1970s.

You may not think you've heard of Augustinčić, but if you've ever seen the monumental horse and rider outside the UN building in New York, or the pick-wielding miner outside the International Labour Office (ILO) in Geneva, then you'll recognise his work.

Augustinčić was born in Klanjec in 1900, and studied sculpture under Croatia's most famous sculptor Ivan Meštrović and in Paris, where he exhibited in the annual salon from 1925. By winning various prestigious public commissions – including those mentioned above – he became Yugoslavia's official state sculptor. In 1970 he donated a wide range of works to his native town, and the museum here was opened in 1976.

The gallery comprises three rooms and a small sculpture garden. The public monuments – including a life-size copy of the UN sculpture, *Peace* – are far and away the most impressive, though if you catch the ILO miner on the right angle it does look exactly like a cricketer hitting a ball for six. In the garden are buried Augustinčić and his wife, looked over by the touching sculpture *The Carrying of the Wounded* – it's only a pity that Augustinčić's *Boy*, an unpleasantly realistic copy of the *Mannequin Pis* in Brussels, wasn't suppressed by the taste police.

On the way out of town there's a monument to Antun Mihanović, a 19th-century polymath who wrote the lyrics to the Croatian National Anthem here, clearly inspired by the ravine along the Sutla River.

Kumrovec

Continuing north, another 10km up the road brings you to the ethnographic museum village of Kumrovec – which you can get to on public transport as for Klanjec, above. The ethnographic museum is a 15-minute walk from the train station.

For half a century the Kumrovec name was synonymous with Josip Broz Tito, since he was born here, but these days that angle's very much downplayed. Although the authorities haven't quite gone as far as removing the marshal's life-sized statue (another work by Augustinčić) from outside his mum and dad's front door, you don't see much mention of him anywhere else. Which is a pity – whatever your feelings about Tito, he was an important player in 20th-century history.

Today the museum part of the village consists of more than 30 houses, each displaying a different feature of life as it would have been lived at the end of the 19th century, when Tito was a boy. Mannequins in period costume, the full range of authentic furnishings, tools and implements, and excellent labelling in English, make this easily the best of Croatia's many ethnographic museums.

In different houses you can imagine what it must have been like (hard work, mostly) to be a wheelwright, a baker, a blacksmith, a linen manufacturer, a toy-maker, a potter or a gingerbread man. One house is given over to a wedding feast, with a shy bride-to-be in her bedroom, doubtless deafened by the jolly music-making going on at the banquet across the hall.

The Broz family house is a low-key testament to Tito's fairly humble origins. The main room is given over to a small collection of Tito memorabilia – a few documents, one of his wartime uniforms, and a handful of photos of Tito with other heads of state from Churchill to Nixon. Without exception, the whole lot look as if they've been amusingly doctored to include Tito after the fact. In 1956, Nasser and Nehru shake hands, but Tito appears to have been pasted in behind; by

JOSIP BROZ TITO

Josip Broz was born in Kumrovec in 1892, to a Slovene mother and a Croat father. Drafted into the Austro-Hungarian army in 1914, to fight in World War I, he was captured the following year, but escaped early enough to join the Red Army in 1917. In 1920, he returned to Croatia, where he devoted his time to communism and unionism, while employed as a metalworker.

With the Communist Party banned in 1928, Broz was frequently in trouble (and jail) but quickly worked his way up through the ranks. On joining the Central Committee in 1934, he took the name Tito. By 1939 he was Secretary-General of Yugoslavia's Communist Party, and when Yugoslavia capitulated in 1941 he was in a good position to rally resistance – not just to the Germans and the Italians, but also to the NDH, and indeed to anyone who wasn't a communist, including other factions of the resistance.

Charismatic, ruthless and utterly determined – though not the military genius he liked to think he was – Tito persuaded the Allies to switch their aid from the Četniks to the partisans in 1943, and ended the war as the de facto dictator of the new Yugoslavia. His enemies – including large numbers of Croatian reservists and civilians – were brutally purged (notably at Bleiburg, see page 17).

In 1948, Tito became the first communist leader to break ranks with Stalin, and was the founder of the non-aligned movement, which included India and Egypt. He continued to embrace communism, though a considerably softer version than that espoused by the USSR and the Eastern Bloc – Yugoslavs, notably, were allowed to own private property, and were free to travel, live and work abroad. But neither Tito himself nor the Communist Party ever brooked the slightest dissent, and prison was a real possibility for anyone who tried.

As Marshal and President for life, Tito made a point of trying to hold the country together, and was quick to quash nationalistic sentiment from the divergent republics – notably the Croatian Spring in 1971 – in spite of being half Croatian and half Slovene himself. Nonetheless he put in place the legislation which would inevitably lead to the break-up of Yugoslavia after his death, in particular by guaranteeing the republics' right to secede. Within 20 years of his death in 1980, only two republics (Serbia and Montenegro) and one autonomous region (Vojvodina) still remained in Yugoslavia – with the likelihood that even they will eventually break up.

1963, it's John and Jackie Kennedy in the frame, with Tito scissored-in on the left-hand side.

The chickens wandering around and the hay drying on the attractive Slovenian-style lattice frames should alert you to the fact that not all the houses are part of the museum – before you wander unannounced into someone else's authentically rustic living room (as I did), check for the tell-tale trainers or gumboots outside.

Within the museum complex there's a nice place to eat, the *Zagorska Klet*, where you'll find a wholesome range of local food at reasonable prices. You can then pick up a *licitar* heart, in the gift shop, for dessert.

Heading up the Slovenian border from Kumrovec, the countryside becomes ever more beautiful, with Austro–Hungarian spires crowning hilltop churches –

stop briefly for the photo-op at **Zagorskje Sela**, where from **Saint Catherine's Church** you get lovely views across the valley into Slovenia.

Not much further up the road from here, as you come into Miljana, is the turnoff to Desinić, which is the road for Veliki Tabor. If you want to visit the lovely Renaissance manor house here – **Dvorac Miljana** is probably the very finest of the restored chateaux of the Zagorje – think again. The separate coach and car parks are blind alleys for the time being, and though there's still talk of opening the place up for public viewing, it was still nowhere near happening in 2004.

Don't miss the turn-off to Veliki Tabor and Desinić – you'll find yourself in Slovenia before you know it, either through the heavily manned border post, or on a mountainous road leading across an unmanned bridge to the spa town of Atomske Toplice. If that's your route into Slovenia, you can forget about trying to argue your way back into Croatia anywhere near here – head all the way back to the Kumrovec border post instead.

Veliki Tabor

A few kilometres up the road from Miljana, on a 333m hill, is **Veliki Tabor**, arguably the most picturesque authentic castle in Croatia. Originally dating from the 12th century, the distinctive defensive round towers were added in the 16th century. From the road there's a lovely view – as indeed there is from the excellent and authentically rustic **Grešna Gorica** restaurant, clearly signed off the main road, a few hundred metres beyond the steep track leading up to the castle.

Unfortunately the castle itself doesn't really deliver on its promise. The lovely five-sided, three-tiered courtyard is undergoing much-needed restoration, and it looks as if it'll take years. The rooms leading off the galleries house a fairly mundane collection, and the art and pikes don't really warrant the 20 kuna entrance fee.

Like all good medieval castles, Veliki Tabor has its own romantic fable attached to it. In this case the local landowner's son wouldn't renounce the peasant girl of his desires, and was imprisoned in the castle until his death. The girl, for her part in the sorry story, was bricked up into the castle walls – they say the skull in the chapel here is hers. Count yourself lucky if you live in a time or country where you can choose who you marry.

You could get to Veliki Tabor by taking the bus from Zagreb to Desinić, and then walking 3km, but until they're done with the restoration I wouldn't particularly recommend it – unless your heart's set on lunch at Grešna Gorica.

Eight kilometres east of Veliki Tabor is the village of **Pregrada**, where the local parish church is so big it's known locally as the **Zagorje Cathedral**. It's 38m long and 19m wide, and its two 45m towers dominate the village. Inside, check out the monumental Focht organ, which used to belong to Zagreb Cathedral, until they sold it to Pregrada for 600 forints in 1854 – better value in this humble author's opinion than the 600 forints spent on the huge altarpiece by the church eight years earlier.

Another 4km east leads to **Dvorac Bežanec** (tel: 049 376 800; fax: 049 376 810; www.bezanec.hr), now one of Croatia's five-star hotels. Originally built in the 17th century, the château was remodelled in 1830 in the classicist style, and it's a wonderfully luxurious place to stay, at a pretty reasonable €100 a night for a double room. Call ahead if you want to take advantage of the horse-riding or ballooning opportunities.

Krapina

A further 10km east brings you to Krapina, which is on the main road running north from Zagreb to Maribor (in Slovenia) and Graz (in Austria). It's a busy, commercial little town, but the main reason for visiting is that on the Hušnjakovo hill above town here, in 1899, the site of a Neanderthal settlement dating back some 30,000–40,000 years was discovered.

The site is one of Europe's most important, and though the bones of the 20 or so Neanderthals are today in the Natural History Museum in Zagreb, you can visit the small local museum, and then walk up the path to the actual site, where you'll find life-sized (and quite life-like) statues of the Neanderthals brandishing clubs. One of them looks alarmingly like the exchange student we had one year at our school.

Krapina is relatively easy to reach, with weekday buses running every hour or so from Zagreb, and taking an hour. At weekends you're probably better off taking the train – change at Zabok. If you want to stay over, you're limited to the fairly basic **Motel Croatia** (tel: 049 370 547; fax: 049 300 146), which has 15 rooms at €50 for a double. You might also try the tourist office (tel/fax: 049 371 330), who should be able to find you a private room in the area.

Trakošćan

Northeast from Krapina is the Zagorje's most-visited attraction, Trakošćan. Billed as a 13th-century castle, you don't have to read much of the small print – or use much architectural intelligence – to work out that what you're seeing here isn't medieval at all but mid 19th-century neo-romantic all over. That doesn't make it any less worth visiting – although it's all a bit shabby and run down, it's still extraordinary inside and out, with a complete collection of the original (19th-century) furniture and fittings.

The castle was given to the powerful Drašković family in 1584, probably as a belated thank-you for its role in putting down the peasants' uprising a decade earlier (see *Gornja Stubica*, below). After the first century or so, the family didn't do much with Trakošćan, preferring to live at the better-appointed Klenovik (see over). But with the romantic revival in full swing, they then spent a fortune – and more than 20 years – building the castle you see today, and damming and flooding the valley below to give themselves a decent lake.

Access is up a lovely spiralling path and through mock-defensive gates, overlooked by imaginatively crenellated walls and ramparts. Inside it's all heavy neo-Gothic. On the ground floor you'll find the **Knights' Room**, with lots of clumsy-looking armour and the usual hideous array of pikes and swords. There's also a curious fireplace, with wooden dragons supporting the mantelpiece. At the other end of the building there's a **Hunting Hall** which verges dangerously close to self-parody.

Upstairs there's room after room of heavy furniture and heavier furnishings, hideous to most modern sensibilities, but a real insight into the mid 19th-century mindset of the ruling classes. You'll also see ten generations of smug Drašković portraits, by the famous local painter Nepozanti Slikar, and presumably his eponymous descendants – since they date from 1680 to at least 1823. (No, I'm kidding – *'nepozanti slikar'* just means 'anonymous painter'.)

Far from anonymous, as far as the paintings here go, are those by Julijana Drašković (née Erdödy, 1847–1901). Much of her surviving work is in the castle and, although most of it doesn't stand extended 21st-century scrutiny, there are several truly excellent impressionistic portraits.

Other things to look out for, amongst the absurdly chunky baroque furniture, are an unusual three-seater neo-Gothic sofa, inspired no doubt by church architecture, superb stoves in every room (usually fed from behind, to avoid the unpleasantness of intrusive servants), and what must have been a boy's room on the top floor, with wallpaper consisting of tapestries depicting massive armies of tin soldiers on parade.

You can clear your head outside by a promenade around the lake – the whole circuit takes a leisurely hour and a half.

You can't get to Trakošćan directly from Zagreb, but there are buses roughly every hour from Varaždin, taking less than an hour. Once you're here there's a perfectly acceptable accommodation option, the **Hotel Coning** (tel: 042 796 224; fax: 042 796 205), right across from the castle, which has around 100 rooms at €60 kuna for good doubles, and there's a sauna and gym too. The dining room tends to cater to large tour buses and noisy school groups, but you can escape onto the terrace easily enough, and enjoy the view across to the castle.

Lepoglava

From Trakošćan it's about 10km southeast to Lepoglava, (in)famous mainly for being the site of Croatia's largest prison. There's hardly a big name in 20th-century Croatian politics who didn't do time here, from Tito himself between the wars, to Archbishop Stepinac after World War II, to Franjo Tuđman, who was banged up here during the 1980s for disagreeing with Serbia's take on history – he suffered four heart attacks in jail here before being released.

The prison's still there, but the quiet town is pleasant enough, and there's a fine whitewashed Austro-Hungarian church to visit, with saints in niches on the outside, and colourful frescos and a big baroque altar inside.

Northeast 10km from here is Croatia's biggest castle, **Klenovik**, which claims to have 90 rooms and 365 windows. Built in the 17th century, it was for a brief time the seat of the Croatian parliament, and is now a sanatorium, dealing mainly with respiratory complaints. You can only visit today as a patient.

Belec

Barely 10km southeast of Lepoglava, but on the other side of the 1,100m Ivanšćica mountains (you have to skirt round through Zlatar, and then head 8km north), is the village of Belec, and more importantly the **Church of St Mary of the Snow**. Simple enough on the outside, it's profligate baroque gone mad once you get inside.

There's hardly an unadorned surface in sight. *Putti* proliferate off every balcony, mantelpiece and archway, extravagantly gestured saints camp it up like drama queens, and the accumulated wealth of gilt, carving and paintwork is completely overwhelming. Restrained simplicity it ain't – it has to be seen to be believed. Be warned that it's usually only open on Sunday mornings.

Marija Bistrica

Heading south 10km from Zlatar brings you into Marija Bistrica, a pleasant little town dedicated to looking after the more than 600,000 pilgrims who come here every year, making it Croatia's premier pilgrimage site. The reason? A late 15th- or early 16th-century **Black Madonna**, which already had a huge following, even before a fire in 1880 destroyed almost everything except the statue itself.

With pilgrims on the increase for centuries, the congregation has frequently outgrown the church, and the church has equally frequently had to be expanded. The current incarnation was completed in 1883 by Herman Bollé, the man behind half the buildings in Zagreb, including the cathedral – though here he's been more imaginative (or perhaps less constrained).

From the outside, the **Pilgrimage Church of St Mary** is half way between a castle and a cathedral. An elegant piazza leads through a gate into a half-cloister, lined with thousands of marble plaques of gratitude from pilgrims whose wishes have been granted over the years, and topped with paintings of specific miracles attributable to the Black Madonna.

Inside, the church is a quiet, awed place, with a continuously shifting congregation of the hopeful (mostly older women) saying their prayers, but also seizing the opportunity to photograph and film the famous Madonna behind the altar.

Behind the church, there's an enormous open-air auditorium, which was built for the Pope's visit in 1998, when he came here to beatify Cardinal Stepinac, and a **Way of the Cross**, leading up **Calvary Hill**. The church and town look lovely from the top, even if you haven't climbed up here on your knees.

There are buses every hour or so from Zagreb to Marija Bistrica on most days, though fewer on Sundays. The tourist office (tel/fax: 049 468 380) can point you at private rooms nearby, though it's good to have your own wheels if this is your option, as most of them are some way out into the country. Marija Bistrica's also a good place to eat, with pizzerias and grills in plenty.

You may want to steer clear of the town, however – unless of course you're a pilgrim yourself – on August 15, when thousands of people come here to celebrate the Assumption of the Virgin Mary.

Gornja Stubica

From Marija Bistrica it's 11km to Gornja Stubica, home to the radically named **Museum of Peasant Uprisings (Muzej Seljačkih Buna)**, housed in the local Oršić Palace.

Back in the 16th century, peasants were treated appallingly, overloaded with dues to foreign overlords, expected to fight their battles for them, and driven to the brink of starvation by people who mostly lived idle lives in opulent palaces. By 1573, in this area, it was all too much, and the peasants revolted.

The uprising was quickly and ruthlessly put down by the bishop of Zagreb, a Drašković, who spread word that the ringleader, Matija Gubec, had been made king of the peasants. Within weeks he was horribly executed in St Mark's Square, in Zagreb, by being 'crowned' peasant king with a band of red-hot iron.

There's a dramatic communist-era statue of Gubec on the hill above the town, framed by a huge bronze frieze depicting revolting peasants – it's the work of local boy Antun Augustinčić (see page 98). It's well-enough signed if you're coming from Donja Stubica or Gornja Stubica, but if you're coming from Marija Bistrica, the sharp left-hand turn up to the monument and museum is easy to miss – if you've crossed over the Oršić River or the railway, or got as far as the Grof Bistro, then you've gone too far.

The museum, over the hill behind the monument, is actually a bit of a misnomer, telling you more about the luxurious lifestyle of the oppressors than the beaten-down existence of the oppressed – though maybe that's the point: this is what you're meant to revolt against. (To be fair, however, there are lots of explanatory panels, in Croatian only, which may do the trick.)

The first thing you can visit is the family chapel, dating from 1756, which has a stunningly convincing *trompe l'oeil* altarpiece and fake dome. The chapel and the room next door house some richly embroidered ecclesiastical garments, originally used at Marija Bistrica at the end of the 19th century. Look out for the distinctive hammer and pliers motif, along with a brightly stitched chicken, sheep, ladder and cross, paintbrush, and wicker basket.

The rest of the museum is upstairs. Above the chapel, out of sight of the peasants below, an Oršić countess sits reading her prayer-book in haughty isolation. A roomful of furniture and trinkets only confirms the distance between rich and poor, though you can't help admiring the pocket sundial dating from 1755. 'What time is it, your honour?' 'I'm afraid I can't tell you – it's raining.'

From here there's a bridge through to the rest of the collection, with a group of ragged-looking peasants on one side, and a couple of well-shod militia on the other. You can see the peasants wouldn't have stood a chance.

You can get here by train from Zagreb half a dozen times a day – change at Zabok on the Varaždin line, and then take the branch line to Gornja Stubica. In the courtyard of the palace there's a small restaurant with an even smaller menu, but the terrace is a nice place to sit. Otherwise, if you have your own wheels, head uphill to **Rody**, signed 250m north off the road between the town and the museum – you get a great view south to the back of Medvednica from the terrace, and the food and wine are good value.

Vrbovec

Situated just 45km east of Zagreb, the small town of Vrbovec is way off the tourist radar screen. While the town's nothing special in itself, it does make a great base for exploring the practically unvisited local area, and it has an incredible-value place to stay. Given that it's only 40 minutes by rail into Zagreb, with trains running more than once an hour, and with frequent buses too, Vrbovec is also a possible base for seeing the capital – hotel rooms here are far cheaper than private rooms in the city.

The train station is a ten-minute walk north from the town centre, while the bus station is on the southwestern corner of town, just downhill from the church. From the bus station it's a five-minute walk along Zagrebačka (the main road from Zagreb to Bjelovar) to the excellent **Motel Marina** (tel: 01 279 1502; fax: 01 279 1522), which has great rooms with all facilities (phone, satellite TV, minibar, aircon) at an astonishing €40 a night for doubles – you even get a 10% discount if you pay cash. If that weren't enough, there's a nice terrace, and the food is excellent – local produce and local recipes dominate the menu.

There's another accommodation option, the **Motel Antonio** (tel: 01 279 9955; fax: 01 279 9956), which has 15 rooms also at €40 for doubles. With surly staff and charmless rooms, it really comes a very poor second to the Marina.

Four kilometres north of Vrbovec, on the road to Križevci, there's the charming 16th-century **Lovrečina Castle**, with distinctive round towers at either end. Today, Lovrečina is run as a Cenacolo rehabilitation centre, mainly for former drug users (see box opposite).

Križevci

Just 20km northeast of Vrbovec, and roughly equidistant from Zagreb and Varaždin, is the thriving town of Križevci. It's only an hour or so from the capital by rail, on trains which run about once an hour, but it's far enough off the beaten track to be tourist-free.

The town, which has been firmly on the map since the middle of the 13th century, has more than its fair share of churches and old buildings, as well as a fine **city museum**.

The most obvious sight is the **Greek Catholic Cathedral**. Many of the locals here, as well as the majority of the people in the Žumberak, southwest of Zagreb, were originally Orthodox Slavs. In the face of Turkish expansion they were protected by the Austro-Hungarians, as long as they agreed to recognise the Pope – hence Greek Catholics. The church was rebuilt by the ubiquitous Herman Bollé in his trademark neo-Gothic style, while the iconostasis inside is marvellous, half an acre of gold leaf surrounding colourful icons of the saints, and keeping the congregation separate from the priests behind.

PUTTING SOMETHING BACK – SUPPORTING CENACOLO

The Cenacolo community at Vrbovec is almost entirely self-sufficient, and grows its own crops, milks its own cows, makes its own cheese and bakes its own bread. They even run a printing press for the Croatian version of the monthly Cenacolo newsletter. The residents are really friendly, and it's well worth going to make a donation to the community.

Cenacolo (literally: Last Supper) is a Christian organisation which was founded in Italy in July 1983 by Sister Elvira Petrozzi. With its headquarters in Saluzzo, the community now has 35 fraternities in Italy, France, Bosnia & Herzegovina, Ireland, Brazil, Austria, the Dominican Republic, the USA, and Mexico – and of course Croatia. In total some 900 young men and women, mostly former drug users, are in the community. The lifestyle is a simple, hard-working one, and has proved remarkably successful in rehabilitating drug addicts.

The Cenacolo website is at www.comunitacenacolo.it.

Also worth visiting is the **Church of the Holy Cross**, which started life in the 13th and 14th centuries but has been much remodelled and restored since. Inside there's a dramatic painting of the so-called 'Bloody Diet of Križevci' which took place in 1397, when the Hungarian King Sigismund successfully tricked and murdered the cream of Croatia's nobility.

Back in the centre of town, the 17th-century **Church of St Anne** is also interesting – the niches outside feature painted saints in the absence of statuary, while inside it's simple Romanesque, with a few fresco fragments on the right-hand wall.

The tourist office (tel/fax: 048 681 199) may be able to help you find private accommodation in the area – otherwise there's the **Kalnik** (tel: 048 681 522; fax: 048 682 095), which has 40 boxy but good value rooms with balconies, at €36 for doubles.

Kalnik

Heading out of Križevci towards Varaždin, there's a turn-off after about 10km leading up towards Kalnik, 9km off the main road. The road climbs up steeply to stop right underneath a fabulous ruined ridge-top fortress. Originally built in the 13th century, it must once have been magnificent, although it's been abandoned since the 17th century.

It's been restored enough to make it safe, and stop further deterioration, and it's well worth scrambling up to the highest point – there are handrails on the dodgy sections. You're only 500m above sea-level here, but you can see for miles – to Medvednica in the southwest, and on a very clear day all the way to Papuk, over 100km away.

Just below the fortress there's a lodge run by the mountaineering association, **Planinarski Dom** (tel: 048 857 003), which has a great terrace, fine food and a few rooms upstairs, at €40 for a double. They also have a nice colour leaflet available with a description (in Croatian, but with English captions) of the nature trail starting from here, as well as detailing several longer walks in the area.

The Podravina

Further northeast of Zagreb, running up to the Drava River and the Hungarian border, is the Podravina, a rich agricultural basin marked by fields of sunflowers and maize. There's not much to bring tourists here, to be honest, though if you're in the region you may be interested in visiting the village of Hlebine, where Croatian naïve art took off in the 1930s and is still going strong today.

The main centre in the region is the busy town of **Koprivnica**, which is on major rail and road routes. The town is nice enough though there's nothing special to see or do here. It does make a good place for a layover, however, as there are a couple of useful and affordable places to stay. The nicer of the two is the 14-room **Bijela Kuča** (tel: 048 240 320), which is close to both the bus and train stations, a ten-minute walk from the town centre. Bigger, boxier and right in the town centre is its sister hotel, the **Podravina** (tel: 048 621 025). Both places have reasonable (and fairly priced) restaurants, and offer double rooms at €66 a night.

From Koprivnica it's about 15km to **Hlebine**, and you should expect to use your own transport or take a taxi, as buses are rare. Ever since a local artist fortuitously discovered the works of the self-taught Ivan Generalić in the local shop, in 1930, Hlebine has been a centre of naïve art, and today there are more than 100 painters and sculptors in the area, continuing the tradition. The **Hlebine Gallery** features a rotating collection of works from the village, but you can always be sure of catching some of the original and most striking pictures by Ivan Generalić – check out the famous Eiffel Tower. Also in Hlebine, but you need to arrange a visit ahead of time (call the tourist office, on 048 836 139), is the **Generalić Gallery**, which features work by Ivan's son, Josip, who still works here, in his sixties, and his grandson, Goran, who has continued in the family tradition.

SAMOBOR AND THE ŽUMBERAK
Southwest of Zagreb, and tucked up against the Slovenian border, is the Žumberak region, a sparsely populated expanse of dense forests, steep hills, and sleepy villages. There isn't much to do in the way of specific sightseeing, and you can't get to most places using public transport – lots of villages don't even have metalled roads to them – but if you do have your own wheels it makes for a lovely region to explore at leisure (especially if you're cycling – see page 90).

The northern part of the Žumberak is mountainous and forested, while further to the south are the beautiful steep vineyards of the Plešivica region.

The obvious gateway to the Žumberak is the pretty town of Samobor, though you can also access it from Karlovac.

Samobor
Less than 20km from downtown Zagreb, Samobor is an attractive little town, with a compact heart set on an elegant, elongated square. A shallow, trout-filled stream is spanned by narrow bridges, and there's little to do in town itself other than soak up the atmosphere and tuck into Samobor's culinary specialities.

Being big on sausages (it has a Salami Festival in April), Samobor also produces excellent local *muštarda* to go with them – you can get nice souvenir jars just off the main square, near the Hotel Livadić, from the Filipec family shop. While you're at it, you should try the local *Bermet* (red wine flavoured with herbs and spices), but try before you buy a whole lot; it's not to all tastes.

As a long-standing day-treat for Zagreb's workers, Samobor has also long capitalised on its ability to produce good cakes, notably the famous *kremšnita* – a mountain of cream filling, sandwiched between two slices of flaky pastry. The recipe published by the tourist board makes it sound all too simple: 'Dress lightly. Throw a sweater over your shoulder. Take a vehicle of some kind. Go to main square of Samobor. Take a seat. Order and enjoy.'

You should definitely try a slice, but my personal favourite is the *rudarska greblica*, which is big on walnuts and not quite so creamy. As its name implies, it comes from the village of Rude, just up the valley toward Plešivica.

Between cakes, you might pay a visit to the **town museum**, housed in local composer Ferdo Livadić's solid town house, at the west end of town. The collection of furniture and pictures is only moderately interesting, but the setting is nice, and the ethnographic section in the annex is good value.

When it comes to working up an appetite for the next *kremšnita*, head up past the church into the woods above town, on the hill called **Anindol**. Take the path to the right which leads to the little **Church of St Anne** in the woods, and branch right again here to reach Samobor's medieval castle, **Stari Grad**. The 13th-century fortress is ruined and overgrown, and none the less atmospheric for that, and there are great views back to town and across the plain towards Zagreb.

More ambitious hiking – but not much more ambitious – is on hand in the **Samobrsko Gorje** mountains immediately to the west of town. Increasingly popular at weekends (it's some of the nearest hiking to Zagreb, and not too demanding), you'll find the well-marked trails almost empty out of season, especially if you're here midweek. Ask at the tourist office (tel: 01 336 0044; fax: 01 336 0050) for more information.

The tourist office also has an excellent cycle route marked out, and a free map with English instructions on it. The circuit's only 24km long, but the first nine of these are all steeply uphill, gaining 450m – unless you're pretty fit you may want to do the route in reverse, which makes the climb at a gentler gradient. The only sad thing is that (at the time of writing) there wasn't anywhere to rent a bike in Samobor.

The town also hosts a huge pre-Lent carnival. It's one of the most popular in the country, attracting hundreds of thousands of visitors, which makes it great fun, but not easy if you're looking for a room. Or indeed some peace and quiet.

Reaching Samobor is simplicity itself – there's a half-hourly bus from Zagreb (hourly on Sundays). There are any number of cafés in town where you can try the famous cakes, but for a sit-down meal you can't go wrong at the **Samoborska Pivnica**, behind the Hotel Livadić, where they serve up all the local specialities, and a particularly large *štrukli*. At Livadićeva 22, west from the main square, and just a tad more upmarket, is the **Medved**, which does especially good sausages.

Finally, you might consider basing yourself in Samobor for visits to Zagreb. The **Hotel Livadić** (tel: 01 336 5850; fax: 01 336 5851) has a beautiful flower-bedecked central courtyard and a dozen utterly charming rooms, with old furniture and good-sized bathrooms, at €65 a night for doubles – a snip compared to almost anything in the city. The restaurant is also excellent.

Another even cheaper option can be found across the river, in the shape of the simple but charming (and newly reopened) **Lavica** (tel: 01 332 4946; fax: 01 336 6611), which has 22 rooms at a bargain €40 a night. The brick-vaulted restaurant – like pretty much everywhere in Samobor – serves up great food.

The Žumberak

There's not much to do or see in the Žumberak itself – beyond enjoying the fine scenery and splendid vistas, and perhaps hiking or biking through the hills – but if you have wheels then there's a good circuit you can do anticlockwise through the region, starting at Samobor, heading round to Karlovac and coming back via Jastrebarsko and the Plešivica vineyards. You need to allow at least two days to see everything, or skip various parts of the itinerary – it's a minimum 200km circuit, with quite long sections on gravel roads. (The circuit works just as well starting in Karlovac, if that's where you're based.)

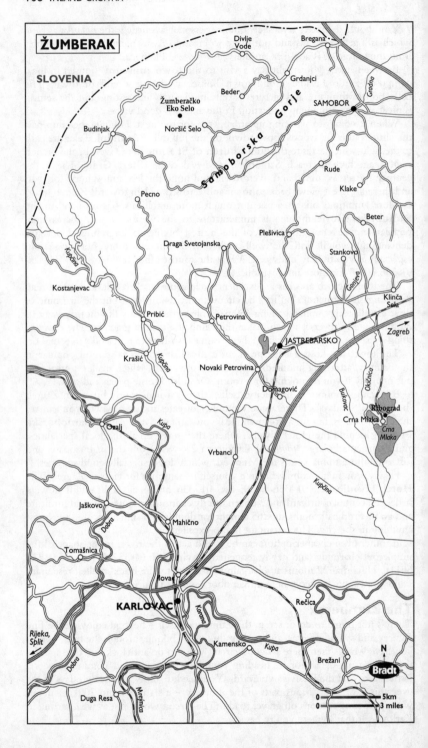

ŽUMBERAK

SLOVENIA

Start by heading due north to Bregana, but turn left before you get whisked into Slovenia. The road then follows the river (the Slovenian border) for about 10km, until you reach **Divlje Vode**, which becomes something of a minor recreation area at weekends. The restaurant here serves excellent local trout.

Žumberačko Eko Selo

Shortly after Divlje Vode, the road forks – take the left-hand fork, heading up to Žumberačko Eko Selo. After a short while the tarmac runs out, and you're on to about 8km of gravel all the way up to the camp, a collection of wooden buildings centred on a biggish restaurant in a valley with a pretty stream running through it (it's just off to the right of the main gravel road, when you get as high as you're going to go).

You can stay up here, in one of the wooden huts (€25 a head) – call ahead or email the Žumberak Nature Park office in Bregana (tel: 01 332 3848; email: pp.zsg@zg.hinet.hr) for more detailed information. You can also book yourself in for horse-riding – there's a stable, which only adds to the thoroughly American-cowboy atmosphere; a Stetson wouldn't be entirely out of place. Even if you don't stay, consider eating – not only is the restaurant first-rate, it's also the last place for a long time ahead.

There's no question that the easiest way onwards is to head back the way you came, but if you're feeling adventurous then press on – at a number of points the network of gravel roads rejoins the tarred road which winds its way around the northern and western sides of the Žumberak. A good sense of direction and the best maps available will help, but are unlikely to prevent you entirely from getting lost up here. Essentially you want to keep heading west and/or south, and don't be afraid to ask smallholders the way to towns on the main road – Kostanjevac, Pribić and Krašić are good names to ask for.

Up here you'll find life going on the way it has for centuries, with tiny villages far, far from the rest of the world, and almost all the work in the small fields still being done by hand.

Pribić

When you rejoin the main road, turn left downhill and wind your way down the tortuous valley to where the land suddenly flattens out, and in no time at all you'll be in Pribić – it's easy to overshoot, so look out for a Byzantine-looking church on the right-hand side of the main road, and park here.

You'd certainly never know it now, but Pribić was once an important Greek Catholic centre. Today all there's left to see is the outside of the church and the doomed 'castle' next door, which is gradually losing its battle with the encroaching vegetation. The church itself is on a tiny islet, reached over a diminutive bridge. The mosaics on the front are still lovely, kneeling angels flanking a Madonna and child amongst stylised lilies. Over the doorway is a fine carved coat-of-arms bracketed by fanciful ropes and tassels. Look more closely and you'll also see some fine sardonic architectural flourishes, in the form of nightmare gargoyles and a couple of carved eagles – which actually look more like cheesed-off parrots.

Krašić

From Pribić it's a short, straight run down to Krašić, the home town of Cardinal Stepinac, and the place where he was kept under house arrest during the final years of his life, after being released from Lepoglava. In front of the church there's a statue of the cardinal, while behind it, in the parish priest's house, his two-room flat has been preserved the way he left it. Ask in the church if nobody's around, and someone will open up the plain, simple rooms for you – there's not much to see, but it's a poignant place all the same. It would be churlish not to leave a donation.

The church itself was rebuilt in 1913, and first impressions of the exterior are misleading – look out for the *Jugendstil* (German art nouveau) touches, with stern female friezes built into the walls. Inside, there's not a whole lot to comment on, though the vaulting is attractive, and the altar is positively understated – by Zagorje baroque standards, anyway.

There's nowhere to stay in Krašić, and – in spite of plenty of cafés – nothing much to eat, either.

Ozalj

From Krašić it's a 10km dog-leg west to Ozalj (another turning that's easy to miss – the main road to Karlovac, which you don't want, goes southeast), where you'll find the best castle in the region.

In a perfect situation, high up above the river Kupa, the medieval settlement here was owned by the Frankopans from 1398, and taken over by the Zrinskis in 1550 – the impressive entrance tower was commissioned by Juraj Zrinski in 1599. During the 18th century, the medieval village was converted into a defensive castle, with the only access being across the drawbridge – the stone bridge you walk across today was built in 1821.

The castle is in the process of being restored, but it's already a wonder, and has everything you'd want in a castle – towers, solid bastions, ramparts, and great views down to the river.

There's not much else to see in Ozalj, but down in the town, by the bridge across the Kupa, have a look at the neo-Gothic building by the water – it's actually a hydro-electric plant, built in 1908 and still operational today.

From Ozalj it's only about 15km to **Karlovac** (see opposite), where you may want to stop and spend the night.

From Karlovac, it's 20km northeast to the one-street town of **Jastrebarsko** (see page 118), which is also the access point for the fish lakes and bird reserve at Crna Mlaka.

Plešivica

The 25km road from Jastrebarsko to Samobor is among the most beautiful in the country, winding its way up into the hills and then down a long, pretty valley through the village of Rude to complete the circuit of the Žumberak.

The route up brings you through the lovely Plešivica wine-growing region, and it's well worth stopping in at one of the dozen or so vineyards for a tasting if you have time (and if you can persuade your designated driver it's a good thing). Make a special effort to sample the local speciality, *Portugizac Plešivica*, a claret-like red, and any of the fresh whites or sparkling wines on offer. The Samobor or Karlovac tourist offices should be able to furnish you with a copy of the useful *Plešivička Vinska Cesta* (Plešivica Wine Tour) leaflet, which helps with navigation.

The countryside round here is delightful. Apart from the vineyards, there are lots of fruit trees in the steep fields, and in the summer every village has hay drying picturesquely on the charming Slovenian-style latticed hay-ricks – designed surely with aesthetics rather than practicality in mind. Wagons and trailers full of brightly coloured beehives are strategically placed to allow the bees access to the best of the local nectar, and romantic hilltop churches crest every horizon.

KARLOVAC

Most people never see more of Karlovac than the big town suburbs and housing blocks on the outskirts as they speed past on the motorway, but dig a little deeper and you'll find a fine provincial old town and two great places to stay.

Karlovac was created from nothing, by the Austro-Hungarians, as a defence against the Turks, with the foundations being laid on July 13 1579. A Renaissance six-pointed star defined the limits of the town, and its moats were kept well supplied with water by the citadel's situation, between the Kupa and Korana rivers.

As the Turkish threat receded, Karlovac grew in size and importance, and became a wealthy and influential provincial capital. Baroque houses and palaces sprang up, and the town walls were pulled down. The shape of the old town is still clearly defined, however, with the moats and earthworks now forming a near-continuous circuit of parks and gardens around the former citadel, or *Zvijezda* (star).

Getting there and around

Getting to Karlovac is easy – it's under an hour from Zagreb, and both buses and trains run pretty much every half hour. There are also good onward connections to Rijeka and Zadar.

The bus station is less than ten minutes southwest of the old town – head up the main north–south axis, Prilaz Vjećeslava Holjevca, and then turn right along Kralja Tomislava, which takes you all the way in. The train station is on the other side of the Kupa River, a kilometre north, also on Prilaz Vjećeslava Holjevca. Just east of the main bridge is the central district where you'll find the Hotel Carlstadt and the tourist office, on Petra Zrinskog, with the old town just behind it, away from the Kupa, to the southeast.

The tourist office (tel/fax: 047 615 115) has good maps and can help you find a private room – there are a handful available, at a little under €25 for doubles.

Where to stay and eat

Opposite the tourist office is the **Hotel Carlstadt** (tel: 047 611 444; fax: 047 611 111; www.carlstadt.hr), which has just expanded its offerings and now has 40 excellent double rooms, with full facilities, at €50 a night, including a substantial buffet breakfast. It's exceptionally good value, and with such good transport connections it's a viable alternative to staying in the capital.

You can also stay at the **Korana Srakovčić** (tel: 047 609 090; fax: 047 609 091; www.hotelkorana.hr), a newly opened four-star hotel in a gracious building right on the banks of the river Korana. Situated in a lovely park, just 15 minutes' walk southeast of town, the hotel has 15 rooms, which go for €116–125 a night – the more expensive rooms have balconies.

Karlovac has plenty of places to eat, but you can't beat **Tiffany's**, between the river and Petra Zrinskog, for pizza – that's all they sell, and they know exactly what to do. Wash it down with Karlovac's most famous product, **Karlovačko Pivo**.

What to see

In the centre of the old town is the main square, Trg Bana Jelačića, which is still rather forlorn and abandoned, following the damage sustained in the 1991 war – most of the town's action is now to be found towards the Kupa River, between the two bridges, on Petra Zrinskog. Persevere, however, and pay a visit to the **Franciscan Monastery and Holy Trinity Church**, on the corner of the square – it has fine baroque altars and a series of dramatic, neck-cricking 18th-century frescos across the ceiling.

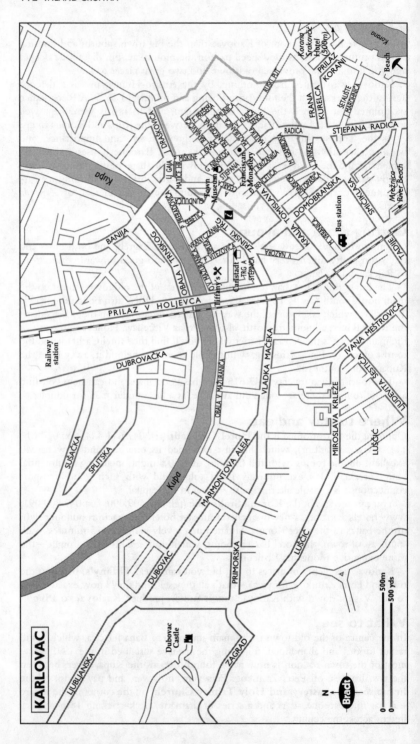

KARLOVAC

Bradt

N

0   500m
0   500 yds

Korana
Korana
Srakovčić
Hotel
(300m)
PRILAZ
KORANI
Beach
RIJEČKI PUT
FRANA
KURELCA
ŠETALIŠTE
MARCINECA
RADIĆA
STJEPANA RADIĆA
Franciscan
Monastery
B BRENCETICA
IM GRMBONJA
TONKE
A
D BRENCETICA
SMIČIKLASA
TADIJE
Mrežnica
River Beach
Kupa
RADIĆA I DRAŠKOVIĆA
LI GAJA
MATICE HR
IVI MIŠKINE
KV PRERADOVIĆA
F PREBORA
KV TOMLINICA
IVI HRVATINA
KLAIĆA
KV KAŠA
KV KVATERNIKA
KV FRANA KV KAŠA
IV TKALCA
IV FRANE
MLINSKOG
STJEPANA
B BENCETICA
A
TRG A
STJEPANA
GUNDULIĆA
P PREBORAVIĆA
P SERBETIČA
OV MAŽURANIĆA
Town
Museum
Carlstadt
Tiffany's
ZRINSKI TRG
RADOSLAVIĆA
TRANZINKA
KOZOVIĆA
V NAZORA
TINKA
TRAKALA TOMISLAVA
DOMOBRANSKA
ARALA TOMISLAVA
V MRENICA
Bus station
BANIJA
OBALA I TRNSKOG
KUPA
PRILAZ V HOLJEVCA
Railway
station
DUBROVAČKA
OBALA V MAŽURANICA
VLADKA MAČEKA
IVANA MEŠTROVIĆA
LJUDEVITA ŠESTIĆA
LUŠČIĆ
MIROSLAVA KRLEŽE
MIROSLAVA KRLEŽE
SUŠAČKA
SPLITSKA
Kupa
MARMONTOVA ALEJA
PRIMORSKA
LUŠČIĆ
LUŠČIĆ
DUBOVAC
LJUBLJANSKA
Dubovac
Castle
ZAGRAD

A block towards the river, on the elegant Trg Strossmayer, you'll find the **town museum** (Gradski Muzej) – at least until it finds its way into one of the buildings on the main square, which is the plan. It's a fascinating collection of everything from fossils to Roman fragments to local art to peasant costumes to civic souvenirs – it's only a pity that the captions are in Croatian only, which can make it a bit hard to follow.

In the middle of the collection there's a scale model of how Karlovac used to look, and there are some old pictures of other castles in the Žumberak region. There are also some great photographs of people hauling grain barges along the river, along with the harnesses they used to do it – when the railway came along, Karlovac lost one of its main sources of wealth.

You'll notice a couple of works by the local artist Vjekoslav Karas (1821–58) – if you're interested in seeing more, there's a whole gallery of his work in an annex in the new town. Staff at the museum will be happy to point you in the right direction, and may even accompany you there.

Recognised for his ready talent with a brush, Karas was sent to Florence in 1838 to study, and spent a decade in Italy perfecting his craft before returning home to his native Karlovac. Unfortunately many of his paintings have been lost, and – given that he never signed his work, and experimented with many different styles – there's a big problem of attribution. Some of the works are way ahead of their time, wonderfully insightful portraits which are practically modernist, while others are embarrassingly amateurish, perhaps reflecting Karas's poor state of mental health. After a failed suicide attempt in Đakovo, where he was the guest of Bishop Strossmayer (a keen art collector), Karas successfully drowned himself in the Korana River at Karlovac, aged just 37.

The last room of the museum features an excellent collection of peasant costumes and crafts, from pottery and weaving to embroidery and basket-work.

Before you leave the old town, make time if you can for a circuit of the **old citadel** – it's a pleasant, meditative 30–40-minute walk.

If you have time, it's also worth visiting the **Dubovac Castle**, up on the hill 2km west of town (it's a short drive or a half-hour walk). You used to be able to stay here, in one of the rooms giving on to the romantic three-tiered medieval courtyard, but these days you can only get inside when the intermittent restaurant is open – but there are great views over the town from the grassy knoll outside, even if it's closed. The castle was originally built in the 13th century, and was a Frankopan stronghold in the 15th century. The French added crenellations in the early 19th century to make it look more appealingly medieval (and there's a picture in the town museum of what this looked like) – but fortunately during the 20th century the castle recovered its genuinely medieval look.

If you're hot and bothered – and it can be baking here – head down to the Korana River to the beach, just ten minutes from the old town centre. Less busy beaches can be found on the Mrežnica River, 3km south of town.

South of Karlovac – Slunj and the Rastoke Mills

About 50km south of Karlovac, and 20km short of the Plitvice Lakes, is the former Austro-Hungarian garrison town of Slunj. Badly damaged during the war of the 1990s, the town's churches at least have now been fully restored, along with the main reason for coming here, the Rastoke Mills. Built to take advantage of the waterfalls where the Slunjčica River drops into the Korana River, some of the watermills are now back in working order and a stroll around them is a delight. If you want to swim make sure you choose the Korana River, not the Slunjčica – the former warms up to a balmy 28°C in summer, while the latter never rises above a chilly 14°C. If its 'first-class trouts' you're fishing for, however, then the Slunjčica is your man.

PLITVICE LAKES NATIONAL PARK

Croatia's best-known and most-visited natural attraction – and a UNESCO World Heritage site since 1979 – is the Plitvice Lakes National Park (tel: 053 751 015/000). Covering a total of nearly 300km², the prize here is a series of 16 lakes, falling from one to the next in a series of gushing waterfalls. The lakes are set in deep forests still populated by bears, wolves and wild boar, and are all the more unusual for being found in the middle of a typically dry karst region, where surface water is extremely rare.

The national park has been very carefully exploited, and although it can get busy – 600,000 people come annually, averaging around 4,000 people a day in the summer months – the crowds are rarely intolerable. Traffic is encouraged round one-way systems to avoid congestion, and the routes are often carried along attractive wooden walkways serving the dual purpose of avoiding erosion and allowing people to walk over, under, across and alongside the waterfalls, and around the lakes.

The whole park ranges in altitude from 380m to 1,280m, but the lakes are all situated between 502m and 637m, with the largest single waterfall (Veliki Slap) being nearly 70m tall. The combination of running water and altitude makes the park wonderfully refreshing almost all through the summer, although it can be cold and gloomy – not to mention frozen solid – in winter. April and October are the best times to visit – the former with the water flow increased by melting snows, and the latter with the deciduous woods enriched with fabulous autumn colours.

Plitvice was occupied by the Serbs from 1991 to 1995, and the staff and management became refugees. On their return, they found the park mercifully undamaged ecologically, although the park offices and the hotels were totally unusable. Since then, the hotels and other facilities have been entirely rebuilt, and the park today is better than ever.

Getting there

Plitvice is situated a little over half way down the main road from Zagreb to Zadar. Regular buses run from both, and also up from Split. The park has two entrances, wittily called Ulaz 1 and Ulaz 2.

In theory Ulaz 1 (the northern entrance) serves the lower lakes, while Ulaz 2 (the southern entrance) is the access point for the upper ones, but for most people Ulaz 2 is the more useful. It's here that you'll find most of the infrastructure, including the three hotels, the tourist office with access to private accommodation, a post office, a shop and a self-service restaurant – and it's in fact within easy reach of both the upper and lower lakes.

If you don't have your own transport, then *leaving* the park may be more difficult than arriving. Regular buses pass through on their way to Zadar, Zagreb and Split, but if these are full, or the driver doesn't like the cut of your jib, they have a habit of cruising right on past.

Testimony to this is borne out by the graffiti which builds up over the season in the bus shelter at Ulaz 2, before being removed each winter. In the unlikely event you won't have time to read some for yourself, here's a selection I culled while waiting myself:

> The only natural wonder we saw was the fog and the rain – still waiting at 2.30 for the 1.40 bus.

> It takes two hours to get to Plitvice but two days to get out.

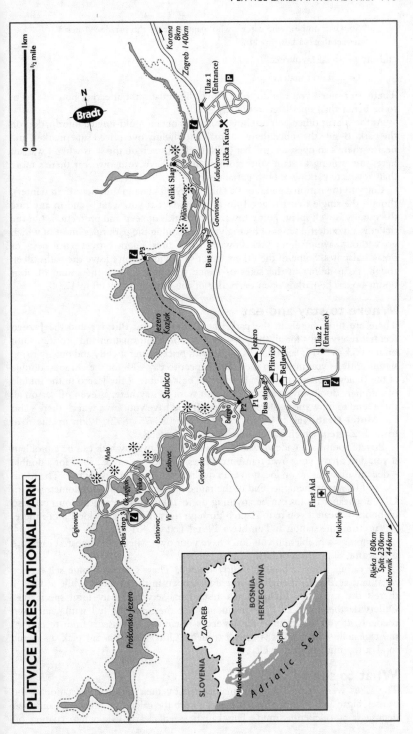

PLITVICE LAKES NATIONAL PARK

Korana 8km
Zagreb 140km

Ulaz 1 (Entrance)

Lička Kuća

Kaluđerovac

Veliki Slap
Milanovac
Gavanovac

Bus stop

Jezero
Kozjac

Stubica

Jezero

Plitvice

Bellevue

Ulaz 2 (Entrance)

Bus stop 2

P1

P2

Burgeti

Galovac

Grodinsko

Vir

Batinovac

Malo

Okrugljak

Ciginovac

Batinovac

Bus stop 3

Prošćansko Jezero

First Aid

Mukinje

Rijeka 180km
Split 230km
Dubrovnik 446km

1km
½ mile

SLOVENIA
ZAGREB
BOSNIA-HERZEGOVINA
Plitvice Lakes
Split
Adriatic Sea

> So what, no bus, who cares – who wants to leave this paradise? Later: I
> retract that – a bus, any bus!

and my personal favourite,

> Great tourist strategy!

There isn't much you can do to improve this situation, but earlier buses do seem to be better than ones later in the day.

At the tourist office you can buy a map and obtain multi-lingual information on the park. Beside the office there's a small and slightly overpriced supermarket, and nearby there's an open-air grill bar (with trick bitumen on the seats when I was last here, just waiting to stain your clothes). If you have your own car there's more than adequate parking at both entrances.

Entry to the national park costs a fairly hefty 90 kuna in summer (45 in winter), though the single ticket is good for as many days as you want – and in any case the money is well spent, going towards the park's upkeep and protection. On the ticket is a wonderful series of hieroglyphs explaining the park rules, most of which go without saying: don't pick flowers, make fires, engrave trees, steal nests or break stalactites. Some of the others aren't so obvious: don't leave the paths, sleep rough, go paddling in the lakes or dance wildly around to the sound of your boom-box. The park is open every day of the year, from 09.00 to 17.00.

Where to stay and eat

There are three hotels in the park, the **Bellevue**, the **Plitvice** and the **Jezero** (central reservations for all three, as well as tourist information and private rooms on tel: 053 751 015; fax: 053 751 013), with prices rising slightly and quality rising significantly as you move up the scale. Expect to pay €48 for the cheapest double at the Bellevue off season, or €104 for the best double at the Jezero in the middle of summer. Book way, way ahead, if you want to stay here, as even off season all three tend to draw the conference crowd. If you have your own wheels there's also the **Motel Grabovac** (tel: 053 751 999; fax: 053 751 892), 12km up the road towards Zagreb, which has doubles in season for €58.

Private rooms are widely available, but often far away, which can be a problem if you don't have your own transport. Prices – expect to pay €25–40 for a double – depend much more on location than quality, which is universally fine. The room I stayed in was at the upper end of the range but only a couple of kilometres from Ulaz 2; cheaper rooms can be anything up to 15km away. Private rooms can also be booked ahead if you're in Zagreb through the national park's local office there, just up from the station at Tomislava 19 (tel/fax: 01 461 3586).

Camping's a problem if you don't have your own wheels – the nearest campsite is **Korana**, 8km north of Ulaz 1.

For eating, your options are fairly limited. There's a good-value self-service restaurant at Ulaz 2, though it's not always open in the evening, while at Ulaz 1 there's the capacious **Lička Kuća** restaurant, serving meaty local specialities. Otherwise the hotels all have restaurants but they may be full with their own residents. If you do get in at the **Jezero's** restaurant, downstairs from reception, the tagliatelle with truffles is truly excellent. Otherwise you can pick up picnic food at the mini-market at Ulaz 2.

What to see

The lakes were created and are maintained by their unusual vegetation – the mosses, algae and other freshwater plants absorb the calcium in the water and then deposit it as calciferous mud. This can be seen clearly as a white coating on submerged tree trunks and roots in the smaller lakes. The water flow causes this calciferous mud to be carried to the lips of the lakes, and deposited there, eventually solidifying as travertine (*tufa*), with the long-term effect that the whole lake system is gradually gaining altitude.

In the short term, the effect is that lots of people are keen to come and see Plitvice, and life has been organised so that this is as easy as possible – to the extent that there's a panoramic train-ride, a couple of boats on one of the largest lakes, and a series of itineraries from one to ten hours long which take in the most scenic parts of the park.

After the initial impression of being almost *too* looked after has worn off it tends to be replaced by something akin to euphoria – the lakes really are beautiful, after all, and you'd have to be very determined not to be impressed by that much moving water. You can even begin to see why people who live in these conditions start believing in water gods.

Each of the lakes seems to be a different colour, ranging from turquoise to emerald through every blue and green you could imagine. In places the lakes seem as still and reflective as a cathedral, elsewhere they run away fast, frothing through steep gullies and shooting out from fissures in the rock. The magical noise of falling water drowns out even the shrillest of small children. On the less frequented paths it's easy to imagine the bears and wolves, as you walk across a deeply shaded bed of leaves, crunching underfoot.

In a perfect world you'd have at least two full days (ie: three nights) to explore the whole park, but you can get a good impression of it all in a single day. Even if you're on an excursion, up from the coast or down from Zagreb, and you have only a couple of hours here, you won't regret it.

Apart from the marked itineraries, which lead you round the best-known sights, there are many other paths open to the public in the national park, though access to them is quietly discouraged by the park management, as there have been incidents of people despoiling nature off the beaten track. If you are wandering away from the marked trails, be ecologically friendly, and stay on the paths.

If you're doing any serious walking – or even if you're just interested – the park publishes an excellent 1:50,000 scale map of the area, including all the footpaths, with a 1:25,000 scale birds-eye view of the lakes themselves on the reverse, along with all sorts of useful information about the lakes' relative altitudes etc. With the aid of this you can easily find a couple of days' walking in the area, none of which is too strenuous.

It's inadvisable, however, to be in the wilds after nightfall – the bears and wolves avoid the main paths and the crowds, but they do patrol at night. The wolves are normally only seen in winter, but a hungry bear, or one which thinks you're too close to its cubs, may be inquisitive.

There have been no incidents in recent years involving tourists, but it was here, on April 16 1988 (a few days before my first ever visit to the lakes), that a national park warden was killed by a bear. The bear was apparently confused by a storm, and anxious to protect its cub, when it was surprised by the unfortunate warden. Being a Serb, he could probably be counted as the first victim in the Serbo-Croat war, which actually took off here in Plitvice, when the Serbs took over the management offices in March 1991.

Fortunately, the warden is the only recorded human fatality from a Croatian bear in more than 50 years, but local people remain understandably cautious, and discourage the idea of camping out in the woods (which is illegal, anyway). Walk in the daytime and stay on the paths marked on the maps and you'll be quite safe. There are absolutely no wild animals round here which would attack in the daytime unless seriously provoked.

If you're in Plitvice on the last Sunday of May there's a folk wedding held by Veliki Slap. This was once no doubt a highly traditional affair, but now has the air of being staged for the tourists. Nonetheless, even the most cynical visitor should be impressed by the traditional dress, the falling water all but drowning out the songs, and the folk dancing and festivities held afterwards.

JASTREBARSKO AND THE TUROPOLJE

Half way between Zagreb and Karlovac, the town of Jastrebarsko gives access to the Plešivica vineyards to the north (see page 110), while to the south there's an excellent ornithological reserve, at Crna Mlaka. Further east you'll find the Turopolje, a region characterised by old villages and wooden houses and churches, bordered by the Vukomeričke Gorice hills to the west, the meandering Sava to the east, and bracketed by Zagreb to the northwest and Sisak to the southeast.

Exploring the region's not really possible without your own transport, although you can get to Jastrebarsko easily enough, and Velika Mlaka and Velika Gorica in the Turopolje are on Zagreb bus route #268.

Jastrebarsko and Crna Mlaka

Jastrebarsko itself is a bit of a commercial one-street town, spread out along the main road from Zagreb to Karlovac. It's worth checking in at the tourist office (tel: 01 628 1115; fax: 01 628 4660), across the street from the bus station, for maps and details of the local vineyards, as well as the particulars of a growing number of agro-tourism offerings.

If you're stuck in town there's a moderately interesting **town museum**, and there's a pleasant park (walk west down Zrinsko Frankopanska, and across the stream) around the decaying fortress-like **Erdödy Castle**, built in the 16th century and apparently unmaintained ever since. There's a hotel in town, the **Jaska** (tel: 01 628 1044; fax: 01 628 3580), with functional doubles at €60.

Southeast, across the motorway, is **Crna Mlaka** (literally Black Marsh). The area was originally conceived as a vast fish farm by the Austro-Hungarians at the end of the 19th century, complete with a narrow-gauge railway running up to join the main line to Zagreb, and a mansion, endearingly named **Ribograd** ('fish city'). The railway's long disused, and Ribograd's falling apart, but Crna Mlaka lives on as a bird sanctuary, and it's now home to all sorts of rare and endangered species, including herons in abundance, and highly secretive black storks, who unlike their white compatriots prefer to stay in the woods, well away from people.

To reach Crna Mlaka, turn left immediately after paying the toll off the motorway (or right immediately before reaching it, if you're coming from Jastrebarsko), and drive 7km down gravel tracks (turn left after 5km, at the sign saying '*IHOR Crna Mlaka*'), keeping your eyes peeled for herons. There's a nice restaurant to greet you, specialising unsurprisingly in freshwater fish, and endless unmarked gravel tracks which make for pleasant, undisturbed walking around the huge ponds.

The Turopolje

The region southeast of Zagreb along the west bank of the Sava is known as the Turopolje, and is worth passing through on your way to Lonjsko Polje (see opposite) – once Zagreb's suburbs have petered out, you'll find old villages and timber churches, and wooden staircases leading up the outside of houses to the upper quarters.

Stop in at the **Velika Gorica** tourist information office (tel/fax: 01 622 2378) if you're interested in specific sights – they'll give you directions to locally famous wooden churches, etc, which can otherwise be hard to find. If you see only one, make it **St Barbara's**, incongruous amongst the suburban houses of **Velika Mlaka**. The all-wooden church was originally built in 1642, and the decorative work inside covers every available surface.

Before leaving Velika Gorica, stop in at the **Museum of the Turopolje**, an interesting ethnographic collection housed in a nice 18th-century arcaded building. If you have to stay then your only option is the businesslike **Bijela Ruža** (tel: 01 622 1358; fax: 01 637 0977), which has 25 €50 doubles.

At the other end of the Turopolje – and marked by the first bridge across the Sava since Zagreb – is the industrial town of **Sisak**. The solid medieval castle on the river doesn't entirely compensate for the huge oil refinery here, or the complete absence of road directions. There is however a good accommodation option, the five-storey **Panonija** (tel: 044 515 600; fax: 044 515 601), which is three blocks back from the river and five minutes south of the bus and train stations, with spacious doubles at €53–68.

Sisak is also the northern gateway to the Lonjsko Polje.

LONJSKO POLJE

Downstream from Sisak, the river Sava meanders slowly through the great marshy swamplands of the Lonjsko Polje. Prone to frequent flooding (the Sava can rise by up to 10m) and full of fish, the area is hugely popular with migrating birds, and especially with storks. The reedy shores of the ox-bow lakes make for excellent nesting grounds for wading birds such as white egrets, grey herons and spoonbills.

Spotted Turopolje pigs root through the flooded oak forests, while dark, chunky Posavina horses – protected, and seen only in this region – graze in the summer pastures. Rustic villages preserve traditional oak houses, with barns on the ground floor and external wooden stairs leading to the living accommodation upstairs. It's a rare chance to see a landscape which was once common across central Europe.

On top of many of the houses in the area, and sometimes on platforms on telegraph poles, you'll see big, tatty storks' nests, and (if you're here between April and August) plenty of big, tatty storks, too. They're most endearing. The storks arrive here in spring, and lay three to five eggs per couple, with both parents sharing the month-long incubation duty. The chicks then spend around two months in the nest, and if you're here in May or June you'll see lots of activity going on, with the young growing fast and permanently hungry, and one of the parents always on the move, looking for food.

During August and September, the storks ship out, using the eastern migration path through Turkey and the Middle East, and then along the Nile to central Africa, with some even ending up in South Africa every year.

The Lonjsko Polje was declared a nature park in 1990, but you wouldn't necessarily know it – apart from the uninformative sign at the park's border. The park headquarters claims to be in Jasenovac, but it most definitely isn't, and though there's an information point of sorts in the main stork village, Čigoć, at number 26, on both times I visited it was firmly closed. The problem seems to be one of understaffing, but there is someone you can speak to on the phone (tel/fax: 044 672 080) for more information.

Fortunately, most visitors will be content enough to drive along the pretty 70km road, most of which is now tarred, which runs through the park from Sisak to Jasenovac – public transport's not really an option. The villages along here are among the prettiest in the region, and all have storks in greater or fewer numbers, along with yards full of ducks, chickens, bantams and the occasional turkey. Many of the older houses are collapsing in on themselves, but a good number have been

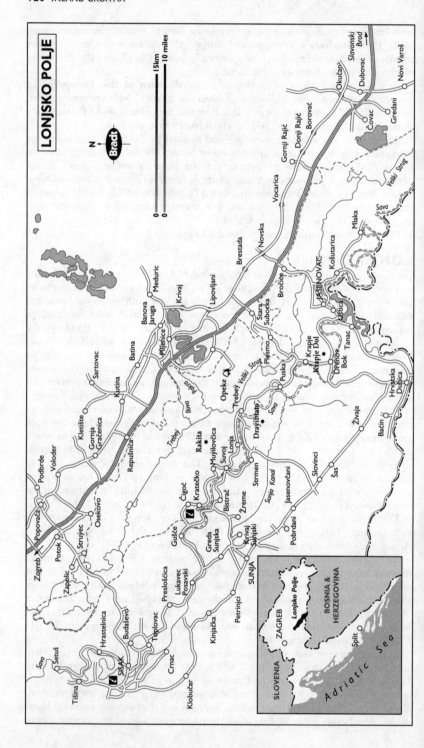

restored as weekenders. If it weren't for the total lack of accommodation, it would make for the perfect cycle ride.

From Sisak it's 30km to Čigoć, via the single-street villages of Topolovac, Prelošćica, Lukavec Posavski and Gušće. After Čigoć it's another 40km on to Jasenovac, passing through Kratečko, Možilovčica, Suvoj, Lonja, Trebez, Puška, Krapje and Drenov Bok on the way. There are a handful of places where you can sometimes eat, though you definitely shouldn't count on it.

More serious birdwatchers should contact the park office in advance (if they can – the staff are even more elusive than the black stork), as there are several special ornithological reserves, protecting some 236 species of bird.

If you're in the area (or just driving along the *autocesta* east of Zagreb) it's well worth stopping in at the 18th-century church of **Our Lady of the Snows**, in the otherwise unremarkable town of **Kutina** – though there is an adequate hotel, the **Kutina** (tel: 044 692 400; fax: 044 684 729), with doubles from €54–74.

The plain, simple exterior of the church hides a plain, simple interior. No, of course it doesn't. Inside, it's wildly over-decorated, with stucco, *putti*, plaster saints, carved pilasters, gilt, medallions, *trompe l'oeil*, the whole bit. The main altar, entirely filling the sanctuary, is practically unwatchable.

JASENOVAC

Where the Sava joins the Bosnian border, you'll find what must be the saddest town in Croatia. Famous only for having been the site of Croatia's worst concentration camp during World War II, Jasenovac was then fought over by both sides in the 1990s war.

Today the town is still half-abandoned and has a moderately desperate air. Many of the bombed-out buildings have yet to be properly repaired, and it looks as if Jasenovac must be way down on someone's agenda of places to fix up. With the **Hotel Sava** still in ruins, there's nowhere to stay (not, frankly, that you'd want to) and nothing to do. You could eat at the one **Kod Ribica** *gostionica*, however, which seems to attract Bosnians from across the border and does a pretty mean fish stew, *Fiš Paprikas*.

The main – in fact the only – reason to visit Jasenovac is to see the site of the former concentration camp. When I was here in 2002, it looked as if Croatia would rather forget the camp altogether. There were no signs to the memorial centre, and no sign even that it was ever opened up any more. Peering through the windows you could see a small collection of photographs and uniforms, but little else.

How pleased I was, then, in the summer of 2004, to find scores of people working on tidying up the area, mowing grass, strimming, and fixing the path out to the memorial. The visitor centre wasn't open, but it was at least being renovated. Obviously there's been a political decision to face up to the past and honour the tens of thousands who died here – and that can only be a good thing.

The main memorial is a dramatic concrete sculpture in the shape of an enormous flower. The path to it is made of old railway sleepers, and on the way you'll find a brass map showing where the huts once stood. There's also a poignant train and cattle wagons (a gift from the Slovenian railway company), like the ones which would have brought prisoners here in the 1940s.

POŽEGA

Set in pretty countryside 175km east of Zagreb (35km from the Nova Gradiska exit off the *autocesta*), the town of Požega makes a great overnight stop if you're heading east, and is within striking distance of the Papuk Nature Park. Under

Turkish occupation from 1537 to 1691, it became thoroughly baroque during the 18th century and still has an attractive old town, centred on the elongated triangular main square, Trg Svetog Trojstva.

On the south side of the square there are two churches, separated by the huge pale-grey wedding-cake frontage of the Franciscan monastery, while the north side is made up of a lovely row of ochre-yellow arcaded houses. In the middle of the square is a baroque **Plague Column** (being restored at the time of writing) from the middle of the 18th century which apparently cost – according to the inscription – the princely sum of 300 forints and 2,000 eggs.

A block away to the east is the **Church of St Teresa**, which became the town's cathedral in 1997 on the creation of the diocese. It has a beautiful, freshly restored front, all pale yellow with decorative mustard-icing swirls. The lower baroque capitals are topped with winged angels, while those higher up are crowned with formalised stone vases, the whole leading up to an elegant clocktower. Inside there's a big baroque altarpiece and choir, and dark paintings everywhere.

Opposite the church entrance, in the small park, there's a fine, soldierly statue of Fra Luka Ibrišimović Sokol, who apparently single-handedly smote the Turks here in 1689, although he was nearly 70 at the time.

Finally, head north to where the road intersects with Kamenita Vrata (literally Stone Gates), and you'll find a new brick-built spiral memorial to the (mostly young) men who lost their lives here during the war of the early '90s. Each of the 102 victims has a plaque at eye-level, and it's heart-rending to read their names and dates.

Like most towns in Slavonia, Požega livens things up with plenty of festivals. Starting the spring off with a bang – literally – is the annual show of cannons and mortars on March 12, St Gregory's Day, which also features mortar fire in Požega's vineyards, to symbolise the routing of the Turks. In May you can choose between the National Dog Show or the unusual festival of Croatian one-minute films held here, and a month later there are contests to see who can cook up the best fish stews and spicy *kulen* sausages. In September the town hosts the 'Golden Strings of Slavonia' festival, which brings in crowds from miles around. Contact the tourist office (tel: 034 274 900; fax: 034 274 901) in the arcades on the main square for more details.

Požega is on a branch line of the rail network, with eight trains a day coming up from the junction with the main line to Slavonski Brod (change at Nova Kapela-Batrina), and is also well served by buses. The bus and train stations are both northeast of the centre of town – head straight down Stjepan Radića to the main square. There are a number of small pensions in Požega, with the nicest and best located being the **Vila Stanišić** (tel: 034 312 168; fax: 034 272 608) on Franje Tuđmana. Head north up the main pedestrian street, which turns into Kamenita Vrata, then turn right and it's on the right, just after the first intersection. The place consists of eight plain but clean rooms above the restaurant; doubles go for around €40 a night. The other option is the town's only official hotel, the **Grgin Dol** (tel: 034 273 222; fax: 034 274 424), east of the main square a few hundred metres, and then signed south, just up the hill. It's pretty run-down, to be honest, and they would have done a lot better spending money on fixing up the infrastructure rather than putting satellite TV in every room – in this author's humble opinion. The rooms are spacious enough, however, and many have balconies. Doubles go for €57 a night, including an astoundingly greasy yet tasty cooked breakfast. For eating and drinking you'll find heaps of cheap and cheerful places in the pedestrianised streets just north of the main square; the **Zrinski pizza bar** is a perennial favourite.

PAPUK NATURE PARK

The Papuk Nature Park covers the hills about 15km north of Požega, and rises from the plain up to nearly 1,000m. There's nothing especially dramatic or spectacular about it, but the walking up here is lovely, through deep deciduous woods and along clear, burbling brooks.

The park was only designated in 1999, so there's not much in the way of infrastructure in place yet, though there are two small park offices, one in Velika (tel: 034 313 030; fax: 034 313 027), 12km north of Požega, and the other over the hill, on the northwestern side of the park, in Voćin (tel/fax: 033 565 296). Whichever one you call first, you're likely to be asked to speak to the other, but they're very friendly and helpful when you finally get through.

The park acts as a watershed for numerous refreshing streams which flow down to the Drava to the north and the Sava to the south, and has lots of well-marked trails through the beech and oak woods. None of the hiking is especially challenging, and the fairly dense forest cover means that spectacular views are few and far between, but it's nonetheless one of the pleasantest places in Slavonia. The flora is exceptional (with around 1,500 species) and there's a 33m waterfall hidden deep in the woods. Geological curiosities include rock columns which were thrown up millions of years ago during volcanic disturbances, and there are even three ruined castles you can clamber up to.

As you come up through Velika from Požega, the road forks right and leads up to thermal baths, which are extremely popular on hot summer weekends with the locals. Above here, on the last stretch of tarred road, there are some lovely picnic and barbecue spots in the small meadows along the river, and even a couple of small grill restaurants. It's a charming place, though there's no obvious public transport which would get you here.

SLAVONSKI BROD

Heading east into Slavonia, especially on public transport, you're likely to pass through Slavonski Brod, as it's a major transport hub. There's no particular reason to break your journey here, however, unless you've come specially for the *Brodsko Kolo*, in June, which is arguably Slavonia's (and some would argue Croatia's) best folk festival. On the other hand, if you have a couple of hours between buses or trains, there are things to see.

Until 1891, Slavonski Brod was a military town, but during the 20th century it became an important staging post for trade and industry, both on the Sava, and across the river into Bosnia & Herzegovina. Today, there's still not a great deal of traffic across the bridge to Bosanski Brod (called Srpski Brod by the mainly Serbian population on that side of the Sava), and the remaining shell-scarred Austro-Hungarian buildings on the Croatian side continue to bear witness to the animosity between the two communities during the war in 1992.

From the bus or train stations, head south down Vukovarska towards the river, 15 minutes away on foot. On the left you'll pass the large grassy park which was the essence of the town for centuries – there's not a whole lot of the ruined **fortress** (*trđava*) left now, however, but you can get an idea of the size and scale of the place from the earthworks and the crumbling, overgrown brick walls.

Southeast of the fortress, on the other side of Vukovarska is the pedestrianised main square, Trg Mažuranić, which gives on to the river. Here you'll find a number of shops, banks and café terraces but not a whole lot else. A block north, on Trg Pobjede, the tourist information office (tel/fax: 035 447 721) on the right-hand side will be able to help you with accommodation if you want to stay over – there's currently no proper hotel in town, but there are a number of small (if

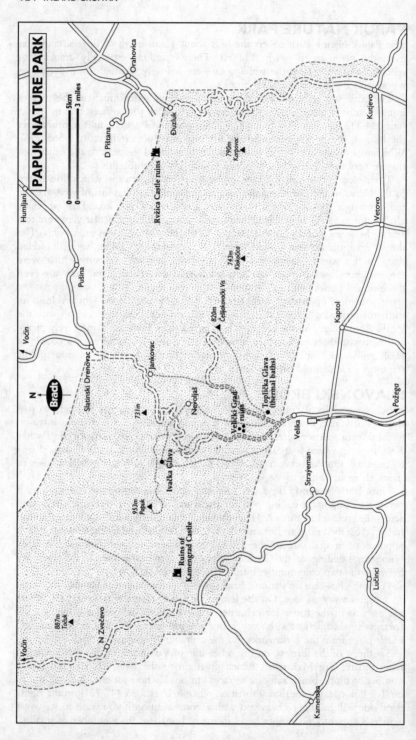

somewhat functional) pensions available. For eateries, the **Zvonimir**, just west of the main square and almost on the river, serves up good local fish dishes at a reasonable price, though don't expect anything sophisticated like an English-language menu. For decent pizza, try the cheerful faux-rustic simplicity of **Mama Mia**, on Ante Starčićeva, heading east out of Trg Mažuranić.

Along the river from the main square is Slavonski Brod's only other main attraction, the 18th-century **Franciscan monastery**, which was the religious and cultural heart of the town when it was a garrison. The church is nothing special, but the baroque cloisters are lovely, with the monks' cells overlooking the garden in the middle, an oasis of tranquillity.

During June, the town hosts the *Brodsko Kolo*, Croatia's oldest folk dance festival, which also features various horse-drawn cart and carriage contests, lots of traditional costumes, a big folk parade, and plenty of eating and drinking. The tourist office has all the details.

ĐAKOVO

The town of Đakovo lies 50km northeast of Slavonski Brod and 35km south of Osijek. With an inspired, twin-spired cathedral and excellent local food and drink, it makes a near-perfect Slavonian stopover – assuming, of course, you don't crash your car here, like I did (before, not after, the gourmet lunch, I might add).

Whichever way you come into town, the fantastic red-brick neo-romanesque **Cathedral of St Peter** stands out for miles. Commissioned by Bishop Strossmayer – Đakovo was his see – it was built between 1866 and 1882, and features a wealth of attractive minimalist detail amongst the brickwork. The 84m twin towers are topped with small spires, while from the centre of the church rises a fine 54m cupola.

Inside, it's a glorious, spacious building, with fluted columns, romanesque arches, and high ceilings. The upper sides of the nave feature almost pre-Raphaelite biblical frescos – the first scene on the left shows Adam and Eve, with Adam stolen shamelessly from the roof of the Sistine Chapel, and Eve a passable copy of Botticelli's *Venus*. The ceilings, with gold stars on a deep blue background, wouldn't look out of place in a Tuscan cathedral, while the walls of the apses and sanctuary are decorated with startlingly realistic *trompe l'oeil* curtains. The whole is quite delightful.

Underground there's a large crypt, with Strossmayer's tomb, but it's rarely open. If you're a Strossmayer completist, you'll also want to visit the **Strossmayer Museum**, across the street from the cathedral, on the corner of the pedestrian zone, where you'll find the bishop's letters and other personal items, but it really is for fanatics only.

At the far end of the pedestrian street – full of cafés, bars and ice-cream parlours spilling out on to the pavement – is **All Saints Church**, which was the town's main mosque (Đakovo was occupied by the Turks from 1536 to 1678) until the plain baroque façade was slapped on in the 19th century.

Đakovo's main annual event is the *Đakovački Vezovi* (meaning 'Đakovo embroidery') at the beginning of July, which features lots of traditional costumes (and embroidery), folk singing and dancing, and parades of the traditional wedding wagons, which are a whole lot of fun. Concerts are put on in the cathedral, while at the race course you'll also get the chance to see competitive trap-and-wagon driving, with elegant pure-bred Lippizaners strutting their stuff – Lippizaner horses have been bred in and around Đakovo since 1506. Book way, way ahead if you want to be there.

If you want to see Lippizaners, there's a stable on the edge of town, 15 minutes due east down Matije Gupica from the cathedral. Ask politely and you may be allowed in to see the horses, or watch them at their morning training sessions. Đakovo is well connected with other towns in the region by bus and train. The bus station is two blocks east of the cathedral, while the train station is 20 minutes northeast of the centre – walk down Kralja Tomislava until you reach the pedestrian zone. Buses come in every half hour or so from Osijek and Slavonski Brod, while trains run to both towns six times a day (for Slavonski Brod change at Strizivojna Vrpolje). The tourist office (tel/fax: 031 812 319) is opposite All Saints Church, on Kralja Tomislava.

There's only one hotel actually in town, the **Croatia-Turist** (tel: 031 813 391; fax: 031 814 063), five minutes south of the cathedral, on the road out towards Slavonski Brod. It's a great place, with a dozen rooms (at a very reasonable €40) above a fabulous restaurant of many separate dining areas, which makes its own spicy sausage (*kulen*). The establishment is run by the larger-than-life Ivan Balog, who speaks remarkable French. In his company you can enjoy litres of the excellent local white wines – a perennial favourite is the local *Đakovačko Rizling*.

OSIJEK

Osijek is the biggest town in Slavonia, and it's a major administrative, economic and cultural centre. Spread along the southern shore of the river Drava, it's a city of wide streets and attractive parks and gardens, with two city centres, the 18th-century Austro-Hungarian military fortress town of Tvrđa, to the east, and the 19th-century commercial centre of Gornji Grad, upstream to the west. Until 1786, when they were joined together (along with the residential town of Donji Grad, downstream from Tvrđa), they were entirely separate towns.

History

The Romans had a settlement called Mursa here in the 1st century AD, and by 331 it was sufficiently important for the emperor Hadrian to raise its status to that of a colony. Destroyed by rampaging Goths and Huns in the 7th century, the next settlers were Croats, who by all accounts built a thriving town near the current site in the Middle Ages, until it was destroyed by incoming Turks. The major Turkish town built here was then destroyed in its own turn, when Osijek was finally captured by the Austro-Hungarians in 1687.

From 1712 to 1721, the Austro-Hungarians built a brand new military-urban complex, Tvrđa, on the site of the Turkish town, as a reflection of its strategic importance in the military border zone. What you see here today has escaped more or less intact, though the Tvrđa town walls were pulled down in the 1920s.

In 1779, the building of a new bridge across the Drava connected Osijek not just to Bilje, but to the rest of Europe, and paved the way for the rapid expansion of Gornji Grad and Donji Grad, upstream and downstream from Tvrđa. In 1786 the three towns were joined together, and in 1884 the first tram started operating between them. During the late 19th and early 20th century, Gornji Grad became the administrative and business heart of Osijek, and indeed still is today.

From the middle of 1991 until early 1992, Osijek was bombarded, but never captured, and though restoration has been quick and effective, there are still scars to be seen, with shrapnel-pocked buildings in evidence around the town.

Getting there and around

As the biggest regional centre east of Zagreb, Osijek is a major transport hub, and it's easy to get here and easy to get around. Eight buses a day make the 4-hour journey from Zagreb, for example, while three a day head up to Pécs (Pečuh in Croatian) in southern Hungary. Every half hour or so there's also a departure for

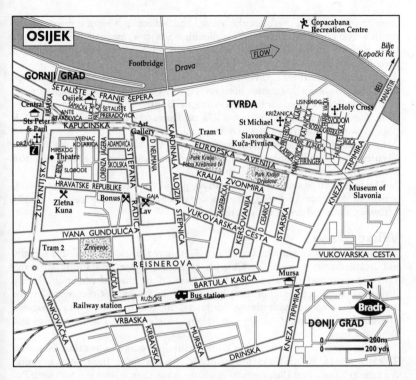

Bizovac, half an hour away, as well as for Slavonski Brod, 2 hours down the road. Five trains a day head across Slavonia to Zagreb (4–5 hours), while there are departures roughly every 2 hours for Bizovac, only 25 minutes away.

The bus and train stations are 15 minutes' walk southeast of Gornji Grad and 20 minutes southwest of Tvrđa – tram #2 does a loop from the stations up to Gornji Grad, while tram #1 runs between Gornji Grad and Tvrđa. You can also walk between the two centres in 20 minutes or so along Kapucinska and the pretty Europska Avenija, or along the riverside.

The tourist office (tel: 031 203 755; fax: 031 203 749), opposite the theatre and almost next door to the cathedral, in a grand administrative building, has maps and useful information on the town and region.

Where to stay and eat

Of Osijek's three hotels, your best option is the **Central** (tel: 031 283 399; fax: 031 283 891), right on the main square, Trg Ante Starčevića, near the cathedral. It retains some of its original 1899 charm while offering recently refurbished doubles at €56 – though being on a busy street, it can be a bit noisy. Right on the waterfront, a block away, is the **Osijek** (tel: 031 201 333; fax: 031 212 135), a tower-block with rather impersonal doubles from €65 to €80. The best rooms, however, do have a lovely view of the river. Finally, there's the **Mursa** (tel: 031 207 640; fax: 031 207 630; www.zug.hr) – owned by the railway company, and appropriately close to the train station – which has perfectly adequate doubles at €52.

Osijek's a treat for eating out, being good value for money and featuring plenty of restaurants and pizzerias. Local specialities tend to be spicy, in sharp contrast with anything you'll find on the coast, and reflecting Osijek's proximity to paprika-mad Hungary. There's an excellent hot fish stew, made of carp, catfish and pike, fittingly called *fiš paprikaš*, while almost everywhere serves up its own variations on *kulen*, a spicy smoked sausage.

In Gornji Grad, there's particularly good *fiš* to be had at the attractively named **Lav** (don't worry, it just means lion) on Trg L J Gaja, while just along the road, at Hrvatske Republike 1, is the prize-winning **Bonus**, which does a great pepper steak. Further along the same street is **Zlatna Kuna** (the golden marten), which is popular with the in-crowd and excellent value.

In Tvrđa, it's well worth heading for the slightly kitschy **Slavonska Kuća – Pivnica**, on Kamila Firingera. The home-made *kulen* and fine *fiš* more than compensate for the somewhat folksy décor.

The best place to sink an **Osječko Pivo**, proudly brewed in Osijek since 1697, is right in the centre of Tvrđa, where a string of bar and café terraces face the old Military Command across the square.

What to see

The main sight in Gornji Grad is the neo-Gothic red-brick cathedral. It's actually not a cathedral, but the parish **Church of Saints Peter and Paul**, but being vast, and sporting Croatia's second tallest spire (90m), the cathedral tag is hardly surprising. Built at the end of the 19th century, in the style of the great German cathedrals, complete with flying buttresses, the church has a fine, spacious interior featuring lovely vaulting and plain, simple frescos on the ceilings and along the nave.

Across and down the street you'll see the freshly restored **Croatian National Theatre**, spoiled somewhat by the garish McDonald's outlet. Inside, it's a beautiful example of classic late 19th-century opulence – the theatre, not the McDonald's.

Heading towards Tvrđa, it's worth stopping in at the **art gallery** on Europska Avenija, housed in a luxurious neo-classical villa. The gallery is one of Croatia's best, and you shouldn't be put off by not recognising many of the names on show – the paintings are on the whole excellent. As you head further east on Europska Avenija check out the *Jugendstil* (German art nouveau) houses along here.

Everything in Tvrđa is on or close to the harmonious main square, Trg Svetog Trojstva, which has a distinctive baroque **Plague Column** at its centre, dating from 1729. The entire north side of the square is taken up with the vast Austro-Hungarian **Military Command**, while the **Magistrate building**, on the eastern side, now houses the sprawling **Museum of Slavonia**. The most interesting of the 130,000 bits and pieces in the museum's care are the Roman artefacts from Mursa, though the collection also spans everything from the Stone Age to the 20th century.

A block northeast of here is the Franciscan monastery and the **Church of the Holy Cross**, which was completed in 1732, on the site of a former mosque. The dark, ornate baroque interior, and women in black praying in hushed voices, lend it some spooky atmosphere, though there's not much to see beyond the big baroque altar.

On the other side of Tvrđa, also on the site of a former mosque, is the Jesuit **Church of St Michael**, with its pair of distinctive square towers crowned with small onion domes. Built in 1748, inside it's a curious mix of plain, simple baroque on the one hand, and garish, ornate rococo on the other. You almost wish they'd gone the whole hog.

When you're done with sightseeing, head across the river on the main bridge or over the elegant suspension bridge to the popular **Copacabana Recreation**

Centre, where you'll find a sandy beach on the Drava as well as outdoor swimming pools.

More watery fun can be had at **Bizovačke Toplice**, a big spa resort 20km west of Osijek, easily reached on public transport to Bizovac. The thermal springs here serve a series of different pools, and there's an enormous and terrifying water-slide. Repair your shattered nerves at the **Termia** (tel: 031 685 100; fax: 031 685 188) which has pleasant double rooms at €56.

KOPAČKI RIT

Just northeast of Osijek is the Kopački Rit Nature Park, one of Europe's most important wetlands, caused by the confluence of the Drava and the Danube. As a result, it's a birdwatchers' paradise, with 141 species nesting here, and some 285 species recorded (birds, not birdwatchers). About the only downside is that the area's also home to the most vicious mosquitoes I've ever encountered, biting even in broad daylight, and through everything but the thickest clothing. Take effective repellent.

Among the nesting species are wild geese, grey, white and purple herons, egrets, coots, kingfishers, woodpeckers and storks. There's also the endangered ferruginous duck (which really ought to be the name of a jazz player rather than a bird), several pairs of rare black storks, and a number of white-tailed sea eagles, as well as a cormorant colony. During the spring and autumn migrations, the park is used as a layover by hundreds of thousands of birds, so that's the best time to come, but even in summer it's a wonderful place, even for the most lackadaisical of ornithologists.

For most of the 1990s, the park was closed, being either under Serbian or UN control (it runs along the border with the Serbian province of Vojvodina), and it's been a tough job to clear most of the mines from the area. Visitors are only now returning, though the numbers are still only barely a quarter of what they were in the 1980s.

With new legislation enacted in 1994, and the park's boundaries being expanded in 1999, there are now ambitious plans on the table to develop Kopački Rit as an eco-tourist destination, with a nature trail, cycle paths, a visitor centre, an ethnological museum, and accommodation in private rooms in the local villages of Kopačevo, Lug and Vardarac.

For the time being, however, most people are still visiting the park on a bus tour (ask at any travel agent in Slavonia or in Zagreb), which takes in the main sights. You can also drive round the park yourself, though the best way of seeing it is from the water. There are currently four five-person boats available for rent (250 kuna – through the park office; essential to book ahead. There's also a new, 50-person boat which is included in the tours.

More specialised field trips are available for groups of 10–15 serious ornithologists, and it's one of the best places in Europe for birdwatching – you can expect to see up to 90 species here in a single day. Contact the park office for more detailed information and bookings.

To reach the park, take the Beli Manastir road out of Osijek until you reach Bilje, just 7km out of town (buses run about once an hour). Turn right, and soon after the junction, on the left-hand side, you'll see Prince Eugene of Savoy's splendid hunting lodge, dating from 1707. The park office (tel: 031 750 855; fax: 031 750 755) is currently housed here, though it should eventually find its way to the village of Kopačevo, 3km further on, which is the real entrance to the park.

The road into the park goes between the two main lakes, Sakadaško and Kopačko, and then heads up through a reedy area of canals and cultivated fields – a great place to see herons – and home to an excellent *konoba* at Kozjak.

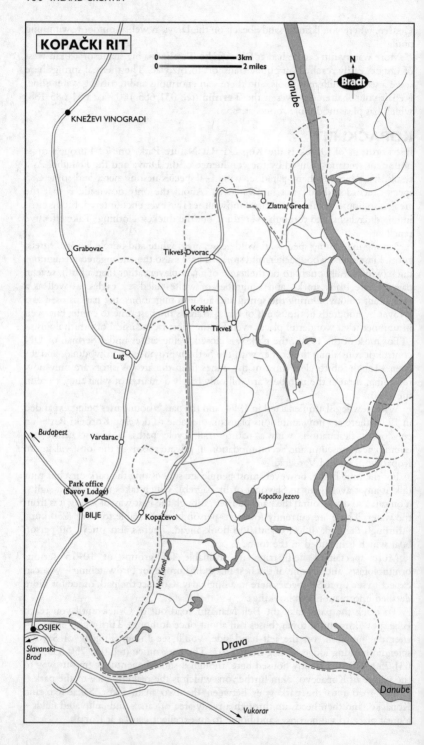

KOPAČKI RIT

0 — 3km
0 — 2 miles

N

Bradt

Danube

KNEŽEVI VINOGRADI

Zlatna Greda

Grabovac

Tikveš-Dvorac

Kožjak

Tikveš

Lug

Budapest

Vardarac

Kopačko Jezero

Park office
(Savoy Lodge)

BILJE

Kopačevo

Novi Kanal

OSIJEK

Slavanski
Brod

Drava

Vukorar

Danube

The road then heads up into the woods around Tikveš, which conceal one of Tito's most-prized hunting lodges, **Tikveš Dvorac** – he and his pals would come up here for a spot of privacy to blast away at the local game. On the road to the castle there's a sentry box, which would presumably have been used to keep away the *hoi polloi*, though it's now, like the lodge itself, in a sorry state of repair. There are plans to use the lodge to good effect, however, as a study centre for research scientists.

The Bilje tourist office (tel: 032 750 027; fax: 032 750 063) can put you in touch with local people with private rooms, if you'd like to stay in the area.

Vinkovci

In spite of the graffiti announcing Vinkovci as 'Punk City', the reality is somewhat more prosaic. Situated 40km south of Osijek, 35km east of Đakovo and a little under 20km short of Vukovar, the town is Croatia's second-biggest railway junction and a staging post for buses, so it's quite possible you may be breaking your journey here.

Both the bus and train stations are a 15-minute walk just north of the harmonious baroque town centre, which still sits within the limits of the (mostly long-gone) Roman walls of the Aurelia Cibalae colony which was once here. Vinkovci was the birthplace of two Roman emperors (Valens and Valentinian) and the composer of the music of Croatia's national anthem, Josip Runjanin, but today it's best known for the Vinkovačke Jeseni, the annual autumn folk festival which brings in big crowds from across Slavonia and features a boozy and excellent Plum Brandy Fair.

If you want to stay over there are two hotels downtown. The **Cibalia** (tel: 032 339 222; fax: 032 339 221) was newly refurbished in 2000, and is just two blocks south of the bus and train stations; its 24 clean doubles go for €66 a night. The **Slavonija** (tel: 032 342 555; fax: 032 342 550) is right in the city centre and towers over the river; rather functional double rooms here go for €55–70. The tourist office (tel: 032 334 653; fax: 032 334 658) also has a list of other pensions in the area, and can give you the dates for the festival.

VUKOVAR

What a difference two years can make. When I'd last come through the region, in the summer of 2002, the reality of Vukovar on arrival, after approaching through bucolic fields of maize and sunflowers, was a terrible shock. Gone was the fine baroque centre and the general air of prosperity delivered by the local shoe and tyre factory at Borovo, which I remembered from the 1980s. In its place was a shambles. The Borovo factory was totally destroyed, and most of the town centre was bombed out, a mess of devastated houses and ruined buildings.

So it was with some trepidation that I returned in May 2004. Coming into town on the main road from Vinkovci, however, it was reassuring to see that almost all the houses had now been rebuilt – if not yet replastered or repainted. In the town centre a gleaming glass-fronted office block had taken the place of a previously gutted concrete shell. Two new hotels were on the verge of opening up. And – most important of all – a huge party was going on in the Hotel Dunav, spilling out on to the riverside terrace and full of cheerful, laughing faces, celebrating a local girl's 18th birthday. It was an enormous relief.

Vukovar suffered more than any other town in Croatia during the recent war (see box), and if there's still much reconstruction to be done it's already looking incomparably better than the way it was at the end of 1991, when the town finally fell, after the horrifying siege and concomitant massacre, or even at the beginning

VUKOVAR AT WAR

Vukovar's position, right on Croatia's border (that's Serbian Vojvodina you see across the Danube), and its ethnic mix (in the 1991 census, 37% of locals considered themselves as Serbs, while 44% said they were Croats) was at the heart of the disaster in 1991. With Croatian independence on the agenda, barricades were thrown up in Vukovar's Serbian suburbs. A rocket attack by Croat extremists led to Croat policemen being murdered in reprisal, after which the Yugoslav army, the JNA, moved in, supposedly to separate the two sides.

By the autumn, Vukovar was surrounded by hundreds of tanks and thousands of soldiers. When ground attacks failed, the town was pounded mercilessly by artillery and bombing raids. The residents took shelter in their cellars, living on meagre rations. In the streets above, resistance was fierce, but eventually doomed in the face of the numerically superior and far more heavily armed Serbs.

On November 18 1991, Vukovar, now completely destroyed, finally fell. With nowhere to run – the ruins of the town were surrounded by enemy forces – the remaining population sought shelter in the hospital. The following day, ahead of the planned Red Cross evacuation, the Serbs cleared the hospital themselves, killing most of the people taking refuge there.

The world – with its attention diverted by the far more photogenic siege of Dubrovnik's beautiful and well-known old town – paid little heed.

Wherever Croats fell into Serb hands, families were separated, and the men were taken away in trucks. Approximately 2,300 soldiers and civilians died in the defence of Vukovar, and another 2,600 people simply disappeared. Many have been found in the mass graves around the town, but others may be buried anonymously in Serbia.

of 1998, when the UN handed Vukovar back to Croatia. The Franciscan Monastery has been beautifully restored, along with the big school behind it – now full of frivolous teenagers. Shops and banks are open again, while a few apartment blocks – and the Dunav hotel – have been rebuilt and refurbished. There's a genuine feeling of optimism, of triumph over adversity, which is hopefully more than simple guidebook-writer naïvety – after all, schooling is still segregated, for example, with separate entrances for Croats and Serbs; and although the children all follow the same curriculum, different languages and alphabets are used for teaching.

Vukovar's history goes back a long, long way – as you'll know if you've ever seen the pigeon-shaped vessel, popular all over the country, known as the **Vučedol Dove** (the original's in Zagreb's archaeological museum, but there are copies everywhere). It dates back nearly 5,000 years, and was found just downriver from Vukovar in 1938. The Vučedol site, after a ten-year gap, is now at last being excavated again, with plans to open it up as a proper heritage site for visitors (there's already a Vučedol Restaurant at the site, which is a good sign).

Vukovar lies along the southern bank of the river Danube (Dunav), with the little river Vuka flowing lethargically through town to join it. The main street, running parallel to the Danube, changes its name from Strossmayerov west of the Vuka, to Franjo Tuđman across the bridge, where you'll find the old town centre.

The train station is 2km north along the river, a 25-minute walk upstream towards Borovo. The bus station is closer to town, a block south of Strossmayerov, next to a big daily market, and is served by buses roughly every hour from Osijek,

36km away. On Strossmayerov itself you'll find the tourist office (tel/fax: 032 442 889), next door to Vukovar's most obvious travel agent, Panturist Plus (tel/fax: 032 441 790). Check with either for details of the two new hotels which should be open by the time you read this – there's the Mijork, almost opposite the tourist office, and the Lav, on the way out of town towards Vinkovci. Until they come on stream the only accommodation option is the Hotel Dunav – see below.

The badly damaged **Eltz Palace**, from the 18th century, is west of here, also on Strossmayerov, heading out of town. If it seems familiar, flip over a 20-kuna note, where you'll also find a picture of the Vučedol Dove. The palace houses the **Municipal Museum**, though since the collections were all destroyed or looted during the war, all you'll find for the time being is temporary exhibitions. Efforts to recover some of the works from museums in Serbia are proving successful, however, and the building itself is being restored – though given the damage sustained this is likely to take years still.

The bridge across to the old town leads on to one corner of Trg Republike, where you'll find the new town hall, the ruins of the elegant **Workers' Party Building** (home to the second congress of the Communist Party of Yugoslavia in 1920, and formerly the Museum of Modern History, but for the time being an empty shell) and the Hotel Dunav. In the middle of the square in 2002 there was a sad shrapnel-damaged monument to an earlier war, though when I was in town in 2004 this had been taken away, apparently for restoration.

The **Hotel Dunav** (tel: 032 441 285, fax: 032 441 762), a curious grain-store of a building, offers small but spanking-new doubles (accessed via a rather tired lift) for a very reasonable €48 a night. Most rooms have some sort of view – either over the town and the Vuka, or across the Danube. Downstairs there's a small souvenir shop, where you can buy Vučedol Doves or reproductions of Vukovar's famously ruined **water tower**, which is on the main road out to Ilok. Behind the hotel, on the riverbank, there's a touching new memorial, with stylised gravestones set like falling dominoes, under a couple of poplars, with the broad sweep of the endless Danube behind.

The Hotel Dunav is also home to Vukovar's only real sit-down restaurant, which fortunately is not only excellent, but will serve you a cracking meal at almost any time of day – though look carefully and you'll notice that the metal pillars and window frames still show shrapnel scars. Nonetheless the grills are great, the *ajvar* sauce is unrivalled, and the *šopska* salad (chunks of cheese and flavoursome tomatoes) is lovely. Breakfast can be an altogether different experience, however. You can just imagine the fun I had with a lone cold sausage and a wickedly hot under-boiled egg – but neither egg-cup nor spoon. I was able to glean some sardines, however – indeed, whole tins of them were arranged tastefully in a basket on the buffet table.

The main street through town (Franjo Tuđman), with its still mostly unrestored and ruined arcaded houses and shops, was once Vukovar's baroque heart. Turn left, uphill, at the brewery (storks nest picturesquely here, on the main chimney), to reach the **Franciscan Monastery**, which has become something of a meeting place for local people since its restoration. The brilliant exterior hides a still largely ruined interior, with bare brickwork where once were pastel plaster and baroque frescos. There are good photos showing what the monastery used to look like, and just how badly ruined it got in 1991.

If you've come all the way to Vukovar you should definitely make the effort to get out to the **Vukovar War Cemetery**, one of the most heartbreaking places in the whole of Croatia. This was built on the site of Europe's largest mass grave since World War II, and 938 crosses have been symbolically placed here to commemorate the dead. There are also the black and grey marble tombs of Vukovar's defenders, strewn with flowers, along with the grim sight of unmarked empty graves ready to receive the bodies of the known missing, should they ever be found. It's a terribly moving place, and there's rarely a time when you can come here and not find tearful family members mourning their dead.

The cemetery is situated about 3.5km out of town on the road to Ilok, and the easiest way to get there is on the regular Ilok bus. If you're walking (it takes about 45 minutes), head along Stjepan Radić out of town. The street is named after the Croatian firebrand who was shot in the Belgrade parliament in 1929; under Serb occupation in the 1990s the name was changed to that of his assassin, Puniša Račić, but now it's been changed back. The street leads 1km to the ruined water tower, which has been left unrestored as a permanent memorial to the conflict.

East to Ilok

East of Vukovar, past the war cemetery, Croatia narrows along the Danube's southern bank, into Vojvodina, and ends in a point at the town of Ilok, 35km later.

If you're coming this way under your own steam, the first place to stop is at the **Ovčara Memorial**, where you can pay your respects to the 200 doctors, nurses and patients evacuated from Vukovar's hospital on November 19 1991 who were found buried in a mass grave here. The grave was found in 1997 after an anonymous tip-off, and 200 small bushes mark the spot, along with memorial plaques. Standing here it's truly awful to think of the tragic end of so many people in such calm, quiet countryside, where today all you can hear is birds singing and crickets chirping. The grave is just past the small farming village of Ovčara – take the right-hand turning (marked with a dove for peace) almost exactly 2.5km after the Vukovar War Cemetery. Follow the road for 5km to Ovčara, then turn left at the end of the road (marked with another dove), and turn left again after 200m or so.

If you're on public transport (ie: the Vukovar to Ilok bus), the first town you come to is **Sotin**, which is not much more than a single street with rebuilt houses, after which you'll pass through **Opatovac**, which has nice vineyards and a shrapnel-pocked church tower. About 10km further on is **Šarengrad**, which was obviously once quite charming. There are two pretty churches and a fish-rich lake, though the signs of war are still omnipresent.

A final 7km brings you to **Ilok**, Croatia's easternmost town. While the Osijek tourist office's description of the town as 'Dubrovnik on the Danube' is a triumph of optimism over reality, it's still well worth coming here to see the fortified old town, up on the hill above the Danube.

The Romans were here, nearly 2,000 years ago, and it was they who planted the first vineyards. After a decade of it being off the shelves, Ilok's excellent wines can again be purchased, and they're generally extremely good – especially the dry Graševina whites.

The old town is set within tall, narrow-bricked walls, which were originally built in medieval times but were then beefed up by the Turks, who ran Ilok from 1566 to 1697. The church in the corner is dedicated to **St Ivan Kapistran**, the so-called 'Defender of Belgrade', who died in Ilok in 1456, though the church is mostly much more recent, having been remodelled in 1906 by the busy Mr Bollé (see *Zagreb*, etc).

There's an unusual statue of St Francis, right in the middle of the nave, and a couple of 15th- and 16th-century tombs to look at before you get to the dark, sagging altarpiece, depicting St Ivan – though without restoration it won't be doing so for much longer.

Istria

Of Croatia's busy coast, Istria, the northwestern peninsula, is by far the most visited, with holiday accommodation for up to 250,000 people at any one time. What's remarkable, however, is how the region has managed to keep tourist development away from the pretty Venetian towns along the west coast, or the medieval villages of the hilly, wooded interior. You'll even find picturesque coves and hidden rocky beaches far off the beaten track. Roman ruins and Byzantine mosaics are complemented by clear unpolluted waters and a gentle climate, helping to explain why millions of people keep coming back here, year after year. Even if the large hotel complexes and campsites aren't necessarily for you, Istria has a great deal to offer.

On the west coast you'll find Byzantine mosaics in **Poreč** and the wonderful Venetian town of **Rovinj**, while on the east lies **Opatija**, the swanky resort of choice for turn-of-the-century Austro-Hungarians. **Pazin**, inland, is the administrative centre, whereas **Pula**, on the southern tip, with its extraordinary Roman amphitheatre, is the economic heart of the region. Off the west coast stand the **Brijuni Islands**, now a pretty national park, while the **Učka Mountains** in the northeast rise above Opatija, providing a welcome relief from the crowds, even at the season's peak.

Early and late season are great times to visit, with the weather often coming good and the towns empty of tourists. April/May and September/October are especially good – in winter the peninsula gets a fair amount of rain, and though Pula and Rovinj are open year-round, resort towns like Poreč, Novigrad and Rabac pretty much close down altogether.

Istria had five sets of rulers during the 20th century, going from Austro-Hungarian to Italian to German to Yugoslav to Croatian in the space of 70-odd years – prompting anecdotes from tour guides across the region about families with four nationalities in the space of three generations. It makes for an unusually tolerant part of the country, and particularly on the west coast you'll still find many people bilingual in Croatian and Italian.

Warning Except in Pula, most coastal accommodation will be fully booked from late June until early September. That includes campsites, private rooms and hotels, so either book well ahead or stay in Pula and make day trips out. Another option, if you have your own transport, is to take advantage of the increasing number of farms and villages in the interior offering agro-tourism (bed and breakfast) accommodation – there are now over 120 places offering this service, and more are coming on board all the time. Get the brochure from the Pula tourist board (tel: 052 212 987; fax: 052 211 855; email: tz-pula@pu.htnet.hr).

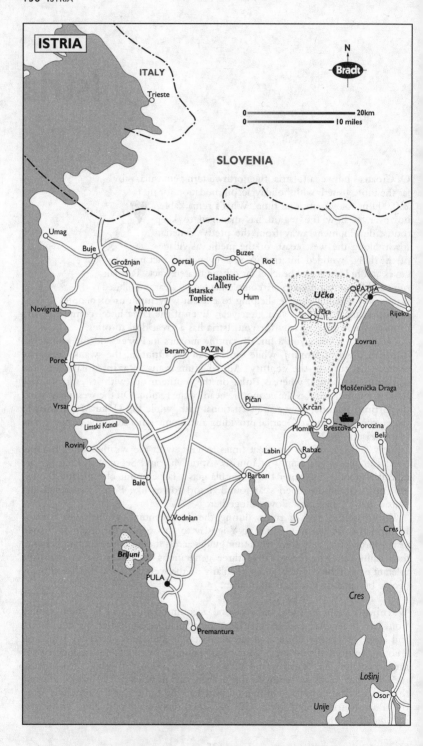

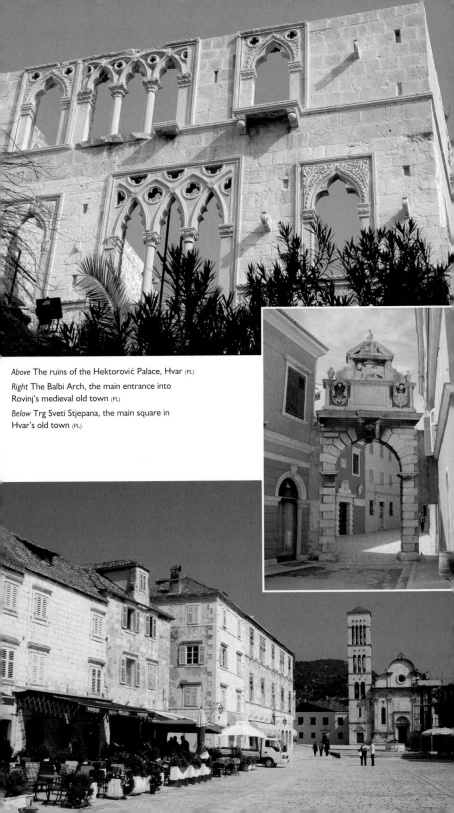

Above The ruins of the Hektorović Palace, Hvar (PL)

Right The Balbi Arch, the main entrance into Rovinj's medieval old town (PL)

Below Trg Sveti Stjepana, the main square in Hvar's old town (PL)

Above left A stork searching for a lunchtime frog in Lonjsko Polje nature park (PL)

Above right On the lookout for bears at North Velebit National Park (PL)

Below Wooden walkways and waterfalls at Plitvice Lakes National Park (PL)

The telephone code for the whole of Istria (except Opatija) is 052. In and around Opatija it's 051, because Opatija's administratively within the Rijeka region.

THE WEST COAST TO POREČ

Working anticlockwise round Istria, the first main settlements are **Umag** and **Novigrad**. These were both once Roman towns, on their own mini-peninsulas, but have long been given over unashamedly to the holiday business, with little to show for their historic past. The lack of industry anywhere near here, the clear waters, and the pleasant enough coastal hotels and campgrounds draw regular crowds, but most visitors will want to head on to the next town south, **Poreč** (Parenzo).

The undisputed capital of Croatian tourism, Poreč (resident population just 7,600) had over 700,000 visitors in 2003, spending an impressive five million nights in the huge resorts spread along the 50km stretch of coast running south from the Mirna River to the Limski Kanal (Lim Fjord). The unashamed devotion to holidaying here means you can find just about anything to divert you (in season), from plain old-fashioned sunbathing and swimming to walking, cycling, riding, water-skiing, diving, jet-skiing, ballooning or paragliding, not to mention tennis, volleyball and the rest. The tourist infrastructure is excellent, with walking and cycling trails (up to 50km circuits), and maps available from the tourist office (at the entrance to the old town, just up from Trg Slobode, at Zagrebačka 9; tel: 052 451 719; fax: 052 434 160), as well as over 100 restaurants and more than 25,000 beds in the vicinity. Lonely, you won't be.

At the centre of all this is the pretty town itself (more of a village, really), tightly fitting onto a peninsula measuring just 440m long and 200m wide. Here you'll find stone-paved streets, fine medieval buildings, traces of the Roman colony and arguably the world's best-preserved early-Christian cathedral complex, featuring those famous mosaics – enough, in any case, to warrant Poreč being on UNESCO's list of World Heritage Sites.

History

Inhabited for over 6,000 years by the Histrian tribes who gave their name to the Istrian peninsula, Poreč was finally subdued by the Romans in the 2nd century BC and – with the new name of Julia Parentium – was upgraded to the status of colony during the 2nd century AD. There's a small walled garden near the peninsula's tip with lots of Roman bits and pieces from this era, as well as more in the town's museum, but the main thing you'll notice is the street layout – and even the street names, Decumanus and Cardo Maximus – which are still Roman rather than medieval.

Early Christians worshipped in secret here, and Poreč's first bishop, Maurus, was martyred in the 4th century – the town still puts on a good show for his feast day, November 21, should you still be around that far out of season.

By the 6th century, with Byzantium in charge (from 539 to 751), Bishop Euphrasius reckoned it was time for a major rebuilding programme, tearing down the existing church and putting up a complex consisting of a basilica, an atrium, a baptistery and – naturally – a bishop's palace.

After the usual takeover by Goths and the like, Venice was in power here for more than 500 years (1267–1797), though in charge of not very much, with the plague scything down the local population to just 100 by the 17th century. Venice repopulated the town from Southern Dalmatia, before collapsing and leaving the way free for the Austro-Hungarians. With the first guidebook to the area available in 1845 and the first public beach opened in 1895, Poreč was well on the way to its true destiny as a holiday haven.

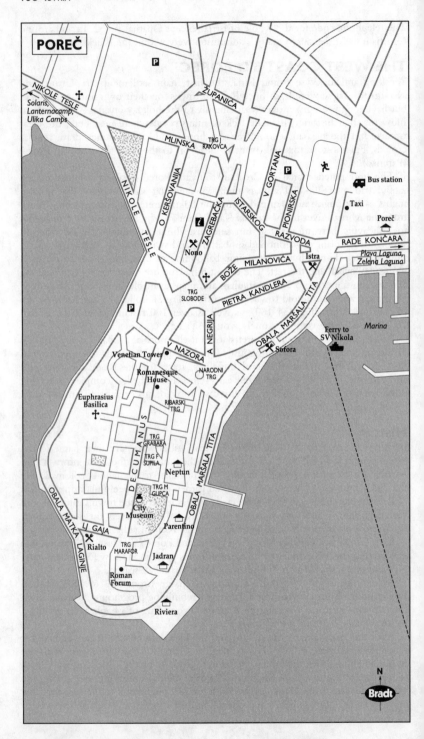

POREČ

NIKOLE TESLE

Solaris,
Lanternacamp;
Ulika Camps

ŽUPANIČA

MLINSKA

TRG
RAKOVCA

NIKOLE TESLE

O KERŠOVANIJA

ZAGREBAČKA

ISTARSKOG RAZVODA

V GORTANA

PIONIRSKA

P

Nono

BOŽE MILANOVIĆA

TRG
SLOBODE

PIETRA KANDLERA

A NEGRIJA

Bus station

Taxi

Poreč

RADE KONČARA

Playa Laguna,
Zelena Laguna

Istra

OBALA MARŠALA TITA

Ferry to
SV Nikola

Marina

P

V NAZORA

Sofora

Venetian Tower

Romanesque
House

NARODNI
TRG

Euphrasius
Basilica

RIBARSKI
TRG

DECUMANUS

TRG
GRABARA

TRG F
SUPILA

Neptun

OBALA MARŠALA TITA

TRG M
GUPCA

City
Museum

Parentino

OBALA MATKA LAGINJE

LJ GAJA

Rialto

TRG
MARAFOR

Jadran

Roman
Forum

Riviera

N

Bradt

Getting there

Poreč is easily reached by bus – it's just under an hour away from Pula or Koper (in Slovenia), both 55km distant, around $3^{1}/_{2}$ hours from Rijeka, nine times a day, or $6^{1}/_{2}$ hours from Zagreb, six times a day. The nearest train stations are Pazin (on the Trieste/Ljubljana to Pula line) or Koper, while the nearest airport is at Pula. In summer there are also ferries from Pula, Trieste and Venice.

If you're coming in by car there's a curious dearth of signs to Poreč itself – just follow signs to the main resort of Plava Laguna and you won't go far wrong.

Getting around

In summer there's a 'tourist train' which plies its way up and down the coast south of Poreč to the main resort areas of Plava Laguna and Zelena Laguna (blue lagoon; green lagoon), with a local boat covering the same turf from the seaward side. Out of season you'll have to rely on the bus to Vrsar or your own transport. If you're just coming in to see the old town, it's all perfectly manageable on foot from the bus station, at the eastern end of the peninsula, next to the small harbour. The bus station has left-luggage facilities.

Where to stay

With 25,000 beds in the vicinity – 5,000 of them in private rooms – accommodation ought to be a doddle in Poreč. Ought to be, but if you're here in season, without a booking, you could well find yourself on the bus back out to Pula in search of shelter.

There are seven main campsites in the vicinity, but four – **Solaris** and **Ulika** (to the north) and **Istra** and **Koversada** (to the south) – are reserved for naturists. If you prefer to keep your kit on, then try **Zelena Laguna** or **Bijela Uvala** (both in Zelena Laguna; tel: 052 410 101; fax: 052 451 044, for advance reservations) or **Lanternacamp** (to the north, reserve ahead; tel: 052 408 000; fax: 052 451 440).

In the area you'll find no fewer than 22 agencies handling private rooms, which go for around €35 for a double in summer but under €25 out of season. From June to September you'll find agencies open seven days a week until 22.00, but outside these months most close soon after lunch and don't open at all on Sundays. Among the most popular are Di-Tours (tel: 052 431 592; fax: 052 431 300, at several locations), Atlas (tel: 052 434 933; fax: 052 451 109), and Generalturist (tel: 052 451 188; fax: 052 451 123).

The nicest establishments in the town itself are the small **Jadran** and the **Parentino** hotels next door to each other in semi-grand, 19th-century buildings right on the waterfront. Both are run by the much larger three-star **Hotel Neptun** which has been completely refurbished and is more luxurious (but less characterful) than its two-star dependencies. Make reservations at all three (tel: 052 400 800; fax: 052 431 351), and expect to pay around €100 for a double room – a little less at the Jadran – including (obligatory, in season) half board. The cheapest option is the two-star **Hotel Poreč**, which has 105 beds in standard-issue comfort for around €80 in a building overlooking the bus station (tel: 052 451 811; fax: 052 451 730). One of these hotels – rarely the same one – stays open all through the year.

Most interesting may eventually turn out to be the **Hotel Riviera**, which was built in 1910 by the enterprising Mr Klein, who already owned swanky hotels at the time in Opatija. Failing to get planning permission from a competition-concerned Poreč council, he was sold a piece of sea instead, and reclaimed the land on which he then built his hotel. The Riviera was 'restored' in 1953 and is supposedly being refurbished again – and it has an unbeatable location – but it still looked in a very sorry state when I last visited.

Out of town there's a huge range of three- and two-star complexes, all run either by the Riviera company (www.riviera.hr) or by Plava Laguna (www.plavalaguna.hr), who between them control almost the entire Poreč economy – your best bet in terms of both price and availability is to go through your local travel agent or one of the tour operators listed on page 28, though Riviera does have direct booking lines (tel: 052 408 000; fax: 052 451 440), while Plava Laguna lists the phone numbers of all its individual hotels, campgrounds and apartments on its vast website.

Where to eat

With around 100 restaurants and 20 pizzerias – not to mention countless snack bars and ice-cream parlours – the Poreč area must have one of the highest eatery-densities on the planet relative to its resident population. In town itself the emphasis is more firmly on cafés and bars, but you'll have no trouble finding pizza, pasta, or Istrian specialities like *pršut*, *maneštra* (bean soup) and a dizzying array of fish dishes. Lobster (*jastog*) is expensive but popular, especially in pasta (*sa rezancima*). In spring and early summer make an effort to try the fine local wild asparagus, dark and slightly bitter, but delicious.

The **Istra**, up by the bus station where Bože Milanovića and Maršala Tita meet, is the right place to splash out on top-of-the-range seafood and other local specialities. Just along the seafront from here is **Sofora**, which not only has a great location but also does remarkably good-value specials. **Nono**, the pizzeria just down from the tourist office on Zagrebačka, is reputed to have the best pizzas in town – and it's certainly popular, even off-season – but it wasn't my personal favourite, being pipped at the post by the **Rialto**, on the west side of town.

What to see

Poreč's main draw is the Euphrasius Basilica and its remarkable series of 6th-century Byzantine mosaics. Access is via the largely reconstructed (albeit with very old materials) atrium, and is free, though it's worth paying to see the small museum in the Bishop's Palace behind the basilica. This houses lots of stone and mosaic fragments including some from Maurus's so-called 'oratory' – probably in fact what was his own house, given the clandestine nature of 4th-century Christianity. Note the mosaic fish, the early-Christians' secret symbol. You might also want to splash out on climbing the campanile which was added to the complex in 1522 (access through the baptistery) for great views out over the town.

But like everyone else you'll end up in the basilica itself, stunned by the mosaics in the main apse. The very plainness of the rest of the church sets these off fantastically. Dating from the second half of the 6th century, they show Byzantine art at its best, following on in the tradition started 100 years earlier in Ravenna, and roughly contemporaneous with the mosaics in Aya Sofya in Istanbul – indeed craftsmen from Constantinople worked on the wall furnishings here too.

Dominated by the virgin and child, you'll see Euphrasius himself on the left-hand side with a handy-sized model of the basilica. To the left of the main windows is the Annunciation, while on the right a nosy servant gets a rare peek at the Visitation. Over the arch are the first 12 women saints, with Agnus Dei (the lamb of God) as the centrepiece, while across the top are Christ and the apostles. Complemented by coloured stones and fabulous mother-of-pearl – whole scallop and oyster shells have been used – the ensemble is still almost unnaturally vibrant some 1,500 years on.

The stone altar canopy, modelled on the one in St Mark's in Venice, wasn't added until 1277, but blends in surprisingly well with the whole.

On your way out you can see where excavations have revealed part of the mosaic floor of one of the earlier churches on the site.

The rest of the town is mainly remarkable for its narrow stone streets, pretty squares and occasional architectural one-offs, like the Venetian Tower at the top end of Decumanus and the so-called Romanesque House further down, with its distinctive 13th-century wooden balcony. Down at the bottom of Decumanus is Trg Marabor, once the Roman Forum. In the low-walled garden behind this you'll find a collection of Roman ruins mainly coming from a couple of temples which once stood here. Finally, there's the **City Museum**, housed in the early 18th-century Sinčić Palace on the main drag, with Greek and Roman artefacts on the ground floor and some monumental canvasses upstairs.

Moving on

Heading south from Poreč you soon come to **Vrsar**, famous mostly as the access point for Europe's largest naturist resort, at **Koversada**. Established in 1960 and catering for the best part of 1,000 people indoors and more than 7,000 campers outside, it's fully booked all season long. Reserve well ahead (tel: 052 441 222; fax: 052 441 122 for the campsite; tel/fax: 052 441 171 for apartments and self-catering).

Koversada sits on the northwest corner of the **Limski Kanal** (Lim Fjord), a 10km-long flooded valley ideal for cultivating oysters and mussels. The only effective way to see it – and the best way of sampling the excellent oysters – is to take an excursion boat from Poreč, Vrsar or Rovinj. It's a quiet place these days, a far cry from the years when pirates and buccaneers hid here between raids on Venetian shipping. Whether or not Francis Drake's treasure is hidden hereabouts is highly debatable, but it doesn't stop treasure-hunters coming each year to look – what you should be looking for however is the dolphins which sometimes come into the fjord to play.

ROVINJ

Dominated by its outsize church and campanile, Rovinj (Rovigno) is one of the most attractive places in Croatia, with the steep cobbled streets of the walled old town giving way to sunny Venetian quayside cafés and restaurants. Serious tourist development hasn't encroached much on this photogenic, once-upon-a-time island city, and though it receives more than its fair share of visitors Rovinj nonetheless accommodates them with ease – mostly away from the old town, along the coast or on one of the nearby islands.

It's also the most Italian place in Croatia, with the people, street signs and menus all being bilingual. A centuries-old fishing tradition is alive and well, though on the wide quaysides you're as likely to witness spontaneous concerts or vibrant café life as fishermen bringing in the catch or mending their nets.

Whilst you're on the quayside have a look at the curiously flat-bottomed, square-stemmed boats unique to Rovinj – the *batana* probably only survived into the 21st century with UNESCO help.

History

The island of Rovinj – it wasn't joined to the coast until 1763 – was known in Roman times and was fortified and inhabited through the decline of the Roman Empire and into the Middle Ages. The frequent subject of barbarian attacks, Rovinj's people developed a densely packed, organic urban architecture on the island, and as the population increased and the space ran out, families found themselves living literally on top of one another. Each insisted nonetheless on its own fireplace and chimney, giving Rovinj's old walled town the distinctively jumbled look it has today.

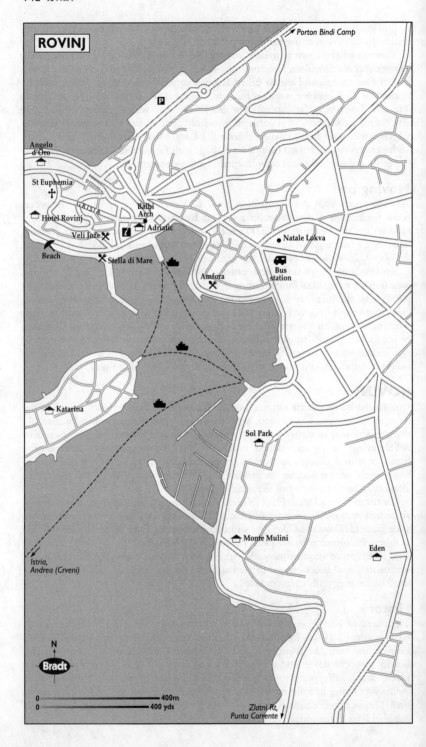

ROVINJ

Porton Bindi Camp

Angelo d'Oro

St Euphemia

GRISIA

Hotel Rovinj

Veli Jože

Beach

Balbi Arch

Adriatic

Stella di Mare

Natale Lokva

Amfora

Bus station

Katarina

Sol Park

Monte Mulini

Eden

Istria, Andrea (Crveni)

N

Bradt

0   400m
0   400 yds

Zlatni Rt, Punta Corrente

Most of the buildings date from the 13th century on, when the Venetians secured control, retaining it right up to the collapse of the republic at the end of the 18th century. (Quarries near Rovinj furnished the marble you can see today in the lovely church of Santa Maria della Salute, in Venice.)

During the scourge of the bubonic plague, Rovinj remained miraculously unscathed. While Poreč, to the north, and Pula, to the south, saw their populations plunge in the mid 17th century to just 100 and 300 inhabitants respectively, Rovinj could boast 10,000 healthy souls – not far off today's 13,000.

With the isthmus paved over, Rovinj spread across to the mainland from the end of the 18th century, while the introduction of Croatia's first tobacco factory in 1872 brought prosperity to the town – even today the factory makes most of Croatia's cigarettes.

Getting there

Rovinj is less than 40km from Pula, and can be reached by bus or car in not much over half an hour from Pula's train station, airport or city-centre bus station – buses run a dozen times a day between the two. If you're coming from the north or east by car you'll see Rovinj clearly signed off the main road.

Getting around

The bus station (with left-luggage facilities) is half way between the old town and the marina, a five-minute walk from the main town quay, home to the highly informative if not always especially friendly tourist office (tel: 052 811 566; fax: 052 816 007). Once you're there everything's easily (and only) reachable on foot. If you're coming in by car you'll almost certainly end up on the northern side of the old town, where you'll find the only large car park, with spectacular views of the ancient walls dropping straight down to the water, crowned by the Venetian campanile.

Where to stay

Popular with well-heeled Croatians, Rovinj has something of a shortage of accommodation in season, and you may find it easier to stay in Pula and make a day trip of it.

If you do get seduced by the idea of staying here – and who wouldn't be? – the two-star **Hotel Rovinj** (tel: 052 811 288; fax: 052 840 757) has a wonderful position right in the old town, above a small rocky beach and overlooking the sea and Katerina Island. Doubles with sea views go for €104 in high season, including (obligatory) half board. The smaller, swankier and older **Adriatic** (tel: 052 815 088; fax: 052 813 573) has just 27 rooms, right on the old quay, which is lovely but can be noisy late in the evening. Expect to pay around €110 for a double – if you can get a room. Finally, there's the five-star **Angelo d'Oro** (tel: 052 840 502; fax: 052 840 111), 24 rooms in a 17th-century Venetian palazzo on the north side of town, expensive at €200 a night for a double, but in a truly beautiful building.

Most of the other hotels are south of the old town, on the Zlatni rt/Punta Corrente cape, a 15–20-minute walk from town, or on Katerina or Andrea islands, a short boat-ride away. The most luxurious of these is the four-star **Eden** complex (tel: 052 800 400; fax: 052 811 349) with doubles in high season (including half board) upwards of €170 a night. Much cheaper is the two-star **Monte Mulini** (tel: 052 811 512; fax: 052 815 882), just behind the marina, with clean doubles at €54. If you want to be on an island then try the two-star **Katerina** (on Katerina; tel: 052 804 100; fax: 052 804 111) or – a little further away – the three-star **Istra** (on Andrea – also confusingly known as Crveni – tel: 052 802 500/813 484).

Rovinj also has plenty of private rooms, though very few in the old town itself. Rooms can be booked through any of the more than 20 travel agents in town, and go for about €25 for a double in high season, though that's based on a six-night stay. Expect to stump up a supplement of 50% for a one- or two-night stay. **Natale-Lokva** (tel: 052 813 365; fax: 052 830 239), just across from the bus station at Carduci 4, doesn't always hit you for the surcharge.

For camping you can't do better than the pleasantly pine-shaded **Porton Biondi** (tel: 052 813 557; fax: 052 811 509), a 15-minute walk north of the old town with its own beach and fabulous views back to Rovinj.

Where to eat
Restaurants in Rovinj mainly cater to well-off tourists – often locals – who come here for the excellent fish. Don't expect bargains on the quayside, but consider splashing out here, as the quality is exceptional; **Amfora** is pricey but sublime. If you're on a tighter budget try the **Stella di Mare**, where the quay runs out past the tourist office. It's in a great location, right on the seashore, and serves inexpensive pizzas and spaghetti dishes (you just have to ask for what you want in terms of pasta, as the menu only lists the pizzas). Up the steps above is **Veli Jože**, a cheerful, cluttered *konoba* oozing atmosphere and specialising in excellent Istrian cuisine. Try dishes with the local *tartufi* (truffles), especially if you're here in spring or autumn.

What to see
Rovinj's main attraction is itself – the charming narrow cobbled streets running up through the warren of the old town, the paved car-free quays, the Venetian *palazzi* and medieval houses, and the 30-odd churches within the old town walls, some so small you'd never know they were there.

The most obvious access to the old town is from the paved isthmus joining Rovinj to the mainland, home to an elegant baroque clocktower and the former town hall. Walk through the 17th-century Balbi arch (on the site of one of the original seven town gates) and notice the Turk's head on the outside of the arch; on the inside there's a Venetian.

The arch leads through and up to the main street, Grisia, eventually running right on up to the cathedral. Take time to wander off through the maze of tiny streets on either side, however, and you can begin to imagine how dense and un-private medieval life might have been. Each house still has its own stone water cistern and oil store, and a chimney for every family. High up on some buildings, above the windows, look out for the pairs of protruding carved stones – rods used to be threaded through these, for hanging fishing nets out to dry.

Rovinj is also home to a thriving artists' colony, and if you're here in August you could hardly fail to notice the paintings, watercolours, drawings and prints that festoon the whole length of Grisia – tradition has it that if you're a Rovinj artist you have the right to display here.

Church of St Euphemia
At the top of the hill is the improbably large church of St Euphemia. Easily the biggest building in town, on a ground plan of 50m by 30m, with a nave nearly 18m tall, the present structure dates from 1725–36 and is a good example of Venetian baroque, though the front is a 19th-century add-on.

The enormous campanile from 1680 – Istria's biggest, at over 62m – is a copy of the 98.6m belltower in St Mark's Square in Venice. Rovinj locals insist of course it's the other way round: that the version in Venice, following the July 1902 collapse of the original, is a copy of the one in Rovinj.

Gloomy and somewhat airless inside, the church retains its fair share of treasures, in spite of much of the original silver having been plundered by Napoleon's troops in 1806. The main attraction however is St Euphemia herself. With the original church on the site dedicated to St George (and you can still see a fine sculpture of the dragon-basher on the main altar), Euphemia stole the limelight in the year 800 by improbably washing up on the shores nearby in her stone sarcophagus.

Euphemia was one of a group of early Christians arrested in Chalcedon, near Constantinople, in AD304, and is said to have suffered terrible tortures under Diocletian for failing to recant. Miraculously surviving death by fire, a pit of poisonous snakes and being broken on the wheel, it's likely she was still only a teenager when she was fatally thrown to the lions.

Christians managed to recover her body, and under Constantine, in the 7th century, a church was built in her honour. The iconoclasts threw her remains into the sea in the late 8th century, but sailors recovered them and took her to the Greek island of Lemnos. By 796 she was back in Constantinople, mysteriously disappearing in early 800, only to turn up in Rovinj. Hardly surprising therefore, that the people there gave her co-patroness status, with St George, and built church after church to house her sarcophagus.

The sarcophagus itself is behind the altar in the right-hand aisle of the church, though there's some confusion about whether it's actually 3rd or 6th century, and it was in any case altered in later centuries. Inside are the saint's relics, wrapped in gold cloth. On the altar is a 16th-century gold-plated stone statue of Euphemia, while by the south door you'll find a 14th-century marble relief of her, incorporating bits of earlier sculpture. Most impressive of all is the 4.7m copper statue of the saint adorning the campanile. Cast in 1758, following the destruction by lightning of an earlier wooden statue (which must have been a dramatic moment), Euphemia also does practical duty as a weather vane, just like the original angel on the *Campanile di San Marco* used to.

On September 16 – the anniversary of her martyrdom – Rovinj celebrates Euphemia's arrival in Rovinj with processions and the performance of miracle plays in the square in front of the church. It's said that in the year 2000 festivities, on the 1,200th anniversary of her arrival, a cloud formed in the shape of the saint.

THE BITINADA AND THE ARIA DA NUOTO

Peculiar to Rovinj are two especially interesting types of folk song, the *bitinada* and the *aria da nuoto*.

The *bitinada* developed, it's said, from music-loving fishermen's inability to play instruments and mend nets at the same time, and depends on an 'orchestra' of human voices. A lead tenor acts as the conductor, singing a phrase which is then echoed by the other 'instruments' in a waltzing rhythm. So convincing is this vocal trickery that there's a popular story told about Mussolini, having commanded a *bitinada* performance in Italy during World War II, insisting on going backstage to find out where the real musicians were hiding.

The *aria di nuoto* (night aria), for its part, echoes the fragments of song which would be passed from boat to boat after dark, with fishermen joining in with new harmonies as the song developed. You can hear both *bitinada* and *arie da nuota* performed during Rovinj's summer-long festival.

Beaches and nature reserves

Rovinj itself just has a tiny rocky beach past the end of the main quay, but if you go past the marina onto the Zlatni rt/Punta Corrente peninsula – a protected park/forest covering around 70ha of land – you'll find footpaths leading to any number of bathing spots. The park itself is charming, featuring cypresses, pines, firs and lovely cedar trees, including the unusual Himalayan cedar.

The 22 islands and rocky outcrops off Rovinj also make up a dedicated nature reserve with an unusual biodiversity – on Katerina alone, there are supposedly 456 varieties of flora. Katerina and Andrea (Crveni) islands also have lovely rocky beaches and the clearest water imaginable. Boats motor out from Rovinj harbour every half hour or so in summer.

Back onshore, 10km south of Rovinj is the Palud ornithological reserve. Palud (from the Latin *palud*, meaning 'marsh') now provides shelter to a variety of both migratory and non-migratory bird species, as well as turtles, eels and mullet, though it was once supposedly a Roman fish farm. Off the coast from here are the Dvije Sestrice (two sisters) islands, a major seagull nesting site.

Finally, if you're into diving, you're unlikely to find the remains of Cissa, the legendary city that supposedly sank near Rovinj during earthquakes in 754 and 801, but excursions from the town will help you swim down to the wreck of the *Baron Gautsch*. The ship was the Austro-Hungarians' pride and joy until – after hitting one of its own side's mines in 1914 – it sank, about 10km off Rovinj, with the loss of 284 lives.

BRIJUNI ISLANDS

Just northwest of Pula lie the pretty Brijuni (Brioni) Islands, formerly a holiday retreat for Austro-Hungarians, then the private residence of Marshal Tito for 30 years before becoming a national park in 1983 and opening to visitors in 1984. Not worth an extensive detour, they're nonetheless well worth a visit if you're in Istria, and can comfortably be managed in a day trip from Pula, Rovinj or Poreč.

Visits remain carefully controlled – the Brijuni is still a state residence as well as a national park – and you can only visit parts of two of the islands, Veliki Brijun and Mali Brijun, on an organised tour or by staying at one of the two hotels or half-dozen villas on the main island. Diving, off-limits for years, is now allowed if you're with a recognised professional operator – check with the national park office (tel: 052 525 888; fax: 052 521 367; www.np-brijun.hr).

History

The Romans made wine and olive oil here, and left behind the remains of a swanky country estate on Veriga bay; Byzantium built an important fortress; and Benedictine monks and Venetian overlords left their mark. But it wasn't until 1893 – when Paul Kupelweiser, an Austrian steel magnate, purchased the islands with a view to starting up a health resort – that Brijuni started featuring on the tour map.

Kupelweiser pursued his dream relentlessly by ridding the islands of malaria (kind of important, that, in a sanatorium), clearing the land, building hotels, villas and heated pools, and providing all the luxury accoutrements demanded by the aristocracy. In the years before World War I they came in droves. On one day in September 1910 no fewer than 11 archdukes and duchesses were logged, while March 31 1911 saw 16 princes and princesses and 15 counts and countesses in residence. Franz Ferdinand was here before being shot in Sarajevo, kicking off World War I; so was Kaiser Wilhelm, Thomas Mann, James Joyce, George Bernard Shaw, Richard Strauss and the ubiquitous Marconi, always on hand with a radio experiment to be performed in Europe's best holiday destinations.

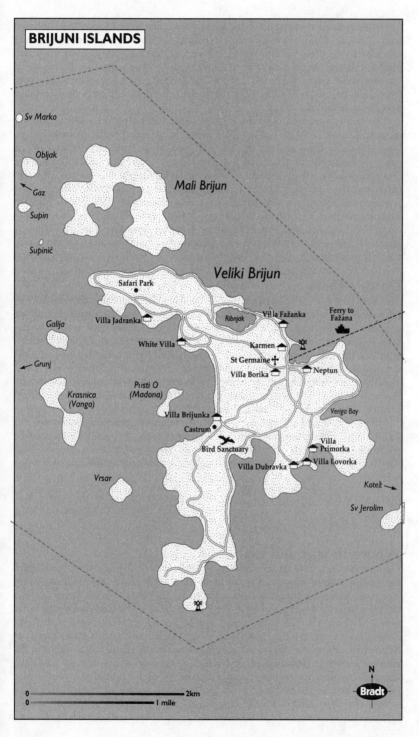

BRIJUNI ISLANDS

Sv Marko

Obljak

← Gaz

Supin

Supinić

Mali Brijun

Veliki Brijun

Safari Park

Galija

Villa Jadranka

Ribnjak

Villa Fažanka

Ferry to
Fažana

← Grunj

White Villa

Karmen

St Germaine †

Villa Borika

Neptun

Pusti O
(Madona)

Krasnica
(Vanga)

Villa Brijunka

Castrum

Veriga Bay

Bird Sanctuary

Villa
Primorka

Villa Dubravka

Villa Lovorka

Vrsar

Kotež →

Sv Jerolim

N

0   2km
0   1 mile

Bradt

On Kupelweiser's death in 1919, his son Karl took over the business, adding a casino and an 18-hole golf course, but ending up bankrupt and suicidal, killing himself here in 1930. The Italians took over, but nothing of much note happened until the islands caught Tito's eye in 1947. From 1949 onwards, for six months of the year or so, he managed the rare trick of effectively running the country from his holiday house, something only the Roman Emperor Tiberius on Capri had previously achieved.

Tito had sub-tropical plants brought in and created a private game reserve on the northwestern end of Veliki Brijun from the animals he was given by fellow heads of state. Their descendants are still here, along with one or two of the originals – notably the elephants, Sony and Lanka, gifts from Indira Gandhi. He also welcomed nearly 100 heads of state including Queen Elizabeth II, Ho Chi Minh and the Ethiopian Emperor Haile Selassie, as well as dozens of celebrities, among them Josephine Baker, Sophia Loren, Elizabeth Taylor and Richard Burton.

After Croatia's independence, President Tuđman continued Tito's tradition by summering here, but President Mesić spends a good deal less time on the islands than his predecessor.

Getting there

The Brijuni Islands are 20 minutes offshore from the small port of Fažana, 8km northwest of Pula, easily reached on Pula city bus #6. Excursion tickets are available from the Brijuni National Park office on the front in Fažana, and cost 180 kuna in summer and 90 kuna in winter. Three to five tours a day set off in summer, with just one trip in winter; it's worth reserving ahead at any time of year. The national park office will organise your transfer to the island if you're staying over.

Almost any hotel from Poreč to Rovinj to Pula will also be able to put you on an excursion, with the trip (including the bus to Fažana, and – sometimes – lunch) coming in at between 220 and 250 kuna.

In Pula you'll find excursions offered to the islands by private operators for 150 to 200 kuna a head, but be careful what you're buying, as some of the trips take you round the islands but not onto them, while others are effectively ferries to Mali Brijun for a picnic and a swim. Nice though these trips are, be sure that's what you wanted to do.

Note On the way over to Veliki Brijun keep your eyes peeled for dolphins – small schools are sometimes seen making their way from the Limski Kanal towards the island of Lošinj.

Where to stay and eat

Eighty years ago there were five swanky hotels to choose from – not to mention the casino, a horse-riding centre, and two polo fields. These days you can either stay at the three-star **Neptun-Istra**, right next to where the boats come in – and the place most of Tito's guests were lodged – or the two-star **Karmen** on the other side of the bay.

Doubles go for €165 at the Neptun-Istra during the priciest three weeks of August but drop right back to €65 from November to April, while rooms at the Karmen are about 10% cheaper. Prices include breakfast and unlimited use of the ferries to and from the mainland, and while they're steep for what you get, they do offer you the only chance you'll get to see the islands outside of a formal excursion.

A choice alternative, if you're in a group, is one of the lovely three- or four-star villas, on the southern end of Veliki Brijun, of which there are half a dozen, sleeping four to eight people. The four-star establishments – right on the beach – come in at around €140 per person per night for bed and breakfast in peak season, while three-star costs around half that; prices go down around 25% in the off season at the four-star places, but plummets to around €30 per person per night at the three-star villas in winter.

If you're booked in for accommodation on the island and have driven to Fažana, then you can leave your car in secure parking there for 50 kuna a day.

As for food, unless you brought a picnic with you – a sound idea – you'll almost certainly be eating at one of the hotels; apart from a summer grill (the *Plaža*) it's all there is.

All accommodation is booked directly through the park office in Fažana (tel: 052 525 888; fax: 052 521 367; www.np-brijuni.hr).

What to see

The standard excursion consists of a three-hour miniature-train ride with an English-speaking guide, which takes in the main sights and culminates with an hour or so to explore the museum/exhibitions.

The first thing you'll notice is the herds of deer – there are at least 800 out in the open here, along with mouflon, pheasants and peacocks roaming free. The keener-eyed will also notice the remarkable number of species of flora – at least 600 local and 30 imported.

The northwestern end of the island is fenced-off as a dedicated safari park, featuring zebra, dromedaries, llamas, antelopes, zebu, sheep and the two elephants. The idea of foreign fauna here isn't new – Kupelweiser had the bright idea as far back as 1911 of using the Brijuni Islands to acclimatise tropical animals on their way to European zoos.

You'll also be taken to see the rather tatty ruins of the 1st-century BC Roman country estate at Veriga Bay, which must have been extraordinary at the time but is hard to imagine now. More impressive is the ruined Byzantine fortress on the other side of the island, the heart of the settlement of Castrum, which was inhabited from the 2nd century BC until the early 14th century, when the plague arrived.

The rest of the west coast features the three residential villas of Tito's time, the White Villa, Jadranka and Brijunka. Tito himself had his quarters, along with his exquisite tropical gardens, on the offshore island of Vanga (also called Krasnica),

GIVE SOMETHING BACK – HELP THE BRIJUNI ELEPHANTS!

For lack of funds, the Brijuni National Park can't provide ideal living conditions for its elephants, and is calling for your help. Although Sony and Lanka are in good health, and are arguably one of the most beautiful pairs in Europe, they don't have enough room, and their 480m^2 living area badly needs to be enlarged, both for their sakes and for the sake of their keepers and visitors. Extra funds are also needed for their healthcare and food costs.

So why not become a Brijuni benefactor? Contributions should be sent to the following account: 'Javna Ustanova Nacionalni Park Brijuni', 2360000-1101435571, at Istarska Banka in Pula, specifying 'SOS Brijunske životinje'. Your help will be greatly appreciated – indeed since the first edition of this guide was published in 2003, dozens of benefactors have answered the appeal.

charging between the two and around the other islands by speedboat. The White Villa was used for formal receptions, while Jadranka was where visiting royalty overnighted.

There's no doubt you'll also be shown the Old Lady, an olive tree more than 1,600 years old – carbon-dating says so. In a botanical triumph, and as a vindication of the programme to revitalise the island's olive production, the Old Lady produced enough olives to make oil for the first time in more than 100 years at the end of 2001.

Back at the starting point, the archaeological museum, housed in a small 14th-century Venetian castle, merits a short visit, while the Church of St Germaine, next door, has an interesting collection of copies of Istrian frescos and Glagolitic inscriptions.

The natural history museum next door is a rather poignant collection of stuffed animals which either died here or on the way here from foreign climes. Upstairs there are two collections, the fascinating photos which make up *'Josip Broz Tito on Brijuni'*, and a collection entitled *'From the memory of an old Austrian'*, dedicated to Paul Kupelweiser.

If you want to see more than is on the tour, you'll probably have to stay over, and hire a guide from the hotel – in-depth freelancing is strongly discouraged. It's a pity, but understandable, given Brijuni's triple function as state residence, national park, and tourist destination.

Birdwatchers will likely want to check out the marshy lakes near the Saline Bay (in the south, unmarked on the maps), which have now been fenced off as a tentative ornithological reservation. Here you'll find excellent nesting grounds for marsh birds including ducks, coots, grebes, quail and noisy pratincoles, as well as warblers, nightingales and other songbirds, while the pine trees provide shelter for goshawks, buzzards and sparrowhawks. Late summer sees the arrival of egrets, storks, herons and bitterns. Contact the national park directly (see *Where to Stay*, above) for details.

PULA

Strategically situated at Istria's tip, and benefiting from a kind climate and a large, sheltered harbour, Pula (Pola) has been continuously inhabited for the past 3,000 years. What you'll find today, however, is a whole clutch of superb Roman ruins (including one of the world's best-preserved amphitheatres) set in a cheerful, cosmopolitan, street-café city of 65,000 people. Pula lives on the fence, caught halfway between its shipyard, docks and busy commercial port, and the beaches, coves and tourist developments strung out along the indented peninsula a couple of kilometres south of the centre.

Bombarded by both sides during World War II – a rare distinction – the city was quickly restored, and during the Yugoslav era became popular as a holiday destination. The recent war didn't come anywhere near here, but drove away the tourists all the same – though they've now returned in force.

History

Mentioned in ancient Greek despatches in connection with Jason and the Argonauts, archaeological findings show that Pula (myths notwithstanding) had already been established as a settlement long before the Histri fortified it in the 1st century BC. Once the Romans had successfully overpowered the Histri, Pula grew rapidly in status and became a colony. Under the first Roman emperor, Augustus, it became an important regional centre, and temples, theatres, a forum and an amphitheatre were built.

At its most prosperous, in the time of Septimus Severus (AD193–211), Pula was an important Roman war harbour, and was by then – according to my 1911

JAMES JOYCE AND PULA

After eloping to Europe in October 1904 with Nora Barnacle, a 20-year-old chambermaid, the 22-year-old James Joyce finally managed to find part-time work teaching English at the Berlitz School in Pula that November.

Moving in with Nora to an unheated apartment in Villa Giulia, just round the corner from the school (in the large yellow building right beside the Sergius Arch – there's a plaque), Jim and Nora spent the winter in Pula half-freezing to death, and spent as much time as they could at the warmer *Caffe Miramare delle Specce*, down on the waterfront (it's now a furniture shop). In letters to his brother he described Pula as 'Siberia by the sea', but it's clear that Joyce grew to love the city, and he would often be seen on long walks around town and up the coast as far as the fishing village of Fažana.

In February 1905, he was taken to the island of Veliki Brijun for his 23rd birthday by his Berlitz colleagues, and on this trip he broke the news that his first child was on the way. The couple, deciding to settle in Pula, moved to a more comfortable apartment at 1 Medulinska (next door to the university's faculty of philosophy), but following a confusing incident – was Joyce suspected of spying for the Italians or British? – they packed their bags and hurriedly moved to Trieste, where their son Giorgio was born that July.

Today you'll find little in the way of Joyce memorabilia in town – the *Uliks* bar celebrates the author of Ulysses in name alone, on the ground floor of the apartment building housing the language school.

Encyclopaedia Britannica – home to a population of 35,000 to 50,000 inhabitants. Mysteriously, contemporary sources never mention a figure of more than 5,000 to 10,000.

After the decline of Rome, Pula's fortunes were subjected to the usual roller-coaster ride of Goths, Ostrogoths, Byzantium and Venice, and the combination of invasion and plague saw the city shrink to 1,000 inhabitants in the 16th century. By 1631 the population was down to just 300 – hardly surprising therefore that the Venetians considered having the amphitheatre removed from Pula and put up in Venice instead.

Over the centuries Pula was visited by the likes of Dante, Michelangelo, Palladio and Lord Byron, spreading the Pula influence into Italian, French and British architecture – Inigo Jones is said to have used the Sergius Arch (see below) as the inspiration for many a loving detail on an English country house.

By 1842, Pula's population had inched up to 1,126, but change was right around the corner. With the collapse of Venice, 50 years earlier, the Austro-Hungarian Empire was seeking major outlets to the Mediterranean, and in 1853 they settled on Pula, rebuilding the town, installing a garrison, starting a shipyard and making it their naval HQ for the empire. By the end of the century Pula's population had exploded to over 45,000.

Badly bombed during World War II, Pula came under Allied administration until 1947, when it passed to Yugoslavia. Today it's the headquarters of the Croatian Navy as well as one of Croatia's three main shipyards, alongside Rijeka and Split.

Getting there

Pula airport is 7km northeast of the city, and a regular airport shuttle bus will bring you into town in around 15 minutes or so. If you're on an Istrian package tour of any kind then you'll probably be transferred straight from the airport to your hotel.

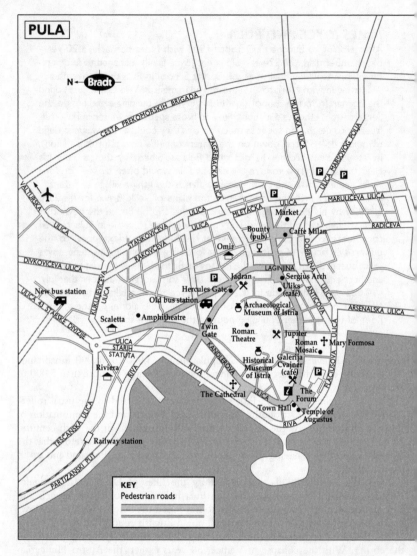

An alternative is to fly to Venice and connect with the twice-weekly car ferry, which takes around 6 hours to make the crossing.

If you're coming in by train you'll find the station on the waterfront, ten minutes north of the old town – just head towards the amphitheatre past the Hotel Riviera. There are left-luggage facilities here, but the hours are much shorter than those at the bus station, only being open Monday to Saturday. Three trains a day come in from each of Rijeka (2½ hours away) and Zagreb (7 hours). There are also two trains a day from Ljubljana (4 hours).

If you're travelling round by bus then you'll find the new station a couple of blocks north of the amphitheatre, though most buses do a loop into town via the old bus station as well. Left-luggage facilities are open here from 05.00–23.00 seven days a week. A dozen buses a day head up to each of Rovinj (40 minutes)

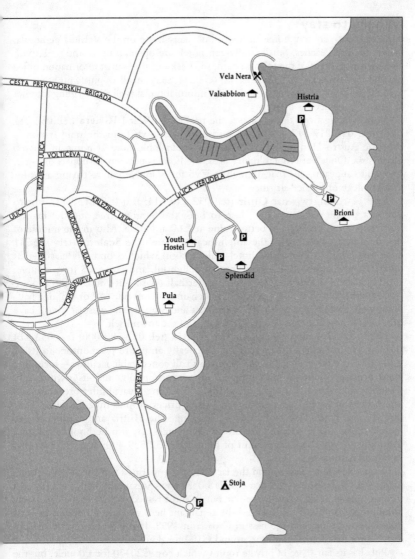

and Zagreb (5½ hours), while six go daily to Poreč (1½ hours), two to Split (11 hours) and one to Dubrovnik (15 hours).

Driving round Pula is pretty easy, though in high summer parking in the centre of town can be a problem – not, however, the insurmountable one you'll find in Opatija.

Getting around

The centre of town is all walkable – and mostly pedestrianised – but you might find yourself on bus #6 if you're going up to Fažana to catch a boat to the Brijuni Islands, #2 if you're hostelling, or #1, #3 or #7 if you're heading towards Stoja or Verudela, where the beaches, the hostel and most of the hotels can be found. Bus tickets go for 10 kuna from kiosks and 15 kuna on the bus, and are valid for two rides each.

Where to stay

Pula has relatively few hotels in town, but many more on the Verdula peninsula, handy for the beaches. Small family-run hotels are opening up all the time, with the encouragement of the tourist board, so check out the tourist information office on the Forum (tel: 052 212 987; fax: 052 211 855; email: tz-pula@pu.htnet.hr), which can also give you maps and useful information, as well as providing internet access (if your need is brief).

Most striking from the outside is the pre-World War I **Riviera** (tel: 052 211 166; fax: 052 219 117; www.arenaturist.hr) just down from the train station, a fantastic Austro-Hungarian edifice which would look more at home in Zagreb than Istria. Once very much luxury class, the hotel is now on-its-uppers one-star, and quite appealing for that, though at €96 for a double you're paying a lot for the privilege of former elegance.

The 12-room, two-star **Omir** (tel: 052 210 614; fax: 052 213 944), just to the east of the old town and close to both the Sergius Arch and the market square, is simple but much better value at €60 a double. Also in the middle of town, almost next door to the amphitheatre, there's the **Scaletta** (tel: 052 541 599; fax: 052 540 285; www.hotel-scaletta.com) which is bizarrely classified as one-star, given that its 12 rooms are all delightful, and cost €75 for a double. The food here is also excellent, so consider half board – if you can get a room.

The other hotels are out on Verdula, a ten-minute bus ride (#7 or #3) or a half-hour walk away to the south. The peninsula and Stoja, to the west (#1 bus), have all the best beaches, within striking distance of the town itself.

Nicest of all is the palatial four-star **Histria** (tel: 052 590 000; fax: 052 214 175; www.arenaturist.hr), which has practically an entire promontory to itself, and views out to sea, back to the marina and all conceivable facilities – including nice private balconies, big indoor and outdoor pools, and its own beach. Doubles go for €164 a night in summer, including a vast buffet breakfast, and the hotel's open all year round – off-season prices drop as much as 50%. Take the #7 bus to the last stop, and walk 200m. The Histria and another dozen hotels (those in the vicinity are mostly three-star) can also be booked through Arenaturist, which manages most of them (tel: 052 529 400; fax: 052 529 401; www.arenaturist.hr).

It's a 15-minute walk round the far side of the marina from the #7 bus route, where the **Valsabbion** (tel/fax: 052 218 033; www.valsabbion.net), with only 15 rooms, might be classified three-star but in most respects it's four-star. Sea-view doubles go for €245 half board – the restaurant here was voted the best in Istria five years running, and the best in Croatia in 1998. If you want to stay, and not eat, rooms on their own go for around €100 for doubles.

Pula has its fair share of private rooms which cost €20–30 for a double, but the locations often leave something to be desired. Book through any of the 20-odd travel agents in town, and expect to pay a 50% surcharge for a one-night stay in summer. If you're on a budget you're far better off trying to get in at Pula's excellent **youth hostel** (Zaljev Valsaline 4; tel: 052 391 124; fax: 052 391 106), which is basic and simple but in an incredible location, with its own beach and a diving club next door. Bed and breakfast costs €14 per person per night. Catch bus #2 or #7 to the Piramida stop, walk back one street, turn left and walk right to the end.

Finally, Pula is great for camping, with an easy-to-reach campground at **Stoja** (tel: 052 529 400; fax: 052 529 401) – just take the #1 bus to the last stop, about 3km out of town. The Stoja has fairly basic facilities, but an absolutely unbeatable location and some of the best swimming near Pula.

Where to eat and drink

The best restaurants in Pula are reckoned by the locals to be south of the town, in Verdula, and if you want a touch of class (and have a pretty fat wallet) you'll be very well treated at **Valsabbion** (see above) or the slightly less-expensive **Vela Nera** (tel: 052 219 209; fax: 052 215 951) nearby, which is unprepossessing enough on arrival but has a lovely seaside terrace, a covered dining room overlooking the marina, and excellent food.

In town the emphasis is as much on café life as restaurants, and every district has huge terraces spreading out onto the pavements, packed in summer and surprisingly well attended in spring and autumn. With most of the old town traffic-free, you can take a leaf out of the *Puležani's* book and take the time to linger over a coffee or an aperitif.

When the rest of the city's stifling you can't do better than the **Jadran**, a terrace right at the top end of Giardini, the street leading down along the old town wall from the Hercules Gate to the Sergius Arch. It's one of the few places in town with guaranteed shade and a breeze.

Down at the bottom of the town in the Forum you'll find the **Galerija Cvajner**, a café-cum-art-gallery run by the former director of the film festival. It has a lovely terrace (right next door to the tourist office) while inside are great 16th-century ceilings and the remains of old frescos, uncovered by chance during restoration.

Up at the other end of the old town, all the way up Sergijevaca, you'll find **Uliks**, in the building Joyce used to teach in, which is a nice bar though not especially Joyce-related. On Narodni Trg, 100m further on, alongside the lovely secessionist cast-iron market building, is the **Caffe Milan**, famous not just for its coffees but also for the underfloor heating on the terrace. It would have suited James Joyce a treat.

Inside the market you'll find fresh meat and fish every day, while on the shady square behind there's a vast range of produce on sale, protected from the flies by the chestnut trees – the perfect place to cruise for picnic food.

Opposite the market, just up Veronska, is the **Bounty**, enormously popular with students and ex-pats. The pub serves up around two dozen types of beer and hearty Anglo-style food.

For pizzas you should try the highly recommended **Jupiter**, on Castropola, the upper street running parallel to Sergijevaca, though I have to confess to not having eaten there myself; it was full both times I passed. Meanwhile if you're near the amphitheatre you might eat at the **Scaletta** hotel's very good restaurant – not inexpensive but well worth the splash. Failing that, you won't go far wrong looking through the windows of busy-looking establishments and choosing for yourself.

What to see

The best way to see Pula is on foot and the best place to start is in the **Forum**, the large paved square just back from the front, on the southwestern corner of town. Stop in at the tourist office and pick up a free map.

The first thing you'll have seen as you came into the square won't have been tourist information but the **Temple of Augustus**. Built in 2BC according to most modern sources, the temple is one of the best complete Roman monuments outside Italy, rivalling the Maison Carrée in Nîmes. After suffering a direct hit during World War II, it was pieced lovingly back together in 1947, and you wouldn't know the difference.

Originally this was one of three temples on the Forum, and you can still clearly see the shape and placing of the Temple of Diana, one of the other two (the third has gone without trace), by walking round to the back of the 13th-century **town hall** next door. While you're there don't miss the sculpted Renaissance siren/mermaid on the northernmost corner, warding off evil.

Walking up Kandlerova will take you past the cathedral towards the amphitheatre. The houses along the way are reflective of Pula's mixed past, with Renaissance blending into Venetian Gothic, and Romanesque mixing into Austro-Hungarian solidity.

The **Cathedral of St Mary** itself would doubtless get more attention if it weren't surrounded by so many Roman ruins – indeed the separate (rather chunky) campanile was built in the 17th century entirely from stones from the amphitheatre. Pop into the cathedral for a peek at the altar, actually a 3rd-century sarcophagus, and some fragments of floor mosaics. The cathedral was started in the 5th century as a conversion job on a Roman temple, but didn't reach its present form until the 16th and 17th centuries.

The Amphitheatre

You can't miss Pula's enormous Amphitheatre – it's the sixth biggest in the world (after Rome, Capua, Verona, Siracusa and Arles, since you ask), and has the most complete outer walls of any still standing. Started under Augustus, and continued under Flavius, it was enlarged and completed to its present 130m-by-105m ellipse under Vespasian (whose lover Antonia, it's said, came from Pula) in the second half of the 1st century AD.

Built outside the city walls, the triple-storeyed building originally had seating for over 20,000 people (odd, given the total population at its completion is widely reckoned to be considerably less than this) and had 20 entrances and exits to allow for rapid access to the seats. Most of the seating has long gone of course – used for building as far away as Venice – but once there would have been stone benches up to the second storey and wooden seating (for women and commoners) above that. Seats were a tight 38cm across and season-ticket holders had engraved name-plates.

Four towers gave access to the upper rows – the southwestern tower housed the royal box, while the northwestern one today features a plaque to the Pula-born Venetian Senator Gabriele Emo, who happily persuaded the Senate in 1583 not to take the amphitheatre away.

The arena in the middle would originally have been filled with sand (*arena* is Latin for sand) and was used for bloody combats until the beginning of the 5th century. Watching a film-screening or taking in a concert here today, it's hard to imagine the awfulness of real gladiator combats – lions and bears were used here against gladiators (mostly luckless prisoners of war), who were also pitted against one another.

After Rome collapsed the arena was used as a marketplace, and for medieval jousting tournaments, but the seating was mostly quarried; today's concerts and screenings seat just 5,000–6,000, and even the biggest gigs – your Stings, your Three Tenors – can't pack in many more than 10,000 fans. If you're here in summer, don't miss out on the opera or film festivals.

Back into town

Walking back towards the town turn half-left into Carrarina and have a look at the **Twin Gate** (Porta Gemina), from the 2nd century. This was once part of the aqueduct providing water to the town and one of the town's 12 gates, and was one of the few monuments built with private money. It's now the entrance to the exhaustive **Archaeological Museum of Istria**, although the exhibits themselves are a bit of a jumble. Re-ordering and re-labelling would work wonders. Even if you don't go inside don't miss the classical sculptures in the garden, or the small Roman theatre here.

The upper road to the right of the museum leads up to the tatty, 17th-century Venetian **fortress**, housing the **Historical Museum of Istria** – only worth seeing if you've done everything else, though the views out over the town and particularly of the amphitheatre are excellent from up here.

Back down at the Twin Gate keep the wall on your right and follow Carrarina down past the **Hercules Gate**. This is Pula's oldest monument, dating from the middle of the 1st century BC; it's now the entrance to the centre for the Italian Minority. The gate's unusual oblique angle is a reminder that the road originally leading out wasn't at right-angles to the wall.

Turning into the shady Giardini, follow the walls down to the **Sergius Arch** (also known as Porta Aurea). This was completed in 27BC as a memorial to three soldiers from the same family, Sergius Lepidus, Gaius Lucius Sergius and Gnaeus Sergius. The arch was originally backed by a gate, so only the inside is decorated – check out the winged victories, imagery which was later co-opted wholesale by Christianity when portraying angels.

The Sergius Arch leads – not surprisingly – into Sergijevaca, the old town's main pedestrian street, running back down to the Forum. Half way down, cut left to the small, 6th-century Byzantine **Church of Mary Formosa**, once part of a larger basilica, built to a similar plan to the one in Poreč (see page 140). The best mosaics from inside are now in the Archaeological Museum. Just down from here is an impressive 3rd-century mosaic floor, discovered by accident in 1959. Amongst some fine decorative geometrical work the main panel depicts the *Punishment of Dirce* – Dirce is the woman in the middle, about to be trampled by the bull, in yet another rendition of the story made famous by the Farnese Bull in Naples. Dirce was the classic cruel stepmother, who treated her husband Lycus's daughter Antiope as a slave. Unfortunately for her, Antiope had already borne two children by Zeus, and once they grew up – after the traditional hillside abandonment – the boys returned to kill Dirce by binding her to a mad bull. Not a great way to go.

Out of town

Out of town, the main attractions are the Brijuni Islands (see page 146), which are well worth a visit, and the 30km of beaches coves and bays to the south of the city. The nearest of these are just a 20–25-minute walk away from the town centre, or a short bus ride away (on #1, #2 or #7).

Further south, right on Istria's point, are the resorts of **Medulin** and **Premantura**. Each has long stretches of beach with fairly shallow waters, making them popular with families. The **Kažela** camp (tel/fax: 052 576 050), on Medulin's sandy beach, has a large (separate) section for naturists. On the other side of the bay, the peninsula's spectacular southernmost spur, Rt Kamenjak, is a dedicated nature park. You pay 10 kuna to gain access to the beaches here.

THE EAST COAST TO LABIN AND RABAC

From Pula to the resort of Rabac, the Istrian coast is at its least developed and least visited. The new main road barrels up through the centre of Istria to Pazin before cutting through the Učka tunnel to Rijeka, while the old main road stays 5–10km inland from the undeveloped east coast, only returning to the sea after Labin.

There's little or no public transport, and nowhere to stay, but if you have your own wheels (and some persistence) you can find deserted coves and beaches here at the end of winding footpaths, even though the steep cliffs often make the coast literally inaccessible. It's a great area to explore on day trips from Pula.

If you're on the bus from Pula to Opatija in the last week of August, it's definitely worth stopping in the village of **Barban**, where the annual Tilting at the Ring (*Trka na prstenac*) festival takes place. The dangerous habit of trying to spear a ring suspended on a rope with a lance from a fast-moving horse used to be commonplace, apparently; today it survives only here and in Sinj (see page 238).

Labin, a charming medieval hilltop town, used to be the centre of a thriving mining industry. You won't see much sign of that now, since the mines closed after subsidence in the 1970s. Today, it's a lovely place to visit, with steep and narrow streets, a sprinkling of churches and a handful of baroque and Renaissance palazzi. The **town museum** features an excellent mining exhibition, complete with a suitably claustrophobic tunnel you can go into, as well as various archaeological bits and pieces from the area. Ask at the museum if Matija Vlačić's birthplace is open – if so you'll find an interesting collection of manuscripts and books by (and about) this 16th-century protestant firebrand, contemporary and colleague of Martin Luther. On the way you can walk up to the fortress (*Fortica*) for a fine view out over Rabac and across the water towards the island of Cres.

Rabac, down on the coast, was once a fishing village but is now unashamedly a tourist resort, with nothing much other than apartments and hotels, though it does have a nice (if busy) pebbly beach.

Pula–Opatija buses stop in Labin's lower town, a steep 15-minute hike below the old town, and you change here if you're going on to Rabac – buses take ten minutes and run half-hourly down to the resort. Alternatively if you've made it up into Labin's old town you can then walk down to Rabac – it takes about three-quarters of an hour, all downhill, on the old mule path.

There aren't any hotels in Labin, though there are a few private rooms – check at whichever tourist agency is open, or at the tourist office (tel/fax: 052 855 560). Rabac, on the other hand, has a dozen or so, though none are open all year round. Expect to pay around €140 at the four-star **Lanterna**, or a very reasonable €70 for the one-star **Mediteran** – in each case for a sea-view double in high season, in a 110-room hotel. Reservations are centralised (tel: 052 862 067; fax: 052 872 561; www.rabac-hotels.com).

TO OPATIJA AND UČKA

Istria's northeastern corner has been popular with visitors for over a century, though it's now more nouveau riche than Habsburg chic. If you're here in the middle of August with your own car, expect to have trouble finding anywhere to park it, but remember you can get away from it all by climbing up into the Učka mountains behind Opatija.

The telephone code for the Opatija area is 051.

The coast to Opatija

Soon after you've left Labin, the road rejoins the steep coast, and you pass the medieval – and abandoned – village of **Plomin**, before turning north on the winding route to the Opatija Riviera. If you happen to be driving past Plomin there's a great restaurant on the main road here called **Dorina**, which serves up hearty Istrian staples at very reasonable rates – it's understandably popular with locals. Their asparagus soup is unrivalled, and the *mineštra* (thick bean soup) is excellent. For main courses try the *fuži* (pasta) with truffles or the amazing *gnojki* (gnocchi) which – in a triumph of excess – is served with both squid and truffles together. If that's not enough to convince you, the house white, at a bargain 35 kuna a litre, will. The first part of the coast here is undeveloped – it's too steep to build on – though you'll see plenty of summer traffic heading down to **Brestova**, departure-point for ferries to **Cres**. At the height of the season drivers sometimes have to queue all day (and even all night) to get on board.

From **Brseč** you can take a higher, less busy, parallel road along the coast for 8km or so, offering terrific vertiginous views – keep your eyes on the road and your hands on the wheel if you're driving. The roads meet up again in **Mošćenička Draga**, the first resort in the Opatija Riviera, with the tiny village dwarfed by the **Hotel Marina** (tel: 051 737 504; fax: 051 737 584). Things get more serious 4km later when you reach the pebbles of **Medveja**, the last long concrete-free beach before the far side of Rijeka.

Next up is the Opatija Riviera's prettiest resort, **Lovran**, featuring lots of late Habsburg-era villas and a well-preserved nugget of an old town. Lovran is just 5km south of Opatija and practically merges with it – you can walk along the pedestrianised front between the two in about an hour.

The name Lovran derives from the laurel tree, and you'll see plenty of these in the resort – along with cypresses, palm trees and lovely flowers. You'll also notice the town's obsession with chestnuts, not just as far as trees are concerned, but also in terms of the food. In October, over a two-week period, the *Maranuda* (chestnut festival) is an excuse to binge on every conceivable chestnut-related goodie.

There's plenty of private accommodation available, through any of the tourist agencies on the main road, though you may have trouble finding a room if you don't book well ahead. Get the latest list from the Lovran tourist office (Šetalište Maršala Tita 63, 51415 Lovran; tel: 051 291 740; fax: 051 294 387). For hotels the three-star **Lovran** (tel: 051 291 222; fax: 051 292 467) has simple sea-view doubles, including (obligatory) half board at €140 for two in high season, while next door the swankier three-star **Excelsior** (tel: 051 292 233; fax: 051 291 989), with indoor and outdoor pools, charges €160. Both hotels are just a block from the sea and only a few minutes' walk from the old town.

Lovran makes an ideal base for walking in the Učka massif (see overleaf), and the tourist office has a good walking map.

North of Lovran, the small towns and little bays (but biggish resorts) of **Ika** and **Ičići** lead seamlessly on to Opatija.

Opatija

Opatija (originally *Abbazia*, after the former Benedictine abbey) is astonishingly popular, and has been for over a century. Rooms in the nicest hotels are booked a year or more ahead, and don't even think about trying to find street parking in August.

It's justifiably proud of its Habsburg villas and palaces, its exotic palms and manicured gardens and its 12km-long pedestrianised front, stretching from Lovran in the south to Volosko in the north, but the fashionable winter resort of Opatija never quite made the post-World War II leap from winter to summer tourism. The beaches here are concrete, and netted in (my trusty 1966 Gateway Guide explains this: 'the visitor should stay within the barriers and never swim far out from the shore since there are sometimes sharks'); the summer crowds can intimidate; and beyond the late 19th-century swank, there's really nothing to see. It's still a great place to come in winter, however, when the town slips quietly back into a nostalgic reverie, and afternoon cakes are picked at with silver forks by retired Austrians.

Until the arrival of the wealthy Rijeka trader, Iginio Scarpa, in 1844, Opatija was the proverbial sleepy fishing village. Scarpa built the **Villa Angiolina** (named after his wife) and created its exotic gardens as a summer retreat, and the high and mighty were soon paying visits.

Given a clean bill of health by doctors to the wealthy – like so many nice places to stay – Opatija soon became a spa town, and *the* place to take a 'cure' (and be seen) in winter. It was helped on its way by the arrival of the railway in Rijeka in 1873 – by 1884 the Kvarner hotel was up and running, and demand was so high that the Imperial was opened only a year later, with the Palace-Bellevue hot on its heels.

Anyone who was anyone in the Austro-Hungarian sphere of influence came here, and it was hugely popular with the aristocracy. Anton Chekhov, Gustav Mahler and Sigmund Freud gave their patronage, while Vladimir Nabakov spent his childhood holidays here (probably up in the hills collecting butterflies).

If you're planning on staying in Opatija in summer it's a good idea to try and book a year in advance – though you may be lucky with private rooms through one of the many tourist agencies in town. It may also be worth writing or calling ahead to the tourist board (Vladimira Nazora 3, 51410 Opatija; tel: 051 271 710; fax: 051 271 699; www.opatija-tourism.hr).

If you have the time to plan, and the budget, Opatija is one place where it's really worth splashing out, as the opulent 19th-century hotels are remarkably good value in their class – rooms at the classic **Kvarner** (check out the astounding 1913 Crystal Ballroom), the **Imperial** (tastefully elegant lobby and bars) and the **Palace-Bellevue** (fabulous reception rooms) can be booked through Liburnia Riviera (tel: 051 710 300; fax: 051 271 503; www.liburnia.hr). Sea-view doubles at the Kvarner in high season go for around €140, while at the Imperial and Palace-Bellevue they're a surprisingly modest €100 or so. Opatija is also home, as you'd expect, to Istria's only three big five-star hotels. The first two have indoor and outdoor pools; the third offers remarkably good-value Viennese-style elegance. Choose between the **Ambassador** (tel: 051 743 333; fax: 051 743 444), which is big, modern and has sea-view doubles at €182 in season; the **Millennium** (tel: 051 202 000; fax: 051 202 406), which spans a pair of fin-de-siècle villas, with a choice of rooms decorated with furniture and fittings classic or modern, where deluxe doubles go for €162 a night; or the **Mozart** (tel: 051 718 260; fax: 051 271 739), which has just 30 rooms, with sea-view doubles at €120.

If you're in Opatija, make the effort to walk along the shore to **Volosko**, still a fishing village even though it's barely half an hour on foot from the summer throngs. It's Mediterranean to Opatija's Habsburg, and though it's no secret, it is a pretty place to go for lunch.

Učka

Rising up above the Opatija Riviera – and giving it its mild winter/cool summer climate, while cutting it off from the rest of Istria – is the Učka massif, culminating in the 1,396m summit of Vojak, the highest point on Veli Učka (Monte Maggiore). On a clear evening they say you can see the lights of Venice from here; what's sure is that you get a great view of the Kvarner Bay and the island of Cres.

With your own transport you can drive right to the top of the mountain on a tarred road (leading up to the TV transmitter) but walking is a far better way of seeing it. Good maps are available from the tourist offices in Rijeka, Opatija and Lovran, with well-marked trails and the chance to really get away from it all.

The most obvious ascent starts off from a junction on the old Rijeka–Pazin road (not the main road, which heads through the Učka tunnel) – this can also be reached from Opatija, or via a dizzying series of hairpins from Ičići.

Exactly 6km after the village of Veprinac, you reach the **Hotel Učka** (tel: 051 299 642; fax: 051 299 658), down a drive to the left, which has rooms in a '70s-futuristic building and a big terrace – doubles go for a very reasonable €50. One kilometre further up the road you'll find the **Pansion-Restaurant Učka** (tel/fax: 051 299 646), which is also an excellent place to stay, with ten rustic rooms at €45 for doubles and a terrace with big views. You can get to both establishments at weekends three times a day on the #34 bus from Opatija.

From the Pansion, it's just over 1km to the **Dopolovaro** restaurant, which is usually busy at weekends and often not open during the week. Just beyond the restaurant you'll find the road on the left which leads up to the summit, almost exactly 6km up the road. On foot it's a pleasant hike up (just follow the road), with great views on the way and even better ones from the top – turn left at the TV and radio mast, and follow the path up to the trig point, on top of a small tower. Avoid sliding down the hang-glider take-off ramp on the way up – unless of course you've brought your hang-glider with you.

Real hikers will of course want to climb the Učka massif from sea-level. To do this the obvious base is Lovran, though there is a path up from Medveja. The Lovran path starts steep and stays that way – it's a fairly tough four hours up to the summit (three hours coming down), so make sure you have plenty of water and food with you (and from Medveja count on an extra hour each way). Most of the walk up is through lovely oak and then beech woods, before you emerge on the grassy shoulder of the mountain itself. By the time you get this far you're less than half an hour from the summit and the TV antenna.

If you're in Lovran and keen to walk you should also consider the paths leading to the abandoned village of Sučići, high above Mošćenička Draga, as well as other paths which will keep you far from the madding crowds.

INLAND ISTRIA

Head just a few kilometres inland in Istria and tourism is wiped almost entirely off the map. Even the biggest town, **Pazin** (the administrative capital of Istria) has a population of under 6,000, while the rest of the rustic interior is characterised by rolling agricultural land, pretty medieval hilltop villages, and a general absence of people – in spite of efforts to resettle some villages with artists, the inland population has been in steady decline since the advent of mass tourism on the coast in the 1960s.

The big hope for central Istria now is agro-tourism, and while it's perfectly suited to it, having central Italy's advantages of great food, fine wine, avenues of cypresses and charming villages, the new Tuscany it ain't (not quite yet, anyway). Accommodation options are limited, while the lack of public transport makes many villages hard to get to without your own wheels. Nonetheless, be prepared at the height of the season to encounter the occasional coach-load of tourists being ferried up on day trips from the coast – and indeed, if you're on a coastal package holiday, the Istrian interior makes for an excursion you shouldn't miss.

Istria's famous throughout Croatia for its truffles, and you'll find truffle dishes here which are affordable – at least when compared with the prices for those in France and Italy. The world's largest-ever white truffle was found in Istria in November 1999, near Buje, putting the town and its finder, Giancarlo Zigante, into the *Guinness Book of Records*. The monster truffle weighed in at 1.31kg, and measured 19.5cm by 12.4cm by 13.5cm. Another speciality – this time found only in Istria – is *biska*, or *biskovačka*, a fairly lethal but (at its best) wonderful spirit made from mistletoe.

In terms of access, public transport is centred on Pazin, with buses from all over Istria connecting here with trains on the Ljubljana to Pula line. Buses run up to

Motovun and Buzet, but you'll find your own transport easier for Oprtalj, Grožnjan, Hum or Roč, though the first two are within a few kilometres' walk of bus routes and the last two within a few kilometres of the train line.

Where to stay

If you have your own transport then agro-tourism is definitely the way to go – check with the Pula tourist office (see the beginning of this chapter for details).

Otherwise, Pazin itself has only one hotel, the two-star **Motel Lovac** (tel: 052 624 324; fax: 052 624 219), with 26 spartan but clean rooms for €26 a double. There's also a sprinkling of private rooms – ask at the tourist office (tel/fax: 052 622 460).

Motovun also has a solitary hotel, the three-star, 29-roomed **Kaštel** (tel: 052 681 607; fax: 052 681 652), set in a lovely 18th-century building, with spacious high-ceilinged refurbished doubles at €66 a night. The pleasant Italianate town of Buje also lists only one hotel, the two-star **Miro** (tel: 052 777 050; fax: 052 777 051), which has 20 clean, comfortable rooms, with doubles at €65. Finally in Buzet you'll find the 1970s-era, two-star 50-room **Fontana** (tel/fax: 052 662 615), with plain €40 doubles.

If you fail at these, it's worth trying the accommodation at **Istarske Toplice** ('Istrian Hot Springs'), between Buje and Buzet. As the name of the location suggests, the hotel (tel: 052 664 300, fax: 052 664 310) is part of a 100-year-old thermal health resort, which explains why there's a 236-room hotel in a canyon in the middle of nowhere. Check into one of the €54 doubles and enjoy the sulphurous waters and a mineral-mud face-pack.

Otherwise it's always worth asking at local bars or cafés whether anyone has a room they're willing to let out – an enquiry at the **Pintur** restaurant in Grožnjan (truly excellent pasta with truffle sauce) delivered a pleasant apartment for two, right in the old town, for €35. Call Diego Pucer on his mobile (098 872 505).

Pazin and Beram

If you're visiting the Istrian interior by public transport you're certain to come through **Pazin**, and there are worse places to stop. Its status as Istria's capital dates back to the end of World War II, when Yugoslavia was keen to moderate the Italian influence – one in the eye for the much larger and more logical Pula. Pazin has its own attractions, but the main source of interest in the area is the extraordinary 15th-century frescos at St Mary's Church near Beram (see opposite).

From the bus and train station walk down towards the town and castle, stopping off at the tourist office (tel/fax: 052 622 460) which can not only provide you with a map, but also has a list of walks and cycle trails in the area. If you're persuasive they can also ring ahead to arrange for the opening of St Mary's Church.

The main attraction in Pazin is **Pazin castle**, a 16th-century pile built on 10th-century remains, right down at the bottom of the town. Inside the monumental building you'll find the **Ethnographic Museum of Istria**, featuring Istrian costumes and handicrafts, along with a curious collection of church bells from Istrian churches through the ages. The castle itself overhangs the dramatic gorge into which the river Fojba disappears, supposedly the inspiration for Dante's entrance to hell (plausible: we know Dante was in Pula) as well as a major scene in Jules Verne's 1885 novel *Mathias Sandorf*; the title character disappears underground here, only to reappear six hours later in the Limski Kanal, near Rovinj, a good 40km away. If you're a Jules Verne fan you should definitely contact Davor Šišiović at the Jules Verne Club in Pazin (tel/fax: 052 622 460), who can tell you all about Pazin's annual Jules Verne Days in June.

Pazin's other main attraction is the **Parish Church of St Nicholas**, which has a magnificent free-standing campanile next to it. Inside the church there are some wonderful, if badly faded, 15th-century frescos – notable are the creation cycle and a battle scene, with baddie angels toughing it out with the good guys.

The old village of **Beram** is 1km off the main road to Poreč, about 5km west of Pazin. Just under 1km west of the village, at the end of a pretty road running into the woods, is the **Church of St Mary**. If you haven't been able to arrange things ahead of time in Pazin, you'll need to go to house #33 in the village, the home of the Gortan family, as they hold the key (*ključ*) to the church. Usually there's someone available who'll come with you to the church to unlock it and lock it back up again after your visit. It's a good idea to give something in return for their time and trouble – 20 kuna or so wouldn't be unreasonable.

The little church itself wouldn't be anything to write home about were it not for the Gothic frescos inside. Dating from 1474 and painted by Master Vincent of Kastav (see the inscription over the south door) and his assistants, they're a triumph of late-Gothic art. That they survived the centuries relatively intact is no doubt due to their having been plastered over; they were only rediscovered in 1913.

In all there are some 46 panels, most depicting scenes from the lives of Jesus and Mary, but what really catch the eye are the 8m-long *Adoration of the Magi* on the north wall, and the *Dance of Death* (more of a walk, really) over the old main door. Medieval pageantry and Istrian scenery dominate the first, while in the second you'll see all classes heading for the same inevitable fate: death. First come the Pope, a cardinal and a bishop, followed by a king and queen, an innkeeper, a child and a cripple. Bringing up the rear are a knight, and a greedy merchant pointing at his worldly goods. Accompanied by fiendishly lifelike skeletons with musical instruments – and one with the obligatory scythe – the frescos are a chilling reminder of life's impermanence.

If you're driving round the area it's also worth stopping at the hilltop village of **Pićan**, about 10km east of Pazin. There's almost nothing to the place, these days, beyond a fine stone gate into town and a monumental 17th-century church – with an even more monumental campanile beside it – but the views across the Istrian countryside are wonderful.

Motovun, Oprtalj and Grožnjan

Motovun, 15km northwest of Pazin, is the classic medieval hilltop town, and you can see it from miles around. It gets its fair share of visitors – usually on a day trip up from the coast – but that doesn't spoil things at all. And in the last week of July it hosts an international film festival.

The town walls have just been restored and offer a lovely promenade – all of ten minutes' walk – with wonderful views out over the surrounding countryside. Otherwise the town itself is pretty much limited to a single street, cobbled and traffic free in its upper reaches, running up from the valley floor. It works its way up through two ancient city gates, the first of which houses a lapidarium of sorts – Roman fragments on the right and Venetian lions on the left. Note the unusual 1755 face-on attempt at portraying the iconic sculpture – it looks more primitive than its 15th-century counterparts.

Between the two gates there's a lovely sloping terrace, where an ice-cream goes down a treat, and an unusual triangular loggia, before the street turns sharply up into the second gate, housing a cheerful restaurant. Through the second gate is the heart of the old town, consisting of the ramparts, a main square under which a cistern used to hold the whole town's water supply, the 18th-century church, and the Hotel Kaštel, with its lovely shady terrace out front and gardens at the back.

It's an idyllic place to stay (or even eat) – arguably the best in central Istria. But travel light – it's an awfully steep hike up with heavy bags.

The Church of St Stephen was designed by Palladio in 1614. Outside it's half way between Renaissance and baroque; inside it's plain and airy, with a flat-ceilinged aisle and naves, and some fine portraits of saints high up. Incongruously, the day I was there the church was filled with the strains of a local singing-group rehearsing Roberta Flack's *Killing Me Softly*. Next door is the sturdy, crenellated campanile, which looks a good deal older than it is (18th century).

Motovun is famous both for the Malvasija (white) and Teran (red) wines produced locally, as well as the delicious but breathtakingly expensive truffles hidden in the nearby woods. Try both, if you can afford to.

Six kilometres north of Motovun, up a windy road, is **Oprtalj**, an almost deserted hilltop village which gives you a good idea of what Motovun and Grožnjan (see below) would have been like had the restorers not moved in. Whilst it's undeniably charming in a run-down sort of way, with a population of barely 100 there's little in the way of life and soul – or indeed tourist infrastructure. There is however a single *konoba* (country pub/restaurant), and the truffles here are especially good.

Half way between Motovun and Buje, a few kilometres north of the main road, on a spectacular bluff, is yet another hilltop village, **Grožnjan**. Adopted by artists from the late 1960s on, it's also home to *Jeunesses Musicales Croatia* in the summer, and it's a lively place during the summer season, featuring lots of art galleries, craft shops, cafés and the strains of music wafting up and down the streets and alleys from the open windows of rehearsal rooms. The only restaurant in town – the Ladonija has sadly closed – is the Pintur, which serves spectacularly good pasta with truffle sauce.

Buzet, Roč, the Glagolitic Alley and Hum

Backed by the Ćićarija mountains to the northeast, the town of **Buzet** (self-billed as the 'City of Truffles' – not to mention 'The World's Favorit Pivo') is at the heart of what will eventually become the Native Park of Istria. It's a good base for walking or cycling.

The medieval town on the hill is excellent, in a slightly run-down sort of way, with two well-preserved 16th-century gates, a maze of narrow streets and a couple of marble-paved squares. At the top of the hill, the pale-yellow church has an unusual onion-domed altar canopy inside and some 19th-century paintings – look out for St Mark, on the left-hand side, with St Mark's Cathedral, in Venice, as a backdrop.

Below the old town, in the more modern Fontana, you'll find the bus station and the eponymous hotel (see page 162). Make sure you try a truffle-based dish while you're in Buzet (most commonly with pasta or an omelette) as well as the eponymous local beer.

When you're boozed-up and truffled-out, head for the tiny villages of Roč and Hum, and the so-called 'Glagolitic Alley' which connects them. Roč, 8km east of Buzet, has an official population of only 17, while Hum, 7km south of Roč, nonetheless steals the tourist limelight with its claim to be the smallest town on earth (even though it has six more residents than Roč).

Buses from Buzet to Rijeka will drop you at the turn-off, a ten-minute walk uphill to Roč, while if you get off the train at the Roč stop you'll find yourself around 2km out of town. Hum is even harder to reach, being more than 5km from the Hum train station, and not on any bus route.

It's hard to believe it now, but **Roč** was an important centre of Glagolitic literature from the 13th century on, and the tiny town, with its low 15th-century walls, is the repository of many treasures of Glagolitic literature from the 16th and

17th centuries. These days there's not a whole lot to see, and the chances are you'll be in and out in half an hour.

Within the main gate there's an interesting collection of Roman stone fragments, and inside, to the right, by the pint-sized concrete playing field, there's a solitary Venetian cannon. On the day I was here, it was Roč and not Hum that was humming, but it turned out to be a swarm of bees. Within the walls you'll also notice various bits of modern sculpture, all donated by the 'Friends of Roč', and it's worth glancing inside the Church of St Anthony – nice vaulting inside the apse and odd sedan chair-like confessionals. Once a year, in May, Roč really does swing, during the '*Triestina*', the annual international knees-up for the harmonica-playing fraternity.

The 7km road south to Hum is known as '**Glagolitic Alley**' (Aleja Glagoljaša), and if you have the time it makes for a pleasant-enough walk – a comfortable three-hour return trip to Hum and back from Roč. The memorial consists of 11 monuments along the roadside which were put up in 1977 to celebrate the Glagolitic priests who were among the first people to raise Croatian national consciousness in the 18th and 19th centuries.

The concrete sculptures are variations on representations of letters of the Glagolitic alphabet, which was kept alive in Istria and the islands of the Kvarner Bay long after it had disappeared elsewhere. Invented by St Cyril and St Methodius in the 9th century, the alphabet was adapted by St Clement into the Cyrillic seen today in much of the Balkans and across Russia.

The road ends at **Hum**, which has all the features you'd expect in a medieval town, though very little in the way of people. An imposing entrance gate (complete with Glagolitic knockers), fortified walls, cobbled alleys, dilapidated stone houses and a small church make up the village. It's in the process of being restored – steeplejacks in harnesses were pulling tufts of grass from between the cracks in the church tower when I was in town – and several of the houses are being done up, but it's still a very, very small place. Commerce exists in the form of a small museum (actually a souvenir shop), and a renowned *konoba*, which serves up excellent Istrian dishes, including *pršut*, and pasta with truffles.

Be warned, however: it may be hard to get to, but Hum can switch from being deserted to being positively overcrowded in the seconds it takes for a tour bus to disgorge its passengers. Trips come up here from the coast, lured by that 'smallest town' tag.

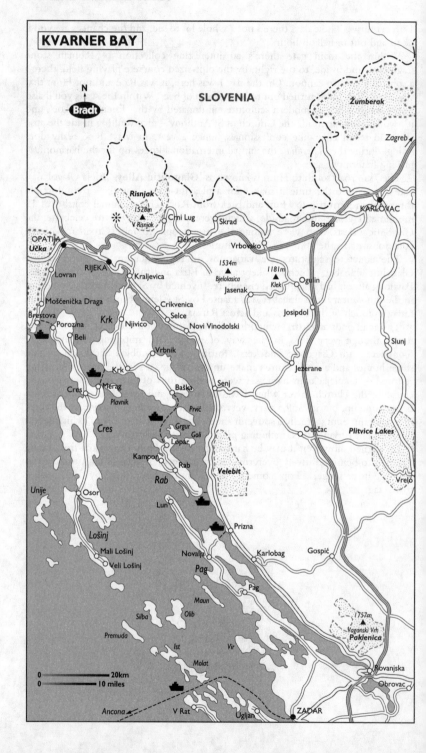

KVARNER BAY

N

Bradt

SLOVENIA

Žumberak

Zagreb

KARLOVAC

Risnjak

1528m
V Risnjak

Crni Lug

Skrad

Bosanci

Delnice

Vrbovsko

OPATIJA
Učka

Lovran

RIJEKA

Kraljevica

1534m
Bjelolasica

1181m
Klek

Ogulin

Jasenak

Josipdol

Mošćenička Draga

Crikvenica

Brestova

Porozina

Beli

Krk

Njivico

Selce

Novi Vinodolski

Slunj

Vrbnik

Cres

Merag

Krk

Plavnik

Baška

Prvić

Senj

Jezerane

Cres

Grgur
Goli

Lopar

Otočac

Plitvice Lakes

Kampor

Rab

Velebit

Unije

Osor

Rab

Vrelo

Lošinj

Lun

Mali Lošinj

Veli Lošinj

Prizna

Novalja

Karlobag

Gospić

Pag

Pag

Maun

Silba

Olib

1757m
Vaganski Vrh
Paklenica

Premuda

Ist

Vir

Molat

Jovanjska

Obrovac

0 ———— 20km
0 ———— 10 miles

Ancona

V Rat

Ugljan

ZADAR

Kvarner Bay and Islands

The Kvarner Bay, with Rijeka at its head and Croatia's largest islands in the middle, has been popular as a holiday destination for over a century. **Rijeka** itself is a lively port and shipyard, and while it's not somewhere you'd spend your holidays, there's nonetheless plenty to see. Offshore is **Cres**, home to wonderful griffon vultures, and **Lošinj**, one of Croatia's busiest and trendiest islands (at least for a fortnight in August). East of Cres and south of Rijeka lies the somewhat lower-key **Krk**, while the island of **Rab** sits to the south, blessed by sandy beaches and one of Croatia's prettiest medieval towns.

According to legend the four islands of the Kvarner Bay (Kvarner = Quattro = four) are the limbs of Medea's brother. She enticed the poor lad on board Jason's ship as he fled away with the Golden Fleece, and Jason chopped him up and cast his limbs overboard to slow down the pursuers.

The coast from Rijeka southwards is backed by the steepest part of the Velebit massif and occupied by a string of smallish resort towns and villages centred on Kraljevica, Crikvenica and Novi Vinodolski, all of which are popular vacation spots in summer with Croatians escaping from the capital.

Inland from Rijeka is the wonderfully protected and unspoiled **Gorski Kotar** region, centred on **Risnjak National Park**, while further south is the enormous Velebit park, with **North Velebit National Park** home to a good proportion of Croatia's remaining brown bear population.

The area code for Rijeka, the Gorski Kotar, Cres, Lošinj, Krk and Rab is 051 (+385 51 from abroad), while for the coast from Senj to Karlobag and Velebit park it's 053 (+385 53).

RIJEKA

Rijeka, Croatia's busiest and most industrial port, with a population rapidly approaching 200,000, isn't really a holiday destination at all – the assumption is that you'll head straight over to Opatija, 14km west, or out onto the islands of the Kvarner Bay. It nonetheless has plenty of sights worth seeing, including the excellent Trsat Castle on its hill, and a number of fine Austro-Hungarian palaces and secessionist buildings down in the town itself.

It's also the main transit hub for the entire region, meaning there's a strong chance of your coming through the city if you're on any form of public transport. Take advantage of any transit time you have here to explore.

History

Like most of the region, the area round Rijeka was home to Liburnian Illyrians until the Romans arrived, and built a port here, on the site of what's now the old town – everything south of the Korzo is on land reclaimed from the sea. Slavs moved in when Rome collapsed, but it wasn't until the 13th century that Rijeka started to grow in importance, though from then until 1947 it was two distinct settlements – Rijeka on the west bank of the river and Trsat (and later Sušak) on the east bank.

Unlike pretty much everywhere else on the Croatian coast, Rijeka never fell under the control of Venice, becoming a key Habsburg possession instead, though it was briefly under Frankopan (see *Krk*, page 187) control. From the early 18th century onwards, Rijeka became a major centre for shipbuilding, and today it's still Croatia's most important shipyard.

During the 19th century, tension increased between Vienna and Budapest, with Hungary insisting it should have its own access to the Adriatic, Austria already having both Trieste and Pula. Rijeka therefore came under the direct control of Hungary, and a railway was built from Budapest via Zagreb to the port (the station, like Zagreb's, is the work of Ferenc Pfaff), dramatically increasing its importance. Under the Hungarians, Rijeka grew wealthy, with its own sugar factory, refinery and paper factory.

In 1915, as a way of persuading the Italians into World War I on the Allied side, Britain promised pretty much the entire post-war Dalmatian coast to Italy. But once the war was won the Allies reneged on the deal, and the coast fell to the Kingdom of the Serbs, Croats and Slovenes instead – though Italy did get Zadar and some islands as compensation.

This wasn't enough, however, to stop D'Annunzio (see box overleaf) from marching into Rijeka in September 1919, using the pro-Italian census (which cleverly excluded Sušak) as an excuse. D'Annunzio then ruled Rijeka for nearly 18 months – in spite of not even having the Italian government's support. Italy finally pushed D'Annunzio out in early 1921, and for three years Rijeka was a free city. But that wasn't stopping Mussolini, who annexed it in 1924.

Rijeka – then called Fiume (both names just mean 'river') – was a divided city once more. The west side was Italian, and fell into decline, while the east side, Sušak, rapidly gained in prosperity as one of Yugoslavia's main shipyards, even though the ships themselves actually had to sail from Rijeka's harbour.

After World War II, Rijeka was returned to Yugoslavia, along with the rest of Dalmatian Italy, and in 1991 the city became part of the new state of Croatia though it still has a large Italian-speaking population.

Getting there and around

If you're using public transport, you'll sometimes feel there's no way of *not* getting to Rijeka. Trains come in from Zagreb four or five times a day, while there are ferries and ships constantly on their way in and out of the harbour. The main coastal line to Dubrovnik (daily) starts here, and there are also ferries to various places on the Kvarner Bay islands, though usually that's not the most practical or efficient way of getting there (see the individual sections in this chapter).

Rijeka also has an airport, on the island of Krk (connected by a big bridge to the mainland) which caters mainly for charter flights bringing in package tours to Opatija and the islands of the Kvarner Bay. There are flights from Zagreb, too, which are met by the Croatia Airlines bus. By the time you've allowed for transfers and check-in time, it's a pretty expensive way of saving a couple of hours on the bus, though if you're coming from outside Croatia the onward leg may already be included in your fare.

A vast array of buses runs frequently to Rijeka from just about everywhere, coming from Pula (2 hours) and Zagreb (4 hours) roughly every half hour, from

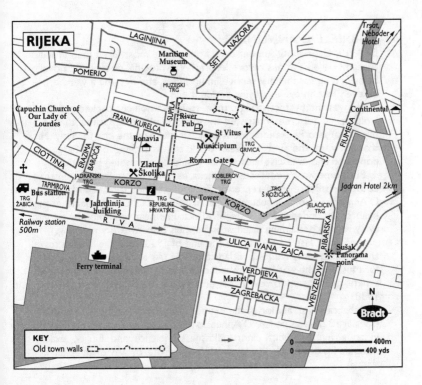

Krk (1½ hours), Zadar (4½ hours) and Split (9 hours) about once an hour, and from a wealth of other destinations besides.

You probably won't need to use local buses much, though it's worth knowing that bus #32 runs from the train station to Opatija twice an hour, and if you want to avoid the walk up to Trsat you can catch bus #1 from Fiumera.

The train station, bus station and ferry terminal are in a line running west–east along less than a kilometre's length of the harbour. The tourist information office (tel: 051 213 145; fax: 051 333 909) has good maps and brochures, and can be found half way along Korzo.

Where to stay and eat

Rijeka's accommodation – or lack of it – speaks volumes about the city's knowing it's a staging post rather than a destination in its own right. There's no campsite, there are no agencies handling private rooms, and there are only two hotels in the middle of town. Most people end up leaving on the next bus or ferry, or heading over to Opatija.

Easily the nicest place to stay in Rijeka itself is the four-star **Grand Hotel Bonavia** (tel: 051 357 100; fax: 051 335 969; www.bonavia.hr), well located just a block north of the main west–east thoroughfare, Korzo. It's a modernised old building, and a few of the rooms on the top floors have balconies overlooking the port – rooms 712, 713 and 714 are especially spacious. None of this comes cheap, of course – expect to pay €130 per night for a double room, or €175 for one of the top rooms with a balcony – but the hotel does have all the luxuries you'd expect for the price. It even has that rarest thing of all in downtown Rijeka, its own parking spaces (if you're driving here, you need to get into the

GABRIELE D'ANNUNZIO

By 1919, Gabriele D'Annunzio was one of the most fêted men in Italy. Already hugely famous before World War I for his poetry and novels, he signed up for military service, in his fifties, and became a war hero – he even lost an eye in a flying accident.

He was the perfect stooge, then, to lead an officer-backed group of 'volunteers' (discreetly assisted by soldiers whose superiors turned a blind eye) into Rijeka in September 1919, claiming the city for Italy. His troops were the first to wear black shirts, kicking off a hideously popular trend in fascist fashion that would last a whole generation.

But Rome wasn't interested in Rijeka, as it was busy negotiating instead at the Paris Peace Conference for Zadar and some Dalmatian islands. So D'Annunzio, cool as a cucumber, set himself up as *Il Commandante*, at the head of the independent state of Rijeka. For nearly 18 months he got away with it, declaiming manifestos from his balcony every morning.

It couldn't last, of course. At the end of 1920, Italy shelled the town and D'Annunzio gave it up in January 1921. As a successful role model for Mussolini, he was later rewarded by *Il Duce* with a place in the Italian senate, and was up for even greater honours when he died suddenly in 1938.

Rebecca West, author of the extraordinary *Black Lamb and Grey Falcon* (see page 322), was no fan. 'D'Annunzio marched his volunteers into Fiume, in an adventure which, in mindlessness, violence and futility, exactly matched his deplorable literary works', she wrote, by way of an epitaph.

one-way system which brings you out on Jadranska Trg, then head up the hill and round behind the back of the hotel).

Your only other option right in town is the considerably further downmarket two-star **Continental** (tel: 051 372 008; fax: 051 372 009; www.jadran-hoteli.hr), which is in a positively Parisian-looking building just across the river, below the Trsat hill. It's actually perfectly acceptable, and doubles here go for €58. Further up the hill, if you're really strapped for cash, is the **Neboder** (tel: 051 373 538; fax: 051 373 551), a rather charmless block of a place with rooms badly in need of restoration – though most do have balconies. Expect to pay €48 for doubles. Better by far is the two-star **Jadran** (tel: 051 216 230; fax: 051 436 203; www.jadran-hoteli.hr), along the coast 2km to the east (you can get there on the #2 city bus). The rooms are nothing special, but the views over the water to the island of Cres are lovely. Expect to pay €52 for a double with a view.

For a town of its size, Rijeka has surprisingly few restaurants – again a product of the relatively few tourists around to keep business booming. Locals wanting to splash out tend to head over to Opatija, but you can find something to eat easily enough in the streets on either side of the Korzo. **Zlatna Školjka** (the Golden Shell) is a personal favourite, right off the Korzo, with stiff tablecloths, cheerful, semi-formal service and excellent seafood in a cellar-like setting. Smarter still is **Municipium**, a swanky place where business deals are cemented over good, solid, Croatian fare. There's also a booming café culture, with terraces spilling out on to practically every pavement in the old town. Finally there's the **River Pub**, just up the steps from the Bonavia, which has an upturned coxless four hanging above the bar. Upstairs there's a grand oil portrait of Winston Churchill – and a rare opportunity to practice your Croatian Karaoke.

What to see

Most of Rijeka was destroyed by a huge earthquake in 1750, and was rebuilt in the monumental Habsburg style, particularly in the reclaimed area south of the Korzo, where you can still be impressed by the sheer grandeur of buildings like the **Jadran** (home of Jadrolinija, the ferry company), or the **Royal Navy Palace**.

Up on the Korzo, one of the few pre-1750 survivors was the **City Tower**, although it was embellished post-earthquake with the baroque trimmings and the distinctive clock and cupola you see today – not to mention the pompously bewigged reliefs of the Austro-Hungarian Emperors Charles VI and Leopold I over the archway. North of here, through the gate, is a warren of streets and squares marking the site of the original walled city. The town's oldest monument, a plain **Roman Gate** (probably the entrance to a barracks, rather than anything more significant), is up here, on the way to the 17th-century **Church of St Vitus**.

Built on the site of an existing church by the Jesuits, St Vitus is an unusual circular building with a cupola supported by massive marble pillars. The 13th-century crucifix inside (from the original church) supposedly had a rock thrown at it in 1296 by a man called Petar Lončarić. He was swallowed up by the ground, but the body of Christ bled convincingly, and the blood was stored in a vial, starting up a useful counter-cult to Our Lady of Trsat (see below).

Heading west from here it's a few blocks to the splendid **Maritime and Historical Museum**, housed in the former Governor's Palace, home briefly to D'Annunzio during his occupation of the city. The exhibits are interesting enough, but it's the palatial rooms and décor that really make the visit worthwhile.

The other church worth seeing down in the town is the **Capuchin Church of our Lady of Lourdes**, conveniently located right by the bus station. The neo-Gothic striped façade stands at the top of a fancy double staircase which wouldn't look out of place in front of one of the palazzi on Lake Como, in Italy. Started in 1904, the lower part was completed by 1908, but the upper part wasn't finished until 1929, in spite of the cash-strapped Capuchins taking advantage of the credulous local people by employing a charlatan calling himself St Johanca, who would raise money by sweating blood on demand, until his arrest for fraud in 1913.

Trsat

Up on the hill above Rijeka is the leafy suburb of Trsat, originally the site of an Illyrian hill-fort, and a strategic defence point for people from the Frankopans on. Up here is the **Church of Our Lady of Trsat**, supposedly the site where the Virgin Mary's house stopped and stayed from May 10 1291 to December 10 1294, on its way from Nazareth to its present resting place in Loreto, Italy. Fortunately, the loss of the Holy home was compensated for by the gift of a miraculous icon of the Virgin by Pope Urban V in 1367, and the Frankopans built the church to house the icon, as well as the monastery next door. The icon embedded into the gaudy altarpiece here is actually a copy; the original is in the monastery treasury, which is hardly ever open. The copy was originally made for a church in Opatija in the early 20th century, so that people there could see it without having to cross Rijeka, which was Italian-occupied at the time.

It still draws the pilgrims in good numbers, as you can see from the clutter of offerings in the **Chapel of Votive Gifts**, across the cloisters, and serious pilgrims will climb here from Rijeka on their knees, all the way up the 500-odd stairs leading from the town below. Less serious pilgrims will jump on a #1 bus.

The other big attraction in Trsat is the **castle**, which has been here forever, though in its present form only since Frankopan times. It was bought in 1826 by

MORETTO

You won't go far these days without seeing a *Moretto* (also called *Mori*, *Morči*, *Morčeki* and *Morčići*, depending on where you're from – and who you ask), as it's become the symbol of Rijeka.

The androgynous turbaned black figure is most commonly seen adorning earrings, but also features on other jewellery, and is prominent during Rijeka's carnival.

Various stories are told of the *Moretto's* origin – rich women over-fond of black slaves, Turkish invaders slaughtered in answer to local prayers, and others – but it seems the truth is more prosaic, reflecting a 17th- and 18th-century love-affair with the orient. The *Moretto* first appeared in Venice, and then in Rijeka during the 19th century, in a more modest and affordable form.

A single *Moretto* earring was frequently worn by men (especially sailors) as a sign of their provenance, though after World War II its production pretty much died out, only being revived with the establishment of an independent Croatia in 1991.

an Austrian army officer of Irish descent, Count Laval Nugent de Westmeth, and was restored to include the family mausoleum, where the sarcophagi were not just above ground, but upright, too, ready to face their makers. Among the people originally buried here was George Bernard Shaw's Aunt, Jane Shaw, though nobody seems to have the foggiest idea why. On the front of the mausoleum there's an inscription reading 'Mir Yunaka', which means 'Peace to the Heroes' – given the area's turbulent history, it's something of an irony. The castle and mausoleum now serve as a low-key museum, though the whereabouts of the sarcophagi is a mystery; they were still here when Rebecca West came through in 1937, but they're certainly not there now. In their place are maps, drawings and photos showing Rijeka through the ages.

The view from the fort across the sea, and down to the shipyards, is great, and can be enjoyed over a cool drink on the terrace.

The Rijeka Carnival

The pre-Lent carnival is easily Croatia's biggest (second only in Europe to the one in Venice, in fact) and Rijeka's most exciting annual event, attracting more than 10,000 active participants and 100,000 spectators. What's most extraordinary about the carnival is its adoption as an instant tradition – it was only revived in 1982, and has grown out of all proportion to expectations.

The main events of the week-long carnival are parades and into-the-night festivities, but you should look out especially for the men wearing sheepskins and ringing bells, who hark back to a centuries-old tradition of driving out the evil spirits from villagers' houses at this time of year – and indeed still do so in the Gorski Kotar hinterland.

GORSKI KOTAR

The mountainous area inland from Rijeka is one of the best remaining examples of forested karst, and is home to a wide diversity of flora and fauna. There's a small national park, Risnjak, and there are many other natural attractions, and mountains to hike up, but although the area's reasonably well known to Croatians it's practically unvisited by foreigners.

Buses and trains run through the Gorski Kotar – it's crossed by the main road and railway from Karlovac to Rijeka, but it's a whole lot easier to explore round here if you have your own transport. Accommodation is also scarce across the region, which makes it more suitable for day trips than extended stays.

Risnjak National Park

Only 15km inland from Rijeka as the crow flies, Risnjak National Park is a wonderful place to come in late spring and summer, with great walking, lovely flowers, spectacular scenery, and a relatively easy peak to scale. The weather can be extreme here, with the park affected by four different types of climate – harsh alpine, Dinaric mountain, mild Adriatic and continental Pannonian. In autumn it tends towards the very wet indeed, and in winter there's a good deal of snow – at the mountain lodge, at 1,418m, there's snow on the ground for an average of 157 days a year, and it can be up to 4m deep.

The local flora includes the protected edelweiss, black vanilla orchids, mountain yarrows, alpine clematis, saxifrage and yellow wood violets, amongst many others, while the fauna includes wild cats, roe deer, red deer, chamois and a small colony of brown bears. After nearly a century away, the lynx has not just reappeared, but is once again well established, and is probably behind the park's name (*ris* meaning lynx). Wolves and wild boar also come through from time to time.

The main entrance to the park is through the village of **Crni Lug**, a narrow and winding 12km west of Delnice, itself on the main road and railway line from Karlovac to Rijeka. Buses run twice a day to the village from Delnice, though not at especially convenient times of day – if you're stuck in Delnice itself you could do worse than the Scorpion Pizzeria, which serves up good-value fare.

Just over 1km beyond Crni Lug you'll find the park office (tel: 051 836 133; fax: 051 836 116; www.risnjak.hr), where you can pick up maps and a good guide, as well as an excellent little leaflet detailing the Leska Nature Trail, which is well worth a couple of hours of anyone's time. The office is also home to a cheerful restaurant, and there are five rooms available (€25 per person, half board), though you should book well ahead if you want to stay in summer, as the lodge is popular with Croatians.

From the park office, at around 700m, it's a well-marked 9km walk (count on a little over three hours up) to the main peak, Veliki Risnjak, at 1,528m – it's the second highest mountain in the Gorski Kotar, being trumped by a mere 6m by Bjelolasica, which is at the heart of the main skiing centre in the area, 25km southeast of here.

A considerably shorter route to the summit, also well-signed, starts from the village of Gornje Jelenje, 16km southwest of Crni Lug (21km west of Delnice). Drive up to the head of the gravel road, at around 1,200m, and count on under an hour and a half from here on foot. The summit can also be reached in three hours or so from the small ski station at Platak, to the west of the park – this is also the best place to start the climb up the 1,505m summit of Snježnik, which can easily be combined with Veliki Risnjak.

Under the peak of Risnjak is a mountain hut, open from May to September – from here it's a rocky 20-minute scramble to the top, and some great views out across the Gorski Kotar to the sea. The best views are on clear days in the depths of winter, but if you're climbing then you need to be a seriously proficient mountaineer, and equipped with an ice-axe and crampons. If you're a winter visitor it's worth knowing there's a winter room in the hut, which sleeps six, but make sure you've cleared this with the park office in Crni Lug first.

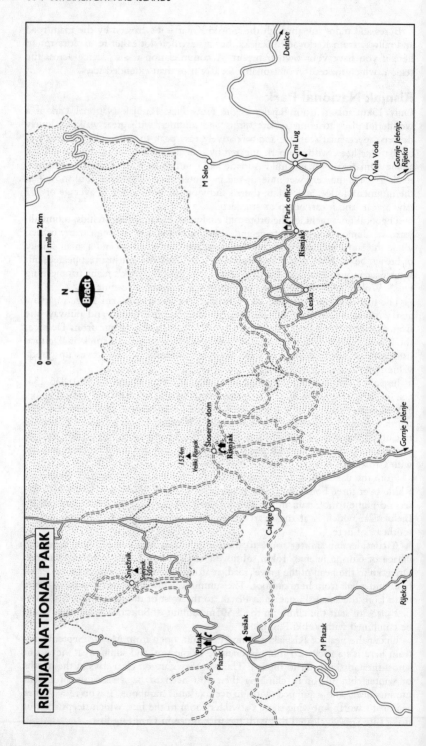

If you're into the underground rather than the mountain peaks, then you'll love the Lokvarka Cave (Spilja Lokvarka), just outside **Lokve**, 6km west of Delnice, on the main road to Rijeka – it's over 1km long, and has truly excellent stalagmites and stalactites. It's open every day from mid June to mid September, and often at weekends in spring and autumn, with guided visits every hour or so; outside these times call ahead (tel: 051 831 278) or ask at the Lokve tourist office (tel/fax: 051 831 250) for more details. The tourist office also has access to a handful of private rooms in the pretty village. If you're here in spring, don't miss out on the Frog Fiesta, which features various froggy frolics and folk music – after all this froggy fun, however, you may want to miss out on the main dish of the day: frogs' legs.

Skrad and the Devil's Pass

About 12km east of Delnice is the small town of Skrad, in itself unremarkable enough. But below the town is a great canyon, nearly 2km long but sometimes as little as 2m wide, known as the **Devil's Pass** (Vražji Prolaz). There's a path, which takes under an hour, down to the top of the canyon from the train station in Skrad, but if you have your own wheels you can drive down a hair-raising 6km to the valley floor (signed Zeleni Vir), and then walk up, which is far more rewarding.

Entrance tickets (7 kuna) are on sale from the mountain association (HPS) van usually parked at the head of the car park; they also sell drinks. To the left is an old power station (Gorski Kotar's first), beyond which you'll find the **Zeleni Vir** waterfall, dropping down from the river's source. But it's up the trail to the right you'll want to head, on a narrow path which frequently has to resort to iron bridges and wooden walkways over the gushing torrent beneath. It's a moderately scary trail, but more of a thrill than actually dangerous, though good walking shoes are essential, especially if it's been raining.

It takes around half an hour to walk up through the canyon, after which you'll see a sign to the left to **Muževa Hišica**, a deep cave which was used as a refuge in times of war – you'll need a torch if you want to explore the tunnel which leads to a biggish chamber containing a good selection of stalactites and stalagmites.

Back on the main trail, the path cuts up through the woods to Skrad, some 400m above – count on an hour to reach the station.

There are several trains a day which stop in Skrad on the way from Zagreb to Rijeka and up to 20 buses a day. Skrad's tourist office (tel/fax: 051 810 680) has access to a number of private rooms, and there's also a small hotel, the **Zeleni Vir** (tel/fax: 051 810 665).

Ogulin, Klek and Bjelolasica

The train line from Karlovac to Rijeka takes a loop southwards away from the main road, before rejoining it near Delnice. On the loop, there's a stop at the small town of **Ogulin**, which has a solid twin-towered fortress from Frankopan times, and a prison cell inside commemorating Tito's imprisonment here in 1932.

More importantly, it's the access point by public transport to the skiing, hiking and biking at **Bjelolasica** – on summer Saturdays and Sundays the morning train from Zagreb is met by a bus which takes you all the way to the Olympic Centre, and in the afternoon there's a return bus and train back.

There's accommodation at the centre, but you need to book well ahead in the winter season, as this is where Croatia's serious skiers train. Call the Olympic Centre on 047 562 118, or in Zagreb on 01 617 7707. You can also stay at the **Hotel Jastrab** (tel: 051 833 161; fax: 051 833 527) in nearby Begovo Razdolje, which is the highest village in Croatia, at over 1,000m. Double rooms cost €40–60 depending on the season. The hotel does bike rental in summer and ski rental in winter, and has maps available.

On the way to Bjelolasica, you'll have passed the peak of **Klek**, which isn't the highest in the area (a fraction under 1,200m), but is one of the most accessible. It can even be walked from Ogulin in under three hours, though if you have a car or can get to the village of Bjelsko first, around 8km west of the town, then you'll save yourself a good deal of time. From here it's only about a 45-minute walk up through the woods to the Klek mountain hut (which usually serves snacks on summer weekends) and a further half hour to the summit, up a rather vertiginous rocky path above the trees. The panoramic view from the summit is excellent.

Bijele and Samarske Stijene

Further south, and reachable only with your own wheels, is the protected nature reserve of Bijele and Samarske Stijene, which has a wealth of dramatic karstic formations and cliffs rising out of the unspoiled woods. It's a reasonably popular place with climbers – some of the cliffs are up to 50m high – but otherwise beautifully untouched by the hand of man, and a great place to find peace, quiet, and edelweiss.

NORTH VELEBIT NATIONAL PARK

The vast Velebit park – covering 2,000km² and stretching over 100km from Senj to Zadar – contains two national parks, Paklenica, to the south (see page 203), and North Velebit, between Senj and Karlobag, to the north. Of the two, North Velebit is the more remote, and far and away the least visited – it only achieved national park status in 1999, and development of any tourist infrastructure is still very much in its infancy. For the time being access is only possible with a four-wheel-drive vehicle, though approval was granted by the government for the upgrading of some of the tracks to proper grit roads, which should improve things dramatically.

Even though the current national park is itself very recent, conservation history in North Velebit goes back a long way – Štirovača park here was one of the country's first, along with Plitvice, back in 1929, and since 1978 it has been part of the UNESCO MAB (Man and Biosphere) programme. There's an inevitable conflict of interest along the park's borders with the highly lucrative local logging industry – most of the jobs in the area are logging-related – but the 1999 legislation promises to keep North Velebit well protected.

Being cool, high up, well forested and very sparsely inhabited, the park is an ideal habitat for brown bears, and there are now reckoned to be around 500 in the area, though they're just as unlikely to be seen here as anywhere else, bears being notoriously people-shy. The park is also home to wild boar, lynx, wild cats, red and roe deer and several species of eagle, along with many other animals – including, deep in one of the caves, *Croatobranhus mestrovi*, a previously unknown (and to this author's eyes, especially revolting) species of leech.

The park also features some of the country's most diverse flora, with a wide range of rare and protected plant species. The **Velebitski Botanički Vrt** botanical gardens – the remotest I've ever visited – were established back in 1967, at 1,480m, to highlight the flora unique to the region, and although the gardens had fallen into disrepair before the creation of the national park, they're now in the process of being restored.

Deep within the park there's an even more strictly protected nature reserve, **Hajdučki i Rožanski Kukovi**, which you'll need special permission (and a very good reason) to visit. Within this reserve is one of the world's dozen deepest caves,

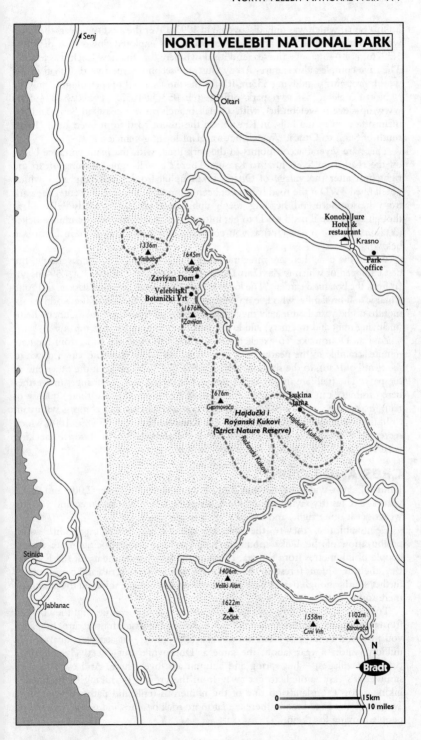

NORTH VELEBIT NATIONAL PARK

Senj

Oltari

Konoba Jure
Hotel &
restaurant
Krasno

Park
office

1336m
Visibaba

1645m
Vučjak

Zavižan Dom

Velebitski
Botanički Vrt
1676m
Zavižan

676m
Gromovača

Lukina
Jama
Hajdučki Kukovi

Hajdučki i
Rožanski Kukovi
(Strict Nature Reserve)

Rožanski Kukovi

Stinica

Jablanac

1406m
Veliki Alan

1622m
Zečjak

1558m
Crni Vrh

1102m
Štirovača

N

Bradt

0   15km
0   10 miles

Lukina Jama, which was only discovered in 1993. Over the next two years the cave, whose entrance is at 1,436m above sea-level, was explored down to a depth of 1,392m, just 44m above the sea (and it's down here that the new leech was found). The cave complex also features Atkov Gust, the second deepest vertical shaft in the world, dropping a giddying 553m. It's for the most serious of speleologists only.

North Velebit has two park offices (tel: 053 884 552; fax: 053 884 551; www.np-sjeverni-velebit.hr), with a small branch on the coast, in Senj, and the main office up in the hills, in Krasno, on the minor road from Sveti Juraj (10km south of Senj) to Otočac. Watch out for giant logging vehicles.

There are several access points to the park itself, with the main entrance being off the road from Sveti Juraj to Krasno. There's a well-signed turning off to the right, just after the village of Oltari, 15km uphill from Sveti Juraj, after which you'll need 4WD if the road hasn't yet been improved. You can also enter the park from the southern end, heading steeply uphill from Jablanac towards Veliki Alan, though again you'll need 4WD to get into the park itself. Buy your entrance ticket (30 kuna for a 1–3 day visit) as you come into the park or at Zavižan Dom (see below).

Within the park there are three mountain lodges where hikers can overnight, the best equipped of which is **Zavižan Dom** (tel: 053 614 200), situated at 1,594m, not far from the botanical gardens. The lodge is also an important weather station, and Ante Vukusić and his family, who live up here, are cut off from the rest of the world for six months of the year. Fortunately they make a fiery spirit from the local mountain herbs (including mint and rosemary) and lovely herbal tea to keep them company.

Zavižan Dom makes an excellent base for hikes through the park, from the ten-minute scramble to the nearby peak of Vučjak, at 1,645m (fabulous views down to the island of Rab), to the six-hour walk over to the Alan Lodge, at the other end of the park. The trails are mostly well marked, but given the rapid changes in weather here (visibility can drop to nothing in a matter of moments, and there's plenty of rain), make sure you're well equipped and have a good map and compass with you.

In the village of Krasno itself there's the **Konoba Jure** (tel: 053 851 100), which serves up a reasonable meal and has some accommodation. It's worth checking with the park administration first if you want to stay or visit.

CRES AND LOŠINJ

Until the 11m-wide channel was dug between them, between 2,000 and 3,000 years ago, Cres (try saying something half way between *tsress* and *trress* and you still won't get it quite right) and Lošinj were a single island.

Geographically, they're the spindly, submerged, 80km-long north–south prolongation of the Učka mountain range, with nowhere being more than a couple of kilometres from the sea. Forming the western boundary of the Kvarner Bay, their deciduous forests in the north give way to dense scrub and barren shores further south, though newer pine plantations on Lošinj have softened the landscape there somewhat.

Today tourism accounts for practically all the islands' revenue, and they benefit from more than a century's worth of hospitality and tourist infrastructure. In season you may find Lošinj just a tad too popular for comfort – it attracts a quarter of a million visitors a year (about the same as Dubrovnik, but effectively only to a couple of villages) – but spring and autumn are lovely here. And even in high summer it's easy enough to get away from the crowds by hiking or mountain-biking across the islands on one of the numerous trails and paths. Once you're away from the paved roads, there are far more rock beaches and pebbly coves than people looking for them.

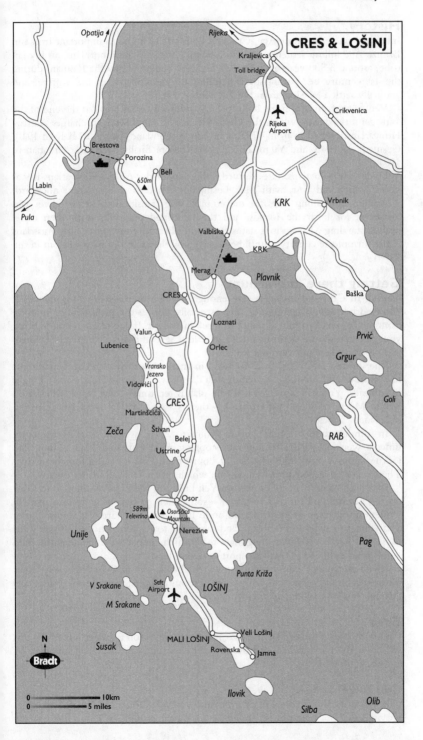

CRES & LOŠINJ

History

Inhabited since the Stone Age, Cres and Lošinj were home to important Iron and Bronze Age hilltop settlements, before being settled by the Liburnians, an Illyrian tribe, around 3,500 years ago. The islands were conquered by the Romans during the 1st century BC, passing to Byzantium on the collapse of the empire, and gradually settled by Slavs from the 7th century on.

Venice took control from 1000 to 1797, with a 50-year break at the end of the 14th century, during which the Croat-Hungarian kings were in charge. Austro-Hungarians stepped in from 1797, after which the islands passed to Italy in 1918, Germany in 1943, and Yugoslavia in 1945, before finally becoming Croatian in 1991.

Under the Venetians, Cres thrived, while under the Austro-Hungarians it was Lošinj which did best, with Mali Lošinj developed as an important dockyard, producing fine sailing ships for the empire. The transition to steam power was disastrous for both the islands, and they declined gradually from then on – notwithstanding Mali Lošinj's status as a winter health resort for wealthy Austrians at the turn of the century – until being saved by the arrival of mass tourism in the 1970s.

Getting there and around

Getting to Cres and Lošinj is easy enough, but be prepared for long queues if you're driving here in summer, and especially during the peak season, running from the last week of July to the third week in August. If you're intending to bring your car, you should factor in a delay of at least several hours at the ferry terminal, and possibly even an overnight wait.

The shortest crossing is from Brestova in Istria to Porozina on Cres, taking just half an hour and running a dozen times a day in winter – and all day and all night in summer. You can also get on to the islands ten times a day from Valbiska on Krk to Merag on Cres's eastern flank – there's a road bridge on to Krk from the mainland.

In summer there are ferries from Venice to Zadar as well, running up to six times a week in each direction and stopping in at Pula and Mali Lošinj. The journey from Venice by boat takes 11 hours; from Pula it's just a four-hour ride. There's also an airport near Mali Lošinj, which brings in small planes only.

Buses run roughly every hour from Veli Lošinj to Mali Lošinj, then up to Osor on the isthmus and on to Cres town – some then go to Merag and on to Krk, while most head up to Porozina and on to Brestova. There are half a dozen buses a day direct to Rijeka (3½ hours), and two a day to Zagreb (7 hours). If you want to get off the islands' 80km-long main road which connects the main centres then you'll need either your own transport or strong legs.

If you're driving, expect traffic jams at the bottleneck at Osor, especially when the swing-bridge is opened (twice a day, morning and late afternoon) to let boats through the 100m-long channel.

Cres

Cres is the less-touristed of the two islands, though don't expect anywhere this attractive, this close to Italy, Austria and Germany, and this warm and sunny, to be entirely visitor-free.

Cres town

Cres town itself (26km south of Porozina) is lovely, almost as Italian-looking as Rovinj, on Istria's west coast, though a good deal smaller. Its raison d'être is the well-sheltered harbour, a stopping-off and refreshment point for Venetian convoys, and the source of the island's long-ago prosperity. Today the old stone buildings soak up the summer sun and it's a charming place to while away a few hours.

Much of the town dates from the 15th and 16th centuries, when Cres was the seat of the Venetian administration for the islands, and there are still lots of well-preserved bits and pieces, including a handful of town gates, a section of the old town walls, and quite a collection of Gothic and Renaissance palazzi. In the main square, Trg Frane Petrića, there's a pretty loggia and clocktower, while through the town gate from here you'll find the sober façade of the 15th-century **Church of St Mary** and its fortified campanile. The church is only usually opened for services – if it is open, however, pop inside to see the fine Gothic (15th-century) wooden carved *pietà* – and a rather sad-looking griffon on the pulpit.

Accommodation in the town itself is limited to private rooms, which you can book through the tourist office (tel/fax: 051 571 535; www.tzg-cres.hr), right where the bus stops. Expect to pay up to €35 for doubles in high season, plus the usual 30% surcharge for stays of under four nights.

Two kilometres west of town along a pleasant seaside path, on the Kovačine headland, and set amongst pinewoods and olive trees, is the **Kovačine Autocamp** (tel: 051 571 423; fax: 051 571 086). The site has accommodation for up to 2,000 people (including a naturist section), four restaurants and bars, a supermarket, and its own beaches, and offers courses in windsurfing and scuba diving. It's a small town in itself.

On the way to Kovačine, a kilometre out of Cres, is the **Kimen** (tel: 051 571 161; fax: 051 571 163) complex, the only hotel near town. It's pretty big (around 400 rooms) but it's set in nice grounds a couple of hundred metres back from the pebble beach, and has unfussy but spacious doubles for around €80 in season. Any time from October to the end of May the price drops to around €60.

Beli – and the Eco-Centre Caput Insulae

Up on Cres's rocky northeastern tip, separated from the dramatic main road along the island's spine by the island's highest peak (650m) is the old hilltop village of Beli, overlooking the western corner of Krk, and sitting high up above a pretty pebble beach. It's hard to reach without your own transport, as buses only come here twice a week. Otherwise it's a good hour and a half's walk from the bus stop at the junction on the main road from Cres to Porozina half way between the two.

The only accommodation options are a handful of private rooms (ask around; there's a tourist office of sorts only in July and August) or the pleasant campsite down in the olive groves towards the shore, which also has a restaurant and a small shop.

Apart from the peace and tranquillity here, the main reason for a visit to Beli is the wonderful Eurasian griffon vulture, one of the largest flying birds. Saved from the jaws of extinction here only in the last few years, the vulture is now protected not just by law but also by the Eco-Centre Caput Insulae Beli (ECCIB), a non-profit, non-governmental organisation established in 1993.

Housed in an abandoned school building – depopulation meant there were no more children to teach – the ECCIB works to protect the area's natural, cultural and historical heritage, and is doing a terrific job of protecting one of the world's most magnificent birds.

There are two permanent exhibitions, one on the Biodiversity of the Lošinj Archipelago and the other on the History of Beli and Tramuntana, while behind

PUTTING SOMETHING BACK – ADOPT A GRIFFON!

The ECCIB has put in place an excellent adoption initiative as a way of protecting the species. A person or an organisation can 'adopt' a bird for a year by making a donation, and will receive in exchange an adoption certificate, a photo of their griffon, a poster, and information about the programme.

To adopt a Eurasian griffon, simply pay 200 kuna (for individuals; 2,000 for institutions) to account number 33800-678-39063 at the Zagrebačka Banka (SWIFT code ZABAHR 2X), and send a copy of the payment slip, along with a completed adoption form (downloadable from the website) to Eco-Centre Caput Insulae Beli, Beli 4, 51559 Beli, Cres Island, Croatia; tel/fax: 51 840 525; email: caput.insulae@ri.htnet.hr; www.caput-insulae.com.

If you have any questions, you should also feel free to contact Tea Perinčić on her mobile phone (091 335 7125).

the building there's a rest hospital for injured or damaged birds, where they're kept until they're ready to go back into the wild. The building also marks the start of a series of eco-routes, guided by a leaflet from the ECCIB, which takes you along trails explaining the culture, flora and fauna of the Tramuntana, the northern part of Cres.

The vultures themselves are truly magnificent, with a wingspan reaching 2.8m, a body weight of up to 15kg, and a life expectancy of up to 60 years. They can be super-fast, reaching speeds of up to 120km/h, but usually cruise at 40–50km/h in search of a carcass. Given the relative rarity of dead animals, the vultures cruise in formation, with fewer than one per kilometre, to cover the maximum ground area, signalling a find by circling.

The birds live only on carrion, which was once provided by the abundance of sheep ranging free here – diseased animals would be cleared up by the vultures, keeping the shepherds happy by saving the rest of the flock from contamination. Today, with depopulation, there are fewer shepherds, fewer sheep and fewer vultures, so the ECCIB programme focuses on making sure there are enough dead sheep to go around.

The vultures are also endangered by tourism, particularly by motor boats coming too close to the cliffs and scaring weaklings into flights which can't be sustained, leading to youngsters drowning. With only one egg per couple per year (during the two-month incubation period both parents alternate in keeping it warm and protected), and a five-year delay before sexual maturity, you can see why they're scarce. Fortunately they're now legally protected, and the fine for killing or disturbing the vultures, or stealing their eggs or chicks, is an off-putting 40,000 kuna.

From just 24 nesting couples in the mid '80s, the population has now increased to 70-odd couples, thanks mostly to the work of the ECCIB, and I can't encourage you enough to support its work.

South of Cres town

The hilly main road from Cres town winds 35km south to the village of Osor, on the isthmus. On the way south you'll see the 5km-long and 1.5km-wide **Vransko Jezero**, the only lake on the Kvarner islands, and the only water supply for the whole of Cres and Lošinj – hence the ban on swimming here.

Before the lake, there's a turn-off downhill to the exquisite village and bay of **Valun**, which isn't easily accessible without your own wheels. Buses only run here three times a week, and although it's barely an hour and a half downhill on foot from the bus stop at the junction on the main road, it's a good two and a half hour slog – all uphill – for the return journey.

Access to the village – even for car drivers – is down a flight of steps leading to the harbour, where you'll find a handful of stone houses and the pretty little church holding Valun's only cultural treasure, the **Valun Tablet**. Housed in the sacristy, this 11th-century engraving was originally a tombstone, and it's one of the oldest pieces of Glagolitic stone-carving in Croatia – with a helpful Latin translation for the Glagolitically challenged.

Accommodation in Valun is limited to a (very) few private rooms, which are tricky to book – there's a tourist office here in July and August, but that's when the rooms are already full of holidaying Italians. Out of season you just need to ask around. Otherwise there's a fine campsite (tel: 051 525 050; fax: 051 525 085) along the lovely beach from the town, but you should book well ahead to be sure of a space.

On a spur off the road to Valun there's a road leading to the nearly abandoned hilltop village of **Lubenice** (there's a tough footpath between the two, the shortest distance if you're walking, but not for the faint-hearted – and remember that there's no public transport away from here).

Sitting on a bluff at nearly 400m above sea-level, it's a popular excursion venue for summer evenings – the views are fantastic – but for most of the year it's deserted and windblown. Below the town (far, far below) there's a wonderful bay and beach – the hike back rightly puts most people off, however. If you really want to explore the coast in these parts you're better off doing so by boat.

Back on the main road south, the first turnoff after Vransko Jezero leads 8km or so west to the little holiday village of **Martinšćica**, set on a pretty shingle bay with an attractive half-kilometre beach. At one end there's a large campsite (tel: 051 574 127; fax: 051 574 167) which also has a few apartments. Again, getting here is very much a matter of having your own wheels.

Osor, on the isthmus, was the capital of Cres and Lošinj until the end of the 15th century, when a combination of plague, epidemic and Venetians shifted the capital up to Cres town, 35km north. Which is why the tiny village of today (population 80) still has a town hall and loggia, a 15th-century cathedral, a bishop's palace, and the extant remnants of old stone walls.

It's a lovely stop, in the process of reinventing itself as a museum-village, and for once it's an easy enough place to get to, being on the regular bus route. The cathedral is shut more often than not, but if it's open it's worth popping in to admire the sizeable altarpiece and the somewhat over-the-top chapel to the left – both a good deal more sightly than the ghastly modern stations of the cross adorning the side walls.

Behind the cathedral, in the town square, you'll find a dozen sculptures by the likes of Meštrović and Kršnić, a couple of cafés, and the small town museum. Housed in the old town hall, and open only on weekday mornings, the museum has an interesting collection of 1st- and 2nd-century Roman artefacts from all over the empire, a testimony to Osor's former importance as a maritime trading port.

If you want to stay, there are a couple of good campsites, **Preko Mosta** (tel: 051 237 350; fax: 051 237 115) and **Bijar** (tel: 051 237 027; fax: 051 237 115), both close to the town and to the beaches, though there's little in the way of private accommodation. In summer Osor puts on excellent classical concerts – check the Cres town or Mali Lošinj tourist offices for details.

Southeast of Osor – off the public transport map altogether – are Cres's best beaches, spread around a crenulated coast, south and east of the village of **Punta**

Križa, that's deserted save for the **Baldarin** (tel/fax: 051 235 679) naturist campsite. The beaches are no great secret, but you should be able to find yourself a quiet spot, away from an incipient off-roading recreational-vehicle community.

Lošinj

Smaller than Cres, but more populous (and more popular) is the island of Lošinj. That has its advantages and disadvantages – the extra tourists mean there are better facilities on hand, while the smaller size makes the island far more manageable on foot. Excellent walking maps are available from the tourist offices in Mali and Veli Lošinj, and the moment you head uphill you'll find you have plenty of space to yourself. Mali Lošinj in the first couple of weeks in August, however, can be seriously busy – seething wouldn't be an exaggeration.

Nerezine

The first settlement you come to, 4km south of Osor, is Nerezine, a cheerily dispersed village and harbour with a fairly large and well-situated campsite **Rapoča** (tel: 051 237 145; fax: 051 237 146) in the woods by the beach along the north shore. There are also some private rooms available – ask at the marina (tel/fax: 051 237 038).

Nerezine lies at the foot of Osorščica Mountain, which culminates in the peak of Televrina (589m), a steep hike up, but one of the best pay-offs in the country, with fabulous views in all directions when you get there – all the way to Triglav (2,864m) in Slovenia, the Velebit massif and Gorski Kotar onshore, Rab and Pag to the east, the length of Lošinj and its offshore islands to the south, and Istria to the northwest. On a clear day you can see as far as the Apennines, in Italy. Just below the peak is the tiny **Chapel of St Nicholas**, still a place of pilgrimage for the Nerezine locals.

Mali Lošinj

Mali Lošinj made its reputation in the 19th century as a dockyard, producing great sailing ships for the Austro-Hungarian Empire. When steam came in, the dockyards went out, but tourism of a sort started here around the same time, with the town gaining favour (like Opatija) with well-heeled Austrians as a fine place for a winter rest cure. Many of the elegant villas they built can still be seen above the Čikat Bay and peninsula, home today to the main resort hotels.

The annual influx of visitors – mainly Italian – hasn't done much to spoil the old town, spreading along both sides of the v-shaped harbour and meeting in a triangular piazza which leads off into the small but pretty clutter of narrow streets making up the old quarter.

There's remarkably little in terms of sights, but the **art collections**, housed a block back from the Riva, are well worth a visit. The gallery comprises two separate private collections, with old masters collected by Guiseppe Piperata on the one hand and more contemporary works collected by Andro Vid Mihičić on the other. Otherwise it's a question of drifting around and soaking up the old town atmosphere before returning to the endless quayside cafés for a well-deserved aperitif.

The main tourist office (tel: 051 231 884; fax: 051 231 547; www.tz-malilosinj.hr), half way along the Riva between the ferry terminal and the main square, has excellent documentation, and you should definitely pick up the *Promenades and Footpaths* map which gives you the walking times between most of the major points on the southern part of the island – an indispensable guide if you're to get away from the crowds in season.

Hotel accommodation is plentiful, but you'd do well to book way ahead in high summer. All the hotels are across the headland on Čika, with the nicest option

Above left Dubrovnik's old town walls – with one of the many
statues of Dubrovnik's patron saint, St Blaise (PL)

Above right View down Stradun from Dubrovnik's city walls (TH)

Below Sunrise over Dubrovnik's old port (PL)

Above St Mary's Island, Mljet (TH)
Below Sundowners at Pomena, Mljet (TH)

being the palazzo-like **Alhambra** (tel: 051 232 022; fax: 051 232 042) which has 41 good-sized rooms with doubles at around €70.

Beyond that are the vast **Bellevue** (tel: 051 231 222; fax: 051 231 268) and **Helios** (tel: 051 232 124; fax: 051 232 104) hotels, and on the other side of the Punta Annunziata, further west, the even vaster **Vespera** (tel: 051 231 304; fax: 051 231 402) and **Aurora** (tel: 051 231 324; fax: 051 231 542) establishments, which have 404 rooms apiece. Expect to pay around €110 for nice doubles at any of these, except the Helios, which is less smart and a good deal cheaper (around €65).

Private rooms are also in good supply and you shouldn't have any trouble in finding one – ask at any of the dozen or so agencies in town and expect to pay around €30 for a double, with the usual 30% surcharge for three-day stays or less. One place well worth trying is the **Ivanka**, just behind the western quayside, right in town, which is a cheerful restaurant with a handful of nice rooms upstairs, which go for €60 a night for a double in summer and around half that in winter.

The main campsite (tel: 051 232 125; fax: 051 231 708) is at Čikat, a half-hour walk across the headland. It's enormous, but well located, right on a good beach.

Veli Lošinj

In spite of the name (*veli* means large; *mali* means small), Veli Lošinj has under 1,000 residents to Mali Lošinj's 7,000, and although it also has many fewer visitors, there's much less space here, too, so the town can get almost as crowded in summer as its larger cousin.

Veli Lošinj is the terminus for the regular bus up to Cres. It's also only about 45 minutes on foot from Mali Lošinj, with the last two thirds of the route along the coastal path, coming in past the Punta hotel complex.

The tiny harbour is dominated by the fortified, barn-like **Church of St Anthony**, built in the 17th century on the ruins of a smaller 15th-century church, and testifying to the former wealth and grandeur of the town. Inside it's stately baroque, and has a fine collection of paintings from the Titian and Tiepelo schools, though you're only likely to see these during the half hour before or after a service, as the church is usually closed at other times.

Behind the church, stand-offishly distant, is a 15th-century Venetian campanile. Also 15th-century Venetian is the crenellated tower built to protect the town from pirates and now restored to house the municipal museum – a minor triumph of form over content.

Everything you need is on the harbour front, including a couple of agencies that will find you a private room for around €30 for a double, though there's a hefty 50% surcharge for one-night stays. The ASL Agency (tel/fax: 051 236 256) can also rent you bikes, an excellent way of exploring the island.

Also right on the front is the only hotel actually in town, the 10-room **Saturn** (tel/fax: 051 236 352), next door to St Anthony's. Nice doubles go for €65, though with the terrace below it's not as quiet as it might be. Up on the northwestern corner of the Veli Lošinj bay is the **Punta** (tel: 051 622 000; fax: 051 236 301), a sprawling affair with 303 rooms, 67 apartments and indoor and outdoor pools. Sea-view doubles go for €110, dropping to €55 in winter. The buffet breakfast features free rum…Veli Lošinj also has a fine **Youth Hostel** (tel/fax: 051 236 312), with its own small park – book as far ahead as you possibly can, as it's usually full.

Southern Lošinj and islands

A 20-minute walk south of Veli Lošinj along the shore brings you to the little bay and pretty fishing village of **Rovenska**. There's a cheerful restaurant here, **Sirius** (tel:

051 236 399) serving up the catch of the day, super-fresh. Ask here about private rooms if you want to stay in the village. If the Sirius is full, try the **Mol** next door.

The attractive coastal path continues another 75 minutes south past the villages of **Javorna** and **Kriška**, terminating in **Jamna** – there's also a wealth of hiking up to and along the spine of the island, with paths leading down to various settlements, coves and beaches on the pretty west coast. Take plenty to drink, however, as there's not much shade and no water at all.

When you're done with the main island, there are day trips to the offshore ones from Mali Lošinj – you can arrange these through any of the travel agencies, or just negotiate on the harbour front with one of the taxi-boats. There's also a Jadrolinija ferry which makes the circuit of the main offshore islands twice-daily.

Most popular is **Susak**, the sandy island off to the west of Lošinj, which is famous for its excellent wines and colourful local costume, featuring orange and yellow pleated dresses and bright-red tights – you're more likely to see this on a local postcard than a local person, however, as most of the population has long-ago emigrated.

Excursions are also available to the island of **Unije**, the westernmost of the islands in the Kvarner Bay. With only one settlement and fewer visitors than most places it makes for a lovely haven to spend a day or so if it's total quiet you're after. It also has a couple of very well-sheltered moorings if you're sailing.

Finally, to the south of Lošinj there's a handful of islands, the biggest of which is **Ilovik**, famous for its flowers and eucalyptus trees, a testimony to the unusual amount of water here.

There are some private rooms available on all three islands – book these through one of the agencies in Mali Lošinj.

KRK

Croatia's biggest island (410km^2 to Cres's 405km^2) has been connected to the mainland by a 1.4km toll bridge since 1980, and it's been one of the most popular holiday spots on the Adriatic ever since – at the height of the season you should definitely try to book ahead to be sure of a room.

Krk – impossible to pronounce correctly without being Croatian (somewhere between Sean Connery saying 'kirk' and a dog coughing) – is home to industry as well as tourism, with a petrochemical plant near Omišalj, and Rijeka's airport also being on the island. People living in the north commute to Rijeka for work, while in summer Krk is busy and popular with holidaymakers, primarily from Austria and Germany – it's not many hours' straight drive from Vienna and Munich.

The island's infrastructure and local transport are good, making a visit here an easy one, and Krk was fortunate in barely being affected by the war at the beginning of the 1990s – tourism continues to boom.

The northeastern side of the island is mostly barren, while the main centres and most of the trees are in the softer and milder southern half. Running down the northwestern shore are a string of fully developed package resorts, Omišalj, Njivice and Malinska.

If you're here at the end of July you'll be within easy earshot of the popular Krk Folk Festival, which is big on the local atonal bagpipes.

History

People have lived on Krk since time immemorial, but the island was first known to have been settled by the Illyrian Liburnians, who were usurped in due course by the Romans. When Rome fell, Byzantium stepped in, to be followed by Venice, and then Croatia–Hungary.

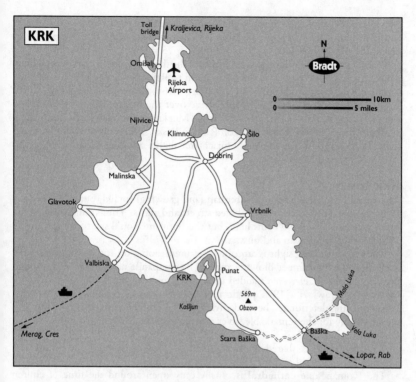

During the 11th century, Krk became the most important centre of Glagolitic culture in Croatia, and much of the country's valuable Glagolitic heritage comes from the island – the script was used here continuously until the beginning of the 19th century and the arrival of the Austro-Hungarians.

In 1358 Venice granted custody of the island to the Dukes of Krk, who ruled semi-autonomously until 1480. They owed their ascendancy, according to Rebecca West (in *Black Lamb and Grey Falcon*): 'not to virtue nor to superior culture, but to unusual steadfastness in seeing that it was always the other man who was beheaded or tossed from the window or smothered.'

From 1430 onwards, the Dukes successfully re-branded themselves (with the Pope's benediction) as 'Frankopans', allying themselves to the Frangepan nobility of Roman times. Their new coat of arms gave a nod both to Venice and the Frangepans (which derives, as New Testament scholars will have guessed, from *frangere panem*, the breaking of the bread), and therefore featured lions with loaves.

The return of Krk to Venice in 1480 wasn't good news for the island. The Venetians tore down the oak forests to build their galleys, and then pressed the islanders into service as oarsmen. In spite of a succession of rulers – from the Austro-Hungarians to the French (briefly) to Yugoslavia itself – little else of great note affected Krk until the arrival of mass tourism in the 1970s.

Getting there and around

Being popular, close to Rijeka and connected to the mainland by a road bridge, Krk is pretty well served by public transport. Around 15 buses a day make the 1½-hour journey from Rijeka to Krk town, stopping on the way at Omišalj,

Njivice and Malinska, and mostly going on to Punat and then Baška, at the island's southern end. Only a couple of buses a day, however, make the 10km journey across the island from Krk town to Vrbnik.

Direct buses from Lošinj and Cres arrive via the Merag–Valbiska ferry several times a day, stopping in Malinska on their way north to Rijeka – change here for access to southern Krk. Four buses a day also come direct from Zagreb, 5 hours away.

By car, the vast majority of people arrive over the bridge, though there is also the ferry connection ten times a day from Merag on the island of Cres, and in summer there's a ferry from Lopar, on Rab, to Baška, which runs two to five times daily. Rijeka airport is used mainly for charter flights bringing in package tours to Krk, Cres, Lošinj and Opatija.

Krk town

The island's capital is a bit of a suburban (and growing) sprawl, but at its core is a well-preserved old town, with cobbled streets and alleys. The Romans walled the town and built extensive baths here, but the remnants you'll see today are mostly 15th-century Frankopan and onwards.

Krk's most striking sight is arguably the onion-dome on top of the campanile, itself topped by a trumpet-blowing angel. The campanile dates from 1515, though the cupola and angel weren't added until 1765, and the angel you see today (not that you'd know) is a 1975 plastic replica, the original copper-plated wooden version having deteriorated beyond salvation. The **church museum** here is worth a visit, if only for the remarkable silver altarpiece of the Madonna, a gift to the last Duke of Krk in 1477.

The campanile is shared by two churches across a covered alley from one another, the cathedral and the church of St Quirinus.

The Romanesque **cathedral** is usually only open around the time of church services, but it's worth the wait, and you can often peer in from the vestibule anyway. Built on the site of an early basilica founded on the site of the Roman baths, today's cathedral dates from the 12th century on. While much of what you see inside is 15th and 16th century, there are some interesting mosaic fragments, and the columns are mostly Roman – the last capital on the left, by the choir, sports an unusual early-Christian Eucharist motif of two birds eating a fish. There are some good 15th- and 16th-century paintings, including the altarpiece, by Pordenone, while the fine 15th-century Gothic chapel on the left-hand side was the Frankopan place of worship, and features their various coats of arms on the ceiling.

St Quirinus, next door, is another fine example of clean, spare Romanesque architecture, also dating mostly from the 12th century. It claims to be the only two-storey church on the eastern Adriatic coast, and it was in the crypt here, dedicated to St Margaret, that condemned men said their final mass before execution in Frankopan days.

Otherwise there's not a whole lot to see, though the remnants of the medieval walls and the old alleys and streets are suitably atmospheric – as indeed are the summer concerts put on in the old Venetian fortress marking the corner of the old town.

Buses arrive at the southern end of town; it's a short walk past the bustling harbour to the old town. The **tourist office** (tel: 051 222 583; fax: 051 221 414; www.tz-krk.hr) is just inside the main gate, on the left, on Vela Placa, but was out of maps on the day I came through – fortunately that's not a problem as the old town is tiny, and it's easy to find your way around. More useful is **Autotrans** (tel: 051 222 661; fax: 051 222 110), at the bus station, which can fix you up with a private room (doubles are around €30, with the usual surcharge for short stays).

Most of the town's hotel accommodation is a 15-minute walk east of town, though there's one place right on the waterfront, the **Marina** (tel: 051 221 128; fax: 051 221 357), which has straightforward doubles at €82 in an unbeatable location. Just 600m east along the shore from here is the newly refurbished and reopened **Bor** (tel/fax: 051 220 200), which offers 20 plain but spacious rooms a stone's throw from the beach. Sea-view doubles go for €100 in high season, dropping back to €56 in spring and autumn.

Best value of the out-of-town package places is the three-star **Koralj** (tel: 051 221 044; fax: 051 221 063), which is on a narrow beach in the woods and has modern doubles for €74 – almost a third less than you'll pay at the equally three-starred Dražica or Lovarka (both on tel: 051 655 755; fax: 051 221 022).

Beyond the hotels there's a naturist campsite, **Politin** (tel: 051 221 351; fax: 051 221 246); more modest campers might prefer **Ježevac** (tel: 051 221 081; fax: 051 221 362), on the other side of town.

Krk also has a **Youth Hostel** (tel/fax: 051 221 212), housed in what was originally the island's very first hotel. With bed and breakfast at €18 per person in high season, and a 30% surcharge for stays of under three days it works out more expensive than private rooms – but the setting is lovely, right in the old town.

Krk town is a good base for excursions around the island, both onshore and off. On the quay – or through any of the travel agents – you'll find boats offering the traditional fish picnic, combined with the chance to swim at one of the southern beaches, as well as trips out to the islands between Krk and Rab. There are also a couple of glass-bottomed boats which go out on excellent two-hour trips, giving you a fine view of the marine life.

If you have your own transport, can work out the twice-daily buses, or fancy the walk, then the old stone hilltop village of **Vrbnik**, 10km across Krk on the empty east coast of the island, is a lovely place to visit. The tourist office (tel: 051 857 479; fax: 051 857 205) can help with finding you a private room if you want to stay, or there's the 12-room **Argentum** (tel: 051 857 370; fax: 051 857 352) which does simple doubles for €60 (off season, in May or October, these are a steal at €25).

The town was famous in the old days for having been one of the havens of the Glagolitic script, but today its reputation is sealed with a cork – you'll have trouble getting away from Vrbnik without trying the excellent local white wine, *Žlahtina*, best sampled at one of the several wine cellars. When you're done with wandering and wining, Vrbnik also has a beach below the town.

Punat and Košljun

Eight kilometres southeast of Krk town, facing west into a big sheltered bay, is the former shipbuilding and fishing village of Punat. It still makes a handsome living from the sea, but it's now the yachting trade which keeps the village afloat, with one of the bigger marinas in Croatia attracting a busy passing trade in summer.

The main attraction, however, is the island of Košljun, out in the bay, and its famous 16th-century Franciscan monastery. You can reach the island by taxi-boat from Punat, itself on a regular bus route from Krk town. Unless you're planning on staying in Punat, however, it's more convenient (if more expensive) to take a boat directly from Krk town.

In the airy church on Košljun there are some superb religious paintings from the 16th and 17th centuries, while the monastery also has one of Croatia's finest libraries, home to countless rare volumes, manuscripts, parchments and old maps. As if that weren't enough, the industrious monks have also put together an interesting ethnographic museum, a natural history collection, and an assortment of numismatic rarities.

With your head spinning from the surfeit of information absorbed, the perfect cure is a walk around the pretty island before catching the return boat.

I wouldn't especially recommend staying in Punat, but if you want to, the tourist office (tel: 051 854 860; fax: 051 854 970) can point you at agencies handling private rooms, and also has maps and brochures available. There's plenty of hotel accommodation in the complex south of town, near where the bus stops, run by **Hoteli Punat** (tel: 051 854 103; fax: 051 854 101), though it may – like everywhere on Krk – be fully booked in summer. Punat also has a **Youth Hostel** (tel/fax: 051 854 037), right in town, though it too tends to be full through the season.

Baška
In a wide bay on the southeastern end of the island is Baška, Krk's most popular resort, with more than 110,000 people visiting the village annually. The reason for its popularity is obvious enough – Baška (population around 1,000) sits at the eastern end of one of what is certainly one of Croatia's best beaches, a 1,800m stretch of sand and pebbles in a wide sweep under the mountains.

The little village dates from the 16th century, and the colourful fishermen's houses and narrow alleys off the small harbour are still very attractive, even amongst the summer crowds. Whilst you won't escape these along the seafront promenade, stretching for a total length of 4km, it's easy enough to get away from it all into the hills behind town, and the tourist office (tel: 051 856 817; fax: 051 856 544) has a great map detailing 15 different marked walks in the vicinity, from 2–10km long and taking anything from 30 minutes to four hours. As always, make sure you have decent footwear and plenty of water.

The four-hour walk over to the twin bays and beaches of **Mala Luka** and **Vela Luka** to the east, passing the naturist campsite and beach at **Bunculuka** (tel: 051 856 806, fax: 051 856 595) on the way, is moderately strenuous but well worth the effort, as is the somewhat easier three-hour hike to **Stara Baška**, a tiny village on a bay over the hills to the west.

A kilometre or so north of Baška is the **Church of St Lucy**, in **Jurandvor**, the site of one of Croatia's most important Glagolitic finds, the Baška Tablet, discovered in the floor of the church in 1851 by a local priest. It took over 20 years to decipher the script, which mentions King Zvonimir and dates from around 1100. The original is now in Zagreb (in the atrium of the building which houses the Strossmayer Gallery) but there's a good copy here – and rather less good, smaller, souvenir copies on sale all over town.

Baška is easily reached on the bus from Rijeka and Krk town, and in summer there's a ferry from Lopar on Rab. With its popularity with tourists, there are also any number of taxi-boats around, which will take you to less busy beaches and hidden coves both on Krk and on the neighbouring islands to the south.

Private rooms can be booked through Primaturist (tel: 051 856 132; fax: 051 856 971), with doubles going for €30, with a surcharge for three days or less (if you can find anyone willing to let you have one) – in summer you should book well ahead. This is even truer if you want hotel accommodation. Call the **Corinthia** (tel: 051 656 111; fax: 051 856 584) far, far in advance for doubles ranging from €90 to €100 depending on the facilities.

RAB
Cruising along the main coast road from Rijeka to Zadar you'd have no idea at all that Rab was worth visiting – it's a barren, denuded place, with no settlements and no sign of life.

Go round to the southwestern side of the island, however, and it suddenly becomes clear why Rab posts more than 1.5 million tourist nights a year from around 250,000 visitors. It's a green and pleasant land, with sandy beaches, hidden coves, and a wonderfully preserved medieval old town.

History

Like Cres and Krk, Rab was first settled by Liburnian Illyrians, before the arrival of the Romans, who established an important base here. The Byzantines and Croat-Hungarians followed, before Venice finally imposed itself on the island definitively at the beginning of the 15th century. The rich architectural heritage of the old town of Rab belies the Venetian plunder of the island's timber, resulting in that denuded northeastern coast, or the republic's limiting of essential supplies of salt (fish preservative), generally keeping the population both poor and subdued for the best part of 400 years.

The late 19th century ushered in new hope for the island as a tourist resort. The Austrians and Czechs were the first to invest in hotels – the Praha opened in 1909, a year after the Grand. They were also the first to encourage naturist holidays, heralding in a long tradition on the island – a tradition embraced in August 1936 by Edward VIII, king of England, and his girlfriend Wallis Simpson, it's said (though to an English sensibility it seems implausible that the king would be getting his kit off in public).

During World War II Rab was occupied by the Italians and then by the Germans, before becoming Yugoslav in 1945. When Tito split with Stalin in 1948 he turned the barren island of **Goli** (Goli Otok), between Rab and the mainland, into an internment camp for Stalinists, and just mentioning it was

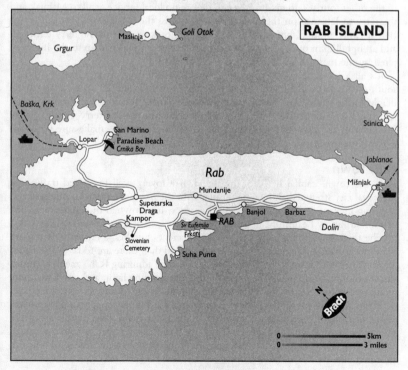

enough to get you a one-way ticket to the horrors of the local *gulag* – it wasn't until after Tito's death that the Goli camp's very existence was made public.

Life on Goli Otok was appalling. Apart from the sheer brutality and cruelty, typical tasks for the prisoners would include breaking rocks and hauling them across the island, where they could be used to spell out a giant 'Tito' or other party slogans, only to have to dismantle them and return the rocks to the quarry.

Today, both it and its neighbour, **Grgur** (which used to be a women's prison), have less traumatic potential as offshore day trips.

Getting there and around

Rab ought to be a perfect stop for island-hoppers on their way from Krk to Pag or vice-versa, but the idiosyncrasies of local transport make it difficult. The ferry from Baška on Krk, to Lopar at Rab's northern end, does run two to five times daily in summer, and usually connects with the bus to Rab town, but there isn't a ferry to Pag, and only one or two a week to Zadar.

The most reliable way of getting to Rab is therefore the twice-daily direct bus from Rijeka, which takes around 3 hours, crossing on the ferry from Jablanac to Mišnjak on Rab's southern end before heading into Rab town. In summer, try to book ahead, as the bus fills up quickly. There are also direct buses to and from Zagreb in summer – again, book ahead if you can.

Onward travel south is problematic – you either have to go back to Senj on the Rijeka-bound bus and then retrace your steps on the next bus to Zadar, or get the first bus to drop you on the highway, above Jablanac, and wait (it can be quite a wait, too) for the next southbound bus willing to stop.

On the island itself there are regular buses from Rab town to Lopar, as well as to the other tourist settlements, though there's no local service at all to Mišnjak and the ferry to Jablanac on the mainland. If you miss the Rijeka bus you can get to Barbat easily enough, but it's then a good 1½ hours on foot to the ferry terminal, and an uphill 2km once you get to the mainland, from Jablanac up to the highway plied by the main coastal buses.

It's all a lot easier with your own wheels. Ferries run from Jablanac (100km south of Rijeka) to Mišnjak nine times daily in winter and 22 times a day at the height of the season, and take just 15 minutes to make the crossing. From Mišnjak it's just 10km to Rab town. That said, the queues for the ferry can be pretty intimidating in July and especially in the first half of August – make sure you have a good book to hand.

Rab town

Rab, the town, capital of Rab, the island, is a lovely well-preserved traffic-free medieval city stretched along a peninsula, with the town's harbour to one side and the long inlet of St Euphemia bay on the other. It's crowned by a distinctive line of four strikingly beautiful campanili, and is best seen at least once from the sea.

The town has an unusually rich stock of ancient churches, a reminder that there were once many more people living on the island than there are today – in winter, anyway. In high summer you'll find you're not alone admiring Rab's medieval heart, but set an early alarm, walk the streets in the soft morning light, and you'll get quite a different impression of the town, soulful and quiet, settled into its long, long past.

Three roughly parallel streets – Gornja, Srednja, Donja (upper, middle, lower) – run the length of old town, connecting the older **Kaldanac**, at the tip of the peninsula, with **Varoš**, the newer (15th- to 17th-century) part of town, where it widens out. The popular Riva running along the harbour-side makes for a fourth thoroughfare.

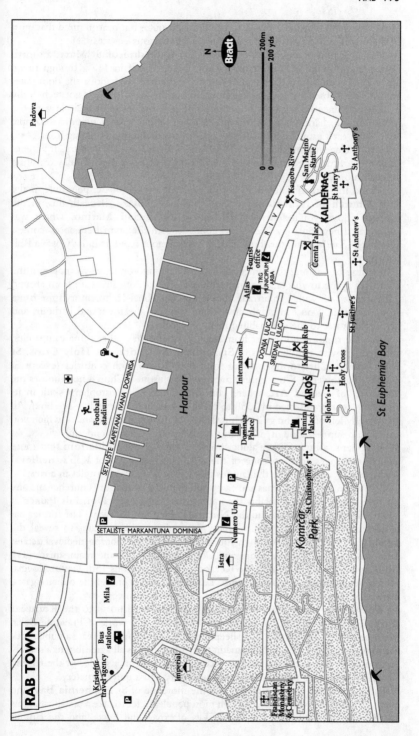

RAB TOWN

N

Bradt

200m
200 yds

Padova

Harbour

Football
stadium

ŠETALIŠTE KAPETANA IVANA DOMINISA

R I V A

Dominus
Palace

ŠETALIŠTE MARKANTUNA DOMINISA

Numero Uno

Istra

P

P

Mila

Bus
station

Kristefor
travel agency

P

Imperial

Franciscan
Monastery
& Cemetery

Komrčar
Park

St Christopher's

Nimfa
Palace

Si John's

Holy Cross

Kanoba Kub

VAROŠ

SREDNJA ULICA

DONJA ULICA

International

Atlas

Tourist
office

TRG
MUNICIPIUM
ARBA

Černita Palace

St Justine's

St Andrew's

St Mary's

San Marino
Statue

Kanoba River

KALDENAC

St Anthony's

RIVA

St Euphemia Bay

As you wander round, prepare to be churched-out – but bear in mind that most of them will only be open just before and after religious services.

The most important church in town is the **Cathedral of St Mary**, a superb Romanesque building consecrated by the Pope himself in 1177, though much altered and rebuilt in the early 16th century – the fine *pietà* above the door dates from 1514. (Observant readers will point out at this stage that it's not technically a cathedral, since Rab lost its bishopric in 1828 – but let's not quibble with the locals.) Inside, harmonious whitewashed Romanesque arches support the triple nave, with each capital subtly different. Dark carved choir stalls, dating from 1445, lead to an elegant grey altar canopy (*baldochino*) from the 11th century. It all goes back much further, even, than this – under the altar floor they're still excavating Roman mosaics.

Behind the cathedral (church, if you must), at the tip of the peninsula, is the small **Church of St Anthony** and a Franciscan convent. Beneath this, in the gardens below, you'll find a brand new statue of **San Marino**, which was inaugurated here on May 9 2004, to coincide with the annual crossbow contest (see box) – San Marino, the founder of the eponymous republic in Italy, was a Rab native.

Heading back along the upper road, the first thing you come to, opposite the cathedral, is the town's tallest **campanile**, an elegant 26m structure from around 1200, topped off with a balustrade with a mini octagonal 15th-century spire rising from within it. You can climb up for fine views of the town and harbour, and across the water to the uninhabited island of **Dolin**.

In a line running northwest from here are the town's other three campaniles, interspersed with the churches of **St Andrew**, **St Justine**, the **Holy Cross**, **St John** and **St Christopher**, dating from the 11th to 16th centuries (except St Justine's belltower, a 17th-century impostor). St Justine's Church now houses the **Museum of Sacred Art**, where you can admire St Christopher's skull in its reliquary, which was used in 1358 to break a siege here (allegedly – see box). All that's really left of St John's Church is the last of the town's campaniles, which you can climb up – though it's fairly vertiginous – for wonderful views. St Christopher's, a little further along, houses a fairly sparse **lapidarium**, but more importantly gives access to one of the few remaining parts of Rab's **medieval walls**, where you can take the famous pictures of all four campaniles in a row.

Below the row of churches and campanili there are even more churches and any number of palazzi, most notably the impressive 15th-century **Dominis Palace** at the northern end of town, and the **Nimira Palace** not far away. The former has a splendid carved portal, with chubby *putti* pulling aside curtains to reveal the family crest. Indeed, all over town you should keep an eye out for medieval details, Latin inscriptions, Venetian lions and Gothic windows. In the main square (Trg Municipium Arba) you'll find the **Rector's Palace**, with its 15th-century loggia, which was originally the public court. Leading off this is one of the old city gates, crowned with a 14th-century clock on a 13th-century tower.

When you're ready for a breather (or a picnic) head north to the **Komrčar Park**. The 19th-century landscaped woodland was the work of Pravdoje Belia, who spent years defying the local sheep farmers in his efforts to create a public park – and was rewarded by a small statue in the park itself. It's all agreeably in a slightly run-down state, but the fine mature trees provide welcome shade. At the far end of the park there's a ruined Franciscan monastery and a quiet cemetery.

Paths lead down through the park to the shoreline of **St Euphemia Bay**, and there are places to swim here – though most people prefer to take a taxi-boat across to the **Frkanj Peninsula**, which has lots of coves and inlets, and the famous

MEDIEVAL PAGEANTRY AND THE ART OF THE CROSSBOW

Living in a place like Rab you'd be mad not to dress up in medieval clothes from time to time, so that's what the locals do for the crossbow contests on May 9 and again on July 27 – and sometimes on other feast days and national holidays too. Amid much pageantry, fanfares of trumpets and formal processions, the tournament is really just an excuse for dressing up and having a good time, and it makes for a great civic occasion. But stay behind the crossbows – they're absolutely lethal.

The tradition dates back to May 9 1358, when Rab was liberated from a nasty Italo-Norman siege through the intervention of the enterprising bishop of the day, who saw off the besieging army by waving the relics of the head of St Christopher from the city walls. The day has been celebrated ever since, and not only could exiles return for the festivities but husbands also had official permission to beat their wives. Today the wife-beating is mercifully outlawed, but the party does go on for three days, with folk processions, much eating and drinking, and the crossbow contest itself on the final day.

naturist beaches on the far side (the scene of King Edward VIII's supposed skinny-dipping).

The main tourist office (tel: 051 771 111; fax: 051 771 110; www.tzg-rab.hr) is handily by the bus station, on the northern side of the harbour, and they have an information-rich map, with the town on one side and the whole island on the other. There's a second office on the old town's central square.

Nicest of the town's hotels is the **Imperial** (tel: 051 724 522; fax: 051 724 126), in fine shape after nearly a century in the business. It's in the woods adjoining the Komrčar park, close to the bus station and the harbour, and a short walk from the old town. Doubles go for €70 in season, and drop to around €50 from October to June. The **International** (tel: 051 724 266; fax: 051 724 206) is even better located, right in the old town, but is currently closed for renovation. The **Istra** (tel: 051 724 134; fax: 051 724 050) is for the time being a better bet, being right on the corner of the harbour, with doubles at €75. In high season, however, you'll be charged a supplement for stays of three days or less at any hotel in town.

If you're after a beach, a decent pool and a bit of tourist luxury, then the **Padova** (tel: 051 724 444; fax: 051 724 418), around the harbour and 1km south of town, is a big, modern affair, with good-sized doubles with balconies at €120 – and half board thrown in for not very much extra.

There are plenty of private rooms also available, though very few in the old town itself, and you may find everything already taken if you haven't booked ahead in high season. Use any of the several travel agencies to secure a room, and expect to pay €30–40 for a double in summer, along with the usual 30% surcharge for short stays. Try Mila (tel/fax: 051 725 499), a block towards the harbour from the bus station, Numero Uno (tel/fax: 051 724 688) on the corner of the harbour, Atlas (tel: 051 724 585; fax: 051 724 028) on Trg Municipium Arba or Kristofor (tel/fax: 051 725 523) by the bus station.

The nearest campsite, **Padova** (tel: 051 724 355, fax: 051 724 539) is 2km away to the south, past the hotel of the same name.

With its traffic-free streets, open squares and no-nonsense holiday atmosphere, Rab's a good place to eat and drink, with lots of restaurants and even more cafés and bars. And though there's little to choose between many of the establishments, I did have a wonderful mackerel one day at the **Konoba Riva**, which spills out of its courtyard on to the Riva itself, and the slightly more upmarket **Konoba Rab**, set inside heavy medieval walls, serves up excellent squid. Finally, if it's pizza you want in an atmospheric setting, you won't go wrong at the **Cernta Palace**, where you eat in the old palace courtyard.

Around Rab

The rest of Rab is hedonistically given over pretty much wholeheartedly to holidays, with well-organised resorts catering mostly for sun-seeking Austrians, Czechs and Germans. There are lots of excellent beaches, and excursions available both to Rab town and to the neighbouring islands.

A few kilometres south of Rab town, facing on to the empty island of Dolin, is the rambling village of **Barbat**, which has a few beaches and quite a large number of private rooms and private moorings. With plenty of buses to Rab Town it's a good accommodation alternative in high season. Contact the **Der Barbat** (tel/fax: 051 721 716) travel agency for reservations.

Immediately to the west of the Frkanj peninsula and Rab town is the tourist complex of **Suha Punta**. It's unashamedly package country, but in a very pretty setting, with plenty of rock beaches, pine woods, and sheltered coves in the vicinity. You can walk or cycle over to the less-crowded sandy beaches at **Kampor**, and it's within easy reach of Rab Town. The place to stay in Suha Punta is the **Carolina** (tel: 051 669 100; fax: 051 669 428), with doubles overlooking the beach at €95 – the **Eva** (tel: 051 668 200; fax: 051 668 518) is cheaper (around €75) but less well situated.

Around 5km northwest of Rab and 1km short of Kampor, on the left-hand side, is the **Slovenian War Cemetery**, on the site of the 1942–43 concentration camp. It's a sobering place, with rows of graves set out as a memorial to the 1,443 victims of fascism who lost their lives in this quiet spot, where today all you'll hear is the wind in the cypresses and distant dogs barking.

Across the headland from Kampor is **Supertaska Draga**, home to a good marina, as well as quite a few private moorings and private rooms – contact the Rab (tel: 051 771 111; fax: 051 771 110) or Lopar (tel: 051 775 508; fax: 051 775 487) tourist offices for more information.

Rab's northern tip is the **Lopar** peninsula, featuring not just the ferry terminal hooking up with Baška, on Krk, but also (across the headland, on Crnika Bay, and centred on the settlement of San Marino), the famous **Paradise Beach**, 1.5km-worth of sand and sea. The enormous **San Marino** (tel: 051 775 144; fax: 051 775 128) complex, tucked into the woods behind the beach, is where you'll probably end up staying (unless you're at the San Marino campsite), with nice doubles at €85. There are at least 20 shallow sandy beaches on the peninsula, within pretty easy walking distance of San Marino, making the area extremely popular with families.

Northern Dalmatia

7

Northern Dalmatia is a region of extreme contrasts – you'd never dream, swimming at the foot of the Krka waterfalls, that the most barren islands of the Kornati archipelago were only a few kilometres offshore. Just as you'd never guess, confronted by a wall of heat on dry and dusty **Pag**, that the island of **Pašman** offered such sweet shelter on its wooded southern bays.

Zadar, the region's economic and transport capital, offers a wealth of things to see in a cultured old town, while **Šibenik's** Renaissance cathedral is one of the highlights not just of Dalmatia but of the whole of Croatia. The region is home, too, to three near-perfect national parks and a dedicated nature park: **Paklenica**, where you can hike serious summits and still go swimming in the same day; **Krka**, where you can visit a 14th-century monastery on an island between waterfalls; **Kornati**, where 89 islands, islets and reefs offer the true desert-island experience; and **Vransko Jezero**, privileged home to 100,000 wading birds. Add in the islands of **Ugljan** (Zadar's quiet holiday retreat) and **Dugi Otok** (a sailor's heaven), and you could spend all your holidays here.

The telephone code for Zadar and surrounds (Paklenica, most of Pag, Ugljan, Pašman, Dugi Otok, Vransko Jezero etc) is 023 (+385 23 from abroad). For Šibenik and the local area (Knin, Krka, Murter) the code is 022 (+385 22). Rather confusingly, the northern end of Pag has the Senj phone code of 053 (+385 53).

ZADAR

Zadar is the economic and transport centre for northern Dalmatia, with a population rapidly approaching 100,000. While its suburbs sprawl along the coast and inland, at its heart you'll find an unpretentious, partially walled old town on a narrow peninsula, full of fine churches and excellent museums.

History

Zadar was first settled by Liburnian Illyrians the best part of 3,000 years ago, but from as early as the 3rd century BC onwards the Romans had their eye on it, finally making a *Municipium* of it in 59BC and giving *Jadera* colony status 11 years later.

On the partition of the empire, Zadar became the capital of Byzantine Dalmatia, and had a period of some prosperity until the rise of Venice. Locals today are still proud of the fight Zadar put up against the Venetians, but in spite of four revolts in the 12th century and further uprisings over the next 200 years, Zadar went the same way as the rest of Dalmatia, ceding to Venice in 1409.

The Venetians' endless feuds with the Turks did nothing special for Zadar, though they did leave the city with a fine set of 16th-century defensive walls. Austria picked up the reins on the fall of Venice, with a brief French interlude, and

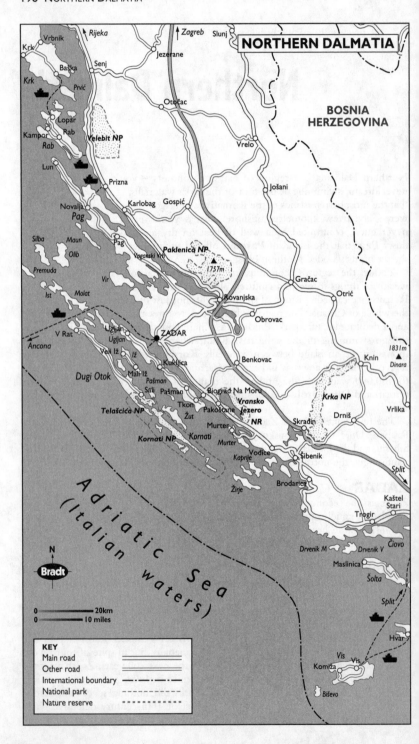

allowed Italian immigrants to take care of the city – something which continued after World War I, with Zadar not joining the nascent Kingdom of the Serbs, Croats and Slovenes, but becoming Italian (*Zara*) instead. Indeed, some older people still speak Italian, though you'll find the younger generation more switched on to German or English as a first foreign language.

When Italy capitulated in 1943, Germany took over Zadar, and the Allies practically bombed it into oblivion, a fate many feared might happen again during the winter of 1991, when the Serbs laid siege to the city. People went hungry and thirsty during the siege, but the old town remained intact, something which can't be said for the inland suburbs, some of which still show the scars of warfare more than a decade after it ended.

Getting there and around

Zadar is a transport hub, with regular bus arrivals and departures (hourly, for the most part) to and from Zagreb (5 hours), Rijeka (4–5 hours), Split (3 hours) and Dubrovnik (6–7 hours), as well as several weekly runs to and from places like Frankfurt and Munich. The best place to buy long-distance bus tickets is at Croatia Express (tel: 023 211 660; fax: 023 211 631), on Široka, right in the middle of the old town.

Trains come in from Zagreb twice a day, but it's a long, long journey, as the route takes a dog-leg via Knin (where you have to change), and works out twice as slow as the bus. Quicker by far is flying, as there's a small airport, about 10km away to the southeast, with daily Zagreb flights being met by the airline bus.

There are lots of ferries out to the islands of the Zadar archipelago (notably Ugljan and Dugi Otok), as well as regular excursions to the Kornati archipelago – see the relevant sections later in this chapter for details. There are also larger ferries which stop in four times a week on the Rijeka–Dubrovnik run, as well as a ship four times weekly which goes up to Pula (8 hours away), via Lošinj, and another which goes to Venice (15 hours) twice a week. Finally, in summer, there's a fast catamaran which runs daily up to Rijeka, taking barely longer than the bus.

Zadar's bus and train stations are 1km southeast of the old town and port, while most of the hotels and beaches – and the town's marina – are 3km northwest of it, at Borik. There's a bus about three times an hour from the bus station up to Borik, via the harbour.

Everything you want to see in Zadar is in the compact old town, sitting on its own peninsula, separating the harbour from the Zadarski Kanal, the strait running between Zadar and Ugljan. There's a footbridge across the harbour from the old town, leading to the road running north to Borik.

Where to stay and eat

Zadar has remarkably little accommodation in or very close to the old town, and surprisingly few restaurants either, so there's a good chance you'll end up eating and sleeping at Borik, or visiting Zadar on your way somewhere else, between buses.

The tourist office (tel: 023 212 412; fax: 023 211 781; www.zadar.hr), on the southeastern corner of the old town, has good maps and other documentation, and friendly staff. Private rooms, of which only a very few are in or really close to town, are handled by travel agencies, including Miatours (tel: 023 212 888; fax: 023 212 788), on the harbour front, and Atlas (tel: 023 235 850; fax: 023 235 772), across the footbridge. You'll be lucky to get away with paying under €35 for a double, plus the usual 30% surcharge for short stays. Both agencies can of course also organise excursions for you, of which there are any number from Zadar, including trips up to the Plitvice Lakes, down to the Krka River and waterfalls, or out to the Kornati archipelago.

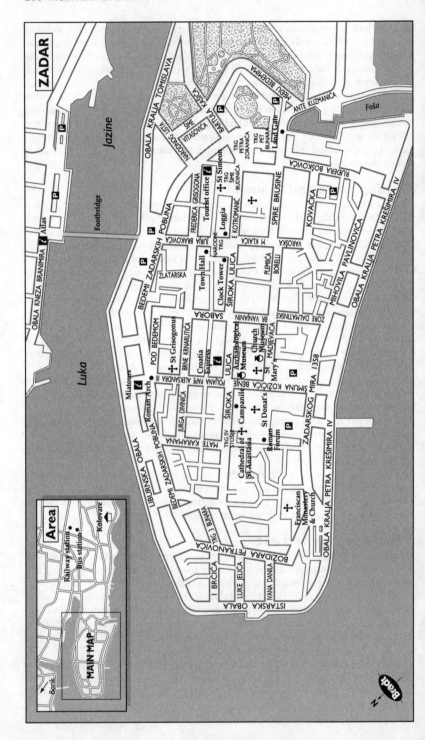

There's only one hotel in town, the large, modern **Kolovare** (tel: 023 203 200; fax: 023 203 300; www.hotel-kolovare-zadar.htnet.hr), which has a small pool and its own beach, and is open all year round. Expect to pay €100 for doubles with a view across to Ugljan, at any time of year.

Otherwise you're almost certain to end up in Borik, which has a plain but well-situated campsite (tel: 023 332 074; fax: 023 332 065) and a clutch of mostly package-oriented hotels, many of which could do with a spot of renovation. One which certainly doesn't need refurbishing is the small but swanky **President** (tel: 023 333 464; fax: 023 333 595; www.hotel-president.hr), but it's priced accordingly, with doubles going for around €200 a night.

In terms of bang per buck, the best hotel is the 30-room **Mediteran** (tel: 023 337 500; fax: 023 337 528; www.hotelmediteran-zd.hr), which has nice doubles with balconies and a view of the sea for €80. Cheaper rooms (a shade under €70) can be found at the **Barbara** (tel: 023 206 100; fax: 023 332 065; www.hoteliborik.hr) and **Donat** (tel: 023 206 500; fax: 023 332 065; www.hoteliborik.hr). They're both package hotels, though the Barbara has a decent-sized pool.

Finally, there's a **youth hostel** (tel: 023 331 145; fax: 023 331 190), between the marina and Borik beach, where you can find a bed for €21 a head, and it's open all year round.

The lack of restaurants in town is compensated for to some extent by good cafés and bars, with terraces spilling out onto the pavements. This is the place to try Zadar's most famous speciality, *Maraskino*, the cherry liqueur which has been produced here since the 1820s. It was long Austrian royalty's most popular tipple, and if it's a touch *démodé* now, that shouldn't stop you trying it. Once.

What to see

All of Zadar's sights are within the old town, within a few hundred metres of each other. They're ordered in the text from the northwestern corner, working back towards the southeast. To get to the start either walk along the tree-lined, sea-facing promenade (a nice place for a picnic) or walk around the remains of the town walls facing the harbour – these are mostly 16th-century Venetian, though you'll see Roman fragments, particularly near the footbridge across the harbour.

The **Franciscan monastery and church** dates back to the 13th century, but it's been much remodelled since and you wouldn't know it wasn't entirely 18th-century baroque these days. The choir stalls inside are late 14th century, however, and the treasury – rarely open – houses some important works, including a big 12th-century crucifix. The monastery's fine cloisters are mid 16th-century Renaissance.

From here it's a stone's throw (if they haven't finished tidying up the piles of Roman rubble) to the site of the **Roman Forum** – the single 14m-high **Roman column** standing here is all that's left. Originally 90m by 45m, the forum would have made a decent-sized football pitch. Until the 19th century, criminals were tied to the pillar here, and...well, pilloried, I suppose.

Many of the original bits of Roman stonework ended up in the solid church which dominates what's left of the forum today. The **Church of the Holy Trinity** was started in the 9th century by Bishop Donat, and has been known as **St Donat's** ever since. It's a 27m-high structure, built on a circular ground-plan, and its tall interior is now used for secular concerts rather than religious worship. Look out for everything from upside-down capitals to gravestones to altars to whole pillars within the structure of the walls – all Roman. Parts of the floor, too, are the original Roman flagstones. You can walk upstairs to the gallery, looking down into the church, but don't lean on the handrails, as they're not very sturdy and it's a long way down.

Round the corner from St Donat's is the triple-naved Romanesque **Cathedral of St Anastasia**, dating from the 12th and 13th centuries. Badly bombed during World War II, it was painstakingly rebuilt afterwards. The façade features an attractive series of blind arches and two rosette windows. Inside there are some 13th-century frescos, a 14th-century altar canopy (sheltering an altar containing bits of 9th century stonework), some 15th-century choir stalls, and the marble sarcophagus commissioned by Donat in the 9th century to house the mortal remains of St Anastasia herself.

Behind the cathedral, the bottom half of the lovely **campanile** dates from the 15th century, though it wasn't completed until the 1890s, to a design by the British architect (and sometime writer of ghost stories), Sir Thomas Graham Jackson. Given the centuries-old rivalry between the bishops of Zadar and Rab, and Rab's having lost its bishopric in 1828, it can only have been professional irony that made Jackson model his campanile on Rab's most famous belltower. Or perhaps simply that he was very good at copying things – his most famous work in England is the Bridge of Sighs, in Oxford.

Across the forum is **St Mary's Church** – the squat, 16th-century Renaissance front hides a church originally consecrated in the 11th century, along with a few more bits of the Roman forum. Behind it stands yet another Rab-like campanile, though this one's original, dating back to the early 12th century.

Next to this is Zadar's excellent **church museum**, which houses a wonderful collection of reliquaries, paintings and sculpture, while nearby, in a modern building, there's the **Archaeological Museum**, a fine collection from Liburnian times on. At both museums the labels are only in Croatian, however.

Heading towards the harbour, the 12th-century Romanesque **Church of St Grisogonus** (also called Chrysogonus – *Krševan* in Croatian) is all that's left of one of Croatia's oldest monasteries, founded in 908. The outside, with its rows of blind arches and a pretty Tuscan-inspired colonnade on the back of the church, is more endearing than the rather shabby 13th- and 14th-century frescos inside.

The town gate leading onto the harbour, down from St Grisogonus, contains all that's left of a **Roman triumphal arch** from Trajan's time. Back inside the walls, head towards Narodni Trg, the heart of business life in medieval times, now overlooked by an impressive clocktower. The **town hall** features fine reliefs of Šibenik Cathedral and Diocletian's Palace in Split, while the 16th-century **loggia** across the square, with unusually tall pillars, does service these days as a gallery.

A block east from here is the **Church of St Simeon**. The baroque building itself can't compete with Zadar's other churches, but **St Simeon's sarcophagus**, inside, certainly can. Commissioned in 1377, and delivered in 1380, it's an impressively chunky burnished silver and gold coffin, with dramatic reliefs on the front and a life-sized portrait of the saint on the lid, complete with swept-back hair and bushy eyebrows. For more detail, come on the saint's feast day, October 8, and you'll find even more silverwork and some fine reliquaries on the inside, when the sarcophagus is opened up for its annual inspection. (If you don't see it here, there's a very good copy in Zagreb, in the atrium of the building which houses the Strossmayer Gallery.)

Trg Pet Bunara ('the square of five wells'), nearby, was the town's main water supply for centuries – the Romans of course had proper running water, but from medieval times until the arrival of the businesslike Austrians, the underground cistern here was as good as plumbing got.

From here the easiest way out is through the **Land Gate**. On the outside of this there's a big relief of a no-nonsense Venetian lion. The miniature harbour here is all that's left of the defensive moat which once protected the city.

NIN AND GREGORIUS

When you've run out of things to do in Zadar, an excursion can be made up to **Nin**, which was important in Roman times, and even more so as a religious centre in the Middle Ages – witness Meštrović's enormous statue of *Gregorius of Nin*, in Split (and the far smaller version of the same, in Varaždin).

These days (and for most of the past thousand years, if truth be told), Nin's a quiet little town, on its own little island, connected to the mainland by a pair of bridges. There's not a whole lot to see and do, but the Church of the Holy Cross is Croatia's oldest (from around AD800), and you can absorb some more history at the local Archaeological Museum – and there are a couple of reasonable beaches nearby.

Nin is easily reached on the bus, which runs every hour or so from Zadar and takes around 25 minutes.

South to Vransko Jezero

South of Zadar are a string of unpretentious resort towns leading to the island of **Murter**, connected to the mainland by a bridge, and the best jumping-off point for the Kornati archipelago (see page 222).

On the way, just past **Biograd** (where you can catch the ferry to Pašman, see page 221), is Croatia's largest natural lake, Vransko Jezero – turn left as you approach Pakoštane, 5km south of Biograd, and then right after just under 2km.

Already an ornithological reserve since 1983, **Vransko Jezero** was declared as a nature park in 1999 in a bid to reinforce the protection of its unique habitat and birdlife. The lake is nearly 14km long and between 1.5 and 3.5km wide, and has a surface area of over 30km^2, but it's never more than 4m deep. A channel which was dug at the end of the 18th century, in an attempt to drain the lake, now provides it with an occasional top-up of salt water at high tide, and it's also partly connected with the sea by underground fissures in the limestone.

A total of 111 bird species have been recorded here, while 41 species over-winter in the park and 49 nest here – including a small colony of rare purple herons. You can also expect to see marsh harriers, ducks, terns and white egrets, and 100,000 coots, which over-winter here.

So far there's very little indeed in the way of infrastructure for the visitor, though there are already plans to have some boats available for hire by 2005, and longer-term plans to build a cycle-path around the lake – for the time being though you'd need a very rugged mountain bike or a 4WD vehicle to negotiate the pitted gravel road. There are also plans to build hides, with coin-operated telescopes.

There's a road running behind the hills on the lake's northeastern shore which goes from the village of Vrana to the settlement of Banjevci. If you turn up the gravel road to the right here, it leads steeply up a *Križni Put* (Way of the Cross) to a small chapel on top of the hills, built as a memorial to the people who were thrown into a deep hole here by the partisans at the end of World War II. It's a moving place, with unrivalled views out west over the lake and the Kornati archipelago.

For more information on the latest state of affairs in the nature park, contact the park office (tel: 023 386 456; fax: 023 386 453; www.vransko-jezero.hr) directly.

PAKLENICA NATIONAL PARK

Situated half way between Karlobag and Zadar – an hour from either, by bus – is Paklenica National Park, a pair of wonderful limestone gorges running up from the sea, deep into the Velebit massif. Popular with Croatian walkers and climbers, it's also one of my favourite places in the whole country, offering everything from a gentle stroll to a seriously strenuous trek, and pitches for rock climbers of every level.

The park was opened in 1949, and is unusually interesting for both climatic and physical reasons. Situated under the highest peak of the Velebit massif (Vaganski Vrh, 1,758m), the area experiences three distinct climates – coastal, continental and sub-alpine. The rock is Velebit Karst (see page 5), and walking is possible from sea-level up to the top of the massif.

Most of the lower reaches are heavily forested with deciduous trees, while higher up mountain pastures support sub-alpine flowers and herbs. One of the most attractive features of the park, however, is the more than 80 species of butterfly found here, making it a lepidopterist's paradise.

There are also lots of beetles and several reptiles (you'll see snakes slithering off the path as you approach) and amphibians, and an extraordinary 209 species of bird to watch out for. Sadly, this no longer includes the griffon vulture (see *Cres*, page 180) – the last pair ate poisoned meat, probably intended to kill local wolves. But in the remoter parts of the park you can still scope for peregrine falcons and sparrowhawks, and you're almost certain to see red-backed shrikes.

On the other hand you're equally certain *not* to come in contact with the bears and wolves which live in the furthest reaches of the park – they're extremely discreet.

Getting there

All buses from Rijeka to Zadar make three Paklenica-related stops. From north to south, the first stop is at Starigrad Paklenica, the second is at the Hotel Alan (the closest stop to the main entrance to the park), and the last is at Seline (closest to the southern gorge, Mala Paklenica). If you're coming from Zagreb then change buses in Zadar.

Although there are lots of buses up and down the coast, leaving in the middle of summer can be harder than arriving, as it depends on the passing buses not being full already. Early mornings are generally better than other times of day, but it's not a guaranteed recipe for success.

Where to stay

The stretch of coast along here is one of the easiest places in Croatia for accommodation, though not one of the most luxurious.

Camping is easiest at one of the two campsites across the road from the entrance to the park, next to the Hotel Alan. One is attached to the hotel (tel: 023 369 236; fax: 023 369 203), while the other is attached to the national park (tel: 023 369 155; fax: 023 369 202); each is equally close to the beach. There are other smaller campsites along the road north and south of town.

There are any number of private rooms in the area, including some on the trail up into the park. There isn't an agency officially handling these, so your best bet is to wander up and down the road and ask at the numerous places with *sobe* signs – expect to pay between €20 and €40 for a double. The nicest ones, some with lovely balconies and sea views, are in the villages of Seline and Starigrad, but these are only practical if you have your own wheels. If you're really stuck, the tourist office (tel/fax: 023 369 255) in Starigrad itself, while not having a private-room mandate, will usually help you out.

There are also three hotels and a number of smaller pensions. The **Rajna** (tel: 023 359 121; fax: 023 369 888) has just ten rooms at €45, and being right by the entrance to the park it's inevitably full of Croatian climbers, but it's a good place to find out about the best pitches currently being recommended.

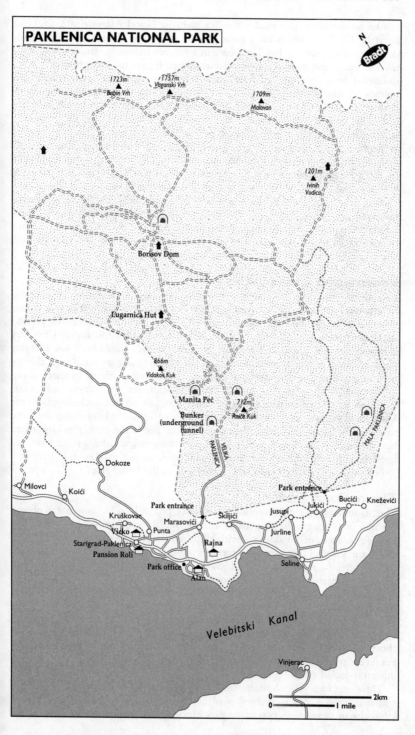

PAKLENICA NATIONAL PARK

N

1723m
Babin Vrh

1757m
Vaganski Vrh

1709m
Malovan

1201m
Ivinih
Vodica

Borisov Dom

Lugarnica Hut

866m
Vidakov Kuk

Manita Peć

712m
Anića Kuk

Bunker
(underground
tunnel)

VELIKA
PAKLENICA

MALA PAKLENICA

Dokoze

Milovci

Koići

Kruškovac

Vicko

Starigrad-Paklenica

Pansion Rolì

Park entrance

Marasovići

Punta

Park office

Alan

Rajna

Šiljići

Park entrance

Jusupi

Jukići

Bucići

Kneževići

Jurline

Seline

Velebitski Kanal

Vinjerac

0   2km
0   1 mile

Out on the main coast road is the '70s high-rise **Hotel Alan** (tel: 023 209 050; fax: 023 369 203), which has a great location on the beach and good views, and double rooms at €86. When I was here in 1988, researching an earlier book, it was my first-ever experience of a totally naturist hotel. It gave me something of a shock on arrival to see a family of four loading up their car, totally in the nude, but presumably they were equally startled by my rude clothed-ness. By the time I came here again, the hotel was firmly '*textile*' (as the naturist community would have it).

Finally, there's the smaller, cheerful, family-run **Vicko** (tel/fax: 023 369 304), which has nice rooms at €65, though the location isn't quite as good for the park as the Alan, and it's not right on the beach. If it's the seaside you're after, you can't do better than the **Pansion Roli** (tel/fax: 023 369 018), in Starigrad itself and right on the waterfront, where the fishing boats tie up. They have 14 rooms, at around €45 for doubles, and do fabulous mussels and other seafood.

You can't camp within the confines of the park itself, but there are several mountain huts along the massif. The biggest and best equipped is **Borisov Dom**, which is the place to stay if you're going for the peaks on the Velebit ridge. Check yourself in ahead of time with the park office (tel: 023 369 155; fax: 023 369 202; www.paklenica.hr), and make sure you have a sleeping bag.

Information and facilities

Everything you need is within easy reach of the park entrance, including a supermarket with good long opening hours and all the makings of a decent picnic, a couple of kiosks, and the park office (see above) itself. Here you'll be given a standard free map which comes with the entrance ticket (30 kuna; a five-day climbing pass is 50 kuna), but you can buy better ones (a good idea if you're doing much walking) as well as more detailed climbing and hiking guides. This is also the place to arrange accommodation at one of the mountain huts, or to check about the opening/visiting times of Manita Peć or the Bunkers (see opposite and over).

There are a whole clutch of places where you can eat out, including both the **Vicko** and **Rajna**, along with informal grills and seafood places along the main road and on the shore, and at least one pizzeria. Inside the park, the **Lugarnica** hut, on the way to Borisov Dom, does great sausages and other grilled food. It's open daily through the summer months and on weekends in May and October.

For swimming, there are beaches either side of the Hotel Alan.

The national park

The national park's geomorphology consists primarily of a horizontal plateau running between the Velebit massif and the sea. Two gorge valleys, Velika and Mala (large and small) Paklenica, with cliffs over 400m high in places, cut through this to the sea, and there are also several networks of subterranean caves. The most famous of these is Manita Peć, which has been explored for nearly 200m of its depth into the mountain and contains two enormous halls.

Because of its triple climate the weather is unusually variable. It's the only place I've ever walked where I've been drenched by rain, then sunburned and finally hailed on, before going for an afternoon swim in the sea. Prepare for all weathers, especially in May and early June, when there's still snow on the north-facing slopes above 1,500m. In high summer the inner parts of the park can be fearsomely hot, but even when the sun's shining on the coast, localised storms can see you miserably hailed on. Be prepared.

There are two official routes into the park, up the two canyons. The main entrance is up a clearly marked road 300m south of the Hotel Alan. A brisk kilometre up here brings you to the park office, where you buy your ticket in, and

STAYING ON THE RIGHT TRACK

Within the park, the trails marked on the map in red are marked in reality with red and white flashes on rocks and trees, and it's very rare that you can't easily see from one mark to the next. Some of the least-used paths may have faded markings, but others will impress you with their fresh brightness. There are also lots of paths used by local people which aren't guided on the ground; these are marked with dotted lines on the map. On the steeper paths you may well appreciate the use of a stick or walking-poles, especially if it's been raining, as some of the trails can be pretty slippery.

A word of warning, though. It's highly inadvisable to leave the marked paths – high up in the park there are still minefields, while lower down you'll have to cross the naked karst. And believe me, wild karst is awful stuff to cross – you'll find it extremely wearing, both mentally and on your clothes and hands. The shallowest slopes will confront you with jagged rocks, and even 2m climbs or drops are difficult.

The first time I came here, a marked path up Anića Kuk took me three hours, including a 700m climb. The same descent, across just 4km of shallow karst, took nearly seven hours. I was never in danger of being lost, since everything was clearly visible, but the rocks were nearly impossible to cross, and my fingers were worn to all but the last layer of skin by the end. For a week I couldn't even hold a cup of coffee.

Assistance in case of an emergency depends in the first instance on members of your party, or other walkers and climbers – there is a mountain rescue service, but they need to be alerted. It's a good idea to let people know where you're headed before you set out.

maps, after which it's a further 2km to the end of the road and the car park. You'll come across the entrance here to what used to be one of Paklenica's greatest secrets, the enormous **bunker complex** built for Tito in the 1950s as a crisis headquarters in times of war. For decades nobody was allowed to even mention its existence, but you can now visit parts of the huge complex, and it's a fascinating glimpse into the paranoia of power. The bunkers are open somewhat irregularly; contact the park administration for more details.

The other entrance to the park is up Mala Paklenica, 4km south, just after and opposite the Church of St Mark. Turn inland and it's nearly 2km to the clearly visible canyon entrance, where you can park, if you have a car.

Anića Kuk

This is easily the most-climbed peak in the national park. There are something like 25 routes up the west and north faces, and these are all serious climbs which shouldn't be attempted without ropes and proper climbing equipment. There are also two walking routes to the 712m summit, which makes for a fine 6-hour return trip from the Hotel Alan (4½ hours if you have a car).

Anića Kuk is not high, but it's an isolated, exposed peak, and it's the nearest major summit to the sea. The side facing into the gorge is a near-vertical drop of over 400m; don't stray too close to the edge.

Both walking routes follow Velika Paklenica upstream from the car park, on a well-made erosion-avoiding paved road, until you reach a sharp uphill left-hand bend, hard on the river, after half an hour. Cross the river here at the sign, and follow a mix of yellow flashes and red and white markers towards the base of the cliff which comes down to a flint-shaped point.

The yellow flashes mark the route to the right, and this is the best route up. It's steep, and there are some assisted sections, but you don't need any special equipment. The summit's an airy, vertiginous place, the best part of a couple of hours uphill, but easily worth it for the fabulous views out across to the barren island of Pag.

The descent heads away from Velika Paklenica at first, clearly identified with red and white flashes, across some naked karst. It's a bit of a scramble, and can be hard on the hands, but within half an hour you're back on to a more regular path down through the woods and scrub – the path then loops round off the ridge and back down into Velika Paklenica, zig-zagging its way back to where the two routes meet.

Manita Peć and Vidakov Kuk

This trail takes in the cave at Manita Peć and the 866m summit above it, Vidakov Kuk. Like Anića Kuk, the summit is close enough to the sea to afford wonderful views without an enormous expenditure of effort. The second part of the walk involves some scrambling and a reasonable sense of balance, but as far as Manita Peć the walk is sometimes steep but never difficult. The walk up to the cave is close to 2 hours from the Hotel Alan; allow another 2½ hours for the return trip from the cave to the summit of Vidakov Kuk – or a total of around 6 hours out and back (4½ if you have a car), not counting cave exploration time.

Manita Peć itself can only be visited with a guide, and is usually open three times a week in summer, on Monday, Wednesday and Saturday mornings – check at the park office before you head up here, to avoid disappointment.

From the car park head up the gorge for around 30 minutes until the path levels out (turning from paved to grit). After a short while there's the sign to Anića Kuk to the right, and indicators to Lugarnica (30 min) and Planinarski Dom (Borisov Dom, 50 min). It's not far from here to the path heading off to the right, which eventually leads to Mala Paklenica (see over), after which you soon reach the sign saying it's 40' to Manita Peć, and that's about how long you should allow to cover the long zig-zags heading uphill to the left, to the cave at 550m.

The cave itself – like most caves – is nothing special outside, but inside it's marvellous. A tunnel-like entrance leads through to two huge chambers, some 40m long and 40–65m wide, with a height of over 30m. The atmospheric artificial lighting shows off the stalactites and stalagmites, and the weird dripstone pillars. Nature's a wonderful thing.

Blinking outside in the daylight, the path up to Vidakov Kuk sets off rather obscurely to the left (with your back to the cave), going down a couple of metres to start with, then traversing a rather steep and insecure scree-like slope, before gaining a shallow scrub forest.

The trail continues consistently upwards and closer to the cliff, drifting right as you look at the ridge. Eventually a way up through a steep split in the cliff is marked, and it's here that you need to be fairly agile, with the terrain rocky and mostly unassisted. As you attain the ridge the summit is only 50m above you, to your left. There isn't a marked trail to the peak, but there are several fairly easy ways to reach it. But make sure you have secure hand and footholds as the rock's rather friable up here. The view from the top, of course, makes it all worthwhile.

The marked trail continues fairly gently from the Vidakov Kuk peak to the farm at Ramići, where you can either go back down Velika Paklenica, or up towards Velika Golić. There's also an ill-marked route down the back of Vidakov Kuk to the village of Tomići, which takes around 3 hours – don't take this unless you're absolutely sure of the way down.

Velika Golić

Some of the more spectacular views in Paklenica can be had from the long ridge of Velika Golić, and an excellent 10-hour walk (under 9, if you have a car) takes in this ridge and returns via Borisov Dom.

The walk starts exactly as if you were going to Manita Peć (see previous page), but heads straight on when the path branches up and left to the cave. After half an hour you'll come to a water trough and a sign saying Borisov Dom 30'. The main path branches up to the left here, and 10 minutes further on you need to take the path branching steeply uphill, away from the river. Follow this up its zig-zags for about 40 minutes, after which you'll come to a straighter section, with markings on the dry stone wall leading to the farm at Ramići (not the only place named Ramići in the immediate vicinity, unfortunately).

The main marked trail leading through the farm leads up to Vidakov Kuk – the path you want, to Velika Golić, is a hard right-hand turn, almost behind you as you arrive at the farm. From here, after skirting between a series of dry stone walls, the path rises steadily, and you're soon a long way above the farm. The ground becomes rougher as the path skirts the 903m summit of Čelinka and crosses a rocky wood before surfacing on an open pasture. This leads directly to the corner of the ridge, level with the top of Čelinka. It takes about 2 hours from the river to this point, from which there are fine views down on to the refuge below, across to the peak of Anića Kuk and over to the sea.

The ridge is an extraordinary formation, consisting of a series of parallel broken limestone ridges at an angle of about 40°. The valley side is nearly a sheer drop, but the side from which you've approached is relatively shallow, as is the line of the ridge itself, which takes the best part of 2km to rise from 900m to 1,285m. There are endless false crests to this, but the summit is superb, with spectacular panoramic views making the 4–5-hour ascent well worthwhile. Make sure you have appropriate clothing, however – this is where I was once caught in a late-May hailstorm.

The best way down is to continue along the ridge, scaling a secondary summit of 1,160m, before the path curves back on itself to bring you down to Borisov Dom. This takes around 2 hours, after which it's an easy $1^1/_2$ hours back to the car park.

Mala and Velika Paklenica

This is a terrific circular walk, including both gorges and some very fine views. It runs from the Hotel Alan to Seline, up Mala Paklenica, across the broad ridge between the two canyons and then down Velika Paklenica. It can be done in reverse, but with Mala Paklenica being the tougher walk, you're better off tackling it while you're fresh.

If you take your time, and aren't in a hurry, the walk takes around 10 hours, including the hour between the two villages, which you can't avoid unless someone gives you a lift, as you end up where you started. It's a pretty long, tough day out, so be prepared, but it's well worth the effort.

You can reach Mala Paklenica either straight along the main road, or slightly inland, via the settlements of Škilići, Jurlini and Jukići – which is quieter and quicker if you don't make any wrong turnings. The two routes meet 1km inland.

At the entrance to the gorge the dirt road peters out and you're on the trail upstream. It's very rustic and empty compared to Velika Paklenica, and less well marked at first, but the route is clear enough, starting on the left hand side of the gully before crossing over to the other side. Unless there's been exceptional rain, the gully is dry from May to September.

As you enter the canyon proper the walls steepen and the path becomes clearer and better marked. At the first big boulders on the valley floor the path climbs to the right, assisted by steel cables and well-secured pitons.

The next 2 hours are hard, ascending sharply, but the way the rock's been sculpted by flowing water, the small flowers and trees growing tenaciously from pockets in the cliffs, and the fine views should cheer you up. After a while you'll notice puddles on the valley floor, which gradually become a rivulet and eventually turn into a bubbling, refreshing stream. The path criss-crosses this on well-marked boulders.

When the gorge forks, take the left-hand one, following the stream. Twenty minutes later the path definitively leaves the stream, but only after a couple of false alarms, and then heads steeply uphill, zig-zagging until you're at 650m. At the top there's a dry stone wall clearly marked Sv Jakov, though there's no obvious church. This junction is easy to pinpoint on the map.

Take the left-hand of the two paths, marked Starigrad. The path is a bit indistinct here, running across pastures, but there are markers. If you lose these, head west-northwest until you join the marked path coming in from your right. At this point the trail starts down a rocky gully. It divides fairly often, but the right path is always well marked, eventually coming out at a small farm.

Leave the farm on the leftmost track, and then fork immediately right on the marked path. From here it's easy to find your way to the valley floor – even if there aren't signs you can follow the donkey droppings, as you're now on the farm's access road. The path comes out suddenly and unexpectedly to the top edge of Velika Paklenica, and it's an ideal picnic spot – it's almost all downhill from here, and the views are great.

The path down is a steep, knee-testing zig-zag – you might be grateful of walking-poles here – until you reach the valley floor, after which it's an easy walk back to the entrance of Velika Paklenica.

Other walks

The walks described above are only a fraction of what you can do in the area, particularly given that none of them even takes you up onto the spectacular Velebit ridge.

You can also wander happily around at lower altitudes to the west of the park, discovering the abandoned and near-abandoned villages in the hills. One of these, **Bristovac Tomići** (the locals leave off the Bristovac) is the start of a good walk up to Vidakov Kuk, and provides a poignant look at a world where electricity supplies, running water and central heating never quite caught on.

The more ambitious, however, will want to scale the region's highest peak, **Vaganski Vrh**, just 73m lower than Croatia's highest point, Dinara. Bear in mind, however, that the ridge hasn't entirely been de-mined, so discuss your route with the park staff before heading off, and stay on the marked trails.

Whilst an ascent of Vaganski Vrh is possible to complete within a day from the park's entrance, the 14-hour minimum round trip isn't for the faint-hearted, and you need to set off very early in the morning indeed, and be extremely well equipped – friends who've done it reckoned that two litres of water per person was nothing like enough.

Better by far is to stay overnight at Borisov Dom or one of the other mountain huts, and start the 5–6-hour climb to the summit from there. On a clear day they say you can see Italy on one side and a good 100km into Bosnia on the other, but those days do tend to come in winter, when a combination of snow and a vicious *bora* are likely to dissuade you from making the ascent at all.

Best of all is a three-day circuit covering the **Velebit ridge** – again, discuss your route in detail with the park staff before heading out, and remember there are still mines in the ground. On the first day head up Mala Paklenica, going straight on instead of left at Sv Jakov (see previous page), and then right instead of straight on at the junction for Borisov Dom. The route then skirts left of the 999m summit of Martinovo Mirilo, eventually reaching the Ivine Vodice hut at 1,200m, where you can stay the night (check it's open, of course, before you start out).

Day two then starts with the climb up to the ridge, and the chance to reach the summits of Malovan (1,709m, around 4 hours from the refuge) and Vaganski Vrh (1,758m), among others, before coming down at Borisov Dom for the second night out. Bear in mind that it's a lot further on to Babin Vrh (1,723m) than you might think – count on 14 hours just from the Ivine Vodice hut – and that you don't want to get caught out at this altitude at any time of year.

ŠIBENIK

Šibenik is something of an odd-man-out on the Dalmatian coast, firstly because it has no classical history – it was founded by the Croats and doesn't show up until the 11th century – and secondly because it's not really a tourist town. Indeed, until the 1990s, and the war with Serbia, it was a light industrial hub with a moderately busy port, and nothing much in the way of either beaches or visitors.

It's well worth stopping here, however, not just for the cathedral – the most important piece of Renaissance architecture in Croatia (and classified by UNESCO as a World Heritage Site in 2000) – but also for its charming medieval old town, and its position as a springboard for trips into the Krka National Park and to the Kornati archipelago (see pages 214 and 222).

By the end of the war in 1995, Šibenik's industrial base was in ruins, and during the second half of the 1990s the town found it hard to recover, with high unemployment and consequently very little money around for spending. The new century seems to have brought with it new optimism, however, and in summer it's hard to find a seat at any of the seafront cafés on a Sunday morning. Recovery isn't complete, but Šibenik's well on the mend.

History

After first being mentioned in 1066, Šibenik was tossed back and forth between Venetians, Hungarians, Byzantines, Croats and Bosnians, before knuckling definitively under Venice (1412–1797) and the Austro-Hungarian Empire (1797–1918). Italy was very briefly in control (only until 1920) before the city became Yugoslav, and finally, in 1991, Croatian.

The Venetians built the defensive walls (best preserved on the north side of town) running all the way up to the three fortresses at the top of the hill, and it was also under Venice that St Jacob's Cathedral was built, in fits and starts, over more than a century.

Getting there and around

Šibenik is easy to reach. A few local ferries come in to the sheltered bay through the narrow Šibenik channel, and dock at the southern end of the old town. The bus station is 200m further south, in the new town, while the train station (only serving local routes inland) is a further 300m to the southeast. Both the bus and train stations have left-luggage facilities.

The old town is entirely pedestrianised, which is excellent, so once you've arrived you'll be on foot – it's all perfectly manageable, though the narrow streets running up to the St Anne Fortress are pretty steep.

The friendly tourist office (tel: 022 212 075; fax: 022 219 073; www.summernet.hr/sibenik), with town plans etc, is on Fausto Vrančića, bang in the middle of the old town, just off the main artery of Zagrebačka, across from St John's (Sveti Ivan) Church.

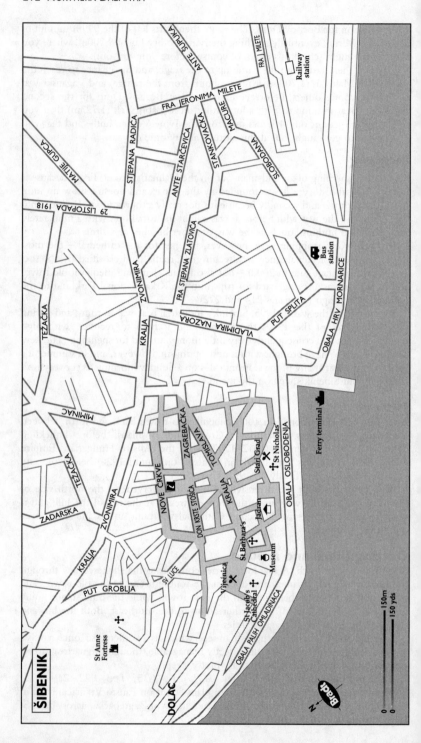

ŠIBENIK

Where to stay and eat

With accommodation in fairly short supply in Šibenik (there are very few private rooms in the old town and only one hotel) you may find it easier to make a day trip from Zadar, Trogir or Split – or indeed go for one of the slew of private rooms in shamelessly touristy **Vodice**, just 12km up the coast. That said, it's worth persevering – with few visitors spending the night here, you'll find Šibenik evenings pleasant at any time of year.

Most private rooms are out of town, along the coast, though with regular buses this needn't be a problem. If you arrive in summer you'll likely be met off the ferry or bus by women offering rooms – check the location before you agree.

The town's only hotel, the **Jadran** (tel: 022 212 644; fax: 022 219 960) is unexciting, but it's clean, modern and well equipped, and it's in a fabulous location right on the harbour. Doubles go for €82 in summer, dropping to €65 off season. Failing that, there's a huge resort, **Solaris**, about 6km south of Šibenik, which is easy to reach by bus. Solaris (tel: 022 361 001; fax: 022 361 801) has four hotels with a total of nearly 1,000 three-star rooms from €90 to €120 for doubles, as well as two campsites, big beaches and pools complete with pedalos and water-slides, and Šibenik's only disco.

Like most Dalmatian towns, Šibenik's favourite food is fish, but like everywhere else it doesn't come cheap. Both the restaurant at the **Jadran** and the **Stari Grad**, further down the seafront towards the ferry terminal, are good places for fresh fish, while the nicest restaurant in town is unquestionably the **Vijećnica**, set in the ground floor of the loggia, right on the cathedral square.

For more modest fare Šibenik's also well supplied with pizzerias and snack bars, and you shouldn't miss the chance of eating or drinking in **Dolac**, the part of town along the shore which is furthest from the ferry terminal, where the city walls plunge down to meet the sea. Here you'll find dozens of cafés, bars and restaurants, many featuring live music on summer evenings.

What to see

Šibenik's must-see is the wonderful cathedral, though the old town itself is perfectly lovely, from the fluttering flags and cheerful cafés along the seafront to the ruins of the St Anne Fortress on the hill, by way of any number of narrow flagged streets, medieval archways and a mix of Gothic, Renaissance and baroque buildings.

St Jacob's Cathedral, a triple-aisled basilica with three apses and a cupola, was started in 1431 but not completed until 1536, and reflects the transition from Venetian Gothic to Tuscan Renaissance. What makes it unique, however, is the extraordinary barrel-vaulting, consisting of stones chiselled to fit together snugly using carpentry techniques, and leading to the cathedral's exterior being almost identical to its interior – something you won't see in any other church. It's difficult to get a good look at the roof from outside, as the town crowds up to the cathedral, but postcards – or a hike up to the St Anne Fortress – will give you a good idea. A result of the design is also that the façade is the only one in Europe able to reflect the true shape of the triple-aisled church behind it – all the others are effectively stage-scenery, stuck on for effect.

The cathedral is largely the work of Juraj Dalmatinac (George the Dalmatian), a sculptor who was born in Zadar, but rose to fame in Venice (perhaps under the tutelage of Donatello). He was chief architect here, on and off, from the early 1440s until his death in 1473. The extraordinary frieze on the outside of the cathedral of 74 individual heads running round the apses (a fabulous glimpse of 15th-century life), along with the stunning baptistery inside the big echoing church, are his finest works. In front of the cathedral you'll find a Meštrović statue of him.

The north side of the cathedral makes up one side of the elegant Trg Republika Hrvatske; the other is occupied by a fine loggia, built between 1533 and 1542. Originally the town hall, the version you see today is mostly a post-war reconstruction, following the 1943 bombing of the town – though it's nonetheless lovely for that.

Otherwise the rest of the old town is really its own attraction, though there are several other churches worth visiting (notably **St Nicholas** and **St Barbara**), as well as a small **archaeological museum**. Up at the top of the town, the **St Anne Fortress** isn't much to look at, but has great views out over the town and across the bay.

North to Knin

From Šibenik the road runs north along the eastern border of Krka National Park (see below), to Knin, some 60km distant. You're also likely to come through Knin on any other road from central or southern Dalmatia to Zagreb, which is why the town had such significance in the conflict of the 1990s, as the capital of the Serbian RSK (Republika Srpska Krajina) – it effectively cut off southern Croatia from the rest of the country.

Driving up past the unremarkable town of Drniš, towards Knin, and on towards Gračac and Zagreb, the scars of the war are still very much in evidence. Many properties along the roadside are devastated, windowless and roofless, and while some of the older Serbs who'd lived here for generations have clearly returned, there are few if any young people around. Houses which weren't destroyed by shells were gutted by fire, and the torched wrecks of cars still stand in their driveways. The farming villages of **Kaldrina** and **Kosovo** are still absolutely lifeless, a bleak and immediate reminder of the awfulness of war.

Knin, by contrast, even on a cold and windy day, positively buzzes, though even here the population is nothing like what it was 15 years ago. If you stop in Knin (and it's easy, with so many onward buses, and trains to Zagreb and Split), then make the effort to climb up the hill to the terrific medieval fortress which dominates the town. It's the way fortresses are meant to be, with great big walls, ramparts, buttresses, towers and a sturdy central keep, and panoramic views out over the surrounding countryside.

KRKA NATIONAL PARK

The 72km Krka River and waterfalls are a popular rival to the Plitvice Lakes further north, and are essentially a result of the same travertine process which formed (and is continuing to form) Plitvice (see page 114). Krka makes a great excursion from Šibenik, and is offered as a day trip by any number of tour operators all the way from Zadar to Split, though it's easy enough to visit under your own steam, too.

Krka used to receive many fewer visitors than the more famous Plitvice, but it's catching up now, with close to 500,000 visitors annually. And it's hardly surprising – there's more to see here, and a far greater water flow. The biggest falls, Skradinsiki Buk, see an average of 55m^3 per second year-round, rising to a splashy 350m^3 per second after heavy rains inland.

After much wrangling between the proponents of hydro-electricity and conservationists, the middle and lower parts of the Krka River were finally declared a national park in 1985, and the park's recently been extended pretty much all the way to the river's source, near Knin. The two most impressive waterfall systems are Roški Slap to the north and Skradinski Buk to the south, separated by a wide section of river on which you'll find the islet of Visovac and a Franciscan monastery.

For the last 20km downstream from Skradinski Buk, the Krka is at sea-level, with a mix of salt water and fresh water.

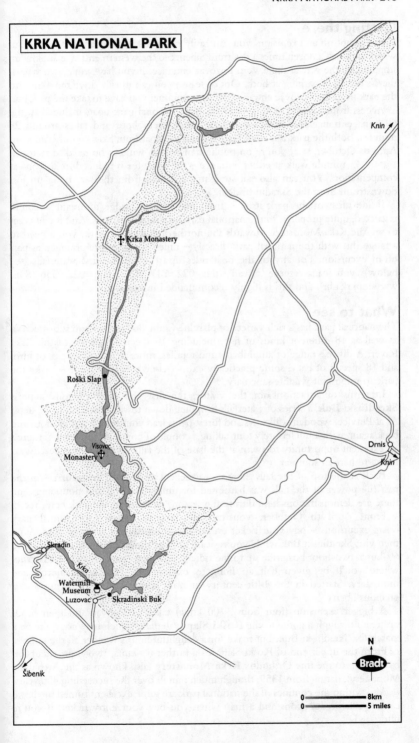

Getting there

If you're not on an excursion, you can easily reach Krka National Park on the bus which runs half a dozen times a day from Šibenik to the western entrance at Skradin, stopping on the way at the eastern Lozovac entrance. If you have your own wheels there's plenty of parking at both. Out of season you can usually drive the 4km into the park from the Lozovac entrance, while in summer you have to take the park bus.

Access from Skradin to the waterfalls is by national park boat, included in the 60-kuna entrance fee, which leaves the quay every hour and takes around 25 minutes. Both the park bus from Lozovac and the boat from Skradin only run from April to October, so if you're on public transport in winter you need to factor in a good 45-minute walk at either entrance – the entry fee is reduced to 20 kuna as compensation. You can also sail straight to Skradin from the sea, tying up just downstream from the Skradin bridge.

Inside most of the park itself – from the Skradin bridge upstream – you're restricted, quite properly, to the national park boats and footpaths. And if you want to see the Krka Monastery, towards the northern end of the park, you'll need to arrange this with the national park directly – unless it's been pre-arranged as part of an excursion. For any of the boat-rides upstream of the first waterfalls (see below) you can reserve ahead (tel: 022 217 720; fax: 022 336 836; www.npkrka.hr), and this is highly recommended in summer.

What to see

The national park has a rich variety of plantlife (some 860 species and sub-species), as well as 18 different kinds of fish, including 10 species endemic to the Krka River. A diverse range of amphibians and reptiles, more than 200 species of bird, and 18 species of bat – some practically extinct elsewhere in Europe – make the park an important wildlife sanctuary.

In terms of attractions for the visitor, the first and most obvious sight is **Skradinski Buk**, a series of waterfalls dropping down towards Skradin in 17 steps. As at Plitvice, wooden walkways and forest paths lead you from top to bottom and back again, with a full leisurely tour taking a couple of hours. At the bottom there's an excellent opportunity to swim at the base of the falls, so bring your beachwear if you're here in summer.

Back at the top of the falls there's an excellent **watermill museum** – in the past the power of the falls was harnessed for milling, rolling and pounding, and there are demonstrations here during the season, included in the park entry fee.

From April to October, you can also take a variety of national park boats/excursions – buy your ticket on arrival if you haven't reserved ahead, and then visit Skradinski Buk while you're waiting. The most popular excursion is the 60-kuna, two-hour boat-ride up to the ridiculously picturesque island of **Visovac**, where you'll be given half an hour to explore the Franciscan church and monastery. Started in the 14th century, it now houses a small museum and a precious library.

A bigger excursion (four hours, 100 kuna) takes in Visovac and then heads upstream through a gorge to the **Roški Slap** waterfalls, which may not quite be a match for Skradinski Buk, but make for a delightful hour's wander all the same.

From the upper end of Roški Slap, it's a further 60-kuna, two-hour excursion by boat up to the fine Orthodox **Krka Monastery** (also known as the Archangel Monastery), dating from 1359, though much rebuilt over the succeeding 400 years.

Also within the confines of the national park are some excellent ruined medieval castles; ask for directions and a map when you buy your entry ticket, if you're interested.

PAG

Pag, stretching some 60km alongside the coast north of Zadar, is one of the most barren of the Adriatic's big islands. It supports fewer than 10,000 people (and rather more sheep) in a handful of villages, and it can be a torpid, stifling place in the dog days of August, with the frequent lack of trees (barring some olive groves in the north, and some stunted figs) being maddening and oppressive.

Nonetheless, it's increasingly popular as a holiday destination, with an interesting old town, some fine sandy beaches and a generally unspoiled air – the lace-makers of Pag town are charming rather than touristy. Visitor arrivals in 2003 were up 70% on the previous year, and with tourism Pag's sole source of real prosperity, that can only be a good thing. Apart from a few weeks at the end of July and the beginning of August in Novalja, Pag is still far from crowded.

Pag's reputation in the past was tied to salt, and there are still big salt-pans in the centre of the island, but today its fame rests squarely on the *Paški Sir*, the distinctive hard cheese which is one of the highlights of Croatia's indigenous cuisine. The unique flavour is a combination of the sheep's diet – mainly salt grasses and sage – and the way it's matured, rubbed with olive oil and ash. Even here, it's relatively expensive, and harder to find than you'd expect, but it's worth making the effort.

History

It's hard to believe now, but Pag was covered with woods when it was first settled by the Illyrian tribes, and was still forested through its Roman occupation, the arrival of the Slavs in the 7th century, and the feuding of the bishops of Zadar and Rab (back when Rab *had* a bishop) over the island's salt-pans in the late Middle Ages.

It was the Venetians who did the damage, here and all the way around the Kvarner Bay and throughout northern Dalmatia, cutting down the trees wholesale for shipbuilding. The scrub grasses and roots which were left behind were then over-cropped by sheep, and the *bora* winds blew away whatever topsoil was left. The land has never recovered, even now supporting little more than a few herbs and salt grasses.

The Venetians were also responsible, however, for the island's capital, Pag town, so we can thank them for that at least. Pag fell under Austro-Hungarian control after the fall of Venice, and became Yugoslav after World War I, though neither left much of a mark on the island until the bridge connecting it to the mainland was built in 1968.

Getting there and around

The access to Pag from the south is across the road bridge, while from the north you're better off taking the ferry from Kovači (just down from Prižna) to Žigljen (6km across the island from the main resort of Novalja), which runs hourly in winter and continuously in summer (day *and* night). Note that when the *bora*'s a-blowing, however, especially in winter, the ferry might not be running at all.

Access by public transport is limited to four buses a day from Zagreb and the two daily Rijeka–Zadar buses which run via the island rather than along the coast, stopping at Novalja and Pag town on the way. Pag town is under an hour from Zadar, 3½ hours from Rijeka, and 7 hours from Zagreb.

The buses from the mainland are also the island's only local transport, effectively providing a connection from Novalja to Pag town five times daily.

Pag town

The attractive, partially walled old centre of Pag you see today is in fact the new town – the original Pag was 3km south of here, and you can still see some of the

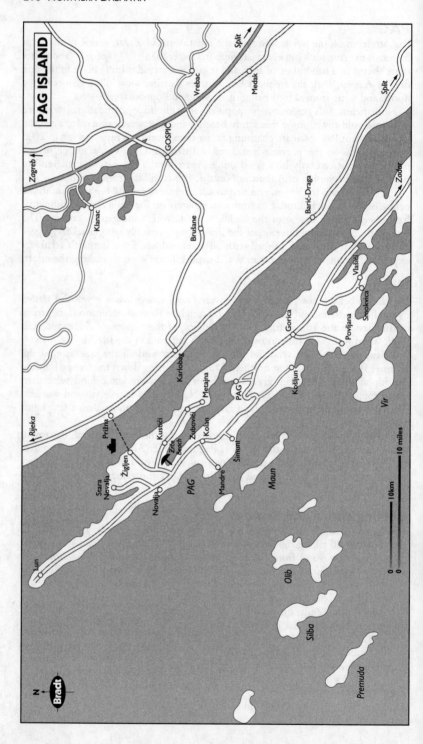

PAG ISLAND

ruins at Stari Grad. The new town was founded in 1443 and built according to designs by Juraj Dalmatinac, the man behind Šibenik's lovely cathedral.

A regular grid of old narrow streets meets at the town's main square (see map, over), Trg Kralja Krešimira IV, which contains the **Church of St Mary** (meant to be a cathedral), the **Duke's Palace**, and the unfinished **Bishop's Palace** – Pag never quite got its act together on becoming a bishopric.

The church has a fine, simple front, with a carved Gothic portal, four unfinished-looking saints, and a Renaissance rosette window which is presumably the inspiration for all those lace motifs. Inside, there are lovely Romanesque arches with Corinthian capitals (at the far right-hand end check out the cavorting dolphins), while on the ceiling there's a huge plaster relief of St George and the Dragon. The solid belltower, behind and to the left, looks firmly rooted in the 16th century.

Given the town's heritage, it would be madness not to pop into the tiny **lace museum**, just off the square, which has a small collection of intricate work. Pag's been famous for its lace for centuries, but it wasn't until 1906 that the lace-making school was reopened – after being closed for decades it was reopened in the late 1990s, following the upswing in tourism. If you want to buy lace, your best bet is to purchase directly from the women making it – you'll see them dressed in black in the old town in the mornings, with their hair distinctively braided. The asking price reflects the amount of time it takes to make.

Also revived has been the Pag Carnival, in February, a cheerful affair with lots of dressing up, folk music, dancing, parades and processions, and performances of the local play *The Slave Girl of Pag*. It's so much fun that the carnival is repeated at the end of July – and why not?

The bus stops just west from the old town, near the Pagus Hotel. Tourist information (tel: 023 611 301; fax: 023 611 286) is on the southern side of the old town, by the bridge across to the old salt warehouses (one of which has been converted into a disco), and has a good reversible map of the town and the island.

Meridijan (tel: 023 612 162; fax: 023 612 161), by the bus stop, and Maricom (tel: 023 612 266; fax: 023 611 331), at Radićeva 8, are two of the agencies handling a growing supply of private rooms – expect to pay around €30 for a decent double. It's also highly likely you'll be approached by old women when the bus arrives, and given Pag's small size it's worth going and having a look.

The nearest campsite is 8km away, at Šimuni (tel: 023 697 441; fax: 023 697 442), on an attractive bay on the western side of the island, half way to Novalja – buses stop here, and there's a popular marina, too.

There are several hotels in or near town, but the **Pagus** (tel: 023 611 310; fax: 023 611 101) right by the bus stop, is justly popular, in a good location with its own concrete beach, and sea-view doubles with balconies for €70 a night. Across the bay, a 15-minute walk from the old town, is the **Biser** (tel: 023 611 333; fax: 023 611 444) which has its own rather nicer beach, and sea-view doubles at €60.

Finally, you can book excursions from the usual agencies – the best of these are the day trips out to the Kornati archipelago. Meridijan also rents out bicycles, a great way of exploring the island, but make sure you have plenty of water and are well protected with sun block – there's no real shade anywhere to speak of.

Novalja and northern Pag

Much busier and far more developed than Pag is the resort of Novalja, 20km north. Within reach of a whole load of good beaches (notably **Zrče**, **Časka** and **Straško**), it's understandably popular, and well equipped for visitors, with thousands of private rooms available, and an enormous campsite (**Straško**; tel: 053 661 226; fax: 053 661 225), around a third of which is given over to naturists.

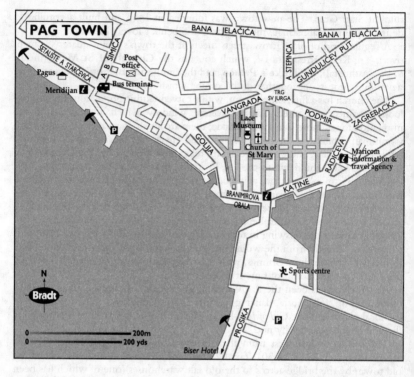

Two kilometres south of Novalja, just off the main road to Pag town, is the beach of **Zrče**, a kilometre or so of shingle which has become one of Croatia's hippest summer night-time playgrounds, with clubbing until dawn. There are three main bars/clubs operational through the summer; the original is **Calypso**, but in recent years **Aquarius** and **Papaya**, offshoots of well-known Zagreb clubs, have also taken to setting up camp here. There's a shuttle bus from Novalja if you don't fancy the walk.

Also close to Novalja are the meagre ruins of the Roman town of **Cissa** (now Časka), with the best bits being underwater, as the coast sank here. The main attraction is the underground Roman aqueduct, constructed in the 1st century AD, and visitable for around 150m of its length – further excavations are underway.

For more on Novalja, and accommodation contacts, go directly through the Novalja tourist office (tel/fax: 053 661 404; www.tz-novalja.hr).

The island of Pag ends in the narrow 20km-long **Lun** peninsula, famous for its olive groves (the few trees not cut down by the Venetians), and ending in the quiet fishing village of Tovarnele.

UGLJAN AND PAŠMAN

Just a few kilometres offshore from Zadar are the pretty islands of Ugljan and Pašman. Like Cres and Lošinj in the Kvarner Bay, they were originally a single island, but while Cres and Lošinj have been separate for millennia, the channel between Ugljan and Pašman was only dug during the 19th century, to help sea traffic on its way.

Most of the visitors are locals over for the weekend, as neither island has yet been developed as a package destination. As a result, Ugljan and Pašman are better geared up for individual visits rather than groups, though they're far from empty, with Ugljan being the most densely populated island in the Adriatic (it's practically a suburb of Zadar).

Ugljan

The island of Ugljan is largely dedicated to the cultivation of olives, and some of Croatia's best olive oil comes from here, although it's rarely commercially available. Many of the rest of the inhabitants work in Zadar, while there are lots of mainlanders' second homes on the island, meaning it can get pretty busy on summer weekends.

Just half an hour away from Zadar, Ugljan's main settlement is **Preko**, an unpretentious little town focused more on day-to-day life than anything like a tourist industry. Ferries come across every hour, year-round, and alternate ones are met by buses heading north up to the town of Ugljan or south to Pašman, passing through Kali and Kukljica on the way.

The tourist office (tel/fax: 023 286 108) is cheerful enough but not really equipped to help you, though it can point you in the direction of the Rušev agency (tel: 023 286 266; fax: 023 286 085) which not only handles Preko's plentiful private rooms (around €25–30 for doubles) but also rents out bicycles and boats, great ways of getting yourself around the island. There's one hotel in town, the pleasant **Preko** (tel: 023 286 041; fax: 023 286 040), with doubles at around €70 – ask for a sea view, if they have one available.

Well worth the hour's uphill hike is the trip up to **St Michael's Fortress**. At 265m it's almost as high as any other point on either island, and the views across to Pag to the north, Dugi Otok to the west, the Kornati archipelago to the south and over to the Velebit massif on the mainland can be absolutely breathtaking. Dating from the early 13th century, the fortress is very much ruined, mostly by time, but also more recently by the Serbs shelling it in 1991.

After your exertions you'll definitely deserve a swim, and Preko has a nice enough town beach, but under 100m offshore is the lovely little wooded island of **Galovac**, with a 15th-century monastery and the best local beaches. In summer it's easy enough to find a taxi-boat to whisk you across.

The village of **Ugljan**, 10km north of Preko, is a forgotten sort of place, though it has a lovely beach and a Franciscan monastery you can visit. Ask at the tourist office (tel/fax: 023 288 011) about private rooms, or stay at the **Hotel Ugljan** (tel/fax: 023 288 024), which has reasonable doubles right on the harbour for €60. You can also rent bikes and boats at the hotel.

Heading south from Preko it's not far to the active fishing village of **Kali**, and a further 5km on to **Kukljica**, which is a fishing village as well, but also the nearest thing Ugljan has to a holiday resort. The **Zelena Punta** (tel: 023 373 337; fax: 023 373 545) tourist settlement consists of apartments and bungalows, which tend to be block-booked months in advance. From here it's barely 2km to the bridge leading over to Pašman.

Pašman

Pašman is a smaller, less-densely populated, even less-developed version of its northern neighbour, and although the number of visitors is growing by 20% a year, that's from a pretty low base.

The island is a popular weekender for locals from Biograd on the mainland, and there are seven ferries a day year-round across to **Tkon**, the main settlement in the south of the island, with a couple of reasonable beaches and a pretty campsite (**Adriana**; tel/fax: 023 285 017) south of the town. There's also a naturist campsite, **Sovinje** (tel: 023 285 542; fax: 023 285 304), 2km south, with one of the few sandy naturist beaches in Croatia.

Not far from Tkon, on Mount Ćokovac, is the monastery of **Kuzma i Damjan**. Originally a Venetian fortress, built in 1125, it became an important Glagolitic centre, and is today the only active Benedictine monastery in Croatia. The church here was built from 1369 to 1419, and has a fine 14th-century crucifix.

A few kilometres north, on the way to the village of Pašman, at **Kraj**, there's a solid, defensive Franciscan monastery dating from 1390, though much remodelled in the 16th century. The Renaissance cloisters here are lovely, and there's an interesting little museum housing several valuable religious works.

The village of **Pašman** itself, 6km north of Tkon, is the last place of any significance heading towards Ugljan – after that it's one sleepy fishing hamlet after another. There are a handful of private rooms available – ask at the tourist office (tel: 023 315 107; fax: 023 315 316) – and a couple of pleasant beaches from which to swim.

Between Ugljan and Dugi Otok lies the sheltered island of **Iž**, which is little more than two harbour settlements – **Mali Iž** and **Veli Iž** – connected by what passes for a road in these parts. There's one hotel on the island, in Veli Iž, the **Korinjak** (tel: 023 277 064; fax: 023 277 248) which has 80 fairly simple rooms, and charges €60–70 for doubles.

In the past Veli Iž was famous for its pottery, supplying large parts of the coast with clay cooking pots. Local lore has it that potters threw unsold goods into the sea on the homeward voyage, rather than face the shame of having failed to sell them. There's a daily ferry to Iž from Zadar – don't bother bringing the car.

DUGI OTOK AND THE KORNATI ARCHIPELAGO

Dugi Otok (literally 'long island') and the Kornati archipelago, stretched in a 75km line marking the outer ridge of the Adriatic's submerged mountains, are among the most dramatic and spectacular places in Croatia.

The endless indentations and extraordinary shapes of the islands are a magnet for sailors in summer, and although there's almost nothing as such to do, the wild scenery alone makes for a remarkable visit.

It's easiest to visit the Kornati archipelago as part of an excursion – these are offered from Zadar and Šibenik, and as far away as Trogir and Split, but are best from Murter (see *Kornati National Park*, overleaf), which is home to the park office. Bear in mind that some excursions – from Zadar in particular – only go as far as Dugi Otok and not into the national park itself. Far and away the finest way to see them, however, is from the deck of your own boat, and the archipelago is understandably popular with nautical tourists, although the sheer number of islands means you'll never find them even the least bit crowded.

Dugi Otok

Dugi Otok is nearly 45km long but never as much as 5km wide. All the attention goes to the two lobster-clawed ends of the island. The tiny resort and harbour of **Božava** is in the northwest, while the island's capital, **Sali**, is in the southeast – this is the closest town to the remarkable Telašćica Bay, actually part of the Kornati National Park.

The island has no fresh water supply at all, so it relies on collected rainwater, and in hot summers drinking water has to be ferried over from the mainland; it's not a place to leave taps running. The north is moderately fertile, while the southern end of the island (like most of the Kornati archipelago) is more dramatically barren.

Dugi Otok's settlements are connected by a single road, although if you're here without your own wheels you'll soon discover there's only one bus a week which connects north with south – if you do bring your own car, remember there's only one petrol station (at Zaglav). With many parts of the island still only reachable by sea, begging, borrowing or renting a boat is still by far the best way of visiting.

There are two different ferry routes to Dugi Otok from Zadar. The car ferry runs two or three times a day, year-round, and takes about 1½ hours to reach **Brbinj**. There's really nothing much here, in spite of the sometimes busy port and surrounding olive groves, so if you're not driving yourself, try not to miss the connecting bus which meets the ferry and makes the 15km run north to Božava.

There's no bus south from Brbinj to Sali, around 20km distant. There is however a passenger ferry running twice daily, year-round from Zadar either to Sali or **Zaglav**, 3km north – when it goes to Zaglav there's a bus onwards to Sali. In summer there are also various privately operated hydrofoil and ferry services from Zadar to the island.

Božava

The fishing village of Božava, with just 166 residents, is a (very) quiet place most of the time, though it's increasingly popular with Italian yachtsmen and women at the height of the season. There's even a mid sized hotel complex, the eponymous **Božava** (tel: 023 291 291; fax: 023 377 682), which has fairly ordinary doubles from €70 to €100, and a few private rooms which can be booked through the tourist office (tel/fax: 023 377 607). The hotel is also home to a diving centre and diving school (tel: 023 377 619; fax: 023 377 682).

A couple of kilometres northwest of Božava is the even smaller village of **Soline**, at the head of **Soliščica Bay**, which has plenty of swimming opportunities on mostly rocky beaches, heading up towards **Veli Rat**, the northernmost settlement on the island. From here it's a few hundred metres north to the lighthouse, and some popular rocks from which to bathe. If you turn left down a gravel road half way between Soline and Veli Rat, it's a kilometre or so south to Sakarun, a half-kilometre stretch of fine shingle on a truly lovely bay, facing south.

Sali

Sali, with over 1,000 inhabitants, is Dugi Otok's social and economic hub. It still derives a good deal more of its revenue from fishing than tourism, though that balance is surely set to change, as more people are visiting every year. The town is understandably popular with sailors, who come here on their way to or from Telašćica Bay, the Adriatic's largest and most dramatic natural harbour, and the Kornati islands.

Sali's tourist office (tel/fax: 023 377 094) will help with finding you private rooms. There's also the **Hotel Sali** (tel: 023 377 049; fax: 023 377 078), 300m across the headland to the north, set in pine woods, which has double rooms including (obligatory, usually, in summer) half board at €80.

The tourist office will also point you in the right direction for the good dive centre (tel: 023 377 079; fax: 023 377 078) here, as well as organising boat trips for you around the island and into the Kornati archipelago – by far the best way of seeing the dramatic scenery. Although you can walk the 3km west to the head of **Telašćica Bay**, you're really missing out by choosing this option.

In the southwestern pincer, about 7km from Sali, but still within the Telašćica Bay, is the **Mir Bay** ('bay of peace'), which harbours a saltwater lake, connected to the sea by underground karstic channels. The rocks around here are popular with naturists.

Kornati National Park

Eighty-nine of the 140-odd islands, islets and reefs of the Kornati archipelago were declared a national park in 1980, with the boundary also including the spectacular Telašćica Bay on Dugi Otok (see above).

The park is managed from the town of **Murter**, on the island of Murter, connected to the mainland by a drawbridge. As it's the closest place to the national park it's also the best starting point for an excursion – you'll see much more if you're not spending most of the day schlepping your way up the coast from Split or down from Zadar.

Murter's also the place to start if you want to stay on one of the Kornati islands, though be warned this represents quite an investment – you can't normally stay for less than a week, you need to pay for transport as well as accommodation, and it doesn't make much sense not to have your own boat while you're out there.

On the other hand there are few places in Europe which offer you this much isolation or privacy with such a great climate. There's no electricity, let alone shops or restaurants, and the cottages have just the bare essentials, though twice a week a supply boat will come and deliver you staples (food, not office supplies), as well as the gas which powers the fridge, cooker and lights. Catching your own fish, grilling it over an open fire, and watching the sun plunging into the sea on a sultry evening is a sure cure for urban stress.

An interesting alternative to the desert-island week can be had by talking to the locals in Murter and negotiating your way out to one of their own houses on the islands – the archipelago is actually the property of the people of Murter, and there's still a certain amount of fishing and agriculture which goes on. Your chances with this particular strategy will be greatly enhanced if you speak Croatian and can handle your *rakija*.

Even if you're only here on a day trip, you'll see some of the most extraordinary scenery in Europe. Most of the islands are covered in sage and feather grasses, or low scrub, turning the grey karst green, though some also permit the cultivation of figs, grapes and olives.

Where the islands face the open sea, to the southwest, dramatic cliffs plunge into the water. Known locally as 'crowns' (you'll have your wrist slapped if you say 'cliff'), they rise up to around 80m tall, and extend underwater almost as far. The crowns are the most obvious sign of the fault zone running down the Adriatic, the result of sudden tectonic movements in the past.

The highly varied submarine flora and fauna, along with the unusual geomorphology, also make for excellent diving and snorkelling.

Murter

Murter is about 25km up the coast from Šibenik, and is served by half a dozen daily buses – change in Vodice if you're coming from the north. The town itself is nothing special, though there are some pretty good beaches on the island if you have some time to while away.

The national park office (tel: 022 434 662; fax: 022 435 058; www.kornati.hr) will sell you entry tickets (50 kuna for individuals), a fishing licence (150 kuna, includes entrance fee), a diving permit (100 kuna, ditto) and good maps, as well as letting you know who's authorised to offer excursions into the park.

There are a number of agencies in town who can arrange both day trips and longer stays on the islands. Costs generally include the park entrance fee. Coronata (tel: 022 435 089; fax: 022 435 555) and KornatTurist (tel: 022 435 855; fax: 022 434 853) are both reliable.

Central Dalmatia

Central Dalmatia is wonderfully rich both in cultural sights and the great outdoors – whether it be the stark severity of the **Biokovo** massif above **Makarska**, or the green islands of **Šolta**, **Brač**, **Hvar** and **Vis** offshore, with their innumerable beaches, bays, coves and fishing villages. Unmissable are the Emperor Diocletian's palace in **Split**, the medieval island town of **Trogir** and the Renaissance elegance of **Hvar town** – along with the extraordinary shingle spit of **Zlatni Rat**, at **Bol**, and the **Blue Cave** on **Biševo**, just offshore from the island of Vis, itself only open to tourists since 1989.

The telephone code is 021 for Split and the whole of Central Dalmatia.

TROGIR

Trogir – just 26km up the coast from Split – is one of the most attractive stops in Dalmatia, with the old town being not just excellently preserved but also delightfully car-free. Come here to soak up a pleasantly uncorrupted medieval atmosphere, where stone-carved balconies overhang the narrow streets, and Renaissance and Gothic palaces compete for your attention with the ancient cathedral.

History

Trogir started out in the 3rd century BC as Tragurion, an offshoot of the Greek colony of Issa (on Vis), before being developed as a key port under the Romans. Later overshadowed by Salona (see page 237), Trogir grew in importance once again during the 7th century, when Salona was sacked and its refugees came north to Split.

Relative peace under the Croatians and Hungarians came to a sudden halt in 1123, when the Saracens pretty much demolished the city, but prosperity soon returned, and the 12th to 14th centuries were a golden age for the town. From 1420 onwards Venice ruled, while from 1797 to 1918 the Austro-Hungarians were in charge – with a short break for Marshal Marmont and the French, from 1806 to 1814. The rest, as they say, is Yugoslavia – until Croatia won independence in 1991.

Getting there and around

Trogir is on the main coast road, so it's easy to reach by bus from Zadar or Šibenik to the north, or Split to the south. It's also the terminus for the local #37 bus from Split – buy a four-zone ticket on the bus – which runs half-hourly, making Trogir an easily feasible day trip from Split. An even quicker alternative is the regular coach which leaves from the Split ferry terminal. (The reverse is also true – if you can get in at one of the private rooms or small hotels in Trogir itself, it's a really attractive option.)

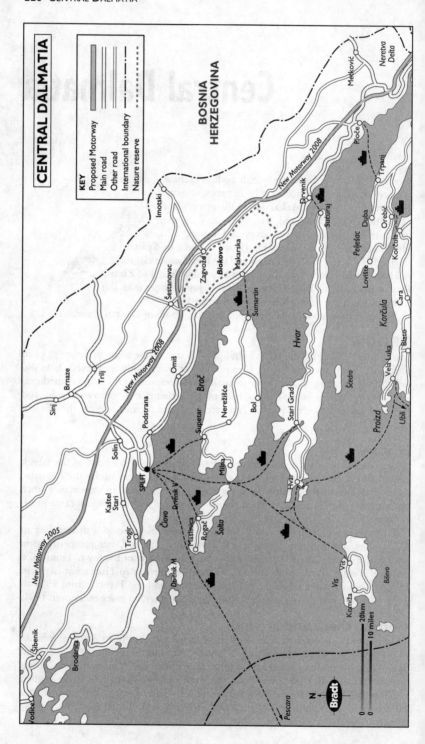

CENTRAL DALMATIA

KEY

Proposed Motorway
Main road
Other road
International boundary
Nature reserve

BOSNIA HERZEGOVINA

Split airport is just 10km east of Trogir, and the #37 bus is again your answer – a taxi from the airport to Trogir is cheaper than one to Split, but will still cost well upwards of 100 kuna.

Your only problem might be in leaving, if you're heading northbound in summer – the coastal buses from Split often arrive here full on their way to Zadar. It's not unheard of to take the #37 back to Split, make an onward reservation, and spend some time sightseeing before heading north again.

Trogir's bus station (more of a bus stop) is right by the stone bridge leading onto the island containing the old town. There are no left-luggage facilities. Just beyond the bridge – and indeed on it – you'll find a colourful local market selling everything from fruit, vegetables and flowers to home-made liquor.

If you're coming in by car out of season then cross the stone bridge and immediately turn right along the quay – there's a certain amount of paid parking along here, and the location's perfect. In summer don't even think about this – traffic snarls up a treat. Instead, stop a few hundred metres west of the bridge on the main road into town, in one of the several car parks along here.

Once you're in town you'll find it charmingly small – the whole place, connected to the mainland by the stone bridge and to the island of Čiovo by a drawbridge, is barely 500m long and under half that width.

Where to stay and eat

Trogir seems single-handedly to have implemented Croatia's policy of introducing small, family-run hotels, and has three excellent establishments to choose from. The only thing you need to do is to book well ahead – Trogir's a lovely place, and the combined capacity for the three hotels in town is just 36 rooms…

Right by the front in the old town is the reliable **Fontana** (tel: 021 885 744; fax: 021 885 755), which has nice doubles for €80; further along, near the fortress, is the lovely **Concordia** (tel: 021 885 400; fax: 021 885 401), which is great value at €70 for a double; while across the drawbridge on the Čiovo front, facing back towards Trogir (a lovely view) is the **Vila Sikaa** (tel: 021 881 223; fax: 021 881 149), with just ten rooms – doubles with spa jets go for €80.

If Trogir itself fails you – or if you want to swim – then head 4km west to the **Medena** (tel: 021 880 588; fax: 021 880 019) resort, where you'll find a rocky beach and nearly 700 rooms; doubles go for around €90 at the height of summer, but more like €65 otherwise. To get there catch the Medena bus, which runs about hourly; otherwise it's a dullish 50-minute walk.

The tourist office (tel/fax: 021 881 412), on the front facing Čiovo, is friendly and has a map for you, but doesn't do private rooms – for that you need to go to the Čipiko agency (tel/fax: 021 881 554), in the Čipiko Palace, opposite the entrance to the cathedral. Rooms in or very close to the old town get snapped up quickly, with doubles going for €40 a night, and there's a 30% surcharge for stays of under five nights here.

For campers, the nearest site is **Seget** (tel/fax: 021 880 394), a couple of kilometres west of town, which has all the usual facilities, including windsurfing.

Eating in Trogir is as easy as falling off a log. Practically every square has its own terrace set up in summer for al fresco dining, and the only hard thing is to choose which one suits you best, though the **Fontana's** restaurant clearly has the most diverse menu.

What to see

The old town (listed as a UNESCO World Heritage Site since 1997) is entered through a 17th-century gate – hook left and right from here and you'll find

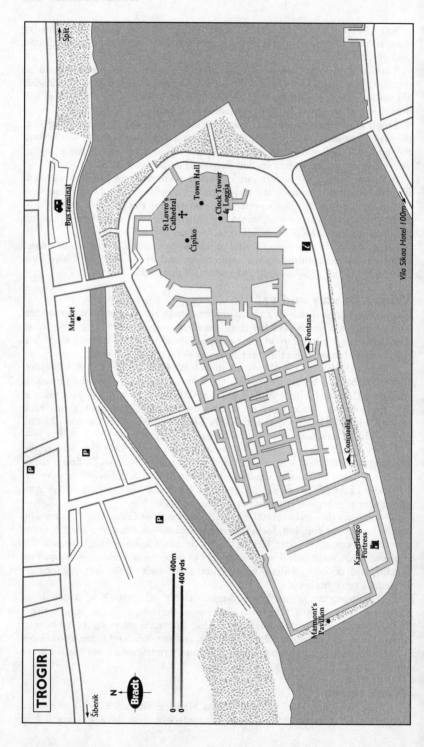

TROGIR

yourself on the pretty main square, Trg Ivana Pavla II, home to most of the famous sights, including **St Lovro's Cathedral**.

The cathedral's portal, dating from 1240, is the stunning work of truthful but far from bashful local boy Radovan (look for the inscription above the door: *'per raduanum cunctus hac arte praeclarum'* – 'all of this was made most excellently by Radovan'). Adam and Eve stand apparently appalled at their nakedness, atop two superb Venetian lions. The inner pillars, resting on the shoulders of medieval bugbears (Turks and Jews), frame graphic scenes from the calendar year (labours of the summer and winter months), while above it all sits a superb Nativity.

Inside, the cathedral's a cluttered, sombre place, still used by older local women every morning for prayers. The most important thing to see here is the extraordinary **Ursini Chapel**, in the north nave, which has been called 'the most beautiful Renaissance monument in Dalmatia'. Sculpted by Nikola Firentinac (Nicholas of Florence) at the end of the 15th century, it's here you'll find those torch-bearing cherubs featured in the tourist board's promotional literature.

Other sights within the cathedral include the elaborately carved 15th-century choir stalls, and an octagonal 13th-century pulpit.

Outside, have a good look at the campanile – the first floor's 15th-century early Gothic, the second's pure Venetian Gothic, and the third is late 16th-century Renaissance.

Opposite the entrance to the cathedral is the Venetian **Čipiko Palace** complex, now home to the Čipiko tourist agency. Pop into the hallway and check out the giant wooden cockerel on the wall, a trophy from the prow of some long-forgotten Turkish warship. Across the square is the **town hall** – in the courtyard, you'll see the coats of arms of the ruling families of Trogir.

Completing the square are the town's 15th-century **clocktower** and **loggia**. Both feature more work by Nikola Firentinac, while the loggia also has a large Meštrović bas-relief. Behind the loggia is the oldest surviving pre-Saracen church (**St Barbara's**), dating from the 11th century.

It's a short walk south form here to the Riva and the few remaining preserved parts of the city walls – Marshal Marmont, the Napoleonic administrator in the region from 1806 to 1814, had the rest torn down in an attempt to introduce sea breezes as a cure for malaria. Draining the swampy western end of the island a century later was a far more successful strategy.

Along the lovely Riva you'll find the huge **Kamerlengo Fortress** – following what looks like earthquake damage it's very much closed. Beyond that Trogir peters out with a football pitch and a small car park, but have a look at **Marmont's Pavilion**, if you're up here – it's a small (and sadly graffito-ed) memorial to the man who really did try and do his best for Napoleon's short-lived Illyrian Provinces.

Finally, if you want to visit the nearby islands of **Drvenik Veli** and **Drvenik Mali** (they both have some nice beaches, and are very much unvisited), you should ask at the tourist office on Riva – there are boats, though you may end up having to charter one, as the times aren't really convenient for day trips, and there's nowhere to stay.

SPLIT

Croatia's second biggest town has a population of over 200,000, but the old centre is surprisingly compact and easily manageable on foot. The main draw is Diocletian's Roman palace, just along the Riva from the port where you're likely to arrive – still stunning after more than 1,700 years of builders' alterations. Diocletian no doubt had a monster ego (being emperor has that effect), but even he can't have imagined his retirement home would be so well worth visiting in the 3rd millennium.

DIOCLETIAN AND THE PALACE

In its heyday the palace must have been extraordinary. At over 30,000m², it included everything from vast reception chambers to temples, arcaded corridors, baths, huge storerooms, extensive private apartments and an entire barracks. No expense was spared in its construction, with materials shipped in from Egypt and Greece, though it was built in a terrible rush, as it had to be ready for the emperor's retirement.

It's thought that Diocletian's wife and daughter never joined him here, in spite of their having lavish residences within the palace, and it's not clear whether he eventually had them killed – or indeed whether or not he himself committed suicide, was murdered, or died a natural death. What is known is that he passed his retirement years in Split having Christians captured, tortured and put to death – so many were martyred, in fact, that Diocletian holds the individual record for saint creation. Fighting Christianity was a losing battle, however – only two years after his death, in AD316, the Milan edict legitimised the religion.

Split's a lively, friendly city, and although it wasn't the victim of a Dubrovnik-like siege during the 1991–92 war (just one casualty was sustained here), it suffered the effects of large numbers of refugees coming in and a huge drop in tourism, and unemployment is still high. Happily, that doesn't stop people from having a good time, and the café terraces along the front are packed, practically year-round. Split has also long been a voice of political dissension, and is home to the weekly *Feral Tribune*, a regular thorn in the side of politicians for years, even before Croatia became independent, and continuing through Tuđman's times to the present day.

History

Although previously inhabited, Split only officially came into existence when Diocletian retired here in AD305, after 21 years as Roman emperor. The palace – started half way through Diocletian's reign, in AD295 – was built on a vast 170m-by-190m ground-plan, with walls 2m thick and up to 26m high, making it the largest private residence in antiquity.

Post-Diocletian, the palace continued to be used on and off as a sort of upmarket hotel for the elite, until the Roman Empire finally collapsed. After the Avars burned Salona in 614, refugees moved in permanently, converting chambers into houses, and corridors into streets, using the huge defences to good effect against invading hordes from the north.

Byzantium, the Ottomans, the Austro-Hungarians, the Venetians and Napoleon all left their mark on Split, but it was the Scottish architect, Robert Adam, who practically created it as a tourist destination overnight. Having seen Palladio's drawings, Adam and his team of draughtsmen stopped over in Split for five weeks in 1757, at the tail end of his 'Grand Tour' (tours really were grander then), and made hundreds of drawings and surveys of the palace. Published to huge acclaim in 1764, they came to dominate Georgian architecture, and influenced the future shape of whole tracts of London, Bath, Bristol and Edinburgh.

The name Split is itself relatively recent – the town was probably originally called Aspalatos (after the yellow broom still common round here), before metamorphosing into Spalatum, Spalato and Spljet, before finally settling down as Split.

Getting there and around

Split's international airport is 20km/half an hour west of town, almost at Trogir, and flights are met by Croatia Airlines buses, which will run you into town for 25 kuna. Shuttles return to the airport from the air terminal (right by the passenger ferry terminal and bus station) 90 minutes before flight departures. If you miss the shuttle, local bus #37 also runs half-hourly from Split to the airport and on to Trogir – buy a four-zone ticket on the bus. A taxi to or from the airport will set you back 200–250 kuna.

Just to the east of the old town, in a row, you'll find the passenger ferry terminal, the air terminal, the train station, the bus station and the car ferry terminal.

Ferries run frequently from Split not just to the local islands of Šolta, Brač and Hvar, but also to Vis, Korčula and Lastovo, as well as up and down the coast to Rijeka and Dubrovnik, and across the Adriatic to Ancona. If you're planning on taking your car by ferry anywhere in the summer, reserve as far ahead as you can, or expect a long wait.

The train station is effectively the only coastal railhead south of Rijeka. Several trains a day come in from Zagreb, and it's a practical alternative to the bus – slightly cheaper, if slightly slower. Book your ticket ahead of time if you possibly can.

As for buses, Split's well connected with everywhere – at least a dozen a day go to each of Dubrovnik (5 hours), Rijeka (8 hours) and Zagreb (8 hours). There are also international departures several times a week to destinations in Germany and Holland. Again, book ahead if you can, as buses fill up fast, especially in summer. The bus station has a left-luggage office with long hours (daily 04.30 to 22.00).

If you come in by car you'll discover that Split has its fair share of traffic problems, and parking can be a major hassle in summer. The best-located car park is right on the Riva in front of Diocletian's Palace (8 kuna an hour), but you'll be lucky to find a spot in season.

Once you've arrived, everything's easily reached on foot, though you may end up taking local bus #12 if you're going to the two galleries west of town, or onto the Marjan peninsula – Split's own nature park, and home to the nearest beaches. Tickets cost 10 kuna for two trips, and should be bought in advance from a kiosk.

Right in the middle of Diocletian's Palace, in a tiny converted church on the peristyle, you'll find the municipal tourist information office (tel: 021 348 600; fax: 021 348 604). Outside, on Riva, the Turist Biro (tel: 021 347 100; fax: 021 347 271) is where you should go for private rooms and more detailed information on excursions etc (you can also buy a detailed city guide there). Both offices will sell you the *Split Card* for 40 kuna – and it's free if you're staying in town for four days or more. This gives you 72 hours' worth of free access to some of the city's museums, half-price access to others, 20% off selected car-hire, 10% off your bill at the Park Hotel, 5% off at the Bellevue, Marjan, Consul and Split hotels, and 5% off at a number of restaurants.

Where to stay
Hotels

As far as hotels are concerned, Split still has a real accommodation problem. During and after the 1991–92 war many of the hotels were pressed into use as hostels for refugees, and a large number of rooms were damaged. The authorities are encouraging their restoration, and the opening up of smaller family-run hotels, but they're not on stream yet, so don't expect out-of-season price reductions here. An alternative to staying in Split is to base yourself in Trogir (only 45 minutes away

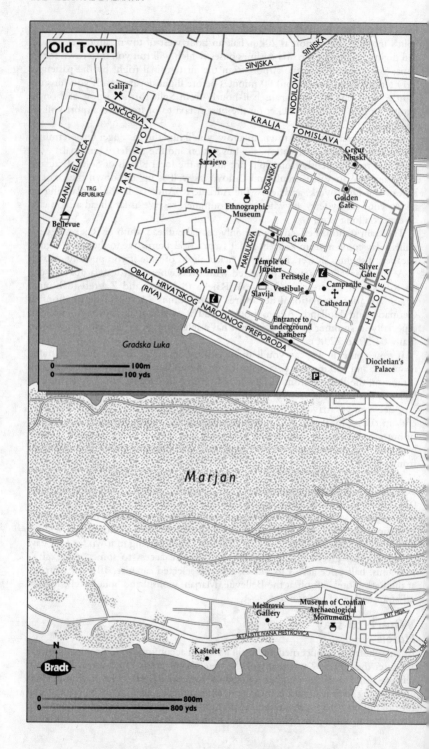

Old Town

SINJSKA
SINJSKA
NODILOVA
KRALJA
TOMISLAVA

Galija ✗
Grgur
Ninski ●

TONČIĆEVA
MARMONTOVA
BANA JELAČIĆA

Sarajevo ✗

Golden
Gate ●

BOSANSKA

Ethnographic
Museum ●

TRG
REPUBLIKE

Iron Gate ●

Bellevue ●

MARULIĆEVA

Temple of
Jupiter ●

Silver
Gate ●

HRVOJEVA

Marko Maruli» ●

Peristyle ● ℹ

Vestibule ●
Campanile ●

OBALA HRVATSKOG
(RIVA)

ℹ
Slavija ●
Cathedral ✝

NARODNOG PREPORODA

Entrance to
underground
chambers ●

Gradska Luka

0   100m
0   100 yds

Diocletian's
Palace

P

Marjan

N

Bradt

Meštrović
Gallery ●

Museum of Croatian
Archaeological
Monuments ●

ŠETALIŠTE IVANA MEŠTROVIĆA

PUT MEJA

DRAČ

Kaštelet ●

0   800m
0   800 yds

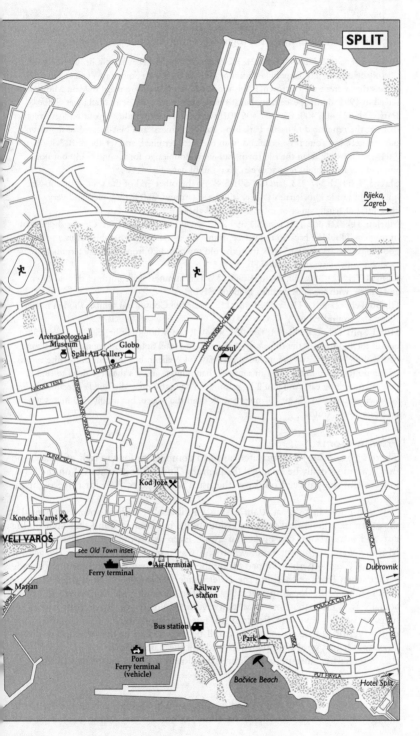

SPLIT

Rijeka,
Zagreb

Archaaeological
Museum
Split Art Gallery   Globo

Consul

DOMOVINSKOG RATA

NIKOLE TESLE

LOVRETSKA

ZRINSKO-FRANKOPANSKA

PUJNAČSKA

Kod Jože

Konoba Varoš

VELI VAROŠ

see Old Town inset

DUBROVAČKA

Ferry terminal   Air terminal

Dubrovnik

Marjan

Railway
station

POLIČKA CESTA

TISKA

SPINUČEVA

Bus station

Park

Port
Ferry terminal
(vehicle)

Bačvice Beach

PUT FIRVLA

Hotel Split

on the local bus), although if that's your choice you'll need to book yourself into a room well ahead of time, as Trogir's accommodation is also limited.

Bellevue Tel: 021 345 644; fax: 021 362 383; www.hotel-bellevue-split.hr. On the western side of the elegant Trg Republike (a minor copy of St Mark's Square in Venice) and a stone's throw from the old town, is this modest hotel. It was here that President Mitterrand stayed in 1992, during peace talks, but it's now quietly two-star, with doubles at €90.
Park Tel: 021 406 400; fax: 021 406 401; www.hotelpark.split.hr. If your budget stretches that far, the renovated four-star Park is probably the nicest and best-located of the town's other hotels, just round the headland from the ferry terminal, and set above Bačvice beach, a ten-minute walk from the old town. Sea-view doubles go for around €140 but noisy summer Saturday-night festivities can go on until dawn!
Slavija Tel: 021 347 053; fax: 021 591 558. At the other end of the scale is this no-star hotel right inside Diocletian's Palace. It's cheap (around €50 for doubles) and very cheerful, but hardly quiet or calm. Book well ahead.
Marjan Tel: 021 302 111; fax: 021 399 210; www.hotel-marjan.com. On the shore west of town and looking back to the palace, is this three-star high-rise, which is in a pretty good location; 10 minutes' walk from the old town and 20 from the ferry terminal. Doubles with views start from €110.
Consul Tel: 021 340 130; fax: 021 340 133. Ten minutes' walk north of the old town and palace, with spacious doubles at about €110.
Globo Tel: 021 481 111; fax: 021 481 118. Near the Consul and similar, though newer. Rooms at around €120.
Hotel Split Tel: 021 303 111; fax: 021 303 011; www.hotelsplit.hr. Finally, a good 3km east of the old town is the three-star, 135-roomed Hotel Split. Most rooms have balconies overlooking the sea, and the included breakfast is excellent, but the blue and white rooms (€125 doubles) are much nicer in summer than winter, and it's the very devil to find if you're coming by car. And you'll be wanting to come by car – the hotel's literature dithers between saying it's a 15- or 25-minute walk from the palace, but a dull 45 minutes would be closer to the truth.

Private rooms

There's a good supply of private rooms to compensate for the lack of hotels, and these can most easily be arranged through the Turist Biro (see above) on the Riva, just west of the palace. You'll pay the usual surcharge of 30% for three nights or less.

If you come in by boat, train or bus you'll also be offered rooms on arrival – these can be a great deal (bargain assiduously), but bear in mind that Split's a big city and some rooms can be far, far away. Even as seasoned a traveller as Dervla Murphy was caught out here, when she was researching her book *Through the Embers of Chaos* – perhaps ripped off by the same woman who did for me a decade earlier when I was researching the *Bradt Guide to Yugoslavia* back at the end of the 1980s. Check the location carefully, and for a realistic idea of where the place actually is, double the time or distance you're told. If you leave your bag at left luggage, you'll have the freedom to reject a room that's too far away, too expensive, or not up to scratch – you'll be back down in this area soon enough anyway. Or just go the simple route and use the Turist Biro.

There are no campsites near Split – the closest is 26km southeast, at Omiš.

Where to eat

There are relatively few really good restaurants in Split, especially in the old town, though this is compensated for to some extent by any number of bars with excellent terraces, particularly along the Riva. **Kod Jože**, a block north of the palace walls, across the small park, however, is one of the best places anywhere for seafood, while in town itself the **Sarajevo**, just off the main square, Narodni Trg, offers authentic Dalmatian cuisine. Good Dalmatian specialities are also available at the **Konoba Varoš**, just up the hill west of the town.

There are also any number of pizzerias in and around town, with the city's clear favourite being **Galija**, an unpretentious place a block north of Trg Republike, just off Marmontova.

If you're looking for your own ingredients there's an excellent daily market just to the east of the palace, while on the west side of town you'll find the famous fish market. The smell here has more to do with the sulphur spa next door than the fish itself, which is guaranteed super-fresh.

What to see

The main draw is clearly the former palace, standing on Riva, though what you see now, inside the old walls, is an entire town, centred on Diocletian's peristyle. Around 3,000 local people still live within the walls – barely fewer than in Dubrovnik's much bigger old town – so you'll find the cafés and bars catering to a healthy mix of both visitors and residents.

Enter the old town from the Riva, which is actually reclaimed land – the gate you go through (known as the Brass Gate) was originally on the sea. It was built to be used as an emergency escape route for Diocletian in case of trouble, but may also have seen service as a delivery entrance.

The gate leads through a semi-underground chamber, now a small crafts market, flanked by chambers you can visit (see below) before climbing some worn steps up into the peristyle.

The peristyle

The peristyle, an open, colonnaded square, was the public heart of Diocletian's Palace, and is still an extraordinary place to sit and wonder. Everything off to the south (towards the sea, behind you) was originally Diocletian's imperial quarters, while to the north were servants' lodgings and soldiers' barracks.

The pink granite columns are Egyptian, while their capitals are Corinthian. You can see that even originally there were four antique columns too few, with local marble pillars making up the difference. The cracked black sphinx dates back to the reign of Thutmosis III, who ruled Egypt from 1504 to 1450BC (though how anyone knows these things for certain sure beats me), and was originally one of ten imported for Diocletian from the land of the Pharaohs. Another four survive, in varying states of repair – one in the underground chambers, one in the Temple of Jupiter, and two in the Archaeological Museum.

The streets out of the peristyle lead to the palace's other three gates – north, to the Golden Gate (the main entrance, coming in from Salona), east, to the Silver Gate, and west, to the Iron Gate. On the peristyle itself you'll find the **vestibule** (above the podrum), the **cathedral** (actually Diocletian's mausoleum), and off down an alley to the other side the **Baptistery of St John** (the Temple of Jupiter – Diocletian reckoned he was Jupiter's son). Inside the barrel-vaulted temple (also known as the Temple of Aesculapius – see page 287) you should be able to see a couple of classical statues, an interesting 11th-century baptismal font, and a statue of John the Baptist by Meštrović.

The vestibule was the main entrance hall to the imperial quarters. The domed roof has long gone, along with the ornate mosaics which would have lined it, but it's worth walking through here and circling round to the left, back to the cathedral, for some idea of where Diocletian lived – this was originally the dining halls and Roman baths. There are some mosaics here, hidden under protective sand, awaiting restoration.

The Cathedral of St Domnius

In a move which must have had Diocletian whirling in his sarcophagus, the emperor's mausoleum was long ago converted into one of Christianity's smallest cathedrals, honouring one of his own victims, St Domnius.

The main structure, including the dome, is original, dating from AD300, but the choir is a 17th-century addition. The entrance doors, with 28 excellent carved wooden panels describing the life of Christ, date from 1214 – the lower four panels have been damaged by centuries' worth of being pushed open by booted feet.

At the base of the dome there's a pagan-looking frieze, and what are said to be medallions of the heads of Diocletian and his wife. Diocletian's ahead of you as you come in, while his wife is two medallions to the left. Down below, the 13th-century pulpit may be a Romanesque masterpiece by Radovan (he of Trogir fame), but to my eye it's too big for the space it's in. The baroque 17th-century chapel is the one housing the Domnius relics; the other two chapels are 15th-century Gothic. Finally, the choir itself may be 17th-century, but the stalls are around the same age as the cathedral doors, and are a fine example of early Dalmatian wood-carving.

Take the time to climb up inside the campanile for an excellent view over the palace and out to sea – this version dates from 1908, following the collapse of the original, which was built in stages from the 13th to 17th centuries.

Underneath the cathedral is the spooky circular crypt, dedicated to St Lucy, patron saint of the blind (legend has it that Diocletian put her eyes out). The function of this chamber in antiquity isn't known – it's unlikely that it would have been a prison, being under a mausoleum, but large numbers of human bones were found here, and it is the kind of damp, gloomy, airless place you could imagine being used as a dungeon. Ask in the cathedral if you want to see the crypt – it's not always open.

The underground chambers

Don't miss the chance to see the huge semi-underground chambers which provided the foundations for the imperial quarters above. The only whole rooms remaining from the original palace, they give some idea of the sheer scale and size of Diocletian's ego. Remarkably, these chambers only survive because of sewage – during the Dark Ages, people simply threw their slops down holes in the floor, and it accumulated here, protecting the rooms from future squatters.

After World War II the western rooms were cleared out and opened to the public, while the eastern wing wasn't excavated until 1997 – at various points you can see the original waste chutes coming in from above, along with the foundations of medieval houses. The halls are now used for temporary exhibitions, but look out for a few original curiosities, including some mosaics which clearly pre-date the palace – they run underneath Diocletian's walls – and a marble *mensa*, a Roman table with raised edges for resting your forearm on.

Beyond the palace

Just outside the Golden Gate you can hardly fail to spot Meštrović's monumental 1928 statue of *Grgur Ninski*. Originally standing in the peristyle (which looked pretty wild – there's a photo in the first edition of Rebecca West's *Black Lamb and Grey Falcon*), the statue commemorates the 10th-century Bishop Gregorius of Nin, who tried (but failed) to introduce Croatian instead of Latin into the liturgy.

According to local tradition, touch his big toe and your wish will come true – which explains why it's been worn golden.

Walk west a block and head down Marulićeva Bosanska, the narrow street separating the palace from the rest of the old town. This is the least well-preserved wall of the palace, with an unbroken row of houses built into the original fortifications. On the left-hand side, unmarked, is Split's first synagogue – Europe's third, after Prague and Dubrovnik.

Half way down the street is the palace's Iron Gate, which leads out into the old town's main square, Narodni Trg (also known as Pjaca, pronounced *piazza*). Palazzi from different periods surround the square, with a Venetian Gothic town hall now housing the interesting **ethnographic museum**, and an Austrian secessionist palace dominating the square's west end. The next square to the south, just off Riva, has an excellent statue of **Marko Marulić**, the father of Croatian literature, who died in 1524 but is still widely celebrated, and indeed read. Yes, you guessed – it's by Meštrović.

The old town's western boundary is the elegant Marmontova, named after Napoleon's Marshal Marmont, the captain of his Illyrian Provinces, and the man responsible for both the Riva – Narodni Trg had got too small to function as a collective town square – and Trg Republike, now used for summer concerts.

West of the town you'll find the popular old quarter of **Veli Varoš**, which leads up the slopes of the 182m **Marjan peninsula**, Split's own city park, featuring woods, picnic areas and beaches – a great place to get away from the crowds, though very popular with the locals at weekends.

Museums and galleries

Split has four museums and galleries of particular note, two about a 15-minute walk north (head up Zrinko Frankopanska, from the top of Marmontova), and two

SALONA

If you know your archaeology, a trip out to Salona (now called Solin) might interest you – though be warned that anything which could be carried off has been carried off (some of the best pieces are in the Split Archaeological Museum), meaning you'll need to rely heavily on your imagination if you're going to people the dusty fields here with temples, houses, markets and an amphitheatre capable of seating nearly 20,000.

Salona is 5km north from the centre of Split, and is best reached on the #1 bus which drops you off at the Caffe Bar Salona, at the entrance to the site. There's a small archaeological museum here (an offshoot of the one in town), called Tusculum, where you can pick up a local map – after which you're on your own to wander across the worn grass and traces of the extensive ruins of the city, home to around 60,000 people in the 1st century AD.

The amphitheatre is the most impressive ruin, though there's very little left beyond the foundations. The Venetians carted off most of the stone in the 17th century, and used it for local building works and fortifications, claiming the dismantlement was only to prevent the Turks from using the amphitheatre as a hideout.

If you've come this far, the quickest way back to Split is on the #37 city bus. Cross the new highway using the underpass, and walk towards Solin centre until you get to the bus stop.

a 20-minute walk west onto the Marjan peninsula – or a short hop on local bus #12 from Trg Republike.

Heading north there's the secessionist **archaeological museum**, housing Croatia's biggest collection of remains from antiquity, and especially strong (unsurprisingly) on artefacts from Salona (see box, page 237). The Roman findings include excellent glass, jewellery, ceramics and statues, including some extraordinarily rich sarcophagi. There's also an extensive collection from very early Christianity.

Over on Lorevtska, less than five minutes away, is the **Split Art Gallery**, which has a terrific collection of paintings from the 14th century on. Unless you're an expert on Croatian art you won't recognise many of the names, but make the effort to come here and you'll find a rich tradition of painting which is especially strong on late 19th- and early 20th-century works, including a couple of masterpieces by Vlaho Bukovac (see page 293).

Heading west from the old town, a 15-minute walk will get you to the **Museum of Croatian Archaeological Monuments**, an unusual collection of Croatian artefacts from the 7th century on, housed in a wonderfully airy modern building. Around 5,000 items are on display (from a collection of more than 20,000 in total), running from old jewellery and stone inscriptions to a unique series of monuments from early Croatian churches, including gables, friezes, altar canopies and baptismal fonts. The captions, sadly, are only in Croatian; buy the English guide for full information.

Five minutes west of here brings you to the vast **Meštrović Gallery**, the mansion built by the sculptor between 1931 and 1939, and intended both as a museum and as his retirement home – instead, he emigrated to the USA, dying there in 1962. If you're even remotely interested in Meštrović – and you should be – then this comprehensive collection is the best anywhere. Outside is the sculpture garden; indoors, the full range of the sculptor's work can be seen, from family portraits to religious tableaux, to allegorical works. The entry ticket is also valid for the **Kaštelet**, just down the road, which Meštrović bought to house one of his most important works, a series of large wooden friezes dedicated to the life of Christ, and which (pre)occupied the sculptor on and off from around 1916 until its completion in 1950.

Klis

Just 9km north of Split, on the road to Sinj, are the magnificent monumental ruins of the fortress at Klis (Tvrđava Klis), situated along the length of a 340m hill. It was captured by the Turks in 1537 and remained in their hands for just over a century until the Venetians got their own back in 1648. Today there's not a great deal to see, but the ruins are highly atmospheric and make for a superb picnic spot. You can reach Klis either by taking the #34 or #36 bus to Klis–Megdan (where you'll find the fortress entrance), or by taking the Sinj bus to Klis–Varoš, and hiking up the hill from there. By car, take the old road from Solin (rather than the new road from Split to Sinj), and turn left at the Tvrđava sign).

Sinj

Thirty kilometres out of Split is the town of Sinj, famous mainly as the scene for the annual Sinjska Alka, a festival celebrating the 1715 victory over numerically superior Turks. Taking place on the Sunday before the Feast of the Assumption (August 15), the main feature is a contest in which metal rings suspended on a wire have to be speared at full gallop by chaps in traditional costume. It's all very noisy and colourful, and one of only two places where the time-honoured *Tilting at the Ring* still takes place (the other is in the village of Barban, in Istria – see page 158).

Half-hourly buses from Split will bring you to Sinj in under an hour.

MAKARSKA/BIOKOVO

The 100km or so of coast south of Split, to **Drvenik**, is a long string of pebbly beaches, broken only by the **Cetina Gorge** which cuts through the mountains to emerge at **Omiš**, once home to audacious pirates but now a rather half-hearted resort, given over as much to industry as to tourism.

Twenty kilometres beyond Omiš, **Brela** marks the start of the 60km-long **Makarska Riviera**, a series of cheerfully touristy villages and beaches sheltered by the solid mass of **Biokovo** to the northeast. At the heart of it all is Makarska itself, a small but busy town, tastefully restored in stone after the devastating 1962 earthquake. With a lovely palm-studded front and a 2km beach across the Sveti Petar headland, it's a perfect sunny stop if you're travel-weary and footsore. If you don't have sore feet, then Makarska's also the gateway to some of the most spectacular hiking in Croatia, on the Biokovo massif, home to four rare species of eagle (Golden, Imperial, Grey and Snake) and culminating in one of the country's highest peaks, Sveti Jure, at 1,762m.

Getting there

Without your own wheels, you'll be arriving in Makarska either by bus or ferry. Ferries come in from Sumartin, on the eastern end of Brač, twice a day in winter and five times in summer, while ten daily buses stop in on their way from Split to Dubrovnik, and vice-versa. There are direct buses to both Rijeka and Zagreb, twice daily.

Where to stay and eat

From the bus station, on Ante Starčevića, the main road running above the town, it's a five-minute walk downhill to the front, where you'll find everything you need. The tourist office (tel: 021 612 002; fax: 021 616 288; www.makarska.hr), at #16, has maps and information and can put you in touch with any number of agencies handling rooms and excursions – including SB Tours (tel: 021 611 005; fax: 021 611 955), just next door, and the Turist Biro (tel: 021 611 688; fax: 021 615 352), at #2. Private rooms (doubles) go for €15–30 depending on level of comfort and location, with the usual 30% surcharge for three nights or less. The nearest campsite is at **Baško Polje** (tel/fax: 021 612 329), nearly 10km back up the coast towards Split.

Most of the hotels in Makarska are on the town's long pebble beach, across the headland to the northeast of town, though an exception is the friendly three-star **Biokovo** (tel: 021 615 244; fax: 021 615 081), right on the waterfront in the middle of town. With any number of busy late-night terraces on the Riva below it, you may be glad of the air conditioning and double-glazing. Nice doubles go for €85 a night.

Just ten minutes away across the headland, on the beach, is the modern three-star **Meteor** (tel: 021 615 344; fax: 021 611 419), which has a triangular front, giving most rooms a generous sunny balcony. The best doubles go for around €120, and the hotel has a good pool. A little further up the beach is the **Biokovka** (tel: 021 602 200; fax: 021 602 287), which is also three star, but less overtly swanky and quite a bit cheaper, with doubles at €75.

Makarska has no shortage of eateries along the front, where terraces spill out across the pavement, and slightly cheaper places a block or two back from the sea. There's also an excellent daily market, if you're looking for picnic food, just up from the town's only old square, Kačićev Trg.

What to see

Makarska isn't a place you come to for culture – it's a town with a great beach and even better hiking up in the mountains – so the sights can be comfortably counted off on the fingers of one hand. On Kačićev Trg there's the 18th-century **St Mark's Church** (usually closed), while at the eastern end of town you'll find Croatia's finest **malacological museum** – that's seashells, to you – housed in the cellars of the Franciscan monastery. The collection of more than 3,000 shells from around the world was put together by one of the Franciscan monks, Jure Radić, and opened in 1963. Radić also founded the botanical gardens in Kotišina (see below).

A couple of kilometres along the coast to the north there's a curious shrine at the **Vepric Cave**. Inaugurated in 1908, on the 50th anniversary of the apparitions in Lourdes, the sanctuary was founded by Bishop Carić (who was buried here on his death in 1921) and dedicated to Our Lady of Lourdes. It's been popular with pilgrims since its foundation, and is especially busy on February 11, March 25, August 15 and September 7–8.

Finally, if you're here in May, don't miss Makarska's spectacular rowing regatta, which proves the town hasn't entirely forgotten its Venetian legacy.

Biokovo

The Biokovo massif rises up steeply above the Makarska Riviera in three ever more spectacular shelves, providing hiking at all levels and fabulous views, but if you're coming here to head up into the mountains don't underestimate them, and start out as early in the day as you can. The weather can change very quickly, there's no water or food to be had once you're out, and the karst limestone is hard on even the toughest hiking boots. It's highly inadvisable to go out far if you're alone. If you run into trouble, it's unlikely anyone would find you, and – without wishing to be alarmist – you should remember there are still wolves in the wild up here.

The two main summits reachable from Makarska are **Vošac** (1,420m or thereabouts, and a 3½-hour hike one way) and **Sveti Jure** (1,762m; allow a good 5 hours up and 4 hours back).

There are two paths up out of town leading to Vošac and on to Sveti Jure, one going via the village of **Makar**, and the other via the village of **Kotišina**. Once you get to either village the trail is well signed with red and white flashes, but pick up a map from the tourist office before you head out.

In either case, start off from Kačićev Trg, pass the church and market, and cross the main road, continuing up **Put Makra** until you reach the next main road, Dubravačka. For the Makar route you should then stay on the continuation of Put Makra until you reach the village. For Kotišina turn right after 200m up Put Mlinica, which leads to the village of **Mlinice**, from which you'll see signs for the path to Kotišina. Both Makar and Kotišina are at around 200m above sea-level and take around 45 minutes to reach on foot from the seafront.

The village of Kotišina was definitively abandoned after the 1962 earthquake, but locals still keep weekenders up here. It's well worth a visit, not just because of the interesting **fortress** built right into the rock here, but also because of the **Botanički Vrt**, the botanical gardens founded by Jure Radić. Radić knew more than anyone about the flora of Biokovo and built the gardens here – more an oversized rockery – as a plant haven. Sadly, since his death in 1990, it has all fallen somewhat into disrepair.

From Makar or Kotišina it's a tough hike to the summit of Vošac, but the views once you get there are absolutely stupendous, way out across the sea and islands. On the way, not far from the summit, you'll pass the **Dom Vošac** refuge (at

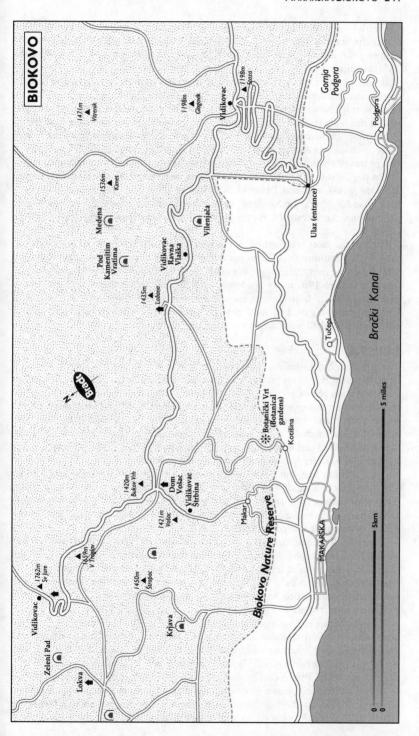

BIOKOVO

1471m
Vitrenik

1536m
Kimet

1198m
Glogovik

Vidikovac

1198m
Sazza

Gornja
Podgora

Podgora

Ulaz (entrance)

Medena

Pod
Kamenitim
Vratima

1435m
Lodono

Vidikovac
Ravna
Vlaska

Vilenjača

Brački Kanal

N

Biadi

Tučepi

Botanički Vrt
(Botanical
gardens)

Kotišina

1420m
Bukov Vrh

Dom
Vošac

Vidikovat
Štrbina

1421m
Vošc

Makar

1659m
V Troglav

1762m
Sv Jure

Vidikovac

Zeleni Pad

Lokva

1450m
Stropac

Kljava

Biokovo Nature Reserve

MAKARSKA

5km

5 miles

0
0

1,370m) – this was closed at the time of writing, but ask at the tourist office. This marks the start of the steep and somewhat difficult path up to Sveti Jure, the highest point on the massif. The little Church of Sveti Jure here is dwarfed by the TV transmitter.

If hiking's not for you, Sveti Jure isn't necessarily out of the question. There's a narrow road that goes up to the summit from Makarska, making for a 30km white-knuckle ride, best performed by jeep and with someone else at the wheel. The road is the highest in Croatia, positively vertiginous, and has no safety barriers...

For more information on hiking or jeeping up the mountain contact the tourist office or Biokovo Active Holidays (tel: 099 471 229/098 225 852), especially if you're travelling alone and would like the security of some company on the trail.

On the far side of the Biokovo mountains, tucked into the border with Bosnia & Herzegovina, and near **Imotski**, which is on the way to absolutely nowhere (a back road to Mostar or Sarajevo, conceivably), are two typically strange karstic phenomena, the so-called **Crveno Jezero** and **Modro Jezero** (the Red and Blue Lakes).

Each of the lakes was formed by the roof collapsing above a vast cave, and even though they're more than 20km from the sea as the crow flies, and on the wrong side of a major mountain range, the lakes are deep indeed – the bottom of Crveno Jezero is a mere 19m above sea-level, with the lake depth itself varying between 280m and 320m. Modro Jezero, for its part, really is blue. With less steep sides than Crveno Jezero, it's used by local boys for swimming – when there's water in it at all – or as a football pitch when it's dried up.

ŠOLTA

The island of Šolta, easily accessible from Split and right next to the much larger Brač, is something of a mystery. It's pretty, it's wooded, it has old stone hamlets (it even has a couple of prehistoric and Roman ruins, and a sprinkling of medieval monuments), it has appealing coves, beaches and bays, and yet it's somehow off the main tourist map – it sees only around a tenth of the visitors of Brač or Hvar, and most of those check in at the increasingly large apartment complex at Nečujam. Come and stay in one of the 120 or so private rooms on the island and you'll never believe Split's under half an hour away on the catamaran.

Šolta is 20km long but less than 5km wide, and has a local population of under 1,500, mainly in a handful of settlements along the north coast and in the interior. The south coast, a crenulated maze of inlets, coves and tiny bays, is almost entirely uninhabited. Olives, figs, wine production and fishing still drive the part of the economy that isn't fuelled by tourism.

Three ferries a day make the one-hour crossing to Šolta's port, **Rogač**, year-round. In summer the frequency more than doubles (depending on demand), and there's also a catamaran service which crosses to Rogač in just 25 minutes. More irregular crossings (aimed mainly at weekenders) are made by both ferry and catamaran in summer to Stomorska, and – by catamaran only – to Nečujam, the two main tourist spots.

Regular ferries and catamarans are met by the bus which connects all the main settlements – if you miss the bus or want to get around the island at other times your options are limited to walking or calling one of the island's two taxi drivers – Dušan Lisičić (tel: 099 477 852) drives a white van; Vladimir Vlak (tel: 091 360 3388) has a white Fiat. You can also get from port to port by local water taxi.

If you are walking, make sure you have plenty of water – it's a hot, dry place. It's around 2km up the hill from Rogač to the administrative centre, **Grohote**, which has a shop and pizzeria, as well as a regular market. From here it's the best

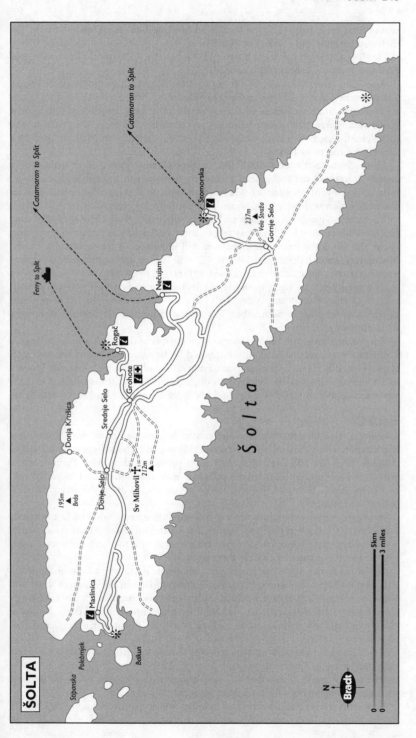

part of 8km west, passing by the hamlets of **Srednje Selo** and **Donje Selo**, to the sheltered harbour and beaches at **Maslinica**.

Heading east from Grohote, it's around 7km to the once-upon-a-time village of **Nečujam**, now unashamedly a tourist resort.

Also 7km from Grohote, at the foot of the island's high point (Vela Straža, 237m), is the old stone village of **Gornje Selo**, itself 150m above sea-level. There's a paved path from the village to the top of the mountain, where you'll find great views and a large plain concrete crucifix. There are also footpaths down to the south coast, though stock up at the bakery or shop before you head off, as there's nothing on the coast itself.

From Grohote it's a downhill 3km to **Stomorska**, Šolta's other main tourist centre. Stomorska sits at the head of a lovely narrow bay, and although it can get busy (noisy, even) on summer weekends, a short walk along the coastal path in either direction will get you to some lovely little rocky beaches.

There are no campsites or hotels on Šolta (although the **Avlija Hotel** in Maslinica, in a fine 18th-century building, may reopen some day), so if you're staying here – you could also do a day trip from Split – it will either be in the apartments in the **Nečujam Centar** (tel: 021 650 149; fax: 021 650 153) or in one of the island's private rooms (call the tourist office, tel: 021 654 151; fax: 021 654 130).

The apartments are open from May to September, and go for €48 (two person, with terrace) or €68 (four person, with balcony) a night at the top of the season – prices halve for May or September. Private rooms come in at under €30 a night for doubles.

For private rooms you can try your luck on the spot at the tourist offices in Rogač, Nečujam, Stomorska or Maslinica, but you'd be far more sensible to try and book ahead, especially if you're planning on staying on the island in high summer. Rooms and transport can also be arranged through Šolta Tours (tel/fax: 021 475 259; www.soltatours.com), and you can find out more about the island at www.solta.hr.

BRAČ

Like Šolta, Brač is attractive, hot and sunny, and an easy hour from Split – but that's where the similarity ends. Brač is far larger (the third biggest island in the Adriatic, after Krk and Cres) and vastly more popular with tourists. Famous for its white marble – used in Diocletian's palace in Split in antiquity, and more recently in Washington's White House and Berlin's Reichstag – the island today depends mainly on tourism.

Away from the two main centres of Supetar in the north and Bol in the south, however, it's still often deserted, particularly in the mountainous interior, where whole villages have been abandoned to time, but also on the large sections of coast not developed or easily accessible by road.

Seven car ferries a day run from Split to Supetar, rising to 13 a day in summer, and supplemented in season by catamarans direct to Bol on the southern shore, via Milna on the western end of the island. Car ferries also run twice a day (five times in summer) from Makarska to Sumartin, on the eastern tip of Brač. If you're already in Bol, and want to go on to Hvar, there are privately run services across to Jelsa in summer.

Brač also has a small airport, which is used mainly for charter arrivals but features daily flights from Zagreb in summer as well. There's usually (but not always) a shuttle to Bol which meets flights. If you're onward to Supetar you'll either have to take a bus from Bol or a taxi direct from the airport.

Supetar is the bus hub, with most destinations served three times a day – once in the morning, once around lunchtime, and once in the late afternoon. This

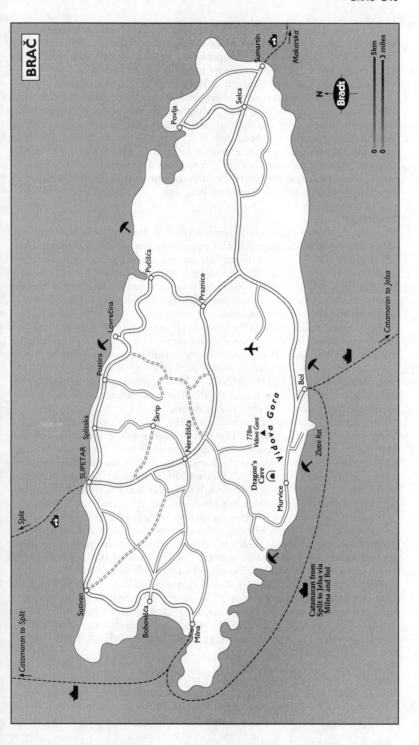

makes getting anywhere easy from Supetar, but can be a problem if you arrive in Milna or Sumartin and want to move on straight away. The afternoon ferry from Makarska, in particular, doesn't connect with onward transport until the following day. Fortunately people in Sumartin are friendly and will help to find you a room if you need one. Buses from Supetar to Bol run six times a day.

If you haven't got your own wheels and want to give yourself vastly more freedom to explore Brač, then renting transport is the way to go. In Supetar you'll find cycles, scooters and cars for rent, and even motorboats. Rental isn't cheap (though less expensive in Supetar than Bol), but gives you the run of the island, and is the only real way of getting away from the crowds in summer. Ultimately, a cycle or scooter is the best way of getting around, though if you're relying on pedal-power don't under-estimate the summer heat or over-estimate your fitness – it's a hilly 40km ride from Supetar to Bol.

Supetar

The chances are you'll arrive in Supetar. A pleasant cluster of stone houses spreads round the harbour, where you'll find everything you need – the tourist office (tel/fax: 021 630 551; www.supetar.hr), the bus station, and a couple of travel agencies. Atlas (tel: 021 631 105; fax: 021 631 088) or Maestral (tel: 021 631 258; fax: 021 631 461) should be able to fix you up with a private room, arrange excursions, or rent you transport. If you want a car, rather than a cycle or a scooter, it's pretty much essential to call ahead.

The main beaches are west of the town, and being shallow these are good for (and popular with) families. Most of the accommodation here is at the **Kaktus** complex (tel: 021 630 200; fax: 021 631 344), which includes the smaller **Olea & Salvia**. Expect to pay around €95 for sea-view doubles. A very pleasant alternative is the **Villa Britanida** (tel: 021 631 038; fax: 021 630 017), which is 300m east of the port, and features a fine restaurant. Book well ahead as it only has around 20 rooms (€66 for doubles), and only a few of these face the sea.

An interesting side-trip can be made to **Škrip**, the island's oldest settlement and home to the **Museum of Brač**. The hilltop village is inland 3km from **Splitska**, itself 6km east of Supetar, and the museum, housed in a fortified old stone building, gives an interesting glance into the toughness of island life in the past. The usual three buses a day come up here, and it's a pleasant half- or three-quarter-hour walk back to Splitska if you fancy a swim afterwards. It's a further 4km east along the coast from Splitska to **Lovrečina**, the only sandy beach on Brač. It's no secret, believe me.

On Brač's southwestern corner is the sheltered little port of Milna, around 20km from Supetar on a thrice-daily bus. On your way you might want to come via **Sutivan**, the last settlement on the north coast, which is a charming stone village with access to some good pebble beaches. Private rooms are available through the tourist office (tel: 021 638 357; fax: 021 638 134; www.sutivan.hr).

Milna – the birthplace of 2001 Wimbledon winner Goran Ivanisevic – is at the head of a narrow inlet, and one of the nicest places in Brač, within easy reach of beaches which are never too busy. There's one small hotel, the eponymous **Milna** (tel: 021 636 116; fax: 021 636 550), which has 25 rooms at around €90 for doubles, or you can get private rooms through the tourist office (tel: 021 636 233; fax: 021 636 505).

Bol

Brač's biggest draw by far is Bol – or more accurately the extraordinary spit of fine shingle called **Zlatni Rat**, the Golden Beach. Featuring in every Croatian tourist promo, the tip of the south-facing 500m triangular spit shifts west or east depending on the season, and the beach attracts around 50,000 visitors a year. It's not the only place to swim near Bol – the town, sheltered by the mass of **Vidova Gora** behind it, is at the heart of a 15km stretch of beaches – but it's certainly the most popular.

Zlatni Rat is a pleasant half-hour stroll west of Bol, which is a pretty little fishing harbour surrounded by old stone houses. New developments spread up the hill, but the centre itself is compact and charming. It's far too small to accommodate all the people who want to see it, however, so be warned ahead if you're crowd-phobic.

The tourist office (tel: 021 635 638; fax: 021 635 972; www.bol.hr) has a good supply of maps, which you'll find useful if you're planning on hiking up Vidova Gora or west to the Dragon's Cave or Blaca (see below).

Accommodation mainly consists of the **Bonaca**, **Borak** and **Elaphusa** resort hotels near Zlatni Rat. There's not much to choose between them – they're all similarly priced (around €150–170 for a double at the top of the season) and well located – though the Bonaca is popular with families and the Borak's a bit more upmarket than the others. All three can be centrally booked through the Zlatni Rat company and offer a discount for online bookings (tel: 021 635 210; fax: 021 635 150; www.zlatni-rat.hr).

There's also the **Kaštil** (tel: 021 635 996; fax: 021 635 997) which is completely different, offering just 32 rooms bang on the fishing port of Bol itself, with sea-view doubles at €120, dropping back to €60 off-season.

For one of the town's 3,000 beds in private rooms you'll need to go through an agency – Adria Tours (tel: 021 635 966; fax: 021 635 977), Atlas (tel: 021 635 233; fax: 021 635 707) and Bol Tours (tel: 021 635 693; fax: 021 635 696) are all in the middle of town (and can also organise the usual excursions and rentals). Expect to pay €40 for a double in season, and a surcharge of 20% for three nights or fewer.

Once you've had your fill of beach-life, one of the best side-trips you can make is to head to the top of **Vidova Gora**. At 778m it's not just the highest point on Brač, but the highest point on any Adriatic island, and the views are terrific – down onto Zlatni Rat far below, and across to the island of Hvar, to the south, and back to the grey karst mountains on the mainland to the north. The easy way up is by road, either with your own wheels or on an excursion, but the most satisfying way to the summit is by hiking up from Bol. It's a good 2½ hours of steady trekking, but it's well worth it – walking boots are recommended. At the top there's a *konoba* which usually opens to coincide with excursions.

Another interesting excursion you can go on is to the **Dragon's Cave** (Drakonija Spilja), above the little village of Murvica, to the west of Bol. It's a bit of a mystery as to who carved the wild beasts and mythological creatures here, but they're likely to date back to the 15th century at least. You can't usually visit on your own as the cave is mostly closed – check with the tourist office in Bol before setting off.

Finally, there's the extraordinary **Blaca Monastery**. This is most easily visited on an excursion, though you can get there on your own (but check the opening times at Bol's tourist office). If you have wheels, you can drive (but only just) to the abandoned village of **Dragovode**, after which it's a half-hour walk to the monastery – otherwise the whole walk from Bol takes around three hours each way, though you can cut that in half or less by taking a boat to Blaca beach, and walking up from there.

Set high up under a cliff, the imposing monastery served as a refuge from the 16th century on, and was still inhabited until the last monk, Niko Milčević, died here in 1963. It now houses a curious collection of astronomical instruments, old weapons and watches, and an exceptional library.

HVAR

South of Brač and stretching finger-like towards the southern end of the Makarska Riviera, Hvar is one of the most pleasant islands in the Adriatic. It has an elegant 16th-century Venetian capital, plenty of beaches, and great weather – it boasts 2,700 hours of annual sunshine and averages only eight snowy days a decade. In winter you'll find hotels offering 50% off your room rate for any day on which it rains for more than three daylight hours, and free board and lodging if it goes below freezing during the day.

Not surprisingly, the island is one of the Adriatic's worst-kept secrets – book well ahead if you want to stay in any of the island's hotels at the height of the season. Or simply follow the example of Riccardo Mazzuchelli, the wealthy Italian businessman (and former husband of Ivana Trump, though at Bradt we wouldn't normally stoop to such tabloid gossip), who's bought himself a fabulous villa and grounds on the island. It's also worth looking at the Hvar website, at www.hvar.hr, where you can get advance details on much of the private accommodation across the island.

Hvar town sits at the sheltered southwestern tip of Hvar, separated from the other main settlements of Stari Grad, Vrboska and Jelsa by the 600m bulk of **Sveti Nikola**, which runs down the spine of the island. Hvar stretches nearly 70km from west to east, but almost everything that happens here happens in the western third, **Sućuraj** (on the eastern tip) serving only as an arrival point for car traffic on its way in from the Drvenik ferry.

The island's main crop – it won't take you long to work this out from the number of places it's on sale in Hvar – is lavender, which is cultivated in great swathes, and makes a spring break here a real treat. There's also a fair amount of wine made, and the usual crops of figs and olives.

Getting there and around

Arrival on the island is inevitably by ferry or catamaran. The most frequent crossing is also the shortest – it's only 5km (20 minutes) from Drvenik to **Sućuraj**, and the ferry runs five times a day in winter (up to 15 a day in summer). Count on doing this only if you have your own wheels, however, as the bus heading up the island leaves Sućuraj before 06.00, and only runs three times a week.

Contact the Sućuraj tourist office (tel: 021 773 203; fax: 021 773 371) for a smattering of private rooms if you get stuck here – and there are many worse places to spend a day or so, with nice beaches only a short walk from the tiny harbour, and a handful of cheerful cafés, restaurants and shops on hand. It's an option for arrival, with onward travel off the other end of the island. More on Sućuraj can be found at www.sucuraj.hr, a popular and lively internet site.

From Split there's a car ferry two or three times a day, year-round, direct to Stari Grad (actually a few kilometres out of town, but buses to Stari Grad, Jelsa and Hvar meet the ferry), with the frequency increasing substantially in summer. The journey takes a couple of hours. Reserve well ahead in summer on this route if you're coming by car.

The daily catamaran from Split to Vela Luka (on Korčula) and Ubli (on Lastovo) also stops in at Hvar town, and it's only a 50-minute journey from the mainland. The daily car ferry on the same route also stops by (taking 1½ hours from Split), but only twice a week in winter. These services offer you a good onward option for your journey, as both Korčula and Lastovo are compelling destinations in their own right. Note that although the ferry carries cars, you can't disembark at car-free Hvar town – come in through Sućuraj or Stari Grad if you're driving.

In summer there's also a daily, privately operated catamaran which runs from Jelsa across to Bol, on Brač.

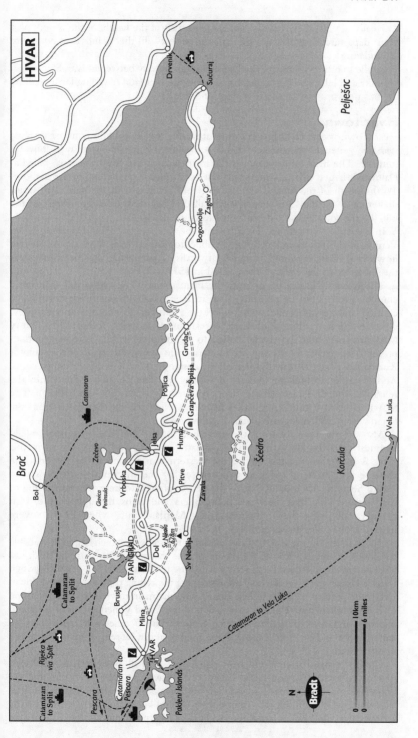

Finally, if you are here with your car, especially at the height of the season, plan your departure carefully, as the queues to get off the island can be pretty intimidating.

Public transport is limited to a handful of buses a day between Hvar, Stari Grad, Vrboska and Jelsa, though all incoming ferries are met (and outgoing ferries fed) by the bus network – with the exception of Sućuraj.

Hvar town

Hvar Town is one of Dalmatia's most attractive, rivalling Dubrovnik or Korčula with its Venetian Renaissance charm – though it can get oppressively busy in summer. The heart of the town is the main square, Trg Sveti Stjepana, billed as Dalmatia's largest piazza, which runs east–west from the cathedral to the harbour. To the north of the square is the swanky old quarter, with the palaces of **Grad** sheltering under the 13th-century city walls and overlooked by the fortress on the hill. To the south is the old residential town of **Burg**.

In the early 15th century, Hvar became the wealthiest town in Dalmatia, under Venice, as all ships to and from the republic stopped in here. What you see today, however (barring the mostly original city walls), is uniformly late 16th century, as the Turks razed the town to the ground in 1571.

The main sights are on or near the main square. The **cathedral** (actually a church, but let's not be pedantic) with its Renaissance trefoil façade is attractive enough (and the campanile, with its increasing number of windows on each storey, is lovely), but nothing particularly special inside, barring a fine 13th-century Madonna and Child, in striking contrast to the morbidly graphic baroque paintings on the other altars. Check out the modern main doors, the work of the sculptor Kuzma Kovačić, the man also behind the design on Croatia's kuna and lipa coins. And if you're around on Maundy Thursday, just before Easter, don't miss the religious processions around the island, maintaining a 500-year-old tradition. The festivities reach a climax on Easter Monday, when the six big crosses from the island's main settlements are paraded around town.

Also on the main square is the great hulk of the **Arsenal** – unusual indeed amongst naval buildings in having a theatre upstairs, and especially so in this case, as it was one of the first in the western world open to all comers. The **theatre** was built in 1612, as you can see by the inscription outside saying 'Anno Secundo Pacis MDCXII' – the peace referred to here was the ending of the century-long spat between commoners and nobs throughout the 16th century, following the 1510 uprising by Matija Ivanić, when 19 men were hanged from galley masts here.

Access to the theatre is through an adjoining **art gallery**, which has highly variable temporary exhibitions from Croatian artists. The theatre itself is charming, with just 86 seats and 28 pint-sized boxes, but it could use the kind hand of a restorer – when I was last there a net was the only thing stopping the ceiling paint from flaking down.

On the other side of the square, dominating the main town gate, you'll find the so-called **Hektorović Palace**, an ornate but unfinished Venetian Gothic building, unroofed and overgrown since the 15th century. The so-called palace pre-dates the famous poet, in fact – and a more fitting memorial can be seen at his actual palace in Stari Grad.

Up the stepped street from here you'll find a small **Benedictine convent**, where the few remaining nuns – they never leave the hallowed walls, and are bound to an oath of silence – spend their hours making the extraordinarily intricate lace which you'll find for sale around town (you'll know it's the real thing by the serious price tags). Just below the convent is a small, plain church, remarkable only

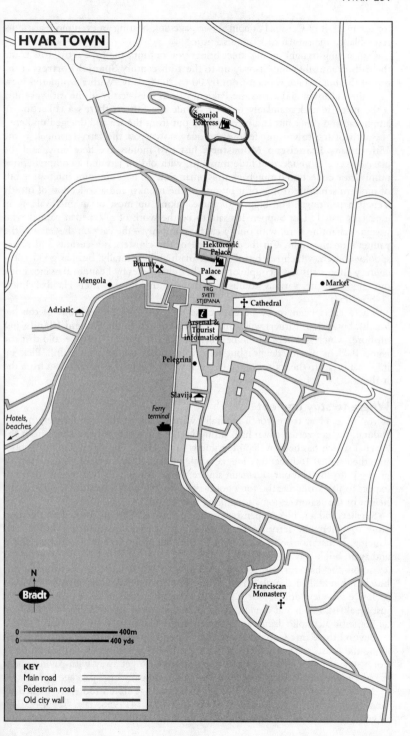

HVAR TOWN

Španjol Fortress

Hektorović Palace

Bounty

Palace

Mengola

Market

Adriatic

TRG SVETI STJEPANA

Cathedral

Arsenal & Tourist information

Pelegrini

Slavija

Ferry terminal

Hotels, beaches

Franciscan Monastery

N

Bradt

0 ——————— 400m
0 ——————— 400 yds

KEY
Main road
Pedestrian road
Old city wall

for the portrait of Cardinal Stjepinac (see page 86), bearing an even more alarming resemblance than usual to Vladimir Putin.

Continuing straight up the street brings you out into the park above town, and the path eventually winds its way up to the 16th-century **Španjol Fortress** at the top of the hill, which is open from 09.00 to 20.00 daily. With a wonderful view over the old town and across the Pakleni islands – especially in the early evening – the place is understandably popular. Inside the fortress there's a collection of amphorae and other bits and pieces fished out from the sea and dragged up here.

South of the town (just follow the quay down past the ferry terminal) is the 15th-century **Franciscan Monastery**. Just two monks live here now, and the place serves as an endearing little museum, with old oil jars and a comprehensive numismatic collection dating back to Roman times. There are some interesting bits of modern sculpture (some of it by one of the monks) and a collection of mostly Venetian paintings. The biggest of these, taking up most of an end wall, is an especially rowdy Last Supper. It's said to be the work of a Venetian painter who was in quarantine here, with only a cat for company – the cat's on the left and the painter's on the right. On the other side of the cloisters is a curious and rather spooky church, which is a bit of a mish-mash architecturally, but has good 16th-century choir stalls and a couple of huge dark altarpieces by Leandro Bassano. Look out amongst the various tombs for that of the local writer Hanibal Lučić (1485–1553).

There are several rocky beaches close to town (notably in front of the big hotels), but serious bathers will want to take a trip out to the **Pakleni Islands**, just offshore, which is where all the best beaches can be found (you'll be told that the name Pakleni means 'devils', but it actually refers to the pine resin). Pick up information from the tourist office (see below), and get there by taxi-boat from the harbour.

Where to stay and eat

If you're in Hvar town you'll naturally want to stay at the appropriately named **Palace**, the converted town hall, sitting in a prime location right across from the Arsenal which has been welcoming guests since 1903. The reception area is built into the original 16th-century loggia, while upstairs there's a fabulous open terrace giving onto the harbour and main square. Prices for the 75-odd rooms vary, but expect to pay around €160 for a good-sized double with a reasonable view at the height of the season. Book a long, long way ahead.

Smaller, and a tad less expensive, is the 56-roomed **Slavija**, located on the quay close to where the ferry docks. With a busy terrace, frequent live music, and dancing, it may not be as quiet as you want, but again the location is excellent – and again book way ahead.

Across the harbour, also on the waterfront, and in a better location for the beaches, but still in the old town, is the 63-roomed **Adriatic**, which offers all-inclusive sea-view doubles for €165. And that means all-inclusive – meals are not just breakfast, lunch and dinner, but also afternoon tea and a midnight snack, and all domestic alcoholic drinks are included in the price.

Beyond these three, you're most likely to end up in one of the package hotels along the coast, most of which are within a 10–15-minute walk of the old town. For a stay of under three nights you're not going to get away with paying under €130 a night for a decent double, unless you're actually on a package here.

All of the hotels above – and most of the package hotels too – are owned by (and reserved through) **Sunčani Hvar** (tel: 021 741 956; fax: 021 742 014; www.suncanihvar.hr). Prices drop 25% for stays of more than three nights, and more than half if you're here between October and May, an option well worth considering.

If the summer prices in Hvar have taken your breath away, then you'll probably be looking for a private room. These are handled by the Pelegrini and Mengola agencies – Pelegrini (tel: 021 742 743; fax: 021 742 250) is close to where the ferry docks; Mengola (tel/fax: 021 742 099) is on the little harbour, across the water from the Arsenal and tourist office (tel/fax: 021 741 059). Expect to pay €50 for a one-night stay in season; out of season you should do a great deal better than this.

What and where you end up eating and drinking in Hvar will depend a great deal on what time of year you're here. In high summer there are dozens of restaurants and even more bars and cafés, and you can pick and choose to some extent – though the fare mostly sticks to the traditional seafood/pasta/pizza variety; hardly surprising, given Hvar's enduring popularity with Italians. Out of season it's a different matter altogether, and when I was here at Easter – notwithstanding the religious festivities going on – there were only two restaurants open in the whole town, and a mere handful of bars. The only place you could get breakfast, having arrived on the 06.00 ferry, was at the Hotel Slavija. Full marks, however, to the **Bounty**, right on the old harbour, which served up the best fish soup I ate in Croatia on that particular trip, and offered the local Hvar house white wine at an all too reasonable 40 kuna a litre. In summer of course it's packed out and a bit more expensive; but well worth it all the same.

Stari Grad

Stari Grad, set around an elongated horseshoe harbour at the head of a long sheltered bay, was formerly the capital of the island, and the location of the 4th-century BC Greek colony of Pharos (the name Hvar comes from Pharos). The town is on the south side of the harbour, with the northern shore occupied by a string of package hotels. If you're driving from Hvar there are two roads, the new fast route through the tunnel, or the picturesque old road over the hills, past the village of **Brusje**. Take the high road if you're not in a rush.

With little having survived from antiquity (barring a small section of the original walls, a few paving slabs, and some Greek gravestones in the museum at the monastery), head instead for the **Tvrdalj**, the summer house of one of Dalmatia's most famous poets, Petar Hektorović (1487–1572). The fortified house has undergone numerous facelifts since being started in 1520, but features interesting inscriptions on the walls from Hektorović's work, in Croatian, Italian and Latin, and a heavy cloister surrounding a fishpond – a memorial to the poet's love of fish, fishing, and fishermen.

The rest of the town is a small but agreeable hotch-potch of little streets and small squares, though there is a **Dominican monastery** to visit, with an interesting museum off the cloisters.

Tourist information (tel/fax: 021 765 763) is on the harbour, while private rooms can be arranged through Mistral Tours (tel: 021 765 281; fax: 021 395 851), right where the bus stops. Hotel accommodation is across the bay in package hotels, including the **Lavanda**, the **Arkada** and the **Helios** (for all, tel: 021 765 555; fax: 021 765 128), which do reasonable doubles with views for around €90.

Jelsa and surroundings

The small town of **Jelsa** – mostly modestly 19th-century, sitting on a pretty port – is today somewhat dwarfed by the hotel complexes on either side. Nonetheless it's an attractive place in itself, surrounded by pine forests and giving easy access to a number of beaches, including by taxi-boat to the best ones on the **Glavica** peninsula, and across to the naturist island of **Zečevo**.

Jelsa also offers one of the very few routes across the island to the south coast. You'll need wheels, as the route winds 4km up to the old village of **Pitve** before entering the **Vratnik** gorge, and a long tunnel, which comes out above the village of Zavala (around 7km from Pitve).

Zavala itself is a tiny fishing village, but it does have an excellent place to stay, the **Villa Stella Mare** (tel: 021 767 128; fax: 021 718 133). A total of seven apartments go for around €70 apiece per night in season, and the friendly staff can even rent you a bike, a scooter or a boat if you want to explore the deserted coves and beaches along Hvar's south coast.

Three kilometres offshore is the island of **Šćedro**. Protected since 1972, the island doesn't see many visitors (the occasional sailing boat and motor cruiser), and has a resident population of just one. It makes for a lovely day trip from Zavala (or Jelsa), with its dense woods, sheltered inlets, and the remains of a 15th-century monastery.

From Jelsa it's only a 45-minute walk west along the coast path (or a short taxi-boat ride away) to **Vrboska**, a charming old village set along both sides of an inlet. Stone bridges connect the two halves, which are dominated by the fortified 16th-century **Church of St Mary**, built after the Turks destroyed the place in 1571. You can climb up to the battlements for a nice view over the village.

East of Jelsa, Hvar becomes very empty indeed, and although there's plenty to explore if you have your own wheels, it's pretty much impossible otherwise. You can, however, get yourself on an organised tour from Jelsa to **Grapčeva Spilja**, an ancient cave complex with excellent stalactites and stalagmites, just south of the semi-abandoned hamlet of Humac. Ask at the Jelsa tourist office (tel: 021 761 017; fax: 021 761 918; www.tzjelsa.hr).

Hotel accommodation in Jelsa is pretty much exclusively at the resort complexes which include the **Fontana**, the **Jadran** and the **Mina** (for all, tel: 021 761 182; fax: 021 761 810), with doubles at around €75. Private rooms, however, are in good supply and considerably cheaper here than in Hvar town, and can be booked through Atlas (tel/fax: 021 761 605), just up from the tourist information office. There are also some private rooms available in Vrboska. Contact the Vrboska tourist office (tel/fax: 021 774 137) there for more details.

VIS

The lovely island of Vis is Croatia's farthest flung possession, and also its oldest recorded settlement, having been colonised by the Greeks (from Syracuse, on Sicily) at the beginning of the 4th century BC. The colony of Issa then went on to found its own colonies (notably at Trogir and Salona) before succumbing to Roman rule, and following much the same historical fate as most of the rest of Dalmatia – Venetians, Austrians, the French, Austrians again, and then Yugoslavia – with the notable exception that Vis was also a British possession, from 1811 to 1814.

The British came back here in 1944, when the island was briefly Tito's headquarters – after the war, when Vis was Yugoslavia's naval staff headquarters, the only foreigners allowed on the island for decades were British veterans, who came back every September for their annual reunion.

Since 1989, Vis has been open for business, and tourism, while still relatively low-key, is growing by around 30% annually. Today the island is often seen simply as the jumping-off point for trips to the famous **Modra Špilja** ('Blue Cave') on nearby **Biševo**, but it's well worth visiting in its own right.

Vis has no freshwater sources, apart from a few springs near Komiža – water has to be brought in during the summer months by ship and stored in cisterns – so don't expect to be able to fill up here if you're sailing; head instead for Hvar and Korčula.

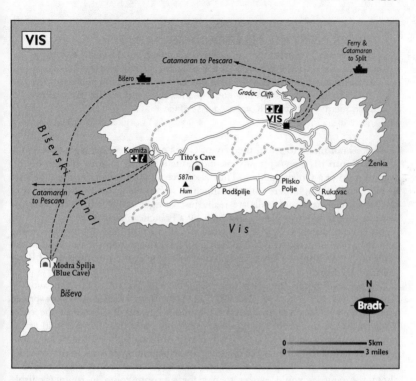

The lack of water, however, doesn't stop the locals making excellent wine in great quantities, notably the red Plavac, and the dry (but sweet-scented) white Vugava.

The capital, Vis town, is in a sheltered inlet on the spectacular north side of the island (the cliffs at Gradac, nearby, rise 100m out of the sea), while Komiža, in a large bay facing west, is the other main settlement, closer to the island of Biševo.

Ferry schedules make Vis an unlikely day trip, unless you take an all-in excursion from the coast or one of the other nearby islands, and you should be warned that outside the summer months the 2½-hour ferry journey from Split can be a truly stomach-churning one. On the other hand if the weather's fine and the sea's calm, this is one journey where you're quite likely to see dolphins alongside the boat.

One or two ferries a day come from Split year-round, stopping twice a week in Hvar, while in summer there's also a daily hydrofoil, which takes around 1½ hours from Split. Twice-weekly trans-Adriatic ferries from Ancona stop here in summer, along with twice-weekly hydrofoils from Pescara. Don't even think about trying to bring your car here in summer – rent a scooter or mountain bike on the island if you really want your own wheels.

Public transport on Vis consists of the bus which meets the ferry and goes over to Komiža, a fairly spectacular half-hour (18km) ride. There's also a 10km track connecting the two towns, making for a pleasant 2½-hour walk, or a great hour on a mountain bike.

Vis town

Ferries arrive in Vis town, the diminutive capital, which consists of Luka to the west and Kut to the east, though the whole place is a ten-minute walk end-to-end, leading to the famous local quip, 'Vis town ain't big enough for the both of us'.

TITO'S WARTIME HEADQUARTERS ON VIS

Up in **Hum Mountain** is the warren of underground tunnels and caves used by Tito in 1944 as a hideout and temporary headquarters. Popular as a tourist attraction when the island was first opened to the public in 1989 and 1990, they have since been boarded up, though there are plans to re-open them – ask at the Komiža tourist office.

There's not much to see in the way of Greek and Roman heritage, though the **Issa Museum** has a few treasures on show, including the famous 4th-century BC bronze head of a Greek goddess. They also have a useful leaflet detailing the sites of local ruins, though there isn't that much to see on the ground – the remains of the Greek cemetery and walls are really just vestiges, while what was once the Roman theatre has been firmly overbuilt by a Franciscan monastery.

More immediately evocative – especially to students of English history – are the remains of the imperial forts. Head past the Hotel Issa and up the headland to the ruins of the **Wellington Fort**, and on further to the even more dilapidated **King George III Fort**.

Vis has two hotels, the **Issa** (tel: 021 711 224; fax: 021 711 740) and the **Tamaris** (tel: 021 711 350; fax: 021 711 349). Both establishments are priced identically, with doubles at around €60, and while the 27 rooms at the older Tamaris, in the middle of town, are considerably nicer than the 130-odd at the newer Issa, the latter does have the advantage of being right on the beach. Both hotels are closed from the end of October to the beginning of May; in the shoulder months, off-season, the price of doubles plummets to a very reasonable €35 – about the same as you'd expect to pay for a private room in town (available through the Ionios agency (tel/fax: 021 711 532).

The town's best restaurant is unquestionably the rather swanky **Villa Kaliopa**, situated in the gardens of the fine 16th-century Renaissance Garibaldi Palace – it's pricey, but excellent, and increasingly popular with well-heeled Italians. Plainer and more inexpensive fare is available at half a dozen other restaurants and pizzerias.

The Vis tourist office (tel: 021 717 017; fax: 021 717 018; www.tz-vis.hr) has some local information and maps, while Ionios is the place to go to rent bikes and scooters – a wonderful way of seeing the island.

Komiža and Biševo

Komiža, at the other end of the island, is a strong rival for Vis. Set under the bulk of Hum Mountain (587m), the town stretches in a lovely palm-studded sweep round the bay, and has plenty of appealingly run-down 16th- and 17th-century houses, as well as a fine 16th-century Venetian fortress, dominating one end of the harbour.

Behind the town, up the hill, is the austere fortified Benedictine monastery of St Nicholas. On the saint's feast day, December 6, the local fishermen drag a fishing boat up here and then set fire to it, in a display which has nothing whatsoever to do with pagan rites, really.

Komiža's tourist office (tel/fax: 021 713 455) can fill you in on local sights, while Srebrna Tours (tel: 021 713 668; fax: 021 717 840) and Darlić & Darlić (tel: 021 713 760; fax: 021 713 206) have private rooms for around €30. The town's only hotel, the **Biševo** (tel: 021 713 095; fax: 021 713 098), has a handful of pleasant rooms overlooking a pebble beach, and is open all year round. High-season doubles go for €80, but from October to May you pay under €43, an absolute snip.

Eating and drinking go on around Komiža's attractive main square, Škor, which is home to a handful of bars, cafés and restaurants.

No trip to Vis seems to be complete without the obligatory visit to **Modra Špilja**, on the island of Biševo, 5km southwest of Vis (the island is now uninhabited, though families still tend the vines here, travelling back and forth by boat). And indeed, if you get there at the right time of day (between 11.00 and midday), and you have a moment in the cave to yourself, then it is surely one of the most beautiful sights on the planet. Sunlight filters down through the water and reflects off the pale sea-floor, giving a vibrant blue and turquoise shimmer to the cave. It's an absolutely incredible place to swim, especially if you've brought along a snorkel and mask.

Unfortunately, that's not the experience most people have. Out of season, access to the cave is often made impossible by choppy seas, while in July and August, on calm days, the cave gets almost as crowded as its namesake on Capri, and you'll be briskly ferried out to make room for the next boatload coming in.

The cave was discovered – and the entrance enlarged to allow boats in and out – in the 1880s. You can access the cave most easily via an excursion from either Vis or Komiža, though you can also easily charter your own boat. If you go, make sure you're wearing swimmers, and have a snorkel and mask if at all possible – even if your time in the cave is short you should have time for a quick dip. Excursions usually then take you on to one of Biševo's many coves and beaches, and often feature the obligatory fish picnic.

Finally, spare a thought while you're here for the terribly endangered Mediterranean Monk Seal – the islet of Brusnik, off to the west, near Svetac, is one of the very few places where it's recently been sighted. Brusnik is also home to a charming endemic species of black lizard, *Podarcis melisellensis melisellensis*.

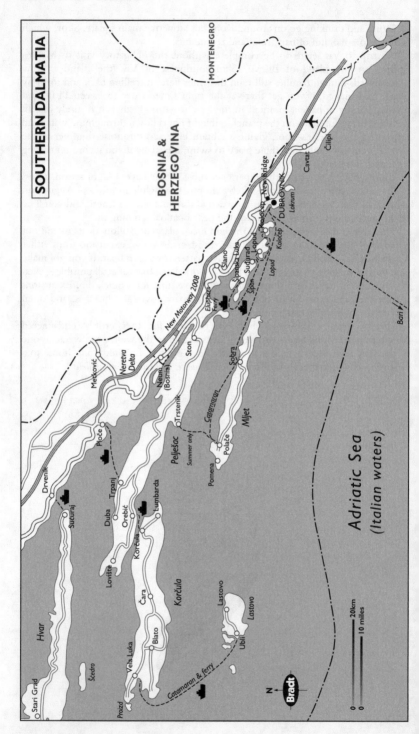

SOUTHERN DALMATIA

Southern Dalmatia

The biggest draw in southern Dalmatia is the extraordinary walled-city of **Dubrovnik**, but the area is unusually rich in other sights as well, and in spite of the Adriatic's cleanest waters, there are fewer resorts and package destinations here than further north. The islands range from the quiet **Elaphites** (**Koločep**, **Lopud** and **Šipan**) and the near-perfection of **Mljet** (most of which is a national park), to popular **Korčula**, remote **Lastovo**, and Dubrovnik's own back garden, **Lokrum**. Onshore there's the long, straggly wine-growing peninsula of **Pelješac**, with oyster-rich **Ston** at its base, while against the Bosnian border you'll find the wetlands of the **Neretva Delta**.

The telephone code across the whole of southern Dalmatia is 020 (+385 20 from abroad).

DUBROVNIK

Dubrovnik is an extraordinary place. Vast walls, up to 25m tall, come complete with fortresses, towers, crenellations and an ancient footpath along the entire 2km extent. The walls encircle an incredible stone-built red-roofed city, which juts out into the clearest, cleanest blue-green waters of the Adriatic. The streets are paved with time-polished pale marble, with the town's harmony owing as much to the 17th-century rebuilding programme following the Great Earthquake in 1667 as it does to Dubrovnik's remarkable history, stretching back well over 1,000 years.

Of course Byron's 'Pearl of the Adriatic' is no secret, and in 2003 over 300,000 people stayed at least one night here. Even more came in for the day, on a record 582 cruise ships. Nevertheless the city copes admirably with the influxes, and you'll find a place full of cheerful cafés, bars and restaurants, wonderful architecture, intriguing museums, atmospheric churches and a world-famous summer festival. The entire old city is a UNESCO World Heritage Site.

As if that weren't enough, Dubrovnik is blessed with an especially kind climate. Winter daily maximums rarely fall below 12°C, the sun shines reliably right through the summer, and there are plenty of beaches, with swimming popular from May to October. The city even has its own perfect forested island, Lokrum, just a few hundred metres offshore.

History

Although some Roman, Illyrian and early-Christian remains have been found in Dubrovnik, it was only at the beginning of the 7th century that the area was permanently settled. Survivors from the Roman colony at Salona (near Split), which had been taken over by avaricious Avars, teamed up with the remnants of the colony at Epidaurus (now Cavtat), which had been ravaged by Slavs, and settled on the rocky outcrop which is now the part of the old town south of

A NOTE ON CROSSING BOSNIA & HERZEGOVINA

Southern Dalmatia is cut off from the rest of Croatia by Bosnia's land corridor to the sea, and while for most visitors (see page 29 for visa requirements) this isn't a problem, for some nationals it will imply getting a Bosnian visa – which is a serious hassle if this is all you need it for (it's not unknown for your passport to be sent to Sarajevo). If you're travelling by bus and don't plan on stopping in Bosnia, then you don't really need a visa, however, as you can plead your transit case with the guards who board the bus – in the worst case you'll have to go around, via Pelješac (see below), but I've never known the guards to insist on this.

If you're driving yourself, however, you do in theory need a visa (I have met people who've winged it successfully, but it's not recommended). Safer by far, and completely legitimate, is to get round the Bosnian section of road altogether by taking a ferry from Ploče to Trpanj (on Pelješac) and continuing south from there – though it does add at least a couple of hours to your journey. By the time the motorway is open (scheduled for 2008) this particular hassle should be a thing of the past.

Stradun. Doubtless scarred by their recent experiences, they started building fortifications right away – and kept on doing so until the 16th century. They called their town Ragusa, which first shows up in print in 667.

Slavs, meanwhile, settled on the lower slopes of Mount Srđ, across the marshy channel which would become Stradun. Over the centuries the populations mixed, the channel was filled in, and the city walls grew to encompass both parts of the settlement. But even today there's a clear distinction between the steep narrow streets leading uphill from Stradun to the north and the palaces and churches and open squares which characterise the rest of the city to the south. To their dying day (which we'll get to in a little while) Ragusan patricians insisted they could trace their lineage back to Roman rather than Slav ancestors.

After switching between Byzantium and Venice and back again, and even throwing in its lot with the Normans on a couple of occasions at the end of the 11th century, Ragusa finally recognised that Venice was top dog in the Adriatic in 1205, and remained under Venetian sovereignty until 1358. It nonetheless kept its own currency and continued to develop its own institutions and culture.

Ragusa was also becoming a trading state of increasing importance, capitalising on its fortunate position between north and south and east and west. By the early 13th century favourable trading agreements were in place with many of the Italian city states and far inland into the Balkans. Over the years it developed a strong seafaring tradition, with trade routes eventually established all the way to Spain, Portugal and England. Dubrovnik sailors were even on board Columbus's ships when they discovered the West Indies in 1492.

Back at home the early 14th century saw a number of important developments. After a huge fire destroyed most of the city in 1296, a new urban plan was developed. Dominicans and Franciscans were allowed inside the city walls for the first time, on condition that they defended the two main land gates at either end of Stradun – where you'll still find their respective monasteries and churches today.

The city's first hospital was inaugurated in 1347, but all too quickly followed in 1348 by a seriously nasty dose of the plague, which reduced the population by 8,000. Soon, however, Dubrovnik was ready for its '**Golden Age**', which began when it escaped Venice's grasp in 1358 by formally becoming part of the

Hungarian–Croatian kingdom. In exchange for paying Hungary 500 ducats a year, however, and providing armed forces when called upon to do so, the republic was allowed to do pretty much whatever it liked.

The first thing it liked to do, it seemed, was to frogmarch the Venetian rector, Marco Saranzo, off on to his state galley, thereby kicking off the best part of 500 years of tension between the two republics – a situation only resolved when Napoleon dissolved *La Serenissima* in 1797.

In 1365, just seven years after sorting things out with Hungary, Dubrovnik signed a treaty with Sultan Murat I – again with a 500-ducat-per-year price tag – which allowed the republic free-trading status across the whole of the occupied territories of the Ottoman Empire. By monopolising large chunks of the trade to and from the interior, Dubrovnik became hugely wealthy. Dubrovnik had freedom, liberty and independence – but it was Libertas (the republic's long-standing motto) bought with gold.

With money came territory, and during the Golden Age Dubrovnik's lands stretched from the town of Neum to the north (now in Bosnia) all the way to Sutorina, on the Bay of Kotor, to the south (now in Montenegro), a distance of around 120km. It included the Elaphite Islands (Koločep, Lopud and Šipan), the islands of Mljet and Lastovo, and the Pelješac peninsula.

At the beginning of the 15th century the remaining wooden houses in the town were demolished and rebuilt in stone. This was not so much for aesthetic reasons as to prevent fires from spreading. With many potential enemies, Dubrovnik had large stockpiles of munitions, and they had an unfortunate habit of going off – the Rector's Palace was destroyed by fire and explosions twice within a generation, in 1435 and then again in 1463.

The 15th century also saw Dubrovnik flourishing as a haven of liberalism. It offered asylum to refugees, including Jews, at times when many other cities turned them away at the gate. In 1416 slavery was definitively abolished, over 400 years ahead of Britain (1833) and America (1863). Many slaves subsequently had their freedom bought for them by Ragusan nobles. A public health service was in place

WHAT'S IN A NAME?

For most of its extensive history – right from the 7th century through to 1918, in fact – Dubrovnik was known as Ragusa. The name was changed to Dubrovnik (according to Rebecca West, at least) only because Ragusa sounded too Italian by half.

The truth, as usual, is somewhat more complicated. Dubrovnik was originally not one place but two, divided by what's now the main street, Stradun. On the seaward side, which was originally almost an island, was Ragusa, which was populated by people of Roman origin. On the landward side, populated by Slavs, was Dubrovnik. Given that the nobles all came (or claimed to come) from Roman stock, Ragusa was the name which stuck – until the city was incorporated into the newly founded Kingdom of Serbs, Croats and Slovenes after World War I.

The name Ragusa is thought to be a corruption of the Greek word *lausa*, meaning rock, while the name Dubrovnik comes from the Croatian word for oak woods, *dubrava* – which were once plentiful on the hills above the town before being cut down and used to build Dubrovnik's impressive fleet of ships. (A fleet of ships which gave us another word, incidentally – *argosy*, a variant on the name Ragusa.)

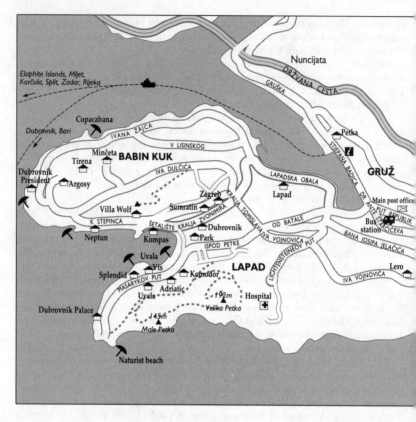

as early as 1432, while the principle of education for all was established three years later, along with one of Europe's first orphanages and a free retirement home for the poor and elderly (it's still running, but no longer free).

The republic's wealth was also put to good use in a major building programme. The city walls were reinforced and defensive fortresses and towers constructed along their length. Onofrio della Cava, a bright engineer and architect from Naples, spent the six years to 1444 putting in place a sophisticated water supply (including an 8km aqueduct) which still works today and powers the two Onofrio Fountains on Stradun. In 1468 Stradun itself was repaved with marble, and in 1516 work began on the Customs House (formerly called the Divona and now known as the Sponza Palace).

Unfortunately an earthquake destroyed most of the city in 1520, and the plague returned in force in 1528, leaving 20,000 dead.

By the end of the 1520s, the Turks had pretty much defeated Hungary, and Dubrovnik was quick to change its allegiance from the Hungarian king to the Turkish sultan – now agreeing to pay an annual tribute of 12,500 ducats to keep the peace (that's inflation for you). The money was taken to the Sublime Porte every two years by envoys who then had to spend the next two years waiting there as effective hostages until they were relieved by the next cash-laden delegation.

In 1588 Dubrovnik joined the Spanish in their 'Invincible Armada' and lost a dozen of its finest ships. As a result, trade with Britain was interrupted for the best part of two centuries. The battle neatly marks the beginning of the long, slow

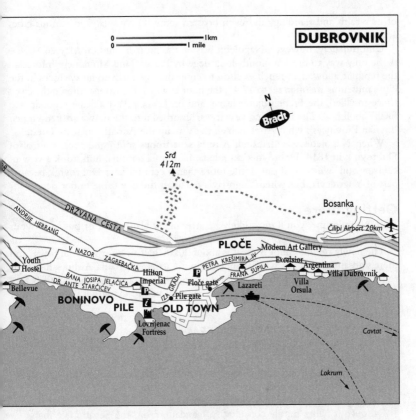

decline of the republic. New trade routes across the Atlantic made Britain, Spain and Portugal into wealthy nations, and Mediterranean shipping was never to regain its former importance.

Real disaster didn't strike, however, until 08.00 on April 6 1667, the Saturday before Easter, when a massive earthquake destroyed Dubrovnik. More than 5,000 people – including the rector, the entire Minor Council and more than half the Great Council – were killed. Only the Sponza Palace, the two monasteries, the bottom half of the Rector's Palace and the Revelin Fortress were left standing.

Seizing his opportunity, the Turkish sultan asked for a vast ransom to be paid if Dubrovnik wanted its freedom to continue as before. A delegation was sent in 1673 to the Porte to…well, 'talk turkey' with the Turks. Among the party were Nikola Bono and Marojica Koboga. Bono was to die in prison, but after the Turks were defeated at Vienna in 1683, Koboga came home to a hero's welcome. Dubrovnik had got away without paying the ransom, and was still free. It consolidated its position in 1699 by letting the Turks have chunks of land at either end of its territories – which is why today Neum is in Bosnia not Croatia, and Sutorina is in Montenegro. This meant that potential attacks from Venice could now only come from the sea and not overland.

Although Dubrovnik would never regain its former glories, the massive programme of rebuilding which went on through the early 18th century was to deliver the harmonious city you see today. Things started to look up for the republic, and by the end of the 18th century it had regained a considerable amount of its wealth and standing, and even boasted some 80 consulates in various cities across the continent.

Unfortunately, however, Napoleon was on the horizon, and on May 26 1806 – as the only way to break a month-long siege by Russian and Montenegrin forces – the republic allowed a French garrison to enter the town. (Even now, clocks in the city's museums are often set to 17.45, the hour at which the troops entered the city.) Once installed, the French didn't leave, and on January 31 1808 the republic was finally abolished. The following year it was absorbed into the newly created French 'Illyrian Provinces', which stretched all the way up the Adriatic coast to Trieste.

When Napoleon was defeated, Austria sent troops south and took control of Dubrovnik in 1814. Dubrovnik's noble families, in a terminal huff, took a vow of celibacy and swiftly died out. Little more than a century later Dubrovnik became part of Yugoslavia, but when Yugoslavia fell apart the city came under siege.

Getting there

With no train line, you'll most likely be arriving by plane, boat or bus, or in your own car.

The newly rebuilt Čilipi Airport is about 20km/half an hour south of town, and there's an airport shuttle which coincides with arriving Croatia Airlines flights. It returns to the airport from the Dubrovnik bus station an hour and a half before Croatia Airlines departures, and costs 25 kuna. If you're flying with anyone other

RAGUSA'S POLITICAL SYSTEM

Ragusa's political system was a variant on that of its rival Venice, though it was somewhat more subtle and complex. The main governing body was the Great Council, which consisted of all the male nobles over the age of 20; their main function was to elect the head of state, the rector, and supervise the Senate. The Senate comprised 45 nobles over the age of 40, though it had a purely consultative mandate. From the Senate, five men over the age of 50 were given a one-year term by the Great Council as Proveditores, keepers of the legal statutes and the constitution.

Executive power was wielded by the Minor Council, which consisted of 11 nobles appointed by the rector, with the youngest taking on the role of Foreign Minister. The rector had a term of office of just one month, during which he lived alone in the Rector's Palace, separated from his family and the rest of society. He was only allowed to leave the palace on state business or to attend church, and couldn't be re-elected within two years. In spite of all these restrictions he was merely a figurehead, wielding no power.

The political system was designed to concentrate power into the hands of a trusted few – in the 15th century there were only 33 noble families – but to avoid any one person or family being able to dominate, and for centuries it worked remarkably effectively.

The class system was rigidly enforced. Inter-marriage between classes was forbidden and social relations between them strongly discouraged – though that doesn't seem to have been necessary, given the divisions even within classes. The nobles defined themselves as Salamancans or Sorbonnais, named after the respective Spanish and French universities, with the former sympathetic to Spanish Absolutism and the latter with a liberal Francophile outlook. Apparently hostility was such that members of the two factions couldn't even bring themselves to greet one another in the street.

THE SIEGE OF DUBROVNIK

In October 1991, with the war in full flow, the Yugoslav army laid siege to Dubrovnik, shutting off the water and electricity supplies, and raining shells down into the heart of the old town from air, land and sea.

The quick capitulation the Serbs expected never happened, mainly because of determined resistance, but at least in part because Onofrio's fountains – supplied by 15th-century plumbing – continued to function throughout the siege. Nevertheless, for three months there was no water for anything other than drinking, and no electricity or telephone service at all.

More than 100 civilians lost their lives in Dubrovnik, either when their houses were bombed or by snipers up in the hills, looking straight down Stradun – people simply didn't believe they were going to be shot in the sunny streets of Dubrovnik's old town. On one day alone (December 6 1991) the Serbs shelled the city from 05.00 to 16.10 with only a 15-minute break. In all the siege lasted from October 1991 to August 1992, though a cease-fire of sorts was in force at the beginning of 1992.

The material damage caused was enormous, with 70% of the old town's 800 houses sustaining direct hits, and more than 50 shells landing on Stradun alone. Many churches and monuments were targeted in spite of being clearly marked with UNESCO flags.

Dubrovnik's newly refurbished airport was completely destroyed, with the brand-new equipment being looted and taken back to Montenegro and on to Belgrade. Many people moved out, and not all have moved back – the old town's population, at 4,000, is still around 20% less than it was in 1990.

The damage sustained to Dubrovnik's reputation as a holiday destination was incomparably worse, and it took a full decade to bring back just half the visitors.

Yet Dubrovnik has made a truly heroic recovery from the war. Today, beyond a few pock-marked buildings, and acres of new tiles on the roofs, you'd never know there had been a terrible siege just a decade ago. (Ironically, some of the old tiles pulled off roofs during renovations were sent to villages further north to repair war damage there – only to be caught in the 1996 earthquake which destroyed much of Slano and Ston, at the base of the Pelješac peninsula.)

The only real reminder that the war happened at all – beyond the psychological scars – are the multi-lingual signs at each entrance to the old town, showing the 'City Map of Damages caused by the aggression on Dubrovnik by the Yugoslav Army, Serbs and Montenegrins, 1991–1992'.

Some justice has been done – in March 2004 a retired Yugoslav navy admiral, Miodrag Jokic, was sentenced to seven years in prison at The Hague for his part in shelling Dubrovnik.

than Croatia Airlines, however, then you'll need to take a taxi, which costs around 220 kuna if the meter's on, or 200 kuna cash in hand – if the meter's off make sure you've agreed and understood the fare with the driver before you set off.

All ferries come in to the city's port, Gruž, which is about 500m north of the bus station, itself just over 2km north of the old town (catch a local bus). There are also an increasing number of cruises featuring Dubrovnik; these too will bring you into Gruž harbour.

Long-distance buses come straight to the bus station, past the port. If you're coming from the north you'll have driven over the fabulous, spanking-new suspension bridge over the Dubrovačka Rijeka inlet, which cuts a welcome 15km off the journey. From one side you'll notice it labelled as the Tuđman Bridge, while from the other it's the Dubrovnik Bridge – telling you something useful about local politics. There's one direct bus a day from Frankfurt, Trieste and Sarajevo, seven buses a day from Zagreb, and 15 from Split. The bus station has Dubrovnik's only left-luggage facility, open from 04.30 to 21.00 daily.

If you're coming in by car, be warned that parking in Dubrovnik can be both a problem and expensive. Hotel car parks tend to be over-flowing, while street parking, especially in summer, is a non-starter. There are two main car parks for the old town, one at the Pile gate (10 kuna an hour) and the other alongside the north wall (5 kuna an hour), though both fill up fast. There's a larger car park at Gruž harbour (5 kuna an hour), however, which also offers a long-term rate of 25 kuna a day.

If you park illegally you can definitely expect your car to be towed away by the ruthlessly efficient 'Sanitat Dubrovnik' tow away service. The number to call when this happens is 020 331 016, 24 hours a day, and the pound, where your car will have been taken, is on Lichtensteineov put, in Lapad. The nearest bus route is the #9; take it to the terminus (the hospital) and walk round to the left to find the top end of Lichtensteineov put.

Getting around

Flat-fare Libertas buses cover the whole of Dubrovnik and most run from 05.00 to midnight. Tickets can be bought in advance from newspaper kiosks at 8 kuna apiece, or on the bus for 10 kuna – and you'll be expected to have the right money for all except the bus to Cavtat.

The main bus routes used by visitors are:

#1A and #1B – from Pile to the bus station and on to Gruž; about every half-hour.

#3 – from Pile to Gruž; about once an hour.

#4 – from Pile to Lapad, passing many of the main hotels and terminating at the newly reopened Dubrovnik Palace; two to three times an hour.

#5 – from Pile to the Lapad post office and on to the Hotel Neptun on Babin Kuk; about once an hour. The return route goes round the one-way system, arriving at the Ploče gate and then going round behind the old town walls to Pile.

#6 – from Pile to the bus station, then up to the Lapad post office, terminating at the Dubrovnik President Hotel on Babin Kuk; about four times an hour.

#7B – from Gruž to the bus station and then up towards Lapad, passing the Hotel Bellevue and the Lapad post office before terminating at the Dubrovnik President Hotel on Babin Kuk; about once an hour.

#8 – from Pile to the bus station, then on to Gruž where it goes into a one-way system which ends by coming down the hill past the Ploče hotels to the Ploče gate, and round behind the old town walls to Pile; two to three times an hour, but less frequently at weekends.

#9 – from the bus station up to the Lapad post office and on to the hospital before taking a shorter return route to the bus station; about once an hour.

#10 – from the bus station to Cavtat; about once an hour. The fare to Cavtat is 12 kuna and you pay on the bus.

Notwithstanding the excellent local buses, Dubrovnik also has plenty of **taxis**. There are five taxi stands, at Pile, Ploče, Gruž, the bus station and Lapad (on Kralja Tomislava, just before the Lapad post office). You can also call taxis from any of the main hotels.

Tourist information

The main official tourist information office is 200m up the hill from the Pile gate, on the left-hand side, at Ante Starčićeva 7 (tel/fax: 020 323 887; www.tzdubrovnik.hr), which dishes out maps and various leaflets and can help you with booking concert tickets etc. The office handily co-locates with an Internet café. There's been talk for years of the main office moving inside the old town walls, but at the time of writing it was still just talk. There are two smaller, subsidiary tourist offices, one actually in the old town, at Miha Pracata (the eighth street on the right off Stradun, coming from Pile) and the other at Gruž, next door to the Jadrolinija ticket office.

You can also usually pick up maps and flyers from the various local tourist operators and agencies, though of late – particularly when a cruise ship arrives – they've taken to charging a token fee for maps.

Where to stay

Dubrovnik's long been popular with visitors, with the first proper accommodation for them opening in 1347, and private rooms coming on stream in the second half of the 14th century. The Grand Hotel Imperial, with 70 rooms just up from the Pile gate, opened for business in 1897, but shut its doors again with the war in 1991. At the time of writing renovations were nearly complete and it should be reopening in 2005, as the **Hilton Imperial**.

During the siege of Dubrovnik (see page 265) the city lost around half of its total hotel stock, with damage being caused first by bombs and then by refugees flooding in afterwards. Indeed, if tourist numbers in 2003 were still a third below their 1990 levels, that's partly because of an accommodation shortage. The scene now, however, is improving fast, with most of the affected hotels restored and reopened.

Your main accommodation options in Dubrovnik are hotels or private rooms – of which there is a plentiful and growing supply. There's also a youth hostel and a solitary campsite (see below). Private rooms offer the best value for money, but if you're in the mood to splash out there's certainly plenty of choice at the top end of the market too.

Hotel accommodation fills up fast in summer, so it's definitely recommended that you reserve well ahead of time, and confirm by fax. Private rooms can be booked on the fly, though those in the best locations fill up well in advance.

Hotels

Dubrovnik has just two hotels in the old town; the rest are distributed around the smart suburb of Ploče just south of the old town, on the Lapad and Babin Kuk peninsulas, a few kilometres away, and in the port area of Gruž.

If you're coming to Dubrovnik out of season, shop around for serious reductions at almost all the hotels listed here – but especially those in Lapad and on Babin Kuk.

In the old town

Until recently, accommodation in the old town itself was limited to a handful of private rooms, but in 2003 two boutique hotels opened up for business. Bear in mind if you stay here that it can be stifling hot in summer, and views will be minimal – but on the other hand there's atmosphere in spades to be had from being inside the old walls.

Pučić Palace ★★★★★ Od Puča 1; tel: 020 326 200; fax: 020 326 323; www.thepucicpalace.com. Fabulously located on the corner of Gundulićeva poljana, the Pučić Palace consists of just 19 rooms in a luxuriously refurbished noble's home. You

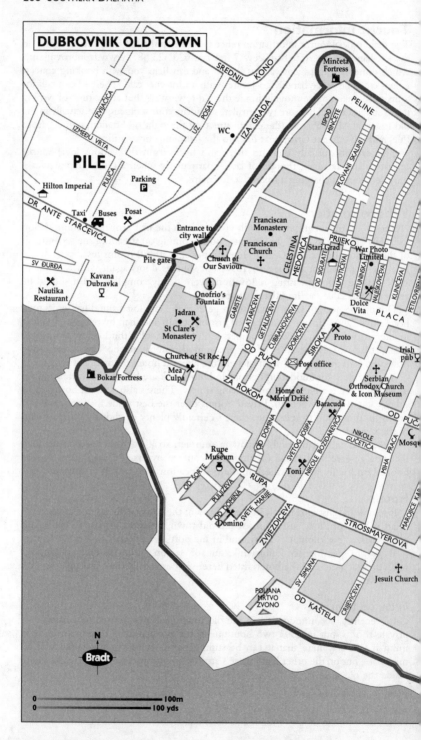

DUBROVNIK OLD TOWN

SREDNJI KONO

Minčeta Fortress

PELINE

IZVIJAČICA

UZ POSAT

IZA GRADA

ISPOD MINČETE

IZMEĐU VRTA

PULIĆA

WC

PILE

PLOVANI SKALINI

Hilton Imperial

Parking P

DR ANTE STARČEVIĆA

Taxi Buses Posat

Entrance to city walls

Franciscan Monastery

PRIJEKO

SV ĐURĐA

Pile gate

Church of Our Saviour

Franciscan Church

CELESTINA

MEDOVIĆA

OD SIGURATE

Stari Grad

PALMOTIĆEVA

War Photo Limited

ANTUNINSKA

KUNIČEVA

NALJEŠKOVIĆEVA

PETILOVRIJENCI

Nautika Restaurant

Kavana Dubravka

Onofrio's Fountain

GARIŠTE

ZLATARIĆEVA

GETALDIĆEVA

CUBRANOVIĆEVA

ĐORĐIĆEVA

Dolce Vita

PLACA

Jadran

St Clare's Monastery

OD PUČA

ŠIROKA

Proto

Irish pub

Bokar Fortress

Church of St Roc

Mea Culpa

ZA ROKOM

Post office

Serbian Orthodox Church & Icon Museum

OD PUČA

Home of Marin Držić

Baracuda

OD DOMINA

SVETOG JOSPA

NIKOLE BOŽIDAREVIĆA

NIKOLE GUČETIĆA

MIHA PRAČA

Mosqu

Rupe Museum

OD RUPA

Toni

MAROJICE KAB

OD ŠORTE

PULIZEVA

OD DOMINA

SVETE MARIJE

Domino

ZVIJEZDIĆEVA

STROSSMAYEROVA

SV SIMUNA

CRIJEVIĆEVA

Jesuit Church

POLJANA MRTVO ZVONO

OD KAŠTELA

N

Bradt

0 ——— 100m
0 ——— 100 yds

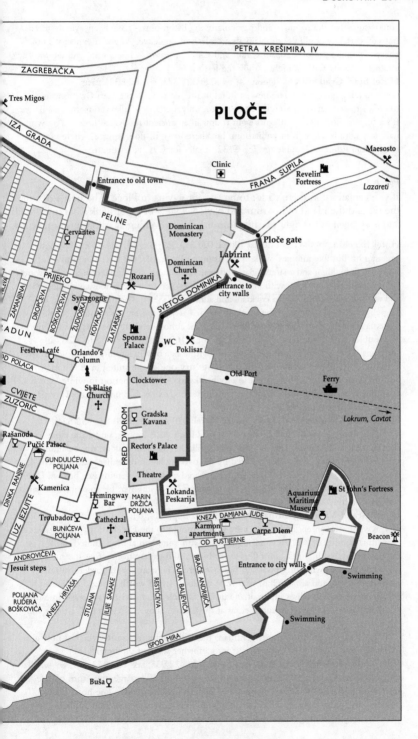

could argue that the rooms – and particularly the bathrooms – have been over-restored, but you certainly couldn't complain about a lack of opulence. As you'd expect it's not cheap – doubles go for €265 in winter and €465 in season, while a suite will set you back a rather dizzying €950 a night during the festival.

Hotel Stari Grad ★★★ Od Sigurate 4; tel: 020 321 373; fax: 020 321 256; www.hotelstarigrad.com. The newest hotel in the old town is the Stari Grad (meaning 'old town'), situated between Stradun and Prijeko, only a couple of alleys in from the Pile gate. It's a tiny establishment, with just eight rooms in an ancient renovated house. You won't have any kind of view from your room, but there is a fifth-floor terrace, where you can breakfast in summer. Doubles go for €132, singles for €91, year-round.

Ploče

If you can afford it, there's a lot to be said for staying in Ploče. The hotels overlook the sea and the island of Lokrum and have *that* view of Dubrovnik's old town walls and port. Seen in the light of early morning or late evening, it's a prospect to die for.

Hotel Excelsior ★★★★★ Frana Supila 12; tel: 020 353 353; fax: 020 414 214; www.hotel-excelsior.hr. Just five minutes' walk uphill from the Ploče gate, the Excelsior consists of a stone 1920s building and a largish glass-and-concrete annexe, for a total of nearly 200 rooms. It's unashamedly luxurious, with private beach, fitness centre, a big indoor swimming pool and terraces where you can sip cocktails and admire the views. The main restaurant, the Zagreb – which also serves as the breakfast room – is a bit too big for comfort, but the Taverna Rustica, set apart from the hotel, has great atmosphere and good regional cuisine.

Doubles with those incredible views go for €169 in winter, rising to €269 in summer; while for €319 you get a double with a balcony in summer (well worth the extra money). If you really want to splash out, try one of the suites, at €339 in winter and €589 in summer. There are also city breaks for €289 per person in winter and €329 in summer, comprising three nights in a room with sea view, a dinner at the Taverna Rustica and airport transfers.

Hotel Villa Orsula ★★★★★ Frana Supila 14; tel: 020 440 555; 020 fax: 432 524; www.hoteli-argentina.hr. Just 150m up the road from the Excelsior, under the same management as (and connected to) the Grand Villa Argentina next door, this beautifully restored 1920s villa is somewhat dwarfed by the two big hotels on either side of it. The 12 rooms, though, are delightful. All facilities are shared with the Argentina (see below). Double rooms with a sea view go for €210 in winter and €270 in summer; for an extra €20 you can get a balcony as well.

Hotel Grand Villa Argentina ★ ★ ★ ★ ★ Frana Supila 14; tel: 020 440 555; fax: 020 432 524; www.hoteli-argentina.hr. In a very similar mould to the Excelsior, the Atlas-owned Argentina consists of a 1920s stone-built hotel with a modern annexe grafted on. It was entirely renovated in 2002, and offers everything you'd expect from a five-star hotel, including a small swimming pool and fitness centre. There are lovely gardens running down to the sea, and almost 2km of private beach. It's well worth trying the Caravelle restaurant which specialises in Croatian cuisine. Double rooms with sea views come in at €207 in winter and €262 in summer; as at the Orsula, above, an extra €20 a night will get you a balcony.

Further up the hill from the Argentina is the **Villa Scheherazade**, which is now also owned by Atlas, who plan to convert it into a further wing of the hotel.

Villa Dubrovnik ★★★ Vlaha Bukovaca 6; tel: 020 422 933; fax: 020 423 465; www.villa-dubrovnik.hr. Another 600m along the coast beyond the Villa Argentina (turn off the main road just after the Villa Scheherazade) is the Villa Dubrovnik. The hotel is in terraces, dropping down to the rocky shoreline. Public areas are tastefully modern, light and airy, and the dining room and bar have gorgeous views back to the old town. If it's considerably less formal and stuffy than the five-star hotels, it's no less pricey. It has no swimming pool, but does have its own rocky beaches and a boat to take you into the old town, as well as a lovely outdoor area. Double rooms go from €180 in winter to €264 in summer, while suites come in at €260 in winter and €420 in summer.

Lapad, Babin Kuk and Gruž

Most of Dubrovnik's accommodation is spread out around the Lapad and Babin Kuk peninsulas, and mainly caters to package tours. It has the advantage of being away from the bustle, and most of the hotels have access to a beach, but you may find yourself further away from the old town than you wish to be. That said, it's only a matter of 5km from the furthest point on Lapad to the old town, and there are regular buses (see page 266). By taxi you're looking at a 10–20-minute ride, depending on the hotel location and traffic density.

Hotel Dubrovnik Palace ★★★★ Masarykov put 20; tel: 020 437 288; fax: 020 437 285; www.dubrovnikpalace.hr. Situated at the end of the Lapad headland, this 320-room, 30,000m^2 complex boasts three outdoor swimming pools, rocky beaches and a diving centre, along with indoor pools, two restaurants, 11 bars and a jazz club. Every room has a balcony and a sea view, and behind the hotel are paths up into the woods leading to stone belvederes with views out to sea. Double rooms go from €160 in winter to €250 in peak season.

Hotel Dubrovnik President ★★★★ Iva Dulčića 39; tel: 020 441 100; fax: 020 435 600; www.babinkuk.com. In a similar vein to the Dubrovnik Palace the Dubrovnik President dominates the Babin Kuk headland. All 165 rooms have a balcony and a view out across the sea to the Elaphite Islands, and there's a fairly large beach area. It's unashamed upmarket package-tour territory, but the location is excellent and the atmosphere cheerful. Prices range from €128 for a double in winter to €238 for the same room in summer.

Hotel Argosy ★★★ Iva Dulčića 41; tel: 020 446 100; fax: 020 435 578; www.babinkuk.com. Behind the President is the Argosy, a 300-room hotel which is a step down in both facilities and price, though it still has access to the beach and tennis courts etc, and boasts a decent-sized outdoor swimming pool. Winter rates for sea-view doubles come in at €80 per night rising to €160 in peak season.

Hotel Minčeta ★★★ Iva Dulčića 18; tel: 020 447 100; fax: 020 447 603; www.babinkuk.com. Further into the Babin Kuk headland, this sprawling four-storey building houses some 300 rooms, and is within reach of one of Dubrovnik's most popular beaches, the Copacabana, where you can indulge your taste for 'water polo, water skiing, scuba diving, wind surfing, and banana rides'. Double rooms with a sea view go for €54 in winter and €128 in summer.

Hotel Tirena ★★★ Iva Dulčića 22; tel: 020 445 100; fax: 020 445 602; www.babinkuk.com. Last of the four hotels in the complex is the Tirena, which is located between the Argosy and the Minčeta. Although only 28 of the Tirena's 190 rooms offer sea views, its main advantage is in being attached to the little local shopping centre. Double rooms with balconies go for €56 in winter and €116 in summer.

Hotel Neptun ★★★ Kardinala Stepinca 31; tel: 020 440 100; fax: 020 440 200; www.hotel-neptun.hr. In a great location on Babin Kuk, facing south and with rocky beaches and a couple of nice swimming pools, is the ten-storey Hotel Neptun. Its 150 rooms are bright and airy and most have sea views, with prices for doubles ranging from €76 in winter to €128 in summer.

Hotel Kompas ★★★ Šetalište Kralja Zvonimira 56; tel: 020 352 000; fax: 020 435 877; www.hotel-kompas.hr. Right down by the attractive Uvala Bay beach is the Kompas. Its 115 rooms mostly have sea views, and it has its own indoor pool, but the hotel has seen better days. It's now under the same management as the Excelsior and Dubrovnik Palace hotels, and plans are to upgrade it. Double rooms presently go for €74 in winter and €140 in high season.

Hotel Villa Wolff★★★★Nika I Meda Pučića 1; tel/fax: 020 435 353; www.villa-wolff.hr. Right next door to the Kompas is the Hotel Villa Wolff, a charming little boutique hotel, with just half a dozen rooms. It has its own terrace and Mediterranean garden, with a great view across the bay. Doubles go for €160 in winter and €230 in summer, while the suites come in at €330 a night.

Hotel Komodor★★★Masarykov put 5; tel: 020 437 301; fax: 020 437 401; www.hotelimaestreal.com. Across the bay from the Kompas, and firmly back on Lapad, is one of the peninsula's oldest hotels, the first in a line of five establishments run by the Maestral hotel chain. The Komodor was refurbished in 1999, and has 64 rooms and an outdoor swimming pool. Rates for a double room with a sea view and a balcony run from €78 in winter to €158 in summer.

Hotel Adriatic★★Masarykov put 9; tel: 020 437 302; fax: 020 437 402; www.hotelimaestreal.com. Just up the road is one of Dubrovnik's last-remaining two-star hotels. With 158 rooms priced at €58 for a sea-view double in winter and €108 in summer, and a beach just across the street, it's something of a bargain – and almost invariably fully booked.

Hotel Uvala★★★★Masarykov put 6; tel: 020 433 580; fax: 020 433 590; www.hotelimaestreal.com. Almost next door (notwithstanding the street number) is the newest addition to the group, which promises to pamper the guests in its 51 rooms, most of which have sea views. Doubles start at €128 a night in winter, rising to €218 in summer.

Hotel Vis★★★Masarykov put 4; 020 tel: 437 303; fax: 020 437 403; www.hotelimaestreal.com. Next up, but over on the seaward side of the street, is the Hotel Vis, whose main attraction is being right on its own decent-sized beach. The hotel has 136 rooms, and sea-view doubles go for €68 a night in winter and €138 a night in summer – but it's very often full up.

Hotel Splendid★★Masarykov put 10; tel: 020 437 304; fax: 020 437 404; www.hotelimaestreal.com. Last of the bunch is the Splendid, which like the Vis is right on the beach. It has 59 rooms, all with sea views and balconies, with doubles going for €88 in winter and €198 in summer.

Grand Hotel Park★★★Šetalište Kralja Zvonimira 39; tel: 020 434 444; fax: 020 434 885; www.grandhotel-park.hr. Situated between the Kompas and the Komodor, and set back from the Uvala beach, is the boxy Grand Hotel Park. Don't be fooled by the name; it has pretty good indoor and outdoor swimming pools, but it's not actually what you'd call grand, making the sea-view double-room price tag (apparently year-round) of €125 look pretty steep. It's being done up in phases, so some rooms are much better than others.

Hotel Dubrovnik★★★Šetalište Kralja Zvonimira bb; tel: 020 435 030; fax: 020 435 999; www.hoteldubrovnik.hr. Nicer by far is the Hotel Dubrovnik (not to be confused with the Villa Dubrovnik, the Dubrovnik Palace or the Dubrovnik President), all of 100m away, which may have neither indoor nor outdoor pools, but does have 15 clean, well-appointed rooms at very reasonable rates, and a welcoming staff. Double rooms go for €84 per night in winter and €110 in summer.

Hotel Sumratin★★Šetalište Kralja Zvonimira 31; tel: 020 436 333; fax: 020 436 006; no website. Further inland still is the 40-room Sumratin, which has neither sea views nor a swimming pool, but has the virtue of being simple, clean and great value for money, with doubles at €50 a night in winter and €81 a night in summer.

Hotel Zagreb★★Šetalište Kralja Zvonimira 27; tel: 020 436 146; fax: 020 436 006; no website. Almost next door to the Sumratin – and under the same management – is one of my favourite hotels in Dubrovnik. It's only two star, but it offers 22 clean doubles at knock-down prices in a lovely refurbished old building. Double rooms cost €53 in winter and €87 in summer.

Hotel Lapad★★★ Lapadska obala 37; tel: 020 432 922; fax: 020 424 782; www.hotel-lapad.hr. Situated down on the shore of Babin Kuk, facing Gruž harbour, the Lapad is based around a renovated old building with a modern annexe, and has nearly 200 rooms. There's a small pool, and the nearest beach is about 600m up the shore. Port-view doubles go for €74 in winter and €124 in summer – if you're here in July or August, ask for a room with air conditioning.

Hotel Petka★★★ Obala Stjepana Radića 38; tel: 020 410 500. fax: 020 410 127; www.croatia-vacation.com. Situated next to the main ferry landing in Gruž, the Petka features 104 rooms, all air conditioned, 64 of which have balconies giving on to the picturesque port. It's nothing fancy, but is only a short bus-ride away from the old town, and is excellent value – doubles with sea views and balconies go for €70 in winter and €92 in summer.

Hotel Lero★★★ Iva Vojnovića 14; tel: 020 341 333; fax: 020 332 133; www.hotel-lero.hr. Although entirely renovated in 1998, the Lero still retains something of its 1971 feel – and its location on a busy main road may put some people off. But it's well placed, and half of the 150 rooms have sea views. At €52 for a double in winter and €96 in summer it's good value; the half-board supplement is a veritable snip at €5 per person per day.

Hotel Bellevue★★ Pera Čingrije 7; tel: 020 413 306; fax: 020 414 058; www.hotel-bellevue.hr. In a wonderful location just 10–15 minutes' walk from the Pile gate and with its own private beach, the cliff-top Bellevue is one of Dubrovnik's great bargains. The rooms are pretty functional but many have their own balconies, and the prices are unbeatable at €66 in winter and €110 in summer for doubles with sea views. The hotel will in the fullness of time be upgraded to five star. If you're on a budget, enjoy it while you can.

Private rooms/apartments

Dubrovnik has a huge supply of private rooms available, and although they're more expensive here than most places in Croatia, they're still a good deal cheaper than the hotels, with most double rooms going for under €60 a night, even in summer.

The obvious way of finding a private room is through one of Dubrovnik's ubiquitous travel agencies, who will generally welcome your business. There are also a number of online resources if you want to book/look ahead – over 100 properties are listed at each of www.dubrovnik-apartments.com and www.dubrovnik-online.com/english/private_accommodation.php, for example.

If you come in by ferry or bus, you're likely to be assailed on arrival by offers of private rooms. These may work out cheaper (even in summer, some double rooms can be had for as little as €30) than anything you can get through travel agents, and unless the season's especially busy you can haggle – but check both the location and total price very carefully before accepting an offer.

Of the places I've stayed recently, the outstanding recommendation has to go to the **Karmen apartments** (tel: 020 323 433; mob 091 332 4106; email – the best way of reserving, for once – apartments@karmendu.tk), in an ancient stone building in a stunning location right on the old port. They're not cheap, at €100 a night in summer, but they're terrific value, with the rooms spacious, comfortably and tastefully furnished, and fully equipped with kitchen, satellite TV, CD player, etc.

Also highly recommended are the rooms run by **Kathy Ljubojević** (tel: 020 423 412; email: info@bedandbreakfast-dubrovnik.com). The house is high up in Ploče with a staggering view down on to the old town and across to Lokrum. There are four clean, tidy rooms which range from €55 to €80 in summer; the

balconies and those stupendous views. You can also buy great gifts
ere, too, as Niko is an expert maker of designer glassware.

...ellcampsite

Dubrovnik's **youth hostel** (tel: 020 423 241; fax: 020 412 592) is in a pretty good
location, about 15 minutes uphill towards the old town from the bus station, just
off Bana Jelačića. For single people on a budget it's as cheap as you'll find in
Dubrovnik, at €16 per person, though as you can imagine it's very hard to secure
one of the 80-odd places, especially in summer.

Dubrovnik also has a solitary campsite, managed by the Babin Kuk complex, but
unless you're absolutely desperate to get under canvas, I can't really recommend it
as an accommodation option for a short break. Having said that, if you are coming
here with your tent, the **Auto-Camp Solitudo** (tel: 020 448 686; fax: 020 448
688) offers 166 pitches, newly refurbished bathrooms and laundry areas.

Where to eat and drink

As you'd expect, Dubrovnik is brimming with places to eat, though with a few
exceptions there's often surprisingly little to distinguish one place from another.
Food in the old town tends universally towards grilled fish, meat and shellfish at
the upper end of the spectrum, and pizza and pasta dishes in the mid-tier
establishments.

Inside the walls

The busiest restaurant district is along Prijeko, but unfortunately it's managed to
get itself something of a bad reputation over the years – which hasn't been helped
by the touts along Stradun trying to entice in passing trade. While there's no doubt
good food to be had, there's a level of unscrupulousness here which probably
comes from knowing the chances are you won't be coming back, and tales of
poor-quality food and routine over-charging are legion. It's a pity, as the location
is perfect and the atmosphere ought to be first-rate. The one exception to the
Prijeko rule seems to be Rozarij, right at the eastern end of the street which serves
up unpretentious local Croatian fare in a nice setting.

Baracuda I Nikole Bošidarevićeva 10. One of the smallest yet cheeriest restaurants in
town, serving up tasty pizzas and very little else (there really isn't room). Situated just off
Od Puča, near the Serbian Orthodox Church. It has a slightly larger sister-establishment
on Lapad (see below). Inexpensive.
Domino Od Domina 3; tel: 020 323 103. At the top end of Od Domina, not far from
the inside of the sea wall, Domino prides itself on its great steaks, but also has decent fish
and seafood specialities, including a particularly good black (squid) risotto. The outside
terrace is enduringly popular. Mid range.
Jadran Paska Milečevića 1. The Jadran has a perfect location inside the old cloisters of the
former Convent of St Clare. The gorgeous setting is a triumph over the somewhat average
fare, but it's a lovely place to sit and while away an hour or two – especially if it's windy,
as it's a well-sheltered spot. Inexpensive to mid range.
Kamenica Gundulićeva poljana 8. Kamenica. A great place in a great location. It
specialises in seafood, and in particular oysters, which in 2004 went for a very reasonable 7
kuna a pop. The menu is short but excellent, with the frittura (whitebait) particularly
good. Highly recommended, so catch it while you can – there were rumblings in 2004
about lease renewals and possible closure. Inexpensive.
Labirint Svetog Dominika 2; tel: 020 322 222. Set into the city walls near the
Dominican Monastery, Labirint offers a top-notch restaurant as well as various bars,

terraces and a discreet nightclub. The fish soup – which goes for 10–20 kuna in most places – costs 45 kuna here (but is worth it), while pasta dishes come in at around 80 kuna. Mussels are expensive at 140 kuna, with mouth-watering scallops a much better deal at 180 kuna. Expect meat dishes to cost 150 to 200 kuna and wine to set you back around 200 kuna or more a bottle. Expensive; booking essential in season and on weekends.

Lokanda Peskarija Na Ponti. My favourite place in Dubrovnik, even if it does have one of the world's shortest menus – or perhaps because of it. Situated right on the old port, the establishment is tiny, with a bar downstairs and a handful of tables upstairs, though in fine weather it quickly spreads out across the quayside. The fried squid is unrivalled here, and the oysters – at 5 kuna apiece – are not just the cheapest but amongst the best in town. Inexpensive.

Mea Culpa Za Rokom 3. Owned by the same people as Lokanda Peskarija (see above), Mea Culpa is an unpretentious place at the other end of town, serving up terrific pizza. Tables spill out on to the street, and it's a popular place with locals and visitors alike, with draught Guinness on tap. Inexpensive.

Poklisar Ribarnica 1. Poklisar has a great location right on the old port, next to the fish market. It serves up the usual range of fish dishes, as well as reasonable pizzas – though you could argue that you're paying as much for the setting as for the food here. Claims to be open from 07.00 to midnight – and in high season that may well be true. Inexpensive (pizza)/mid range (fish).

Proto Široka 1; tel: 020 323 324. Proto is one of Dubrovnik's most famous landmarks, and makes a big deal about having been in business since 1886 and having had Edward VIII and Wallis Simpson to dinner in the 1930s. But in spite of the hype there's a lot to be said for both the fish and meat dishes here, which are probably as good as anywhere in town – and the upstairs terrace is always packed in summer. Expensive; worth reserving.

Rozarij Zlatarska 4. On the corner of Prijeko but with an address on Zlatarska, Rozarij breaks the Prijeko mould (see the introductory section, above), serving up unpretentious local Croatian fare in a nice setting near the Dominican Monastery. Inexpensive to mid range.

Toni Nikole Bošidarevićeva 14. Just a couple of doors up from the Baracuda I (see above) is Spaghetteria Toni. Check out the tasty – and vast – home-made lasagne or the various pasta dishes with seafood sauces. It's cheerful, informal, and highly popular with locals.

Snack bars and ice-cream

If you're on a tight budget – or just don't fancy sitting down for a meal – there are also a variety of snack bars and sandwich joints in town. Two of the best are near each other, towards the Pile end of Stradun. The first is the **Buffet Škola**, which is on Antuninska, on the left-hand side heading up towards Prijeko. Here you can get terrific home-made sandwiches filled with cheese or *pršut* for just 15 or 20 kuna. Across Stradun, in Široka, right by Proto (see above), is the **Fish Sandwich Bar**, which sells wonderful…well, fish sandwiches. Fillings include fried fish or mussels and prices range from 15 to 25 kuna. Both places are open – broadly speaking – from about 10.00 to 14.00 and 18.00 to 21.00.

Dubrovnik's also great for ice-cream. There are three main establishments in the old town. The best located, right by Onofrio's fountain, is perhaps predictably the least good of the three. Somewhat better is the place down at the other end of Stradun, on the right-hand side; but best of all is the **Dolce Vita**, on Nalješkovićeva, one of the streets between Stradun and Prijeko, which serves quite the tastiest and freshest ice-cream (and frozen yoghurt) in town.

Outside the old town walls

Right by the two main gates are two of Dubrovnik's more famous restaurants, Nautika at Pile and Maesosto at Ploče. Both, sadly, trade far too much on their reputations.

Baracuda II Ispod Petke 16. Up in the heart of Lapad you'll find Baracuda I's (see above) sister restaurant. It serves up perfectly acceptable pizzas and has considerably more space inside than its old-town partner, as well as an open rooftop terrace. Inexpensive.

Bistro Riva Lapadska Obala 20. Situated on Gruž harbour, but opposite the port, the Bistro Riva serves up a wide range of tasty dishes including good pizzas. The only pity is that the courtyard is closed in, blocking off what would be great views across the water. Inexpensive.

Casa Nika i Meda Pučića 1. Casa has a great location right on the waterfront at Uvala Bay. It only serves food in summer, and then more of the snack variety than the full meal, but it's an excellent place to sit. Inexpensive for food; mid range for drinks.

El Toro Ivo Vojnovića 5. Just up the road from the Hotel Bellevue, with a nice leafy high-up terrace, you'll find the Café Pizzeria El Toro, which is cheap and cheerful and serves up reasonable pizzas at a good price. Inexpensive.

Levanat Nika i Meda Pučića 15; tel: 020 432 352. With an unbeatable waterfront location on Babin Kuk, Levanat is secluded, upmarket, pricey, and altogether wonderful. It's easy to get to on foot by walking along the footpath which starts at Casa (see above) for about ten minutes, or from the Babin Kuk or Neptun hotels; otherwise you might want to consider getting a taxi, as it's quite a schlep from the old town. The menu focuses on excellent – and by Croatian standards – original fish dishes. You can also come here just for a drink. Expensive; reservations recommended (not least to check it's open).

Maesosto Put od Bosanke 4. Well-known and popular restaurant just outside the Ploče gate with a view across to the old town harbour. The fare is the traditional grilled meat and fish, but the place is (in this author's opinion) somewhat over-rated. Mid range.

Nautika Brsalje 3; tel: 020 442 573. For years the ritziest place in town, the Nautika has an excellent location, on the water, right outside the Pile gate, and a gorgeous pair of terraces overlooking the Bokar Fortress on the left and the Lovrijenac Fortress on the right, as well as smart dining rooms indoors. The food is excellent, as you'd expect for the price, and the service impeccable, but I've had reports of carelessly added-up bills, so check the sums assiduously. Expensive; reservations recommended.

Posat Uz Posat 1. Well located outside the Pile gate (just up and to the right) is the Konoba Posat, which has a large and leafy terrace. It's as good a place as any for grilled meats. Inexpensive to mid range.

Shanghai (or Šangaj, if you want the local spelling) Ante Starčićeva 25. About 200m beyond the main tourist office, on the same side of the street, you'll find one of Dubrovnik's few Chinese restaurants. The food is everything you'd expect, though not comparable, sadly, to what you can get in the UK. Mid-range.

Taverna Rustica Frana Supila 12; tel: 020 424 222. Part of the Hotel Excelsior, the Taverna Rustica is in a great location in Ploče, with views back to the old town. The food isn't half as rustic as the name implies, focusing on upmarket pasta dishes and local fish. Expensive; reservations recommended.

Tres Miyos Hvarska 6. On the road running behind the old town (usually marked on maps as Iza Grada) you'll find a minute but friendly Mexican restaurant. It's a brave effort serving tortillas and chilli beans in a place where everyone's come for the fish, but it can make a pleasant change if you're here for a week. Inexpensive.

Cafés and bars

With great weather and lots of visitors, there's no shortage of places to sit and have a drink in Dubrovnik, though fashions change quickly, and today's groovy hangout can all too rapidly become tomorrow's leftover.

In the old town

Carpe Diem Kneza Damjana Jude 4. Situated on the narrow street running down to the aquarium, Carpe Diem does a light breakfast in the morning and exotic cocktails in the evening. It's long, narrow, smartly decorated and popular late into the evening.

Cervantes Dropčeva 5. Hard to know whether to put this under restaurants or bars, as Cervantes – located on one of the streets between Stradun and Prijeko – specialises in tapas. Their anchovies, in various formats, are excellent.

Festival Café Stradun. Benefiting from a perfect location on Stradun, the Festival Café is especially popular through the day and in the early evenings, when it's a great place to see and be seen.

Gradska Kavana Pred Dvorom. In arguably the best location in town, next door to the Rector's Palace and opposite St Blaise's Church, the Gradska Kavana has a spacious interior and a raised terrace which is perfect for people-watching.

Hemingway Bar Pred Dvorom. Right opposite the Rector's Palace and next door to the cathedral is the new and popular Hemingway Bar, which attracts the cocktail-drinking set. It's impossible to imagine what Hemingway himself would have thought.

Irish Pub Od Polača 5. Just one street back from Stradun you'll find the Irish Pub, which although it's not a pub as you or I would know it, still serves a good range of beers and is popular with local students. Happy hour 15.00–18.00.

Rašanoda Od Puča. Next door to the Pučić Palace hotel and under the same management, Rašanoda is a swanky, upmarket wine bar with a good list of the best Croatian wines – and price tags to match.

Troubadur Bunićeva poljana. This is an excellent bar with a pub-like atmosphere and live music most evenings. The tables outside are made from old sewing machines, which is an unusual touch.

Outside the old town walls

Needless to say, Dubrovnik has its own life beyond that aimed at tourists, and there are a couple of areas where this goes on, notably on Bana Jelačića, running up into Lapad, and on Ivo Vojnovića, in the heart of Lapad:

Buša Situated on the rocks outside the western (seaward) walls of the city, Buša is the place to come if you want to watch the sun go down. The entrance is pretty well hidden and usually unsigned – go up behind the Jesuit church and out of the square on the opposite corner, and then turn right under the walls along Od Margarite. After a short while you come to a hole in the wall on your left (Buša means 'hole') which leads out on to the rocks – and there you are. Only open – you'll see why – when the weather's fine.

Casa Nika i Meda Pučića 1. Casa has a great location right on the waterfront at Uvala Bay, and although the drinks are pricier than you might be used to (20 kuna for a beer), the situation alone makes it worth the visit.

Kavana Dubravka Brsalje. Occupying prime real estate right outside the Pile gate, the Kavana Dubravka has a lovely terrace overlooking the bay between the Bokar and Lovrijenac fortresses. For 2 kuna you can use the toilets – which are a good deal more pleasant than the public ones over on the other side of the Pile gate.

Self-catering

If you're looking for picnic food you'll probably be reliant on the Mediator supermarket – there's a branch on Gundulićeva Poljana, and one outside each of the two main gates.

Nightlife

Though there's plenty of late-evening café activity and drinking going on in the old town, actual nightlife is decidedly thin on the ground in Dubrovnik, with most places closing up by 01.00. Just outside the Pile gate, at Brsalje 10, there's the **Latino Club Fuego**, which is open from Thursday to Saturday nights from 22.00 to 04.00. It's one of the few places open that late and therefore popular with backpackers who've had a bit too much to drink. Otherwise there's **Labirint**'s tiny nightclub in the town walls, which is open until 03.00; **Esperanza**, at Put Republike 30, just up from the bus station, which is popular with locals and sometimes puts on gigs; and the **Exodus** nightclub, out on Babin Kuk (and part of the Babin Kuk hotel complex) which offers the nearest you'll probably find to trance and techno.

Beaches

If you simply fancy cooling off after a hot walk around the city walls, walk just round the corner at the old port and there's a swimming area off the rocks, by the jetty. The city's main public beach, though, is the Banje Beach, just outside the Ploče gate, facing the old port. It's recently been refurbished and you can now rent parasols and deckchairs here, and order cocktails at the summer bar. Another option is the tiny beach underneath the Hotel Bellevue, half of which is public (the other half belongs to the hotel). It's on the gorgeous little cove facing southeast, and hosts Dubrovnik's annual water-polo championships – each little beach and cove around the city has its own team.

For pure hedonistic beach games and watersports, you can't do better than the Copacabana Beach on Babib Kuk, though in high season it does get mighty crowded with package tours from the Babin Kuk hotel complex. The Uvala Bay Beach, on Lapad, is the locals' beach of choice, and offers lovely swimming out to sea. Finally, the nicest beaches are out on the island of Lokrum (see page 290).

What to see

The main sight of course is Dubrovnik itself, and the best way of seeing it is from the city walls, which are among the best preserved and most picturesque in the world. There's a promenade along their entire length, and you should make every effort to circum-perambulate at least once, as it really gives you the best possible perspective (physical and historical) of just what Dubrovnik really means. Another wonderful view can be had from the top of Srđ (412m), the mountain looming above the city. Time was, you could take a cable car all the way up – and it's to be hoped that the war damage is repaired soon and it's pressed back into service, as the walk up the barren hillside can be a punishing one (see page 289).

Once you've seen Dubrovnik from above, choose your time of day for the city itself with care; after 11.00 there's a predictable tendency towards more visitors and less atmosphere – though early evening is a lovely time, regardless of the crowds, with soft light treating old stone kindly.

There's a lot to see in the old city, but don't be too obsessive – not all of the 48 churches within the walls need a visit (or indeed are open), and the museums are mostly fairly low key.

The city walls

The walls surround the entire old town and run for a whisper under 2km. At their highest they're 25m tall, and at their fattest 12m wide. There are five fortresses and around 20 towers. Work started on the walls in the 8th century and continued more or less continuously until the 16th, though much more than you might imagine is also late 20th-century restoration – even before the Serb shells pounded the city in 1991–92. Indeed, when I was here in the 1980s, the promenade around the walls wasn't actually complete. Since the war, huge amounts of restoration have been done throughout the old city, including the complete re-paving of Stradun – not that you'd know – and the replacing of most of the houses' roof-tiles.

There are three places where you can get up on to the walls – on Stradun, right next to the Pile gate; on Svetog Dominika, the road leading up to the Dominican Monastery; and on Kneza Damjana Jude, near the Aquarium. The walls are open from 09.00 to 19.00 in summer, with slightly shorter hours in winter, and the entrance fee is 30 kuna. The earlier you get up on to the walls the less crowded you'll find them.

The whole circuit takes a leisurely hour or so if you stop to take pictures (and you will).

Inside the walls

The main sights are all close to one another – the main street, Stradun, is all of 300m long. The following itinerary starts at the Pile gate and works its way back and forth across the old city, before ending at St Blaise's church. At a leisurely pace – and without stopping for any length of time to admire the attractions or visit museums and churches – it would take about 1½–2 hours. If you dip into a handful of the main sights you should count on a good half day; if you want a detailed visit to everything on the itinerary you'll need a couple of full days at least. If you do nothing else, visit the Rector's Palace, the two monasteries and the cathedral treasury.

The **Pile gate**, dating back to 1471, is approached across a wooden drawbridge which used to be pulled up every night. Set into a niche here is the first of many statues you'll see of St Blaise (Sveti Vlaho), the city's patron saint. Indeed, as you enter the gate you'll immediately see another – this time by Ivan Meštrović, Croatia's most famous sculptor.

Once inside the gate you come straight on to Dubrovnik's famous main street, **Stradun**, which is paved in marble (be careful when it's wet; it can be lethally slippery). This was originally the marshy channel which separated the Roman settlement of Ragusa on one side from the Slavic settlement of Dubrovnik on the other.

On the square inside the Pile gate stands **Onofrio's Great Fountain**, which was completed in 1444 by the Neapolitan architect Onofrio della Cava as part of the city's smart new plumbing. Unfortunately all the fancy ornamental work from the upper part of the fountain was lost in the Great Earthquake of 1667.

To your left as you come into the city is the tiny **Church of Our Saviour** (Sveti Spas). It was completed in 1528 as a thank you from the survivors of the 1520 earthquake, and itself survived the far more dramatic quake of 1667 – a tribute to the building skills of the Andrijić brothers, from Korčula, who also worked on the Sponza Palace (see page 281). The simple Renaissance trefoil façade and rose window are quietly pleasing, and hide a Gothic interior which is mainly used these days as a venue for candlelit concerts.

The Franciscan Monastery and pharmacy

Next door to Our Saviour is the Franciscan church and monastery. The church is entered from Stradun itself, where you'll find the south door crowned by a wonderful *pietà* – evocatively described by Rebecca West in 1937 as 'definite and sensible. The Madonna looks as if, had it been in her hands, she would have stopped the whole affair.'

The *pietà* survived the Great Earthquake, but the church itself was entirely gutted by fire and countless treasures were lost for ever. What you see today dates from the 18th century onwards, which explains the baroque nature of it all. The church is famous locally as the final resting place of Ivan Gundulić (see page 284), though he's actually interred in a part of the church which is closed to the public – you can still pay your respects at a plaque on the north wall, however.

The rest of the monastery is accessed down a narrow passage next to Our Saviour. At the entrance you'll find the famous pharmacy, self-billed as the oldest in the world. Whether it is or not, it probably was one of the earliest to be open to the public, and it's still operating today, though from a 1901 refurbishment. The original pharmacy was established in 1317, and in the museum off the cloisters you can see an interesting collection of jars and poisons from the 15th century on, along with ancient pharmacopoeias. The museum also contains various religious artefacts, as well as a testy portrait of Ruđer Bošković, Dubrovnik's mathematical genius (see box), painted in 1760 in London. Most interesting of all, however, is a canvas showing the old town before the earthquake – note how much greater Onofrio's Great Fountain was before 1667.

The cloisters themselves are truly exceptional, consisting of rows of double octagonal columns with individualised capitals. They are the work of Mihoje Brakov, a sculptor from Bar (in what's now Montenegro), who died here of the plague in 1348. One of the capitals near the entrance, depicting a medieval man with terrible toothache, is said to be a self-portrait of the sculptor. Inside the courtyard are palm trees and well-trimmed box hedges, and it's a great place to get away from the heat in high summer.

Stradun and Luža square

Stradun itself (also known as Placa – pronounced *platsa*) continues in a widening straight line all the way to the clocktower at the far end. As you'll notice, the houses along the street are nearly identical; a result of the careful post-earthquake planning at the end of the 17th century. Note the distinctive '*na koljeno*' single-arched frame which combines the entrance door and window to provide a counter over which goods could be served to customers.

In the Luža square, at the far end of Stradun, you'll find **Orlando's Column**, a statue of Roland symbolising the city's desire for freedom (*libertas*) and which has

RUĐER BOŠKOVIĆ – MATHEMATICAL GENIUS AND LATIN POET

Pictures of Ruđer Bošković (Ruggero Boscovich in Italian) – a brilliant mathematician and physicist born in Ragusa in 1711 – show a man with a slightly pudgy face and the permanent slightly exasperated look of the over-intelligent.

He was educated in Ragusa by the Jesuits and then went on at the age of 14 to study at the *Jesuit Collegium Romanum* in Rome – so successfully that he was appointed professor of mathematics and physics there at the tender age of 29. As one of Europe's brightest scientists, Bošković was a member of London's Royal Society and wrote around 70 papers on astronomy, gravitation, meteorology, optics and trigonometry. His most famous work is *A Theory of Natural Philosophy* – or *Philosophiae naturalis theoria redacta ad unicam legem virium in Natura existentium*, as it's more correctly known. Bošković was also something of a Latin poet, too, and was capable of describing his complex astronomical ideas in elegant metered verse. He died in Milan in 1787.

marked the centre of town since its erection in 1418. For centuries Roland's forearm was Ragusa's standard measure of length (the *lakat*, since you ask), a convenient 512mm long – you can see the reference groove at the base of the statue. All state declarations were read from a platform above the column in the days of the republic, and condemned criminals were executed at its base.

Behind Orlando's Column you can't miss the **Clock Tower**, originally built in 1444, which features a complex astronomical clock, and a pair of green men (the *zelenci*) who strike the hour. The tower was rebuilt in 1929 (which is presumably when the digital clock was added), so the only thing that's really original now is the bell, dating from 1506, which weighs over two tonnes. The original clock mechanism and green men are in the Sponza Palace (see below). Next to the clocktower is **Onofrio's Small Fountain,** dating from 1441.

The Sponza Palace

On the left-hand side of Luža square is the Sponza Palace, which functioned variously as a cistern, the customs house and the state mint. Today it houses the Memorial Room of the Dubrovnik Defenders, the original innards of the city clock, and the State Archives. It's one of the most charming buildings in Dubrovnik, boldly mixing pure Venetian Gothic and late Renaissance into a harmonious whole. It was built in 1522 to plans by the local architect Pasko Miličević, and features work by the Andrijić brothers, the master sculptors who were also responsible for much of Korčula Cathedral – as well as the Church of Our Saviour at the other end of Stradun. The Sponza was one of the few buildings to survive the Great Earthquake of 1667.

The entrance is through a wide-arched Renaissance portico, above which there's a lovely Venetian Gothic first storey, topped with a row of four late-Renaissance windows and a statue of St Blaise in a niche. Inside there's a courtyard with a double cloister.

The name Sponza comes from the Latin word *spongia*, meaning sponge, as there was originally a cistern on this site. The Sponza's main purpose, however, was to serve as the republic's customs house (which is why it's also sometimes referred to as the Divona or Dogana). On the ground floor here goods were measured for duty, under the inscription '*Fallere Nostra Vetant et Falli Pondera Meque Pondero cum Merces Ponderat ipse Deus*' – which translates roughly as 'the scales we use to weigh your goods are the same scales used by God to weigh us'.

The ground-floor rooms originally served as warehouse space, while those on the first floor were used for literary and scientific meetings. Up on the second floor was the state mint, which issued Dubrovnik's currency (*perperae, grossi* and *ducats*) from 1337 until 1803.

After World War II, the Sponza housed the **Museum of the Socialist Revolution**, though of course that's disappeared following the more recent war. Instead you'll find the original 16th-century mechanism for the city clock here, along with the two green men, Maro and Baro, who struck the bell until 1928.

The **Memorial Room of the Dubrovnik Defenders**, on the ground floor, is a commemoration of the tragic events here from October 1 1991 to October 26 1992, when more than 200 defenders and 100 civilians were killed. It's a terribly sobering place, with the remnants of the flag from the Imperial Fort on Srđ and the pictures and dates of all the young lives which were snuffed out during the siege.

The building also houses the **State Archives**, which are among the most complete in the world, chronicling pretty much everything that happened during the 1,000-year history of the republic. Altogether there are some 8,000m of shelved documents, ranging from the 13th-century city statutes to Marshal Marmont's orders dissolving the republic in 1808. The archives are open to researchers daily – you should call ahead or email in advance if you want to visit (tel: 020 321 032; email: arhiv-dubrovnik@dad.hr).

The Dominican Monastery

The winding street Svetog Dominika leads up to the Ploče gate. On the way you can't miss the Dominican Monastery. Notice the way the steps on the way up are walled in, up to a height of about two feet – to protect the modesty of travellers and save the monks from impure ankle-related thoughts.

The monastery was used by the occupying French troops from 1808 – you can see from the outside where windows were sealed up to make a Napoleonic prison, and the church itself was used as stables. In the cloisters you can still see the horse troughs which were hacked into the retaining walls by the cavalrymen.

The original church here was completed in 1315, but had to be rebuilt after the Great Earthquake of 1667. It was then paved with the coats of arms of all the noble families, but unfortunately was repaved in 1910 with plain marble. Today it's a vast, boxy place, and most of the best art has been moved to the museum – though not the greatest treasure of all, a terrific 5m-by-4m crucifixion by Paolo Veneziano, which was installed here in 1358. There's also an interesting painting of St Dominic by local boy Vlaho Bukovac, though it's not, frankly, the artist's best work – you can see some of this at the Museum of Modern Art (see page 288) in Dubrovnik, and even more in the painter's home town, Cavtat (see page 293).

The cloisters are a late-Gothic masterpiece, built to a design by the Florentine architect Maso di Bartolomeo, but with extra flourishes added by local stonemasons. In the courtyard oranges and lemons grow, and – like the Franciscan cloisters – it's a wonderfully cool, shady place on a hot day.

The monastery also houses an interesting museum and an extraordinary library; with over 16,000 works and 240 incunabula, it was one of the greatest European libraries of the Renaissance. In the museum you'll find a rare 11th-century bible, along with a much-reproduced triptych featuring St Blaise with a model of pre-earthquake Ragusa in his right hand – still recognisable as Dubrovnik today, though both the Franciscan and Dominican monasteries sported bigger spires back then. Also of note is a marvellous altarpiece by Titian featuring Mary Magdalene with St Blaise and the Archangel Raphael – the chap on his knees is the member of the Pučić family who commissioned the work.

Up a couple of stairs there's a room full of votive gold – a fraction of what was here originally, as most of it was sold off after World War II to support the faculty of theology, unfunded in communist times. There's an interesting Flemish diptych here – with Jesus on the left while on the right there's a reversible panel, with love on one side and death on the other, usefully adaptable according to your moods and whims.

The synagogue

As you leave the monastery turn right and you'll find yourself at the eastern end of Prijeko, which is best visited early in the day, before the eager restaurateurs can get their teeth into you, so to speak (see page 274). Take a detour down Žudioska, and you'll find one of Europe's oldest (and smallest) synagogues. It's Europe's second oldest (after Prague) and in spite of restrictions placed on Jews here during World War II, it was the only European synagogue to function all the way through the war.

The synagogue – with original 17th-century furnishings – is on the second floor, while below it, on the first floor, there's a fascinating two-room museum, where you can see richly decorated Torah scrolls and binders, and ancient Ark curtains, as well as a copy of the letter signed by Marshal Marmont granting the Jewish community full emancipation from 1808. There's also a chilling selection of documents from 1941, issued by the fascist NDH (see page 16), restricting the movement of Jews and ordering them to wear yellow ribbons and badges.

Dubrovnik War Photo gallery

Continue down Prijeko for most of its length – or if it's already approaching lunchtime consider avoiding the touts by walking along the old city's uppermost street, Peline, which gives great views down the steep-stepped streets crossing Prijeko – and then turn left down Antuninska, where you'll find the extraordinary Dubrovnik War Photo gallery.

It's one of the city's newest and most moving galleries, and I can't recommend a visit too highly. Specialising in first-rate temporary exhibitions by the world's greatest modern-war photographers, the gallery aims, as the New Zealand-born director, Wade Goddard, says, 'to strip away the Hollywood image of war, to replace the glamour, the heroic bravura, the "only the bad guys suffer" image of war, with the raw and undeniable evidence that war inflicts injustices on all who experience it.'

It would require a heart of stone to come away unmoved by the extraordinary (and often painful) images. When I visited in the summer of 2004, Ron Haviv's breathtaking '*Blood and Honey*' collection was on show – '*bal*' being Turkish for 'honey' and '*kan*' being Turkish for 'blood'. Haviv won the World Press Photo award for his iconic pictures of the fall of Vukovar in 1991, and is one of the co-founders of agency vii (see www.viiphoto.com).

Check out www.warphotoltd.com for details of current and upcoming exhibitions.

To the Orthodox Church and Icon Museum

On the other side of Stradun, a short walk along Gariište brings you to Za Rokom, where you'll find the little **Church of St Roc**. Round on the right-hand wall of the church is a fine piece of carved graffiti dated 1597 and reading 'PAX VOBIS MEMENTO MORI QUI LUDETIS PILLA' – which translates roughly as 'Peace be with you, but remember that you must die, you who play ball here', clearly the work of an irate adult, keen to warn off noisy football-mad kids.

Continue along Za Rokom until you get to the end of the street, then turn left into Široka. On the right-hand side you'll find the house where Marin Držić (see page 288) once lived – although unless you're a serious fan of the playwright's work, you won't get a great deal out of a visit. Equally, unless you have a lot of time on your hands you probably needn't visit the **Rupe Ethnographic Museum**, a block away – though the former granary building itself is interesting, as you can see some of the vast chambers which were dug into the rock to store grain back in the 16th century, keeping the food dry and cool.

Turning on to Od Puča, you'll find the Orthodox Church on your left, and (two doors down) the Icon Museum (see over). This part of town is where most of the small remaining Serbian community lives and works. Just down Miha Pracata, on the left-hand side, you'll also find Dubrovnik's **mosque**, which is open from 10.00 to 13.00 daily – though there's really nothing special to see there.

The Serb **Orthodox Church** of the Holy Annunciation is one of Dubrovnik's most recent, only being completed in 1877. A plain exterior shelters a rather spare interior, with a traditional iconostasis (with icons from the 15th to 19th centuries) separating the clergy from the congregation. The church was one of the last buildings in the old town – perhaps unsurprisingly – on which restoration work got underway after the end of the siege in 1992, but happily is now receiving both attention and funds; hopefully it will be fully restored in the near future.

The rarely visited **Icon Museum**, two doors down, is on the second floor (past a sign in Cyrillic saying CRŪCKA – Srπska, or Serbian). It's a pity as the two-room collection brings together a wide range of icons from the 18th and 19th centuries, as well as some earlier ones from the 15th and 16th centuries. They come from all across the Balkans and Russia and the differences between the various schools are fascinating – the Russian icons featuring long noses; the ones from the Bay of Kotor having deep, dark shadows. In the second room there are also half a dozen dark, dark portraits of local 19th-century Serb notables by Vlaho Bukovac (see page 293), quite unlike anything else you'll see by the famous local painter.

To Gundulićeva poljana

Continuing down Od Puča brings you past the Pučić Palace hotel and out on to Gundulićeva poljana – literally Gundulić's little field. In the centre of the square stands a statue of Ivan Gundulić himself (see box), which dates back to 1893. There's a marvellous allegorical vignette at the base of the statue; a bethroned Dubrovnik has both Turkey and Venice at her feet – with Turkey represented as the dragon on the left and Venice as the winged lion on the right. A certain irony, therefore, that the city's most expensive hotel, the Pučić Palace, overlooking the very same square, should today be Turkish-owned.

The Jesuit church

Turn right out of Gundulićeva poljana and head up the great flight of steps – said to be modelled on the Spanish Steps in Rome – leading to the Jesuit church (properly the Church of St Ignatius of Loyola, or Ignacija Lojolskog), a massive structure clearly intended to make a point. It was built to plans by the Jesuit artist Andrea Pozzo, who had already done great works in Rome and would go on to design the cathedral in Ljubljana.

Completed in 1725, the church features a dramatic double-storeyed set of Corinthian columns lifting the façade skywards, and the church behind it is enormous, covering a surface of over 600m². Inside it feels very big and gloomy,

IVAN GUNDULIĆ – MASTER OF BAROQUE POETRY

Ivan Gundulić was born in Dubrovnik in 1589, and was famous even in his lifetime as a remarkable poet, churning out vast quantities of – perhaps excessively rhetorical? – baroque verse. Coming from a prominent noble family, it's likely he would have eventually become rector, but he died in 1638, just a few months before the 50th birthday which would have made him eligible.

Gundulić played an important part in standardising the Croatian language, and was enthusiastically taken up by the Croatian nationalist movement in the 19th century – indeed it was only then that the great lyrical poem *Osman* was finally finished, with the last two chapters being penned by Ivan Mažuranić, who later went on to become the Ban of Croatia.

As well as being honoured by the statue in Dubrovnik, a fetchingly bewigged Gundulić also appears on the 50-kuna note.

as you'd expect, with the interior modelled on the Gesù Church in Rome and featuring lots of fabulous *trompe l'oeil*, Pozzi's speciality – he was the author of a seminal work on perspective, *Prospettiva de' pittori et architect*, which revolutionised painting in the 18th century and is still used today. The main attraction is the inside of the apse, which features spectacular scenes from the life of Ignatius, the founder of the Jesuit order, by the Sicilian painter Gaetano Garcia.

Altogether less spiritually uplifting – though popular enough with local devotees, it seems – is the 'Grotto of Lourdes', which was added in 1885.

To the Maritime Museum and aquarium

You can leave the rather tatty square in front of the Jesuit church by the far corner and wind your way all the way along Ispod mira, the alley leading along the inside of the city walls. This is perhaps the quietest and shabbiest part of the town, with lots of buildings still unrestored after being badly damaged in an earthquake in 1979.

At the end of the line, so to speak, you'll find **St John's Fortress**, which houses the Maritime Museum upstairs and the aquarium on the ground floor. Spread out over two floors, the **Maritime Museum** covers the entire history of seafaring in the area, from the Golden Age of the republic through to the arrival of steam-powered ships. It's well worth a visit if you're into ships and sailing, with lots of maps, evocative old photos and models of various types of ship, along with bits of rigging and ship's supplies and cargoes.

Downstairs, you'll find Dubrovnik's dismal seawater **aquarium**. Mostly it amounts to large Mediterranean fish (groupers, eels and the like) swimming listlessly round in tanks that don't seem big enough. The whole bleak experience is epitomised by the solitary giant turtle which paddles its way to and fro miserably in a pond-sized pool, while school groups chuck small change at the benighted beast.

The cathedral and treasury

Heading back into the heart of the city, the first thing you come to is the cathedral. The former Romanesque number – said to have been bankrolled by a shipwrecked Richard the Lionheart (see box overleaf) – was demolished by the Great Earthquake in 1667, so what you get today is the baroque replacement, completed in 1713 to plans by the Italian architect Andrea Buffalini. The statues of the saints along the eaves are rather fine, though notice that St Mark has been relegated to an inferior position – perhaps a none-too subtle snub to Venice.

Surprisingly, for baroque, the cathedral is a rather spartan affair inside, with a chunky modern altar and acres of whitewash – and it's curious in having a west-facing altar. The compelling attraction is the treasury, though if you're here it's nonetheless worth having a look at the impressive (school of) Titian altarpiece.

Altogether, there are well over 100 priceless relics in the **treasury**, many of which are carried around the town in a grand procession on February 3, the feast day of Dubrovnik's patron saint. The most important of these is the Head of St Blaise himself, which was bought from Byzantium (along with the saint's arms and a leg) in 1026. The head is housed in a fine casing decorated with 24 Byzantine enamel plaques from the 12th century, featuring austere, intense portraits of the saints.

The treasury also includes one of John the Baptist's hands, a bit of the *True Cross* incorporated into a crucifix, one of Christ's nappies in a silver box, and a dark wooden lectern which once belonged to England's Henry VIII – after the Reformation, treasures from the dissolved monasteries went up for sale, and a small selection ended up in the hands of enterprising sailors from Lopud (see page 296).

Over on the right-hand side is an extraordinary painting by Raphael, the *Madonna della Seggiola* (Sedia), which is almost identical to the 1514 version in the

RICHARD THE LIONHEART AND DUBROVNIK

Ask anyone about Dubrovnik's cathedral and it won't be long before Richard the Lionheart's name comes up. According to local legend, the English king ran into a terrible storm near here on his return home from the crusades at the end of 1192, and vowed that if he survived he would build a church on the spot. Miraculously, he was saved, and washed up on Lokrum.

On hearing the news of the arrival of such an important – and apparently loaded – visitor, Dubrovnik sent over a welcoming party, who persuaded King Richard that his money would be better spent on building a cathedral in Dubrovnik. In exchange, the Ragusan nobles would build a votive church on Lokrum at their own expense. Richard agreed, and handed over 100,000 ducats, before continuing on his journey to Italy and – eventually – England.

In all probability, however, the Lokrum part of this charming tale is a Benedictine fabrication. The monks on Lokrum had good cause for inventing – or at the very least embellishing – such a story. Because of it, they enjoyed various privileges in Dubrovnik's cathedral, including the abbot of Lokrum being allowed to hold the Candlemas pontifical mass, which is celebrated on February 2, the day before St Blaise's feast day. This mass apparently enraged successive bishops of Dubrovnik, who demanded the privilege be rescinded. In the end, in the 1590s, the Ragusan government had to resort to writing letters to the pope, who finally decided in favour of Lokrum's Benedictines – thereby legitimising the Lionheart story.

Palazzo Pitti in Florence. Why there's a copy here – painted on what looks like the bottom of a barrel – is a mystery, but the painting itself is a pure wonder.

Last but not least is an extraordinary pitcher and ewer from the 15th century, prominently on display, which is an allegory of Dubrovnik's flora and fauna. Featuring snakes and tortoises, eels and lizards, and some pre-Dalí lobsters, along with alarming amounts of vegetation, it looks like it would be the very devil to clean. It's thought to have been made as a gift for the Hungarian king of the day, Matthias Corvinus the Just, but ended up here as the king died before he could receive the tribute.

It's always aroused a certain amount of passion. In 1929, Count Voynovitch, author of a handy little guide to the city, said 'The basin is delightfully finished'. Just eight years later, however, (the ever-opinionated) Rebecca West was writing: 'Nothing could be more offensive to the eye, to the touch, or to common sense… it has the infinite elaborateness of eczema, and to add to the last touch of unpleasantness these animals are loosely fixed so that they may wobble and give an illusion of movement. Though Dubrovnik is beautiful, and this object was indescribably ugly, my dislike of the second explained to me why I felt doubtful in my appreciation of the first. The town regarded this horror as a masterpiece.'

And it's true; it does.

The Rector's Palace

Diagonally opposite the cathedral is the Rector's Palace, with the **municipal theatre** next door. If you get the chance, pop inside and admire the charming, miniature version of the grand Austro-Hungarian opera houses and theatres –

complete with gilded boxes and velvet seating, which dates back to 1869.

The Rector's Palace (*Knežev Dvor*) was the seat of Ragusa's government. It would once have looked more like a castle than a palace, but after the original was accidentally blown up in 1435 (always a mistake keeping your gunpowder next to your government) it was rebuilt in the Venetian Gothic style by Onofrio della Cava – he of the fountains fame.

It wasn't to last, as the gunpowder went off again in 1463. This time the palace was restored by Michelozzo Michelozzi, who also did lots of work on the city's defensive fortresses, and Juraj Dalmatinac (who was also busy up the coast in Šibenik and Pag), who added various Renaissance touches.

You enter through a fine loggia topped with superb carved capitals on pillars of Korčula marble; the outer pairs are the original Gothic while the middle three are Renaissance. Most interesting of all is the rightmost capital, thought to portray Aesculapius, the God of Healing, who was born in Epidaurus (now Cavtat).

The main door leads into an atrium which is the (surprisingly small) venue for summer recitals. In here you'll find the only statue ever raised to an individual in Ragusa's long history. On dying in 1607, Miho Pracat (see page 296), a remarkable ship owner and adventurer from Lopud, left 1,000 shares in the Bank of St George in Genoa to the city. The city was suitably grateful – back then those shares were worth around 100 lira apiece, at a time when gold was fetching three and a half lira an ounce. The interest on the capital was used by the city to free slaves, and Pracat got his statue.

The ground floor of the palace was formerly a prison, handy for the court room off to the right, with a curious marble barrier and wooden bench being about all you can see today. Upstairs are the state offices and rector's chambers – from the day they were elected, rectors were effectively prisoners here, only allowed to leave with the Senate's permission. Fortunately each only served a one-month term.

The main staircase was only used for the rector's inaugural procession on the first of the month, taking him upstairs to his confinement. Nobody ever came down them unless the rector died in office – the hidden staircase behind was the way out. On your way up the main stairs notice the handrails, supported by realistic (if not entirely tasteful) carved hands.

At the top of the stairs, over the door which originally led into the Grand Council chamber, there's an inscription reading '*Obliti Privatorum Publica Curate*' – a quote from Pericles, reminding councillors to forget their private concerns and think of public affairs instead.

The upstairs rooms are a curious collection – mainly because the palace was plundered, first by the French in the early 19th century, and then again by Yugoslavia's King Aleksandar after World War I, for the Royal Palace in Belgrade. As a result they're for the most part furnished with private donations. You'll find an odd mix of Venetian repro, Louis XV copies, painted wood, Neapolitan ebony and marble veneer, along with an unusual collection of canvasses featuring local bigwigs. Note also the keys to the city – the gates were locked every night and the keys were kept in the rector's office – and the candlelit clock.

The Church of St Blaise

Across the square from the Rector's Palace, and facing Orlando's Column, is the church dedicated to Dubrovnik's patron, St Blaise. The original church on this site was built in the 14th century, and although it (mostly) survived the Great Earthquake in 1667, it was subsequently consumed by fire. Miraculously, the 15th-century gold and silver statue of St Blaise escaped unharmed.

The new baroque church was completed in 1717 to plans by the Venetian

MARIN DRŽIĆ – DUBROVNIK'S REBELLIOUS PLAYWRIGHT

Born into a large family of merchants in 1508, Marin Držić was originally destined for the Church, and after being ordained at the age of 18 he was sent to Siena to study Church law. He was soon thrown out for his involvement with the theatre, however, and returned home to Dubrovnik, where he wrote his first plays. These weren't popular with the nobles, who rightly saw the Držić comedies for the political vehicles they were – and presumably weren't wild about being portrayed as inbred fools either.

The latter part of the playwright's life is something of a mystery, though we know that he left Dubrovnik and took up something of a crusade against it. He even wrote a series of letters to the Medicis in Florence, asking them to help him overthrow the republic – though he never received an answer, and died in Venice in poverty in 1567.

Needless to say once Držić was safely dead his reputation was quickly rehabilitated, and today his plays – and in particular *Dundo Maroje* – form a central part of the Dubrovnik Summer Festival.

architect Marino Grapelli, who based the interior design on the Church of San Maurizio in his home town. It's even more unusual than the cathedral in its orientation, however, with a south-facing altar.

The church is an elegant tribute to the city's patron saint, with a classic baroque façade. Inside it's not as austere as the cathedral but not too over the top either. The main attraction is the altar, where you can admire the famous statue of St Blaise holding the city – which shows you what it looked like in about 1485.

Also worth your attention is the painting across the organ loft representing the Martyrdom of St Blaise, which was painted by local boy Petar Matejević in the early 18th century. Spare a moment too for the stained-glass windows, which depict saints Peter and Paul and saints Cyril and Methodius, the creators of the Glagolitic alphabet (a later variant of which, Cyrillic, is named after St Cyril). These are the work of Ivo Dulčić, one of Dubrovnik's most famous modern artists, who died in 1975.

Ploče and the Museum of Modern Art

The **Ploče gate** leads out from the old town into the expensive suburb of Ploče. The gate is a complex structure actually comprising several gates and bridges which were built in the 15th century – though the current design dates from 1628. There's the familiar statue of St Blaise, and a drawbridge leading out into what used to be a market square.

The main road leads up to the **Lazareti**, Dubrovnik's quarantine houses. Dubrovnik was one of the first ports in Europe to introduce quarantine restrictions, and if you wanted to visit you had to spend 40 days here first before being allowed in. These days the houses and courtyards are used as artists' studios and performance spaces.

A little further up the hill, on the left-hand side, is Dubrovnik's excellent **Museum of Modern Art.** Even if there were no art to see, the building itself is magnificent and well worth a visit. Built in 1939 as the summer villa for a wealthy ship-owner, Božo Banac, it was designed in a Renaissance style reminiscent of the Rector's Palace and you wouldn't know it wasn't ancient. Since 1950 it has housed the museum's ever-expanding (and excellent) collection.

The permanent collection includes paintings and sculpture from Croatia's greatest artists as well as focusing on the burgeoning local scene. The works are rotated and there are usually temporary exhibitions, so what's on show at any one time varies. Look out for sculpture from two of Croatia's most representative and best-known sculptors, Ivan Meštrović and Frano Kršnić, as well as landscapes by Mato Celestin Medović and interiors and still lifes from Emanuel Vidović. The show is stolen, naturally, by Vlaho Bukovac (see page 293), and the gallery holds some of his very best work, including a number of gorgeous, complex portraits – though they're not always all on show.

Culture – and the Dubrovnik Summer Festival
Dubrovnik has a richly vibrant cultural scene, with its own symphony orchestra, theatre group and dance ensemble. Most performances take place during the season – broadly speaking from May to October – when there's usually something on every night. Most important of all is the annual **Dubrovnik Summer Festival**, which was inaugurated in 1950.

The festival is big, prestigious and serious, with every conceivable space in the old town – indoors and out – being turned into a performance-stage. The 45-day festival kicks off on July 10 with the performers being given the keys to the city and closes on August 25 with a fabulous firework display.

During the festival you can find everything from opera and classical concerts to chamber music and soloists, while theatre performances tend to concentrate on Shakespeare and local boy Marin Držić (see box). A festival standard is the traditional performance of *Hamlet* in the Lovrijenac Fortress, which is a wonderfully atmospheric setting for the play.

Tickets for the main events sell out well in advance, so if you're serious about attending check out the website (www.dubrovnik-festival.hr) or contact the organisers (tel: 020 323 400; fax: 020 323 365) as soon as the programme becomes available (usually in April) – and make sure you get your accommodation sorted out way ahead of time, too. If you haven't got tickets in advance there are usually places available for the lower-key performances on site – you can buy these from the festival kiosks on Stradun and at the Pile gate.

Even outside the festival there are plenty of opportunities to listen to classical music, largely thanks to the tireless **Dubrovnik Symphony Orchestra** (www.dso.hr), which puts on an astonishing range of concerts, year-round. The two most common venues – outside festival time – are the Revelin Fortress, just outside the Ploče gate, and the Church of Our Saviour (Sveti Spas), just inside the Pile gate, where there are regular candlelit performances.

Dubrovnik also has one of the country's most famous troupes in the form of the 300-strong Linđo ensemble. They're a regular mainstay of the festival, and also perform twice a week from May to October at the Lazareti, the old quarantine houses just up from the Ploče gate. It makes for an amazing and authentic spectacle. Linđo's office is at Marojice Kaboge 12, two streets back from Gundulićeva poljana.

Mount Srđ
Looming large above Dubrovnik, and visible from all over the city, is the mountain of Srđ. Up until 1991 there was a cable car which whisked visitors up to the top for the incredible view over the city and the islands, but it became one of the first victims of the war.

The cable car hasn't been put back into service since then – apparently because of a long-running dispute, with the top and bottom stations owned by different companies. It's a great pity, as the only way up now is on foot – unless you happen to have access to a vehicle, in which case you can take the road up to the village of Bosanka, before turning left on to the road to the summit.

If you do decide to walk up, bear in mind that the zig-zagged path is long, steep, and without shade for the last two-thirds. At first it's through pine trees, with butterflies and cicadas – magic and very cool. There's no water to be had, either on the way up or at the top, so take plenty with you. And although the path is perfectly safe, and the hillside is said to be clear of unexploded ordnance, you should stick to the main track just in case.

The path starts above the main road running above Dubrovnik – referred to variously as Državna Cesta or Jadranska Cesta (and formerly Put Jugoslavenske Narodne Armije). Starting at the Pile gate, turn right just after the bus stop and work your way up Zrinsko-Frankopanska. Cross over Zagrebačka and then Gornji Kono, then take the next right and follow this slip road under Jadranska Cesta. After this the footpath starts off to your left. From the Pile gate it will take you anything between one hour and two, depending on how fit you are, to reach the summit.

At the top you'll find the Imperial Fort, which was built by the French in 1810. In the 1970s it became a popular discotheque (rumours that this author was once seen strutting his stuff there many years ago are clearly unfounded). Today, the fort is still badly damaged and can't officially be visited, so the only reason to climb up this far is for the magnificent views – and of course the exercise. What you won't miss is the huge cross at the top, which now dominates the old town, especially when it's illuminated at night. As you climb up in the heat, spare a thought for the mothers of those killed in the war who follow the route as a pilgrimage for their sons, walking barefoot to the top and stopping to pray at each of the 13 crosses placed at corners along the way.

Lokrum

When you're in Dubrovnik, keep at least half a day free for a trip to sub-tropical Lokrum, the town's own offshore nature reserve. Said to have been visited unwillingly by Richard the Lionheart in 1192 (see box on page 286) the island is today just a 15-minute boat-ride away from the old town quay.

Lokrum remains undeveloped, and makes for a wonderful break from the crowds onshore. Even when the boats are arriving full, every half-hour, the 2km-long island can easily absorb all comers, leaving an impression – away from a small central part – of calm and tranquillity, punctuated only by the cries of birds and the fluttering of butterflies.

A network of footpaths criss-crosses the island and provides access to the sea and into the dense woods. There are several rock beaches, and these are cleaner, fresher and less crowded than Dubrovnik's, as well as a warm saltwater lake (Mrtvo More, the Dead Sea), on the other side of the island from where the boat arrives. This has a 10m cliff which encourages the local lads to dive off it, apparently without harm. There's a naturist beach on Lokrum, too, on the southeastern end of the island, away from prying eyes – follow the FKK signs.

Lokrum's main attraction lies in its enormous variety of vegetation, which is all the more astonishing when you realise there's no fresh water supply – hence the absolute ban on making fires of any kind or even on smoking. When you're wandering the paths look out for numerous species of birds (including peacocks) and butterflies. On a visit here in June I saw white admirals, several sorts of fritillary, and some skittish large yellows.

In the middle of the island, there's an old botanical garden, most of which seems

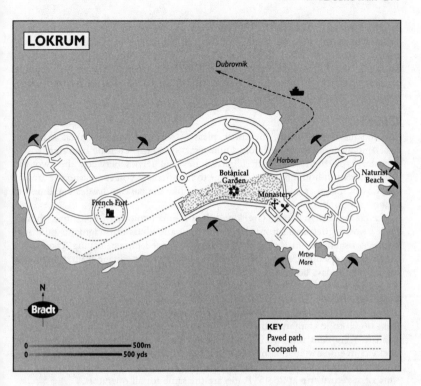

like a series of wonderfully unmaintained secret gardens. Amongst slightly dilapidated walls you'll find palms with soft furry trunks, trellises of twisted vines and crippled trees supported on crutches, while broken cloches sprout thyme and basil and lettuce run to seed.

In the heavy silence and deep shade there's an agreeable air of mystery – which is shattered fairly unceremoniously when you round a corner and discover the restaurant and bar, and a small natural history museum, all within the structure of what was once a large Benedictine monastery.

On the summit of the island – a steepish 20-minute hike – there's a ruined fort. Built by the French in 1808, it gives great views out over Dubrovnik, and the nearby coast and the islands. Be careful here though – it's in a parlous state, and the steps leading inside and up to the lookout are on the point of collapse.

It was from the northern tip of Lokrum that I finally realised what it was I'd found vaguely make-believe about Dubrovnik all along: it's a film set. So many movies have plundered that fortified look – the big walls, the red-roofed houses nestled between them dominated by a smattering of palaces and churches – that it doesn't seem real. It looks like it's meant to be looked at, but could never really have been lived in.

To get to Lokrum, take the half-hourly boat (every day in season, otherwise only on weekends) from the old harbour, and make sure you know what time the last one is coming back. Tickets cost around 30 kuna return. If you're here on a weekday out of season just ask around at the harbour and you'll soon find someone willing to take you across. Expect to pay up to 100 kuna a head, and make sure the skipper knows what time you want to be picked up.

SOUTH OF DUBROVNIK

From Dubrovnik it's just 40km south to the Montenegrin border. On the way there's a string of resorts (Kupari, Srebreno, Mlini, Soline and Plat) collectively known as the Župa Dubrovačka, which lead to the town of Cavtat (pronounced *tsavtat*), after which there's just Čilipi Airport and a handful of fishing villages before you reach the border.

Cavtat

Situated just 16km south, the small, pleasant seaside town of Cavtat makes an excellent and easy excursion from Dubrovnik – and can even be considered as an alternative place to stay, with regular buses and ferries between the two and accommodation both cheaper and easier to find here. If you're visiting the area by car, Cavtat makes an ideal base, with nothing like the parking hassles you'll find in Dubrovnik itself.

Cavtat was originally the Greek and then Roman colony of Epidaurus, though there's nothing left at all from that era barring a few classical fragments built into houses – fishermen, in Rebecca West's nicely turned phrase, having 'taken what they would of sculptures and bas-reliefs to build up their cottage walls, where they can be seen today, flowers in the buttonhole of poverty'.

Getting there

The #10 Libertas bus runs between Cavtat and Dubrovnik about once an hour from 06.00 to midnight, and costs 12 kuna each way (pay on the bus) while the standard ferry runs until 18.00 and costs 60 kuna return (40 kuna single) – and docks conveniently in Dubrovnik's old town harbour. If their hours don't suit, other ferry companies run to a different timetable in summer, including one that runs a last return trip at 23.45. Rates are the same for all operators.

Where to stay and eat

If you want to stay in Cavtat there are lots of private rooms available (just ask around – or contact the tourist office; tel: 020 479 025; fax: 020 478 025). There are also a number of hotels, including one of Croatia's largest, the stunning multi-tiered, 482-roomed, five-star **Hotel Croatia** (tel: 020 475 555; fax: 020 478 213), which does sea-view doubles at around €200 in season, dropping back to €112 in winter. The hotel is happily sheltered from view by the headland, and has its own beaches (both standard and naturist). It's also home to the **Feral** restaurant, which has live music every evening.

Also run by the same management as the Croatia is the rather more endearing, if very traditional, stone-built **Hotel Supetar** (tel: 020 479 833; fax: 020 479 858), which has 28 three-star rooms right on the Cavtat quayside, with doubles priced very reasonably at €75 in summer and €46 in winter, including a good breakfast. One of the best of the town's many restaurants is **Leut** (tel: 020 479 050), which is situated at the southern end of the town, right on the water. It's been in the Bobić family since 1971, and the food is excellent, as you'd expect for the price – though even an advance reservation won't necessarily guarantee they'll keep your waterside table for you here. If you lose your table at Leut, head straight for the **Taverna Galjia**, which also serves first-rate seafood.

What to see and do

Cavtat (the name seems likely to be derived from the Latin word *civitas*) occupies a peninsula between two bays, and has a charming palm-studded front lined with cafés and restaurants. There's not a whole lot to do, though the **Franciscan**

Monastery, at the end of the quay, hides a pair of lovely Renaissance paintings, and the **Rector's Palace**, at the other end of the waterfront, houses the town museum – notable in particular for a selection of excellent works by the local painter Vlaho Bukovac (see box).

Many more Bukovac paintings can be found at the artist's house, which is now the **Galerija Bukovac**, though if this is the main reason for your visit check ahead, as it was still closed for restoration during 2004. When it reopens, over 80 of the artist's oils, spanning his entire career, will be on show here.

Right at the end of the peninsula, in a gorgeous hilltop location overlooking the sea and surrounded by cypresses, is the town cemetery. Here you'll find one of Cavtat's most important treasures, the **Račić Mausoleum**. Its commissioning by a daughter of the ship-owning Račić family seems to have been their downfall. No sooner was the building underway than she, her father and her brother died in quick succession, and just as soon as the mausoleum was completed her mother followed them into it.

The mausoleum is one of the most important works by Croatia's most famous sculptor, Ivan Meštrović. The white marble Byzantine sepulchre dates from 1922. Topped with a cupola and featuring sculpted angels, dogs and eagles, along with the four Račić sarcophagi, it's a quite extraordinary work. It excited mixed feelings in Rebecca West when she was here in 1937. 'There are some terrible errors, such as four boy musician angels, who recall the horrid Japaneseries of Aubrey Beardsley …but there are moments in the chapel which exquisitely illustrate the theory that the goodness of God stretches under human destiny, like the net below trapeze acts at the circus.'

If you're after something a little less esoteric, there's a pleasant **walk** around the headland, with plenty of places where you can swim off the rocks, and regular trips across the bay for 50 kuna to the tiny, almost barren island of **Supetar**, which boasts a simple restaurant. Rather more strenuous are a couple of local **hikes**. The shorter of these leads from Cavtat to Močiči and Čilipi, taking around 1¹/₂ hours. The other involves a 3–4-hour trek up the 'Ronald Brown Pathway' (*pjesačka staza Ronald Brown*) that starts from the main road above the town and leads up into the

VLAHO BUKOVAC – VIRTUOSO PAINTER

Vlaho Bukovac was born in Cavtat in 1855, and showed prodigious talent from an early age. In 1877 he went to the Beaux Arts in Paris to complete his studies and a year later became the first Croatian painter to be accepted into the prestigious Paris Salon. Travelling widely around Europe, Bukovac nonetheless played a vital part in the development of Croatian art – not just by being enormously prolific himself (he left over 2,000 works) but by supporting younger artists as well.

In his forties Bukovac spent five years living in Cavtat before accepting the post of Professor of Fine Arts in Prague, though he returned to his childhood home regularly until shortly before his death in 1922.

At their best, Bukovac's paintings are simply marvellous, combining an almost photographic realism with impressionistic touches, and some of his portraits are truly stunning. As a virtuoso painter, he seems to have had a penchant for technically difficult or daring compositions, and there's a wonderful picture of a woman coming in (or going out?) through a doorway, which is in the Museum of Modern Art in Dubrovnik, along with a brilliant portrait of his daughter.

mountains to the cross commemorating the delegation led by the American Minister of Trade in 1996.

South to the Montenegrin border

Past the airport of the same name you'll find the pretty village of Čilipi. After Sunday mass the locals put on a show of folk music and dancing in the main square here, so it's not surprising that it's become something of a Sunday-morning tourist excursion from Dubrovnik and the nearby resort hotels.

Three buses a day run from Dubrovnik to Čilipi and on to **Molunat**, a tiny fishing village in a lovely cove right at the very end of Croatia. With just a handful of private rooms, and no hotels nearby, it's within an hour of Dubrovnik, and would be an utterly charming place to stay. To be honest, however, given the bus times and the minuteness of the place, you'd need to be in Dubrovnik on an extended visit or to have your own wheels to make the excursion really worthwhile.

THE ELAPHITE ISLANDS (KOLOČEP, LOPUD, ŠIPAN)

The Elaphite Islands lie in a string north of Dubrovnik. Only three are now inhabited (Koločep, Lopud and Šipan), and these are connected by a ferry which runs up and down their length from Dubrovnik three times daily – if you're clever with the Jadrolinija timetables you can also use these ferries to combine the islands with a trip to Mljet.

The Elaphites make for a great excursion, getting you away from the crowds and into nature; there are no cars on Koločep and Lopud, and barely a handful on Šipan. If you're interested in staying in private rooms or apartments it's well worth contacting Elaphiti Travel (tel: 020 452 983; fax: 020 456 345) in advance, as the agency specialises in accommodation on the islands.

The first Elaphite island you'll see is **Daksa**, just 500m out of Dubrovnik's port, which may or may not still be for sale – the whole 6ha island was being advertised at a cool US$3.5 million, including a large house, a ruined monastery, a boat-house and a dock through 2002 and 2003, but by 2004 it seemed to be off the market again. Either way, would your karma ever recover from buying a place where dozens of Dubrovnik intellectuals were massacred by the partisans in 1944?

Koločep

The first inhabited island in the Elaphites is Koločep, just 7km and 25 minutes away from Dubrovnik on the ferry, making it a very easy day trip. The ferry – which costs a thrifty 11 kuna – docks at Donje Čelo, and although there's another settlement on the other side of the island, it's here that you'll find the main infrastructure.

Outside the tourist season Koločep has an official population of just 148, and the doctor only comes once a week. Indeed, if you come here before May, you'll find only a single shop and a post office open in the mornings, and nowhere on the island to eat or drink at all – so bring a picnic, and make sure you know what time the last ferry leaves.

Donje Čelo is spread around a gentle bay, and has a biggish and reasonably sandy beach. A concrete path heads up from the ferry landing and winds across the island, leading through lovely woods and dry-stone walled fields to the settlement of Gornje Čelo on Koločep's southeastern shore – where you'll find a couple of bars in summer and nothing whatsoever in winter. Smaller paths head on into the scented woods, and the island's sufficiently large for you to lose sight of anyone else, but small enough to avoid getting lost.

If you want to stay (from May to October), there's a single hotel in Donje Čelo, across the bay from the ferry landing, called the **Ville Koločep** (tel: 020 757 025; fax: 020 757 027). At the height of the season expect to pay €115 a night for doubles, including obligatory half board, in one of the eight buildings comprising the 150-room three-star hotel. In May and October the rate drops to €53 a night. When the hotel's open there are also three restaurants on the island; two near the ferry terminal and the other one beyond the hotel. There are also a handful of private rooms available – just ask on arrival if you haven't made prior arrangements.

Lopud

Half an hour – and a mere 8 kuna more on the ferry – beyond Koločep is the larger island of Lopud. Important in Ragusan times, it once had a population of 4,000 and harboured nearly 100 ships, as well as being home to Miho Pracat, the man whose bust sits in the Rector's Palace in Dubrovnik (see box, overleaf).

Today the 4.5km-long island has a population of just 348 (though locals put the figure even lower, at barely half that). Everyone lives in one settlement, the eponymous Lopud, on a curved bay with a decent beach facing the village of Suđurađ on the next-door island of Šipan. There's no traffic, no pollution and no crime – and out of season nothing much open beyond a bar and a couple of shops. In summer, however, Lopud really comes into its own, and the village positively hums; it's a great place to come for the day or even for a holiday in its own right.

Where to stay and eat

If you want to stay on Lopud there are quite a few private rooms and apartments for rent (ask on arrival, or contact Elaphiti Travel – see introductory section), as well as a single hotel, the three-star **Lafodia** (tel: 020 759 022; fax: 020 759 026), at the far end of the bay from the ferry terminal and harbour. There's a new swimming pool, and altogether some 200 rooms, with sea-view doubles with balconies going for €100, including the obligatory half board. In May and October that drops to €60; the hotel and most of the island's restaurants are closed from November to April.

By 2006, it seems likely that the **Grand Hotel** will have been restored to its former glories, 70 years after first opening its doors to grand tourists. It's set back from the seafront in what was once a lovely garden (and presumably will be again), and is a striking modernist curiosity, architecturally, having been the first concrete hotel to be built on the Adriatic.

There are restaurants and bars all along the front, but it's also worth climbing up the street near the harbour to **Terrasse Peggy**, which does a great grill in summer and boasts breezy views out across the sea to the island of Šipan. Try the local versions of *limoncello* and a curiously potent, nameless local drink made from honey and herbs.

What to see

There's not a huge amount to see or do, but if you're here (and it's open) check out the church above the harbour, which has some fine 16th-century Venetian paintings and lovely 15th-century carved choir stalls. The church – one of 33 on the island – forms part of the **Franciscan Monastery**, which was dissolved by the French in 1808.

Also of interest is the small **town museum and treasury**, which are just off the quay opposite the end of the harbour, on Zlatarska. If they're closed – and they usually seem to be – pop through the gap between the two into a walled courtyard and seek out Lopud's priest, Don Ivan Vlašić, who holds the keys.

The treasury houses an assortment of ancient icons, vestments and sacred remnants, and a handful of very battered 9th-, 11th- and 12th-century frescos. In the museum you'll find an extraordinary and eclectic assembly of stuff ranging from Roman amphorae to 500-year-old pudding bowls to 19th-century English pottery. There's a nasty-looking French bayonet from 1806, a couple of pulleys from Miho Pracat's ship, and a cloak from the Giorgis, one of Dubrovnik's last noble families. Most curious of all, however, is a shaving gown which belonged to King Charles V of Spain, which was a gift to Miho Pracat (see below). If you're coming just to see the gown, check it's back from the restorers, as that's where it was in the summer of 2004.

Behind the museum you can see the crumbling ruins of the Dubrovnik **Rector's summer palace**, testimony to the fact that even now there are far more houses on Lopud than there are people. Walk further along the quayside, and there's a lovely park featuring tall pines and palms – planted each one, it's said, by grateful sailors who'd avoided shipwreck.

Just beyond the park, before the Grand Hotel, there's a path leading up to the left which crosses the island and comes out half an hour later at Šunj, one of the loveliest beaches on the Adriatic. On the crest of the hill, on the left, there's a concrete monument to Viktor Dyk, the Czech poet, author and political journalist, who died unexpectedly of a heart attack while on holiday here in May 1931, aged only 53.

The sandy beach at **Šunj** has a fine shallow descent into the water and a temporary bar/restaurant open in season. It's an ill-kept secret, however, with sizeable crowds of locals coming over from the mainland on summer weekends.

The name Šunj provides the clue to Lopud's apparently mysterious use of a snake swallowing a child on its coat of arms – something you're more likely to have seen as the right-hand half of the Alfa Romeo logo. According to the legend, Otto Visconti was shipwrecked here in 1098, on his way back from the Crusades, and so grateful was he to survive that he had a votive church built on the hill above the bay. This was decorated with a copy of a shield which had been used by one of the defeated Saracens – featuring the snake and the child – and which subsequently became the Visconti crest. Over time the locale became known as *biscione*, the Italian for 'big snake', which was later abbreviated to Šunj.

The present church of **Our Lady of Šunj** (*Gospa od Šunja*) above the bay – turn left just after the Dyk memorial, if you're coming from Lopud – dates from the end

MIHO PRACAT AND THE KING'S SHAVING GOWN

Born into a wealthy family on Lopud in 1528, Miho Pracat sought fame and fortune at sea but twice returned home penniless and in tatters. On the third try, however, he succeeded, and came back to Lopud a fabulously wealthy man – having saved Spain, it's said, from starvation after a bad harvest by using his ships to supply grain (no doubt at a healthy premium).

At an audience with a grateful King Charles V, Pracat was offered gold and a post as a colonial governor, but being wealthy and a patriotic Ragusan to boot he refused both. Instead, he asked for the king's shaving gown – which is why it's in Lopud's Town Museum today.

Pracat's only problem, it seems, was fertility – neither of his two wives produced an heir for him. When he finally died, in 1607, Pracat left his enormous fortune to the republic, mostly in the form of trusts. He was rewarded with the only statue ever raised to one of its own citizens – you can see it today in the Rector's Palace in Dubrovnik.

of the 15th century. If it's open (which sadly is not all that often) it's well worth looking in to see the marvellous carved wooden altarpiece featuring Mary and the apostles. This, oddly enough, is English, from the 16th century. Lopud sailors – arguably among the best in the world at the time – heard that Henry VIII was in conflict with the pope and busily dissolving the monasteries, so off they went to go and buy relics and religious treasures while they were going cheap. The background to the altarpiece shows the Lopud ship which brought the Madonna here.

There's a direct path leading back from the church into the town; off to the right of this, heading away from Šunj, there's a track leading up to a great ruined **fortress**. Built originally in the 16th century, it was reinforced and expanded by the French from 1808 to 1813. Today it's soulful and dilapidated, and there's nothing special to see – though the views across to the island of Šipan are fabulous.

Šipan

Furthest away, largest and least-visited of the Elaphites, Šipan is lovely. Known as the 'Golden Island', it once had 300,000 olive trees and a sizeable population, but centuries of emigration have left it with fewer than 500 inhabitants and – like Lopud – with many more houses than people. During Dubrovnik's Golden Age, it was fashionable for wealthy nobles to spend the summer season on Šipan, and you'll come across their (mostly dilapidated) summer residences all over the island – along with a smattering of Roman ruins and a score of churches from the 11th century onwards. The main reason to come here, however, is very much to get away from it all.

It takes the best part of two hours to get to Šipan from Dubrovnik (and costs a princely 14 kuna), with the ferry stopping at both the southwestern and northeastern ends. The main centres – and the only places where you'll find anything at all to eat or drink – are the ferry terminals: **Šipanska Luka**, to the northwest, at the end of a deep inlet, and **Suđurađ** to the southeast, opposite Lopud. The two settlements are about 7km apart, and connected by an irregular minibus. There are a smattering of other hamlets across the island, some not even connected by gravel tracks to one another.

Where to stay

There's only one hotel on the island, the two-star **Šipan** (tel: 020 758 000; fax: 020 758 003), which is in a great location on Šipanska Luka's harbour. There are 80 fairly functional rooms, with sea-view doubles going for €86 a night at the height of the season, dropping to €48 in May and October. Everything on the island is pretty much closed from November to April. There's also a handful of private rooms at both ends of the island, and you may find people touting these as you get off the boat – otherwise just ask around.

What to see

An excellent excursion is to take the ferry to one end of the island and then walk across to the other end and catch the return ferry home from there. It takes a leisurely two hours by the most direct route, on Šipan's only paved road. The interior of the island is a fertile valley where you'll see grapes, figs and olives being grown, and there are plenty of places to stop and have a picnic and a bottle of wine.

You can also wander up any of the many tracks leading up to the island's two limestone ridges, where you'll find abandoned olive groves surrounded by crumbling dry-stone walls – though above Šipanska Luka itself work is progressing apace on bringing some of the olive trees back into production. You may also come across the rooting-marks made by wild boar here. They're a recent arrival on the island, and something of a nuisance to the olive farmers, having swum across from the mainland after a forest fire at the end of the 1990s.

As you traverse the island, look out for the ruined **Napoleonic fortress** on the southern ridge, along with a hospital and barracks dating from the same era. There are also secretive military tunnels which dive into the hillside nearby, though for the time being these are off limits to the public.

If you're walking from Šipanska Luka to Suđurađ you'll pass a great fortress of a church dating from the 16th century, dedicated to **Sveti Duh** (the Holy Spirit), as you climb up out of the central valley. Just after this the road forks – if you go right it passes the local clinic and loops down to the port; if you go straight on it goes directly through Suđurađ itself before emerging at the harbour.

The dominating feature of Suđurađ is the summer residence of Vice Stjepović-Skočibuha, which is the only one of Šipan's 42 original mansions to be entirely preserved. It was built in 1563, with the tower being added in 1577, and is today used for conferences and functions. It houses an excellent restaurant and bar, **Na Taraci**, which is about the only place you'll find anything to eat at this end of the island.

If you want to explore further afield, you'll find boats down on the harbour happy to take you out to those of the Elaphite Islands which are uninhabited, as well as to delightful unspoiled coves and beaches on Šipan itself – if there's nobody around ask at the little bar along the harbour front, which is where most of the fishermen and seafaring types hang out.

MLJET

Mljet is one of the most attractive islands in the whole Adriatic. Despite being unusually beautiful, and entirely unspoiled by deforestation (it was never ruled by Venice, hence also the lack of towns of any size), it has hitherto remained relatively unvisited – though with the new, fast connection from Dubrovnik more people are coming every year. Nonetheless, the island is easily big enough, at over 100km^2, to absorb many more visitors without getting overcrowded.

The entire western end of Mljet is a national park, and features a pair of gorgeous saltwater lakes, the larger of which has an island with a ruined monastery on it. It's easy to visit on a day trip from Dubrovnik, but if you want to stay longer there's a hotel and some private rooms, and the island has great walking as well as good cycling and canoeing, along with a nascent (if perhaps rather casual) diving school, and the opportunity of learning to sail – though it's a pity they don't have dinghies on hand.

History

Legend has it that Ulysses stopped here for seven years on his Odyssey, and while there's absolutely no historical basis for the assertion, it makes a nice story. More credence can be given to the theory that on his way to martyrdom in Rome, St Paul was shipwrecked here, not on Malta. It's not just the name (Mljet used to be called Melita), but also the snakes – St Paul was bitten by one soon after arriving, which would be improbable (then as now) on Malta, whereas Mljet was notoriously snake-infested right up until the 19th century.

Less speculative is the island's use by the Illyrians and the Romans – the remains of the Illyrian fort can still be seen on the summit of Mali Gradac, near **Babine Kuče**, while the settlement of **Polače** is named after the ruins of the 4th- or 5th-century Roman palace there.

The next significant development was in 1151, when Mljet was given to the Benedictines, who built the monastery on St Mary's Island. They stayed on even though Mljet itself was handed over to Dubrovnik in 1333, and lived a peaceful life until the arrival of Napoleon's troops in 1808, after which the monastery was abandoned.

The administrative centre of the island, **Babino Polje**, dates from the Middle Ages, but apart from the monastery, nothing on the western end of the island reaches back beyond the late 18th century, and the new port of **Pomena** wasn't established until after World War II.

Wildlife

Mljet is famous for being the only place in Europe where you can find mongooses in the wild. The Indian grey mongoose was introduced to Mljet in 1910, by the Austrians, in an attempt to eradicate the infestation of venomous snakes. This had been a problem since time immemorial – and was probably the reason why the Benedictines built their monastery on the island in the first place ('Never mind the beauty and the isolation, Brother Jacob, let's get away from those blasted snakes!').

Seven male and four female mongooses were introduced, and they adapted well to the Mljet lifestyle, proliferating and practically eradicating the snake population over the next 20 years. So successful were they, in fact, that they lost their statutory protection in 1949, and excessive numbers have proven difficult to curb. Small animals, as well as both resident and migratory birds, fall prey to the feral hunters, and they're not over-popular with the islanders, either.

Mljet's other fauna used to include the Mediterranean monk seal, though none has been spotted here since 1974. You may however see the Turkish gecko, the sharp-snouted lizard, or Dahl's whip snake (if the mongooses haven't got to him first), and there are now quite a few fallow deer in the forests – following their introduction here in 1958.

Getting there

There's a daily Jadrolinija ferry from Dubrovnik, though as this arrives in Mljet in the afternoon and returns at 06.00 in the morning it does mean an overnight stopover. The crossing takes around four hours. In summer, however, you can take the one-and-a-half-hour crossing on the fast catamaran, *Nona Ana*, which comes out to Mljet in the morning and returns in the afternoon, making day trips perfectly feasible. The fare is around 50 kuna return. It is also possible to go direct from Bari to Mljet as the Jadrolinija ferry to Dubrovnik stops at Sobra three times a week.

All ferries dock just east of **Sobra**, about a third of the way along Mljet's north shore, and are met by the local bus – but be warned that on busy days in summer there can be fewer buses than passengers, and if you're stranded your only realistic option is to rent a bike – at sellers' prices (and it's a long, hard, hot and hilly ride). To solve this problem the catamaran has taken to sailing on to Polače, and if you're on a day trip this is definitely the way to go. There's also an SEM ferry linking **Polače** with Trstenik on the Pelješac peninsula between mid July and mid September.

The easiest way of seeing Mljet is by taking an all-inclusive package from Dubrovnik (available from all the usual agencies). These go for around 200–300 kuna and include the ferry fare, a trip out to the island on the lake, and a guided tour, as well as the chance to swim. Bring a bottle of wine and a picnic, and it makes a wonderful day out.

Getting around

Local buses run between Sobra and Pomena to coincide with the Jadrolinija ferry arrivals and departures, but otherwise there's no public transport.

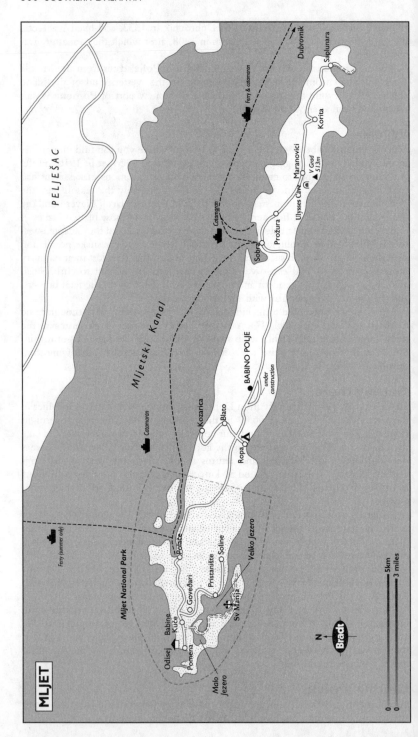

If you want to cycle on the island the best place to rent bikes is at the Hotel Odisej, in Pomena, or by the lakes themselves. Rates run from 20 kuna an hour to 110 kuna a day, and the paths around the lakes are absolutely perfect for cyclists. (There are several other places which rent out bikes too, if the stock at the Odisej's already out on loan, or if you haven't yet got as far as Pomena, including Sobra and Polače.) Even on the main roads, there's no traffic to speak of. You can rent buggies or cars and scooters outside the hotel, too, as well as at Sobra and Polače, with cars going from around 400 kuna a day, including fuel and 100km.

Where to stay and eat

The monastery on St Mary's Island served from 1960 to 1988 as the lovely Hotel Melita, but since it was handed back to the Dubrovnik bishopric it's fallen into ruin. Although restoration commenced in 2004, nobody's sure what will become of it – there's no doubt it would make the most wonderful boutique hotel, but there are also plans to turn it into a research or information centre, or to leave it as a visitor attraction. At present, there's just a restaurant serving the numerous visitors to the island throughout the day.

For the time being, therefore, Mljet has only one hotel, the three-star **Odisej** (tel: 020 744 022; fax: 020 744 042; www.hotelodisej.hr), in Pomena, which has 150 rooms spread across a number of buildings, with sea-view doubles with balconies going for around €140 a night at the peak of the season, and €80 outside July and August. The hotel shuts down from November until just before Easter.

Mljet also has a reasonable (and steadily increasing) supply of **private rooms**, but it's often essential to book ahead. This can be arranged through the Mini Brum tourist agency in Babino Polje (tel: 098 285 566; fax: 020 745 260). For rooms outside the national park, you can also try the rather intermittent tourist office in Babino Polje (tel/fax: 020 745 125) or – within the park itself – that in Goveđari (tel: 020 744 086; fax: 020 744 186; email: tz-mjesta@du.htnet.hr). Polače, a few kilometres away from the Hotel Odisej, but still within easy walking distance of the lakes, has excellent private rooms on the shore, and also has a bakery and a couple of cheerful restaurants. Pomena, too, has some good private accommodation, including the highly recommended Apartments Stražičić (tel/fax: 020 419 122; email: slavica.strazicic@du.htnet.hr), where a double apartment costs €60 a night in July and August, or €45 at other times. Half-a-dozen restaurants line the harbour, which is very popular with visiting yachtsmen (as indeed is Polače), but food shopping is limited to the early-morning bakery van, a couple of fruit stalls and the absolute basics.

There are two basic **campsites** on the island – one in Babino Polje, the other in Ropa. Other, more personal sites are run by private individuals – just ask around when you arrive at the port.

Activities

If you're here for more than a day trip, take advantage of the island's excellent **walking and hiking**. From the gentle paths around the lakes to the harder trails into the hills, Mljet's unspoiled beauty is overwhelming, and away from the lakes you'll pretty much have the place to yourself. Even on the lakeshore, you don't have to walk far to have almost total seclusion. There's a good marked trail from near Soline up Montokuč overlooking the lakes (the ascent takes around 40 minutes), with great views from the top. Rather than retrace your steps, you could return to Pristanište or continue to Polače or Goveđari. Within the park, trails lead to unexplored coves on the island's northwest tip, while even outside the park the ratio of nature to people is very high.

If it's **watersports** you're after, there's plenty of choice. Exploring by **kayak** or **canoe** makes for a great way of seeing the lakes at your own pace – they can be rented by the little bridge or at the hotel, with prices roughly the same as for bikes (see above). Windsurfers can be rented out from the hotel, too, and there's also a sailing school based here, though it's a pity they don't have dinghies on hand. For divers, the local diving centre (book through the hotel or phone Mario on 098 479 916) can take you out to a Roman wreck, complete with original amphorae, or to a defunct German U-boat. Expect to pay €43 for a dive with a guide, including equipment – though if you're a novice you might want to take heed of reports of a certain laxity in this department. Visits to either of the wrecks cost an additional €10.

What to see and do
Mljet National Park

Mljet's main draw is the national park, and specifically the two saltwater lakes, **Veliko Jezero** (with St Mary's Island and the ruins of the monastery) and **Malo Jezero** – literally 'Big Lake' and 'Small Lake'. If you're on a day trip you won't have time to see a great deal else.

As you'll probably guess – the salt water's a bit of a giveaway – neither Malo nor Veliko Jezero is actually a lake. The sea feeds into the larger one, and that feeds into the smaller one. The tidal changes allowed the monks to run a useful watermill in the past, and although the mill's long gone you can still easily see which way the tide's headed from the bridge over the shallow channel between Malo and Veliko Jezero.

Unfortunately the bridge originally spanning the seaward exit of Veliko Jezero was lost when the channel was widened and deepened in 1960, so you can't now do the full 12km circuit round the lake without getting wet. *A word of warning:* If you do decide to swim the 13.6m-wide and 2.6m-deep channel, be very sure which way the current's going, and how fast it's moving – there's an awful lot of water coming in and out of here, and it's frighteningly easy to be swept out to sea.

The boat out to **St Mary's Island** (Sveti Marija) runs several times a day, and the fare is included in the national park entry fee. On the island itself there's not much to see, with the church badly in need of restoration and the monastery/hotel seriously dilapidated and overgrown. The monastery is currently being restored, however, and the church is now open for services at 11.30 on Sunday. You can visit the monks' gardens, complete with lemon trees, in the original cloisters (if they're open). The island does have a restaurant, however, and this is highly popular as the luncheon venue for excursions, as well as an ice-cream stopover.

Take the ten-minute path around the little island and you'll see two other plain but evocative votive chapels dating from the 17th or 18th century. These were built by grateful sailors who'd survived shipwrecks or storms. If you're here in spring, you'll find lots of wild asparagus, while in summer you'll be overwhelmed by the noise of cicadas in the afternoon haze.

Established in 1960, the national park (tel: 020 744 041; fax: 020 744 043; www.np-mljet.hr) is run from the settlement of **Goveđari**, roughly equidistant from Pomena and Polače. Entry is 65 kuna, and the money goes to the upkeep of the park, so don't be tempted to try and avoid paying. Anyway, if you're caught without a ticket, you'll be charged – double. Detailed maps are available from the park office (on the shore of the main lake, at the locality called **Pristanište**) or from the kiosk selling tickets in Pomena, though the footpath network shown on these maps is none too accurate. There's another kiosk on the road in from Polače.

The national park is unusual among nature reserves in including the main villages, the hotel and the basic tourist infrastructure within its boundaries, but don't be lulled into a sense of false security. You're in an ecologically fragile area here, and it's important to follow the rules, especially relating to fire – in 1917 an accidental blaze destroyed much of the old forest and the restoration took decades. So don't light fires, don't smoke, don't camp – and do stay on the paths.

Beyond the national park

Three-quarters of Mljet is forest-covered, meaning good shade in the summer heat (but take plenty of water with you; there are no supplies at all), while the few settlements are rarely visited, and you'll be made to feel welcome by the locals. This is especially true on the 15km stretch of the island east of Sobra, where the settlements of **Prožura**, **Maranovići** and **Korita** are practically never visited by foreigners. Right at the far eastern tip, at Sapunara, are two sandy beaches, the only ones on the island. You'll need a car (or a bike, and strong legs) to get here as no buses run beyond Sobra. The first is below the village itself; the other, round the next bay, has a shallow and very sheltered lagoon, and is almost deserted. Debris washed in on the tide is a problem in parts at present, but with the current promotion by the tourist board, this – and the seclusion – are likely to change.

The highest point on the island (Veli Grad, 513m) is just above Mljet's diminutive administrative capital, **Babino Polje**, which sits on the side of the island's largest field system – the endless dry-stone walls here are the result of centuries of clearing stones from the fields. The main produce is olives and (surprisingly expensive but incredibly tasty) goat's cheese. Much of the island's very drinkable wine comes from the village of **Blato**, just outside the national park.

Once the new bypass is open, the capital is likely to be even less visited by tourists.

Directly south of Babino Polje is **Ulysses Cave** (Odisejeva spilja), a good half-hour's tough walk across fields and down the cliff, but well worth the effort – though not suitable for young children. Also visited on a boat-trip from Odisej Hotel, it's a magical cave to explore in calm seas.

TRSTENO

Just 18km up the coast from Dubrovnik is the little village of Trsteno, which would be entirely unremarkable were it not for the wonderful arboretum here. Originally created as the summer residence and gardens of Ivan Gučetić, a Dubrovnik noble, in 1502, and expanded over the centuries, the estate was nationalised by the communists in 1948 and re-branded as the Arboretum of the Yugoslav (now Croatian) Academy of Arts and Sciences.

The gardens here are delightful, and make a charming excursion out of Dubrovnik. The bus to Split, which goes every half-hour or so, sets down and picks up in the middle of the village, where the first thing you'll see is a splendid pair of huge 500-year-old plane trees. Beyond these, heading towards the sea in a series of terraces, is the arboretum itself.

There's nothing special to do other than to wander round the gardens, which vary from the formality of the oldest part, beneath the villa, with geometrical box hedges enclosing different planted areas, to the wilder areas off to the sides. There's a lovely orchard with citrus fruits, avenues of palms and firs, and all manner of exotic semi-tropical plants, most of them usefully labelled. There's even a rather fanciful 18th-century grotto, where you'll find Neptune with his trident presiding over a water-lily strewn fishpond and playful water-spouting fountains in the form of dolphins.

PLOČE AND THE NERETVA DELTA

Roughly half way between Split and Dubrovnik lies the industrial port of **Ploče**. Known during the 1980s as Kardeljevo, after one of Tito's pals, it still handles most of Bosnia & Herzegovina's sea-bound freight (the coastal town of Neum, actually in Bosnia's land corridor, is a dreary little resort with no proper port) and acts as a transport hub.

The re-established rail link to Sarajevo (a spectacular journey) starts from here, and there are Jadrolinija car ferries across to Trpanj, on Pelješac – three a day in winter, seven in summer. Otherwise there's no reason to break your journey.

South of Ploče is the extraordinary **Neretva Delta**. Long a marshy, malarial swamp, the pancake-flat river delta is now a series of fertile agricultural wetlands, producing Croatia's best citrus fruits (you'll see delicious tangerines for sale along the roadside), and providing shelter to waterfowl and wading birds, as well as spawning grounds for many species of fish, including the locally popular eels.

Deep in the delta are six, hard-to-find dedicated ornithological reserves. You'll need time, patience, and your own transport – and watch out on the main roads for the flying customs squads, on the lookout for Bosnian contraband and speeding tourists. A total of 299 species of bird have been recorded in the delta, with 92 nesting here, including the pigmy cormorant, coots, crakes, warblers and shrikes, several species of heron and egret, all five species of European grebe and almost every species of European duck. In 1999, a government proposal was initiated to proclaim the entire delta as a nature park, but obstacles include various development and road improvement plans.

Easily the best way of visiting the delta is by persuading one of the locals to take you around in a punt (the indigenous *trupica*), poling you along the reedy channels which separate the reclaimed market gardens, and giving you a chance to soak up the mysterious atmosphere.

Far simpler, however, is to book yourself on a day-long excursion from Dubrovnik (around 300 kuna, including a comprehensively guided boat tour), or to contact the Maestral agency in Split (tel: 021 470 944; fax: 021 470 980), which organises trips from one to five days featuring the delta.

PELJEŠAC PENINSULA

An island in all but name, the 65km Pelješac peninsula runs up from the isthmus at Ston to the island of Korčula. Never more than 7km wide, Pelješac is mountainous and rocky, an unlikely home to two of Croatia's best wines, the hearty Dingač and Postup reds.

Three buses a day travel up and down the main road from Dubrovnik to Ston and on to Orebić, the main departure point for Korčula, and buses also hook up with Trpanj, the arrival point for ferries from Ploče, on the mainland. But if you want to explore the dozens of small villages, or the myriad hidden bays and beaches, you'll definitely need your own wheels.

Ston

The land entrance to Pelješac is at Ston, which guards the isthmus with a series of remarkably well-preserved walls from the 14th century on. On the south coast is the village of **Veliki Ston**, while on the northern bay is **Mali Ston**, famous now for Croatia's best oysters and mussels – the two settlements are a 15-minute walk apart, should you get off the bus at the wrong stop.

Ston was badly hit by the 1996 earthquake, which destroyed many of the houses in the old town, along with most of the town of Slano, further down the coast towards Dubrovnik. Restoration has been a good deal slower here than in

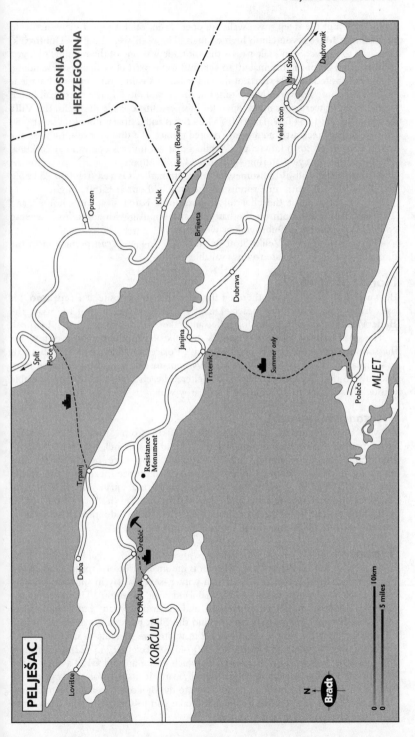

Dubrovnik, but the steep town walls are open again, offering great views across to the island of Mljet if you climb high enough. The walls were built by Dubrovnik, primarily to protect Ston's salt-pans – the salt trade was one of the republic's biggest earners – and 20 of the original 40 towers and some 5km of walls are still standing.

When I visited in 2004, parts of the old town of Veliki Ston were still boarded-up, as were some houses in Mali Ston, but the restaurants and the two small hotels on the harbour were very much open for business. Just outside the walls, the **Villa Koruna** (tel: 020 754 359; fax: 020 754 642) has half a dozen fine doubles at €80 (not including breakfast) and a great covered terrace of a dining room, right on the water. Oysters go for 6 kuna a pop, while a plate of mussels comes in at 25 kuna. The lobster (at an eye-watering 400 kuna a kilo) is superb.

Just inside the walls is the somewhat more upmarket **Ostrea** (tel: 020 754 555; fax: 020 754 575), with nine rooms on the little harbour at €150 a night.

You can also eat at the cheerful **Kapetanova Kuća** ('captain's home') and **Taverna Bota**, also both on the harbour, and popular with aphrodisiac-seeking couples from Split and Dubrovnik at weekends.

The tourist office in Veliki Ston (tel/fax: 020 754 452) can point you in the direction of the few private rooms available locally.

North of Ston
Between Ston and Trstenik there's a flat, tree-shaded campsite at **Prapratno**, set back from a wide, secluded beach. Directly above, on the side of the road, the **Bella Vista** is a good stopover for coffee and cakes, or something more substantial.

The small holiday village of **Trstenik** on Pelješac's southern coast is of note for the summer ferry linking the peninsula with Polače on Mljet, a pleasant hour or so's trip away. Run by SEM Marina (www.sem-marina.hr), it's operational from mid July to mid September. There's a sheltered beach here, with diving available through Mario (see page 302), and the nearby winery is open to visitors.

Resistance monument
As you progress up the peninsula, about 40km from Ston, there's a huge monument to the resistance, right where the road crests a hill, near the locality of **Pijavičino**. If you're under your own steam, stop here by the abandoned restaurant, and take a moment to look at the stylised bronze frieze depicting scenes from World War II, showing brutal oppression, firing squads, the first signs of resistance and uprising, and finally the joy of freedom. On the back of the curved walls is the endless list of the local dead, while the whole is dominated by a pair of curved concrete pillars stretching about 30m into the sky.

Trpanj
In a sweeping bay on Pelješac's north coast is the small town of Trpanj, arrival point for the ferries from Ploče (three a day in winter, seven a day in summer, with an extra service to Drvenik, further up the mainland coast, in season). The cheerful little town has a couple of cafés and restaurants, and a charmingly tatty but helpful tourist office (tel/fax: 020 743 433) hidden behind the **Flok** pizzeria on the front, which can arrange private rooms. Opening hours in winter are sporadic to say the least.

Trpanj has one hotel, the **Faraon** (tel: 020 743 408; fax: 020 743 422), with around 150 rooms, all with balcony and sea view, which go for around €130 a night at the height of the season, including obligatory full board. It sits right on the large pebble beach to the west of the harbour, facing across to the Biokovo massif on the mainland.

Buses connect with the ferries here, and take you to Orebić, which leads on to Korčula or back to Ston and Dubrovnik.

Orebić

Pelješac's best-known resort, Orebić, is an unpretentious little town with an excellent climate – it's protected by the mountains from the *bora* wind, giving it mild winters, early springs and long-lasting summers. The town is right across the strait from Korčula, and in summer 14 ferries a day go in each direction (seven in winter). To get back to the mainland the easiest routes are to either take the direct bus to Dubrovnik (three a day) or to catch the ferry to Korčula and then go on the next ferry to Split from there. Alternatively, you can catch the bus to Trpanj, and the ferry from there across to Ploče (or Drvenik, in summer).

To the west of Orebić are a series of resort hotels, on a mixture of nice sandy and pebble beaches, while 500m to the east you'll find the **Trstenica** beach, which ought to be one of the nicest little stretches of the Adriatic coast – it's backed by cacti and palms, and home to a row of fine 18th- and 19th-century villas – but it has been known to be filthy in the early summer, strewn with litter and beer bottles, and badly in need of a clean-up.

The sometimes unwelcoming tourist office (tel/fax: 020 713 718) has (pretty unreliable) walking maps and access to a supply of private rooms, while the nearest hotel to the centre is the two-star **Bellevue** (tel/fax: 020 713 148) which has around 80 rooms and faces on to a rocky beach. Sea-view doubles go for around €55.

From the Bellevue it's an uphill hike westwards to the 15th-century **Franciscan Monastery** which houses the icon known as 'Our Lady of the Angels' – for centuries sailors came here with votive gifts after being saved from shipwreck, storms or pirates. The terrace of the monastery, at 150m above sea-level, looks down across the strait to Korčula town, a lovely view.

Even finer panoramas can be had from the 961m summit of **Mount St Ilija**. It's a steep hike, four to five hours up from Orebić, but the simply wonderful views from the summit include the whole of the island of Korčula, Mljet to the south, and the gaunt karst mountains of the mainland to the north.

If you're hiking up here wear proper hiking boots (there are reported sightings of sand vipers), start very early (there's little or no shade), take plenty of water, and use common sense as much as the map or the route marks on the ground – neither are anything like as reliable as you'd like (you'll need better eyesight than mine for some of the faded markings). Follow the path up to the monastery, and then continue to Bilopolje, after which the track bears off to the right, following not entirely reliable red and white flashes to the summit.

KORČULA

Like Hvar, Korčula has a lovely old town and lots of hard-to-reach coves and beaches. Like Hvar, too, Korčula's no secret, but it doesn't yet have quite the visitor numbers of its northern neighbour (though Korčula's numbers are growing significantly faster, year on year).

The island is nestled up to the western end of Pelješac (less than 1.5km of sea separates them at the narrowest point) and stretches about 45km west into the Adriatic. On average it's about 6km across, from north to south, and has a mountainous spine rising to 568m just west of the village of Pupnat.

The main attraction on the island is the old town of Korčula itself, almost opposite Orebić (on Pelješac), though a close second has to be Korčula's powerful white wines, notably Pošip, Rukatac, and Lumbarda's Grk. Korčula also makes a pretty good base for exploring Pelješac, and offers easy excursions over to Mljet (see page 298).

History

Korčula's history stretches back as far as anywhere in Croatia, with Neolithic settlements here followed by the arrival of Greek colonists in the 6th century BC. The Greeks co-existed peaceably with Illyrians on the island for several hundred years before the Romans barged in during the 1st century BC, enraged by the island's propensity for harbouring pirates. Most of the population was either killed, exiled or enslaved, setting something of a pattern until the late Middle Ages, when Korčula went through the usual southern Adriatic tussle between Venice, Dubrovnik and the Turks.

In 1298, just off Lumbarda, a total of more than 180 galleys from the rival Venetian and outnumbered Genoan fleets clashed in one of the biggest sea battles of the Middle Ages. Genoa won the day, and took 7,000 prisoners, including a certain Marco Polo, who was back in the Adriatic after more than 20 years in Asia with his father and uncle, and was on that day at the helm of one of the Venetian battleships.

Today, Marco Polo is unquestionably Korčula's most famous son, though some scholars now think he may have been born in Šibenik, further up the Dalmatian coast. Whatever the truth, Korčula does more for Marco Polo than anywhere else, and the setting of the old town here is suitably evocative as the kind of place he might have been brought up.

Recent history on Korčula has been dominated by tourism, though there's still a fish-processing factory in Vela Luka, at the western end of the island, and the wine business is increasingly important. Olive oil has been a valuable source of revenue, too, though it's unclear how much of a long-term impact the forest fires of August 1998 will have – more than 800ha of olive groves and woods were destroyed by the lethal combination of lightning strikes and a gale-force *bora*.

Getting there and around

Daily buses arrive on Korčula from Dubrovnik and Zagreb, rolling on to the car ferry from Orebić for the last couple of kilometres. The journey from Dubrovnik, up through the Pelješac peninsula, takes a little under four hours; from Zagreb it's a 12- or 13-hour overnighter.

Car ferries from Orebić (arrive early if you're bringing your car) come in at Dominče, 3km south of Korčula town, seven times a day in winter, 14 in summer. If you're not on the bus already you can avoid the hike into town by hopping on to one of the hourly buses from Lumbarda to Korčula, though don't rely on this service at weekends. As a foot passenger, you're better off taking the smaller boat which runs from Orebić directly to Korčula town's west harbour (seven a day in winter, ten in summer).

A daily ferry service runs from Split to Vela Luka, at the western end of Korčula, taking around 3½ hours; the same journey can be done in under 2 hours on the daily catamaran. From Vela Luka to Korčula town there are half a dozen buses a day, though fewer at weekends – the ferries always connect with a bus, however. In summer there's also a service (one to three times a day) from Drvenik direct to Korčula.

If you're reliant on public transport you'll be pretty much limited to Korčula town, the sandy beaches of **Lumbarda**, 6km southeast (hourly buses; flaky weekend service), and the main road to **Vela Luka** – for access to Korčula's many hidden beaches and coves, which tend to be at the end of long gravelly roads, you'll definitely need your own wheels. A great, liberating option is to rent a bike, which you can do from the bike rental place next door to the **Hotel Park** – along the coast towards Lumbarda, five minutes out of Korčula old town. Well-conditioned bikes go for around 100 kuna a day. The bike-rental service is

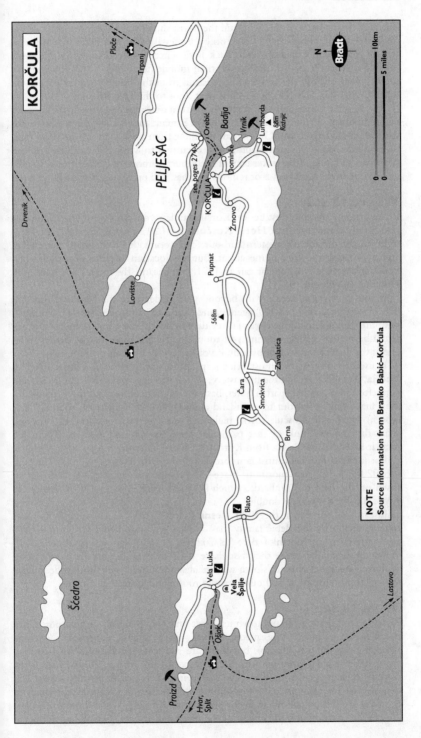

operated by the same people who run the florist shop on the western corner of the town (see map), and if they're not too busy they'll bring you bikes into town to the shop and you can drop them back here when you're done. Contact Vesna Šulekić or Milan Vojinović directly on their mobile (tel: 098 344 867). Pick up the superb maps of both the town and the island from the friendly tourist office (tel: 020 715 701; fax: 020 715 866), right next door to the Hotel Korčula.

If you don't have your own transport and can't face biking, you might consider taking an organised tour (from Marko Polo in Korčula town) to get more of a feel for the island's hidden charms. On offer are anything from a fish picnic to an island tour, to boat-trips round the local islands, to an excursion to Mljet. Alternatively you can negotiate with one of the water taxis at the eastern harbour of Korčula town to take you to one of the local islands or remoter beaches, and pick you up a few hours later.

Where to stay

Private rooms are your best bet on Korčula, unless you can secure one of the 20-odd rooms at the three-star **Hotel Korčula** (tel: 020 711 078; fax: 020 711 746), right on the old town's western harbour. The rooms (€140 doubles) themselves aren't anything to write home about, but the location is perfection itself. The building was already a popular café in 1871, and became the town's first hotel (the Hotel de la Ville) in 1912.

If you can't get in here (or it's beyond your budget) try the **Marko Polo** (tel: 020 715 400; fax: 020 715 800) agency, and expect to pay around €40 for a double, with a 30% supplement for stays of three days or less. If you come in by boat or bus you'll be met by people offering you rooms, and while these can be better value, check the agencies as well, especially if you're staying for four or more days.

It used to be that the most eclectic place to stay was on the little island of **Badija**, just offshore, but the monastery, which was expropriated in the 1950s and converted into a rather spartan hotel, has now been given back to the Franciscans. You may want to go out to the island anyway, however, as it has the best (and closest) beaches to Korčula town, including one reserved for naturists – though what the monks think of that particular arrangement isn't known. There are regular taxi-boats to Badija from Korčula's eastern harbour.

For more traditional tourist comfort there's the **Bon Repos** (tel: 020 711 102; fax: 020 711 122), an enormous place (370 rooms and apartments) 2km out of town on the road to Lumbarda, which is easiest reached by taxi-boat. Expect to pay €100 for a sea-view double.

Just out of Lumbarda, the **Villa Vesna** (tel/fax: 020 712 183) guesthouse and restaurant, run by the Bebić family, has doubles with half board for around €70, while the **Pansion Marinka-Bire** (tel/fax: 020 712 007) has nice apartments with views down to the sea – they also have their own wine, and frequent tasting sessions. Check out Korčula's own website at www.korcula.net/firme/indexp.html for much more on these and other private rooms and apartments online.

What to see

Korčula's top draw is the old town itself, set on a tiny peninsula jutting north into the Pelješac channel. The medieval walls have largely disappeared (Austria wouldn't pay for the upkeep), but there are still towers and buttresses here and there, and the old quarter is a harmonious mix of 15th-century Gothic with 16th-century Renaissance trimmings. The leaf-veined network of narrow streets was designed to keep the place cool in summer yet sheltered in winter – the roads to the west are straight, allowing in the summer sea breezes, while those to the east are curved, to minimise the effects of the nasty winter *bora*. The arched entrances to the old cellars were built that way to ease the passage of barrels, a reminder of Korčula's long-standing importance as a centre of wine production.

In various places around the town you'll see sculptures by Frano Kršnić, who was born in Lumbarda – they're softer and gentler than the works of Ivan Meštrović, with more than a passing nod to Rodin, and a tribute to Korčula's centuries-old tradition of stone-carving.

The obvious access to the old town is through the southern land gate and the 15th-century **Revelin Tower**. The sweep of stone steps leading up to the gate was only added in 1907, replacing the drawbridge. On the left-hand side as you come in through the gate there's a fine loggia (and a pleasant café). The main street then leads straight to **St Mark's Cathedral** (like Rab's and Hvar's, actually a church, since the island long ago lost its bishopric, but who's quibbling?). It's crammed into a space that's manifestly too small, and one of around 150 churches still used on the island.

Over the main door there's a throned statue of St Mark, flanked by a pair of fine Venetian lions on buttresses, the early 15th-century work of Bonino, the Italian sculptor. Supporting the lions are a wonderfully primitive, cowering Adam and Eve, while the blind pillars feature unusual carved clove-hitches half way up. Inside, at the end of the curiously skewed nave (look at the ceiling), there's a famous but frankly rather heavyweight altar canopy from the late 15th century and a couple of paintings attributed to Tintoretto – the altarpiece featuring St Mark, and an Annunciation in the southern nave. Also inside you'll find halberds from a 1483 battle and cannonballs from the Battle of Lepanto in 1571. Near these is a rare and celebrated 14th-century icon which came from the monastery on Badija; it's due for return to the Franciscans there once restorations have been completed.

On the left-hand side of the church is the large chapel dedicated to Roc, the patron saint of the plague; here you'll find a convincing St Blaise by Meštrović and a dusty sculpture over the doorway of St Michael killing Lucifer. If you're in town on July 29, you'll see the relics of the cathedral's co-patron, St Theodore, being carried in a procession around town.

IL MILIONE – THE BIRTH OF TRAVEL WRITING

While he was in prison in Genoa, Marco Polo's stories were written down by a Pisan romance writer who was sharing the same cell as the great explorer. Published in Franco-Italian, *Divisament dou Monde* (*Description of the World* – now better known as *The Travels of Marco Polo*) was received with widespread disbelief. But it was too late – modern travel-writing had been born. The book soon became known as *Il Milione*, possibly because it was seen as a million fables rather than a travelogue – whoever heard of paper money? Or nuts the size of a human head (coconuts)?

Because the book came out before printing was invented, it circulated as a series of hand-copied manuscripts, and more than 100 different versions still exist (but no original), in several languages, making it even harder than it might otherwise have been to know exactly what Marco Polo actually did or saw.

What's important, however, is that he inspired people to travel and explore foreign lands, and was the first westerner to describe the east in any detail. Controversy still reigns over how much of *Il Milione* is true – how can Marco Polo have missed out the Great Wall, for goodness sake? – but it remains one of the great classics of travel writing all the same, and is perhaps one of the reasons I ended up travelling (and writing about it) myself.

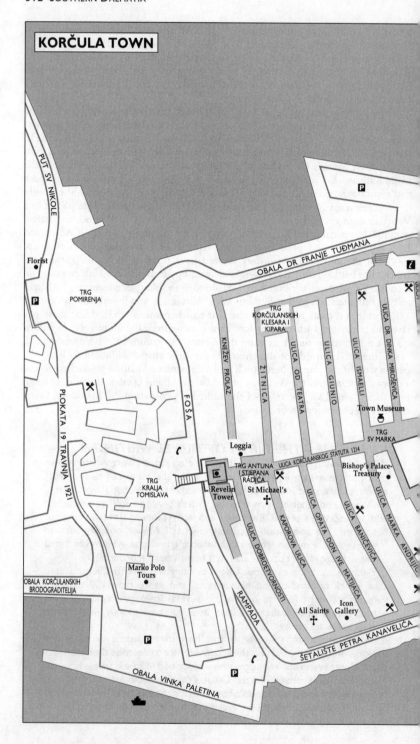

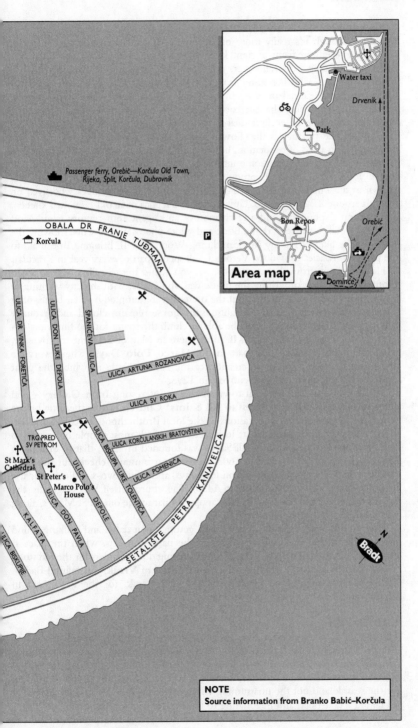

Passenger ferry, Orebič—Korčula Old Town,
Rijeka, Split, Korčula, Dubrovnik

OBALA DR FRANJE TUĐMANA

Korčula

ULICA DR VINKA FORETIĆA

ULICA DON LUKE DEPOLA

ŠPANIĆEVA ULICA

ULICA ARTUNA ROZANOVIĆA

ULICA SV ROKA

ULICA KORČULANSKIH BRATOVŠTINA

ULICA BISKUPA LUKE TOLENTIĆA

ULICA POMENICA

TRG PRED
SV PETROM

St Mark's
Cathedral

St Peter's
Marco Polo's
House

ULICA DEPOLE

KALFATA

ULICA DON PAVLA

ULICA BISKUPIJE

ŠETALIŠTE PETRA KANAVELIĆA

Water taxi

Drvenik

Park

Bon Repos

Orebič

Area map

Dominče

NOTE
Source information from Branko Babić–Korčula

Next door to the cathedral is the **Bishop's Palace**, which houses an impressive **treasury**, though it's really more of a museum. It's an extraordinary collection, covering everything from ancient kitchenware to contemporary art. There are collections of coins, church silver, relics from the Roman catacombs, medieval ballot boxes and a birth register from 1583. Strangest of all is a statue of Mary Queen of Scots, carved in ivory in the early 17th century – her skirts open to reveal a tiny triptych. The last room is lined with antique ecclesiastical robes, which get an airing on ecclesiastical shoulders during the Easter processions.

Opposite the treasury is the **Town Museum**, on several floors of a nice old building. It's in need of restoration, however, and the collection's a bit piecemeal to say the least – but there are some interesting bits of sculpture on the ground floor, where you'll also find the (reproduction – the original's in Zagreb) Greek tablet known as the Lumbarda stone, which lists the names of the families who lived on Korčula around 2,300 years ago. Upstairs there's a replica of an old-fashioned kitchen, a section on shipbuilding and a re-creation of an elegant 18th-century salon. Most evocative of all, however, are the black and white photos on the stairs, showing the arrival of the likes of Fitzroy Maclean during World War II, bringing British aid to the partisans (Maclean's widow, Veronica, still spends part of every year in Korčula).

Heading away from the centre of town you'll find the so-called **Marco Polo House**. At the time of writing the house was up for sale, with the city wanting to buy it and open it as a museum, but the owners were tempted by a far better offer from a Dutch investor. In the meantime the house remains closed and gradually falling apart, so it's unlikely you'll be able to climb the tower for the fine view out over the tiled roofs of the town. If you're here in May or September, however, you'll definitely want to take part in the **Marco Polo Days**, when everyone dresses up to stage a minor re-creation of the famous battle in which the great explorer was captured by the Genovese in 1298.

In the southeastern corner of town there's an interesting **Icon Gallery** – and entry to this also gives you access to **All Saints' Church**, across the little bridge which is still used on special occasions by the local Brotherhood, or Guild. Indeed, the Guilds play an important part in Korčula life, with most people belonging to one or another – the Guild of All Saints was founded in 1301, that of St Roc in 1571, and that of St Michael in 1603. In the icon museum check out the huge candles which are paraded around on feast days, and a fine two-sided cross for use in processions, which dates back to 1430. The church itself was originally the town's cathedral, and features an altar canopy similar to the one in St Mark's, along with a fine carved wooden altarpiece.

Beyond the main sights it's really worth getting up at dawn and walking round the outside of the old town and through the narrow streets, when the place is practically deserted. The pale light of early morning does wonders for the old stone – most of which was quarried locally, on the island of **Vrnik**, just behind Badija. Vrnik also provided stone for the walls of Dubrovnik, for the Parliament in Vienna, and for Stockholm's Town Hall.

Lumbarda

The rest of Korčula doesn't live up to the capital's promise, though it has any number of lovely holiday places if you have your own wheels. Even without your own transport, however, it's easy enough to get to Lumbarda – there are hourly buses in the week, and a restricted service at weekends. Assuming you're heading for the seaside and not the unassuming village itself, however, you're much better off taking a taxi-boat, and negotiating to be dropped right at the beach.

Lumbarda sits on the north shore of Korčula's southeastern peninsula, and the

MOORISH DANCES – THE MOREŠKA

For around 400 years the people of Korčula have been dressing up and performing the *moreška*, a famous sword dance which continues a tradition once common across the whole of Europe. Few of the dances retain anything remotely Moorish (least of all Britain's Morris Dancers), but the name has stuck fast. Korčula is special, however, in still using real swords in what is effectively a war dance.

Originally an annual festival, the *moreška* is now performed around twice a week (in a much condensed version – 40 minutes instead of the original 2¹/₂ hours) in Korčula town in summer, and makes for a spectacular evening show. The plot's pretty simple – bad king runs off with good king's squeeze; good king's soldiers fight bad king's soldiers; squeeze is saved from bad king's embraces – but nonetheless enjoyable for all that.

In other villages on Korčula they perform a similar dance, the *kumpanija* (the main difference being that it's sabres rather than swords which are used), particularly in Blato, towards the western end of the island. These are hard to get to without your own transport.

sandy soil here makes not just for the excellent local Grk wines, but also for some of the island's best beaches, all around the Ražnjić headland.

Vela Luka

Right at the other end of the island is Korčula's largest town, Vela Luka. It is much maligned, and in the past was known only for its shipyard and fish-processing factory. With a great situation, at the head of a well-sheltered bay, and industry slowing down, however, the town is increasingly a tourist destination in its own right. It has a cheerful heart, a handful of good places to stay, brilliant beaches on nearby offshore islands, and good transport connections: Vela Luka sees direct buses from Dubrovnik and Korčula town, and it's also on the main ferry and catamaran lines running from Split to Hvar to Vela Luka to Lastovo.

The tourist office (tel/fax: 020 813 619), on the front, can provide you with maps and local information, but if you want a private room then the place to go is **Apartments Vela Luka** (tel: 098 701 108 or 091 559 7614; www.apartments-vela-luka.com), who will sort you out in a jiffy – expect to pay €30 for a double room in summer. There's also a hotel right on the front, the **Dalmacija** (tel: 020 812 022; fax: 020 812 042), which has clean if rather plain doubles at €74 in season.

If you're here for any time, it's well worth making the effort to walk out of town to an impressive Neolithic cave, **Vela Špilje** – check with the tourist office for visiting times.

If you're feeling more hedonistic, an attractive alternative to the big cave (Vela Špilje means 'big cave'; Vela Luka means 'big bay') is to take one of the thrice-daily boats to the lovely little island of **Proizd**, right off Korčula's northwestern tip. This has several pebble beaches and some of the clearest waters I've ever swum in. There's a cheerful restaurant operational between the first and last boats, and a couple of naturist beaches, if that's your thing. Otherwise just enjoy the sea and sunshine – there's absolutely nothing else to do here. You can also rent yourself a boat from the quayside in Vela Luka (at around 200 kuna a day, plus 30 kuna for fuel), and motor out to the even closer island, **Ošjak**, which is almost within Vela Luka's harbour – it has lovely beaches and is popular with romantic couples; hardly surprising as the name means 'island of love'.

LASTOVO

A dozen kilometres south of Korčula is the island of Lastovo, barely 10km long. Like Vis (see page 254), it was off-limits for half a century and only opened up in 1989. Tourists are still pretty rare, though the numbers are growing rapidly.

It's a low-key destination, with no hotels as yet, and nothing remotely like nightlife. But if you like lobster, fresh white wine, a chance to meet the local people, and peace and quiet, then Lastovo's your place – unless you come during the carnival, when it goes berserk in a small-town sort of way, especially on Poklad's Tuesday (see below).

The island lost nearly a third of its trees during the August 1998 forest fires, but is recovering well.

Getting there/where to stay

Lastovo is the last stop for the daily ferry and catamaran from Split to Vela Luka (on Korčula), with boats arriving at **Ubli** in the early evening and leaving at the crack of dawn (before 05.00), effectively meaning you can't 'do' the island in less than two nights. It takes over five hours for the ferry to come from Split (75 minutes from Vela Luka), but under three hours on the catamaran (45 minutes from Vela Luka).

A bus meets the incoming boats in Ubli, and takes you the 10km to the village of **Lastovo**, spread out on a steep hillside facing away from the sea and sheltered from the *bora*. The tourist office (tel/fax: 020 801 018; www.lastovo-tz.net), right where the bus stops, has sporadic hours, but always opens when the bus comes in – they can furnish you with a basic map and fix you up with a private room.

What to see

There's nothing much to see in town – a handful of small 15th- to 17th-century churches pretty much sums it up – but do make the hike up to the ruined French fort right at the top of the hill, dating from 1810. It's now a weather station, with fabulous views.

You can also walk to various other hamlets on the island – the total population is well under 1,500 – which give access to the few points from which swimming is really an option. More attractive by far is to persuade a local boat owner to take you out to one of the string of islands to the east (the **Lastovo archipelago**). Here you'll find old lighthouses, pebble and rock beaches, and very few other people.

Poklad Festival

Lastovo's biggest annual festival is Shrove Tuesday (known here as Poklad Tuesday), which brings home expatriates from around the world to take part in the ritual humiliation and slaughter of Poklad.

Legend has it that Poklad was an unfortunate messenger sent by pirates to tell Lastovo to surrender, or else. The local people prayed hard and the pirate fleet was duly scuppered by a storm, leaving the luckless Poklad to be paraded round town on a donkey, run down a long rope, and then burned to death. Charming.

The festival pretty much follows the legend, though it's a luckless puppet rather than messenger which gets to play the lead. First off the puppet is paraded round town on the donkey, after which it's slid down a 300m-long rope from the top of town to the bottom, complete with firecrackers going off from its feet. On arrival it's met by uniformed men brandishing drawn swords, before being hauled back up the hill for another two descents. The whole thing ends with Poklad being put back on the donkey before being speared and burned à la Guy Fawkes – though you won't see the Lastovo sword dances on bonfire nights in Britain. It's an extraordinary spectacle.

Appendix 1

LANGUAGE
Pronunciation

Croatian words aren't anything like as hard to pronounce as you might expect them to be – just concentrate on pronouncing each letter the same way every time, and you won't go far wrong.

A	as in party	K	as in kept
B	as in bed	L	as in leg
C	as in fats, bats	M	as in mother
Ć, ć	as in nurture, culture	N	as in no
Č, č	as in chew, chump	O	as in hot
D	as in dote	P	as in pie
Đ, đ	as in George, jam (sometimes written Dj, dj, to help non-natives)	R	as in air
		S	as in sand
		Š, š	as in shovel
E	as in pet	T	as in too
F	as in free	U	as in look
G	as in goat	V	as in very
H	as in hat	Z	as in zoo
I	as in feet	Ž, ž	as in treasure
J	as in yet		

Words and phrases
Courtesies

hello/bye (informal)	zdravo/bok	how are you?	kako ste
cheers!	živjeli!	I'm fine, thank you	dobro, hvala
good morning	dobro jutro	please/thank you	molim/hvala
good day	dobar dan	thank you very	
good evening	dobro večer	much	hvala lijepo
good night		excuse me	izvinite
(on leaving)	laku noć	goodbye	doviđenja

Basic words

yes/no	da/ne	more/less	više/manje
	(nema = emphatic no)	good/bad	dobro/loše
that's right	tako je	hot/cold	toplo/hladno
OK	OK	toilet	zahod
maybe	možda	men/women	muški /ženski
large/small	veliko/malo		

Numbers

one	*jedan*	nine	*devet*
two	*dva*	ten	*deset*
three	*tri*	twelve	*dvanaest*
four	*četiri*	fifteen	*petnaest*
five	*pet*	twenty	*dvadeset*
six	*šest*	fifty	*pedeset*
seven	*sedam*	one hundred	*stotina*
eight	*osam*	one thousand	*hiljada*

Questions

how?	*kako?*	where?	*gdje?*
how much?	*koliko?*	who?	*tko?*
what's your name?	*kako se zovete?*	why?	*zašto?*
when?	*kada?*		

do you speak English?	*govorite li engleski?*
how do you say in Croatian?	*kako se to kaže na hrvatskom?*
can you tell me the way to…?	*možete mi reci put do…?*
how do I get to…?	*kako mogu doći do…?*
is this the right way to…?	*je li ovo pravi put do…?*
is it far to walk?	*je li daleko pješice?*
can you show me on the map?	*možete mi pokazati na karti?*

Getting around

bus	*autobus*	left/right	*lijevo/desno*
bus station	*autobusni kolodvor*	straight on	*ravno*
train/train station	*vlak/željeznička stanica*	ahead/behind	*naprijed/iza*
plane/airport	*avion/aerodrom*	up/down	*gore/dolje*
car/taxi	*auto/taxi*	under/over	*ispod/preko*
petrol	*benzin*	north/south	*sjever/jug*
petrol station	*benzinska stanica*	east/west	*istok/zapad*
entrance/exit	*ulaz/izlaz*	road/bridge	*cesta/most*
arrival/departure	*dolazak/odlazak*	hill/mountain	*brežuljak/planina*
open/closed	*otvoreno/zatvoreno*	village/town	*selo/grad*
here/there	*ovdje/tamo*	waterfall	*slap*
near/far	*blizu/daleko*		

Hotel

bed	*krevet*	toilet	*zahod*
room	*soba*	wc	*wc* (pronounced
key	*ključ*		'vay-say')
shower/bath	*tuš/kada*	hot/cold water	*topla/hladna voda*

Shopping

bank	*banka*	shop	*dućan*
bookshop	*knjižara*	market	*dućan/market*
chemist	*ljekarna/apoteka*	money	*novac*

Post

post office	*pošta*	postcard	*razglednica*
letter	*pismo*	paper	*papir*
envelope	*omotnica*	stamp	*poštanska marka*

Miscellaneous

tourist office	*turistički ured*	dentist	*zubar*
embassy	*veleposlanstvo*	hospital/clinic	*bolnica/klinika*
consulate	*konzularni ured*	police	*policija*
doctor	*liječnik/doktor*		

Time

hour/minute	*sat/minuta*	today/tomorrow	*danas/sutra*
week/day	*tjedan/dan*	yesterday	*jučer*
year/month	*godina/mjesec*	this/next week	*ovaj/slijedeći tjedan*
now	*sada*	morning/afternoon	*jutro/poslije podne*
soon	*uskoro*	evening/night	*večer/noć*
Monday	*ponedjeljak*	Friday	*petak*
Tuesday	*utorak*	Saturday	*subota*
Wednesday	*srijeda*	Sunday	*nedjela*
Thursday	*četvrtak*		
January	*siječanj*	July	*srpanj*
February	*veljača*	August	*kolovoz*
March	*ožujak*	September	*rujan*
April	*travanj*	October	*listopad*
May	*svibanj*	November	*studeni*
June	*lipanj*	December	*prosinac*
spring	*proljeće*	autumn	*jesen*
summer	*ljeto*	winter	*zima*

Food and drink
Essentials

breakfast	*doručak*	tea	*čaj*
lunch	*ručak*	tea with milk	*crni čaj su mlijekom*
dinner	*večera*		(ask for black – *crni*
water	*voda*		– otherwise you get
beer	*pivo*		fruit tea with milk)
wine	*vino*	tea with lemon	*čaj sa limunom*
white wine	*bijelo vino*	cheese	*sir*
red wine	*crno vino*	soup	*juha*
rose wine	*roze vino*	thick soup	*ragu*
home-made wine	*domaće vino*	egg (eggs)	*jaje (jaja)*
spirit (generic)	*rakija*	ham/air-dried ham	*šunka/pršut*
spirit (from herbs)	*travarica*	fish	*riba*
brandy	*lozovača*	chips	*pomfrit*
pear spirit	*kruškovača*	meat	*meso*
cold	*hladno*	vegetables	*povrće*
hot	*vruće*	fruits	*voće*
bread	*kruh*	home-made	*domaće*
jam	*džem*	grilled	*sa roštilja*
	(some say *pekmez*)	baked	*pečeno*
coffee	*kava*	fried	*prženo*
sugar	*šećer*	boiled	*kuhano*
salt	*slan*	stuffed	*punjeno*

Fish

trout	*pastrva*	tuna	*tuna*
salmon trout	*losos*	squid	*lignje*
mackerel	*skuša*	mussels	*školjka* (in general – there are many variants)
perch	*grgeč, smuđ*		
bass	*luben*	oysters	*oštrige / kamenice*
grey mullet	*cipal*	crayfish	*škampi*
red mullet	*barbun*	crab	*rak*
bream	*zubatac*	lobster	*jastog*
sardines	*sardina*	spicy fish stew	*fiš paprikaš*

Meat

beef	*govedina*	spicy smoked sausage	*kulen*
pork	*svinjetina*	goulash	*gulaš*
wild boar	*divlja svinja*	moussaka	*musaka*
lamb	*janjetina*	meat stews	
mutton	*ovčetina*	pepper and tomato	*sataraš*
veal	*teletina*	rice and tomato	*đuveč*
chicken	*piletina*	beef with dumplings	*pašticada*
stuffed vine leaves	*sarma*		

Vegetables

potatoes	*krumpir*	onion	*luk*
rice	*riža*	garlic	*češnjak*
green peppers	*paprike*		

Salads

cucumber	*krastavac*	mixed	*miješana*
cabbage	*kupus*	with chillis and	
tomato	*rajčica* (*paradajz* is often used)	cheese	*grčka*
		with tomatoes and	*šopska* (many also
lettuce	*zelena*	cheese	use name *grčka*)

Fruit

orange	*narandža* (or *naranča*)	melon	*dinja*
lemon	*limun*	pears	*kruške*
plums	*šljive*	peaches	*breskve*

Appendix 2

FURTHER INFORMATION
Books
Many of the books listed here are long out of print, but most can be found second-hand – either by trawling through old bookshops, or online at places like Abe Books (www.abebooks.com).

History/politics
Glenny, Misha *The Fall of Yugoslavia* Penguin, 1996 (3rd edition). Former BBC correspondent's account of how it all fell apart – compelling, if depressing reading.

Goldstein, Ivo *Croatia: a History* C Hurst & Co, 1999 (2nd edition). Well-balanced Croat historian's view of Croatian history from Roman times to the present day. Hard to find, however, in spite of its relatively recent publication.

Harris, Robin *Dubrovnik – A History* Saqi, 2003. Solid doorstop of a hardback with a wealth of fascinating insight and wonderful illustrations – but quite a dent in the wallet at 25 quid.

Macan, Trpimir, and Šentija, Josip *The Bridge – A Short History of Croatia* Journal of Croatian Literature, Zagreb, 1992. Notwithstanding the rather fanatical introduction by Yale professor Ivo Banac, this is an excellent history of Croatia in two sections, the first up to 1941, and the second from 1941 to 1991, with semi-official status. Hard to find, however.

Margaritoni, Marko *Dubrovnik, Between History and Legend* Dubrovnik State Archives, 2001. Lots of wonderful tales and legends by a local author. Order the book for 200 kuna from the man himself, at marko.margaritoni@du.htnet.hr.

Rheubottom, David *Age, Marriage and Politics in 15th century Ragusa* Oxford University Press, 2000. Intriguing – if at times weighty – insights into the inter-relationships between politics, kinship and marriage in the republic. Expensive, however, even second-hand.

Silber, Laura et al *The Death of Yugoslavia* Penguin, 1996. Tie-in with the BBC series, and while it's not wholly successful without having seen the programmes, it's still a frightening blow-by-blow account of the events of the war.

Tanner, Marcus *Croatia: A Nation Forged in War* Yale University Press, 1997. An excellent and detailed history of Croatia, by *The Independent*'s correspondent during the conflict – probably the best book currently available.

Travel and travel literature
Bridge, Ann *Illyrian Spring* Chatto & Windus, 1935. Rather fey (very 1930s) novel about a lady painter working her way down the Adriatic coast in search of inspiration and love – but great descriptions of Pula, Split, Dubrovnik etc.

Clancy, Tim *Bosnia & Herzegovina: The Bradt Travel Guide* Bradt, 2004. Comprehensive guide to this newly accessible Croatian neighbour.

Coyler, William *Dubrovnik and the Southern Adriatic Coast from Split to Kotor* Ward Lock & Co, 1967. Delightfully dated mini hardback with lots of black and white photos.

Delalle, Ivan *Guide to Trogir* Trogir Tourist Board, 1963. Brilliant black and white pocket guide to the city first published in 1936; full of words like 'historiography'.

Goldring, Patrick *Yugoslavia* Collins Holiday Guides, 1967. Marvellous pocket guide featuring mainly Croatia – worth buying just for the splendid peasant smoking a roll-up on the cover.

Kaplan, Robert *Balkan Ghosts* Picador, 1994. The author uses his 1990 odyssey through the Balkans to explain the conflictual politics across the region in depth. Relatively easily available second-hand.

Kastrapeli et al *Dubrovnik Tourist Guide* Minčeta, 1967. Classic 1960s mini guide – gushing prose, black and white photos.

Letcher, Piers *Dubrovnik: The Bradt City Guide* Bradt, 2005. Just the guide you need if you're doing Dubrovnik in detail – or venturing across the border into nearby Bosnia & Herzegovina or Montenegro.

Murphy, Dervla *Through the Embers of Chaos – Balkan Journeys* John Murray, 2002. Brilliant account of a long cycle tour through the Balkans, including Dubrovnik, Split, Zagreb etc. Truly a wonderful, inspirational book.

Rellie, Annalisa *Montenegro: The Bradt Travel Guide* Bradt, 2003 (2nd edition 2005). Essential reading if you're digging deeper into Montenegro.

Voynovitch, Count Louis *A Historical Saunter through Dubrovnik (Ragusa)* Jadran, 1929. Nearly impossible to find, but marvellous short guide to the city from a 1929 perspective. It's amazing how little has changed in spite of both a world and a local war.

West, Rebecca *Black Lamb and Grey Falcon* Canongate Books, 1993. Without question the most comprehensive (1,200pp) and best-written account of Yugoslavia in the 1930s. Rebecca West travelled widely in Croatia (and the other republics of the former Yugoslavia) in 1936 and 1937, and spent five years researching and writing this book. Fatally flawed in places, and terribly naïve in its conclusion, it's nonetheless by turns funny, passionate and tragic – and always brilliantly opinionated. If you come across the original two-volume hardback from the 1940s, go for it; there are excellent black and white photographs.

Natural history

Mitchell-Jones, A J et al *The Atlas of European Mammals* Academic Press, 1999. Heavyweight guide to nearly 200 species, with distribution maps and a real wealth of detail.

Still, John *Butterflies and Moths of Britain and Europe* Collins, 1996. Handy guide for lepidopterists.

Svensson Lars *Collins Bird Guide* Collins, 2001 (new edition). Simply excellent guide to European birds, with truly wonderful illustrations. The many Collins field guides (trees, flowers etc) are also highly recommended.

Art and culture

Beretić, Dubravka *Art Treasures of Dubrovnik* Jugoslavija Guides, 1968. Obscure guide dating back to the communist heyday – still remarkably accurate, however.

Pavičic, Liliana and Pirker-Mosher, Gordana *The Best of Croatian Cooking* Hippocrene Books, 2000. You're back home and missing those Croatian dishes? This is the book for you.

Susnjar, Ante *Croatian-English/English-Croatian Dictionary and Phrasebook* Hippocrene, 2000. Good, helpful reference guide to the language.

Web resources

Croatia has been quick to get itself online and there's a mountain of information and a wealth of resources on the web. Here are just a handful of useful links:

General

www.croatia.hr The National Tourist Board's exemplary website, with a huge amount of practical information and the phone number of most hotels, travel agencies and campsites across the country.

http://imenik.t-com.hr Croatia's online phone directory (including an English-language option). Just what you need when it turns out the phone number listed in this guide has already changed.

www.dalmacija.net Dalmatia's own tourist information site, with online hotel bookings etc. See below for the sailing section.

www.hr The so-called 'Croatian Homepage', an English-language site featuring 7,500 links in hundreds of categories, all about Croatia. You can spend many hours here.

www.hr/wwwhr/useful.en.html In the same site, features especially useful categorised links.

www.uhpa.hr Association of Croatian Travel Agencies. A good way of finding out what can be organised for you.

meteo.hr (and mirror site at **www.dhmz.htnet.hr**) Croatian Meteorological Service. Click on the flag for English and find out everything you ever wanted to know about Croatia's weather, including forecasts.

www.hfhs.hr Croatian Youth Hostel Association. Gives the latest situation concerning youth hostels across the country, and works as a central reservation office, though make sure you have your confirmation with you when you actually show up at the hostels.

www.diving-hrs.hr Croatian Diving Federation. Small (the English part, anyway) but useful site listing the rules and regs for scuba diving.

Transport

www.adriatica.it, **www.jadrolinija.hr**, **www.sem-marina.hr** The three main ferry companies plying the Adriatic.

www.akz.hr Zagreb bus station, mostly in Croatian. Nonetheless excellent site with all arrivals and departures, including costs – go to *Vozni red* (timetable) from the homepage.

www.hznet.hr National Railway. Even in Croatian you'll be able to find your way round the timetables, however, and the standard fares are displayed when the times come up – online booking is a bit trickier.

www.ina.hr The state-owned oil company. Complete with fuel prices and the locations and opening hours of every petrol station in the country.

www.hak.hr Hrvatski Autoklub (Croatian Automobile Club). In Croatian only, though it does have an interactive traffic snarl-up area in English.

Government, media etc.

www.mvp.hr Ministry of Foreign Affairs. Everything you need to know about visa requirements etc.

www.dzs.hr Croatian Bureau of Statistics. Everything you ever wanted to know.

www.mint.hr Ministry of Tourism. More statistics and all the forms you'll need if you're planning on starting a business in the Croatian tourist industry.

www.hrt.hr Croatian national TV and radio (in Croatian).

www.htnet.hr Excellent customisable portal in Croatian and English, with daily news bulletins, weather, traffic, entertainment etc.

www.hic.hr/english/index.htm Another news portal (also available in Croatian and Spanish).

Sailing

www.aci-club.hr Adriatic Croatia International Club homepage, with full details of everything ACI offers.

www.dalmacija.net/sailing.htm An excellent section of the Split & Dalmatia County Tourist Information Service, with lots of information on marinas, regulations for foreign boats, where to get charts, weather, safety etc.

www.planetadria.com Lots of good sailing resources, including rentals, etc.

www.itinerances-dalmates.com Excellent French site with lots of rentals and good information on sailing, winds, guides etc. In French, of course.

www.portfocus.com/croatia Site providing links to harbours and ports in Croatia, as well as weather and satellite photos.

Index

Page numbers in bold refer to major entries; those in italics indicate maps.